THINGS OF THE OLDEN TIME

Painted by Hiamovi (High Chief) and his wife Wowesta (White Buffalo Woman), Cheyenne Indians.

A. 1.   Painted by Hiamovi, is a case for a bow and arrows. It was slung on the back by passing the loop over one shoulder. The bow was carried in the long upper part of the case, the arrows in the shorter part below. The claws of the mountain-lion hung down as ornaments.

A. 2.   Painted by Hiamovi, is a screen ornamented with porcupine-quill work. Such screens were tipi decorations in old times, and hung on the tipi-wall back of the bed.

B.   Painted by Wowesta, is a bag of buffalo-hide, painted and decorated with buckskin fringe. Such bags were used for carrying wild cherries.

C.   Painted by Hiamovi, is a head-dress case in which was carried the war-bonnet or other head-dress; upon the case are painted deer-tracks and stars.

D., E.   Painted by Wowesta, are satchels of painted buffalo-hide (parfleches).

F.   Painted by Hiamovi, is a satchel of buffalo-hide decorated with porcupine-quill work, and black horse-hair trimmings.

G.   Painted by Hiamovi, is a chief's pipe. The bowl is of pipe-stone, the stem is of wood decorated with bead-work and with streamers of buckskin and horse-hair.

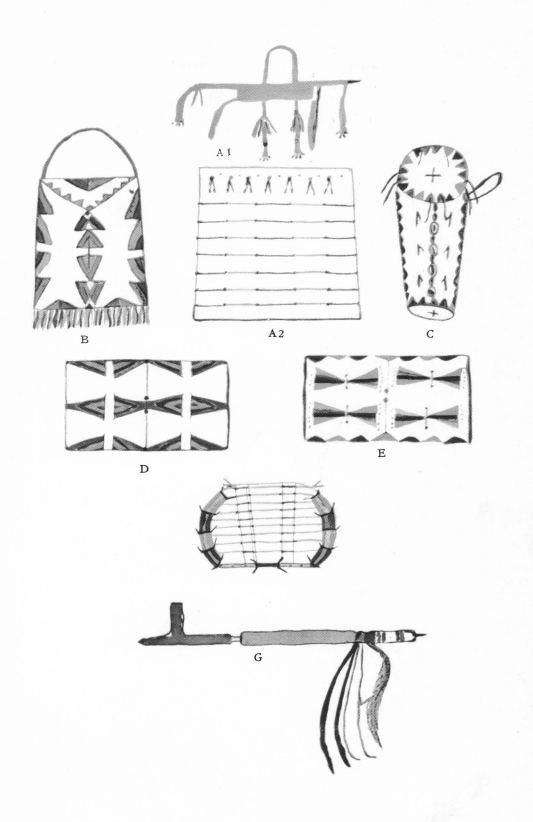

A 1

A 2

B

C

D

E

G

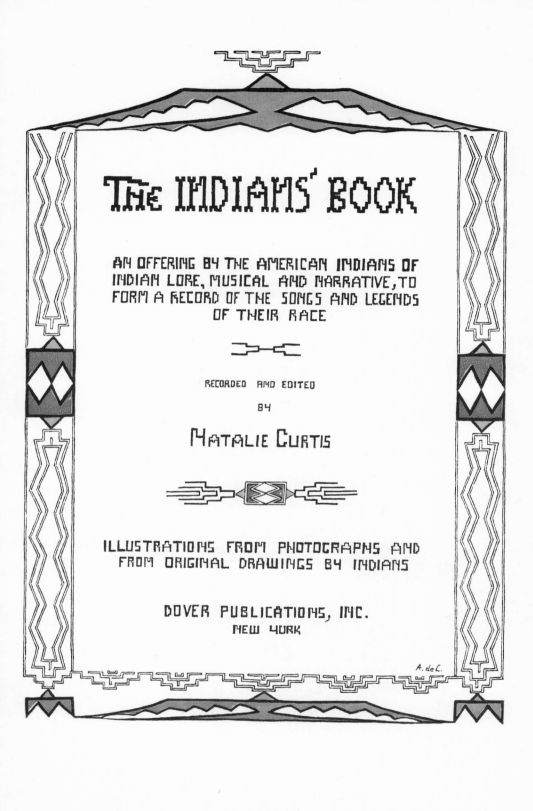

THE INDIANS' BOOK

AN OFFERING BY THE AMERICAN INDIANS OF
INDIAN LORE, MUSICAL AND NARRATIVE, TO
FORM A RECORD OF THE SONGS AND LEGENDS
OF THEIR RACE

RECORDED AND EDITED

BY

NATALIE CURTIS

ILLUSTRATIONS FROM PHOTOGRAPHS AND
FROM ORIGINAL DRAWINGS BY INDIANS

DOVER PUBLICATIONS, INC.
NEW YORK

A. de L.

This Dover edition, first published in 1968, is an unabridged and unaltered republication of the second edition, published by Harper and Brothers in 1923. The colored plates of the second edition are here reproduced in black and white.

Standard Book Number: 486-21939-9
Library of Congress Catalog Card Number: 68-19547

Manufactured in the United States of America
Dover Publications, Inc.
180 Varick Street
New York, N. Y. 10014

This Dover edition is dedicated to the memory of
Natalie Curtis Burlin
born, April 26, 1875 — *died,* October 23, 1921

PREFACE

Natalie Curtis (Mrs. Paul Burlin) died in Paris, October 23, 1921, almost immediately after being struck by a motor car while crossing a street. Shortly before her death she had planned to return to her study of Indian music, which she had laid aside temporarily to fulfill an urgent request that she record in similar manner the Negro folk-songs of our South and the songs and legends of some of the native Negro tribes of Africa. The completion of her collections in that field, *Negro Folk-Songs*, published in 1918, 1919, and *Songs and Tales from the Dark Continent*, published in 1920, left her free to take up the preparation of a re-issue of *The Indians' Book*, to which task she would have brought an even greater knowledge of the Indian and an even deeper insight into the art of primitive man.

Her untimely death makes impossible the revision which she would have undertaken and the inclusion of new material which she had gathered since the first publication in 1907. A few notes, however, as well as new drawings made by Indians especially for the purpose, have been added to this edition, and new illustrations from photographs have been supplied to replace some which have become unserviceable by repeated reproduction.

A creation myth of the Yuma Indians, recorded by Miss Curtis, and the record of her conversation with *Chi*paropai, one of the leaders of that tribe, have been reprinted in the appendix with the kind permission of the successor of the *Craftsman Magazine*, in which they were originally published. A Yuma Indian lullaby and a Hopi Indian "Owl Katzina Song," recorded by Miss Curtis, have also been appended. These songs first appeared in her article on "American Indian Cradle Songs" published in the *Musical Quarterly*, to which acknowledgment is due for the courtesy of republication. Except for those additions, the book remains as it was.

It is a satisfaction to realize that the purpose of the work to which Miss Curtis gave so many years of unselfish effort has so largely been fulfilled. In the introduction to the first edition she expressed the hope that in music, art, and letters, as well as in history and archæology, *The Indians' Book* should find a place. It has done so. Widely reviewed both here and abroad, it won instant recognition not only for the amazing accuracy of the musical transcriptions, but for the revelation of the Indian's artistic genius and for the light which it shed on the inner thought and aspirations of primitive man. Indeed, with the passing years, *The Indians' Book* has become a treasury to musician, artist, poet, and ethnologist alike, and the historian of the future will owe a debt of gratitude to the young woman who made her rare musical gifts and wide knowledge, her spiritual understanding, intellectual penetration, and flashing artistic intuition the medium through which the Indian's contribution of art and creative thought should be recorded for all time. Nor did the service of the book end there; for she made, as one writer has said, art the means of a ministry of service in human advancement; and the book was but a part of a broader appeal for a humane treatment of a deeply misunderstood and gifted race, and for some method of adjusting the primitive Indian to the alien civilization around him, not by stamping out all that was native to him in the futile belief that he might thus be transformed into a white man, but by developing his character through the preservation and fostering of all that was valuable in his own distinctive culture.

Incredible as it now seems, when Miss Curtis first began her self-imposed task of recording Indian music, native songs were absolutely forbidden in the government schools. On one reservation she was warned by a friendly scientist that if she wished to record the Indian songs she must do so secretly, for if the government official should hear of it, she would be expelled from the reservation; and on another the Indians were afraid to sing to her lest it should bring them into disfavor with the authorities. At that time, except for the notable work of Miss Alice C. Fletcher and her Indian collaborator, Francis La Flesche, and for a few cursory gleanings here and there, and for purely scientific treatises (unknown, for the most part, to the general reading public), the wealth of indigenous music, poetry, and legend was not only neglected, but was being rapidly obliterated by the steady pressure of the government's effort to crush the Indian as rapidly as possible into the white man's mold.

Miss Curtis's direct appeal to Theodore Roosevelt, then President, brought not only his official sanction, without which the recording of the Indian songs on the reservations would have been almost impossible, but his warm personal interest in her undertaking. His influence, with the added impetus created by the wider dissemination of a real knowledge of the Indian, resulted in the shaping of an enlightened policy in the administration of Indian affairs which led finally to the adoption of many of the reforms which Miss Curtis advocated.

Thus, for example, the singing of Indian songs in the Indian schools came to be not only officially permitted, but encouraged. The talented Indian artist, Miss Angel de Cora, of the Winnebago Tribe, who designed the lettering of the tribal title-pages of this book, was appointed art instructor at the government's school for Indians at Carlisle, and for a time at least was given a free hand to develop the art of her race and apply it to the useful industries taught there. Even Congress, which could appropriate sufficient

PREFACE

funds to preserve the natural beauties of America, but had never thought of the value of preserving the art of the original American, found funds sufficient for a short-lived effort to record officially the music of the various tribes. At last the Indian child in the government school and the adult on the reservation were allowed a freedom of racial consciousness and a spiritual liberty theretofore almost tyrannically denied. That this change in policy came too late to benefit the older generation of Indians or to preserve their distinctive qualities of character in the younger, was a matter of regret to Miss Curtis; but she was happy in the knowledge that the labor of compiling the book was completed just in time before much of the material held only in the memory of the older Indians should with their death be forever lost to the world. The full history of Miss Curtis's endeavors for the Indian is yet to be written, but for those who care to follow in outline her effort to preserve Indian art a brief list of some of her contributions on the subject to various periodicals is appended in a note.

"Each people," says Professor Michel, of France, "through its great artists, affirms its intimate faith, reveals its manner of understanding and loving life, and enriches just so much the patrimony of the world." It was Miss Curtis's belief that the art of the native race, whose utterance springs from our very soil, could enrich our patrimony, and that if the striking characteristics of that art should eventually be absorbed into the artistic expression of our country, we should, in her own words, "have woven into the fabric of our national culture a strand of color instead of adding to the monotone of gray." Much of what she hoped for has already come to pass. The paintings of the colony of artists who have settled at Taos and elsewhere have sought to reveal Indian life in the primitive beauty of our own Southwest. In Santa Fe a new museum has been dedicated to the preservation of the culture of that region. Indian designs have found their way into our textiles. Anthologies of Indian verse have been compiled, both here and abroad. Poets have begun to experiment with the idiom and pattern of the Indian song-poem form. And musical compositions based on Indian themes are heard in our concert halls. Truly, at last, we have awakened to the artistic riches which, as Dr. Lyman Abbott said, lay hidden like the gold in the rocks of our native land.

Those who believed with Miss Curtis in the essential unity of mankind, who felt, as she expressed it in the preface to her study of African folk-songs, ". . . that only when we admit that each race owes something to the other, only when we realize our vast mutual human indebtedness, may we hope for that interracial and international tolerance, understanding, and co-operation which can at last bring permanent peace"—those who felt beneath the tragedy of the World War a strengthening of the right of each people to racial self-expression, and a quickening of the impulse toward an understanding exchange of cultural gifts, must find in the closing paragraph of High-Chief's foreword to this book a quality of prophecy and the vision of a great leader of men:

There are birds of many colors—red, blue, green, yellow—yet it is all one bird. There are horses of many colors—brown, black, yellow, white—yet it is all one horse. So cattle, so all living things—animals, flowers, trees. So men: in this land where once were only Indians are now men of every color—white, black, yellow, red—yet all one people. That this should come to pass was in the heart of the Great Mystery. It is right thus. And everywhere there shall be peace.

To those who shared Miss Curtis's ideals and to the Indians of the various tribes who contributed to the preparation of the original volume and who held their friend, "Tawi-Mana"—the "Song-Maid," as they called her, in affectionate remembrance, the labor of the present editor is dedicated. Grateful acknowledgment is made to the Rev. Winfred Douglas for his friendly counsel, and to Mrs. Osgood Mason, whose help made possible the original undertaking, and without whose continued devotion the present edition could never have been accomplished.

B. C.

August, 1922.

NOTE

The Perpetuating of Indian Art. *The Outlook*, November 22, 1913.
Folk-song and the American Indian. *Southern Workman*, September, 1915.
The Indian's Part in the Dedication of the New Museum. *Journal of Art and Archæology*, January, 1918.
Mr. Roosevelt and Indian Music. *The Outlook*, March 5, 1919.
Our Native Craftsmen. *Southern Workman*, August, 1919.
Theodore Roosevelt in Hopi Land. *The Outlook*, September 17, 1919.
An American Indian Artist. *The Outlook*, January 14, 1920.
A Plea for our Native Art. *Musical Quarterly*, April, 1920.
Pueblo Poetry. *The Freeman*, January 25, 1922.

FOREWORD

By Hiamovi (High Chief)
(Chief among the Cheyennes and the Dakotas.)

To the Great Chief at Washington, and to the Chiefs of Peoples across the Great Water

This is the Indians' Book

Long ago the Great Mystery caused this land to be, and made the Indians to live in this land. Well has the Indian fulfilled all the intent of the Great Mystery for him. Through this book may men know that the Indian people was made by the Great Mystery for a purpose.

Once, only Indians lived in this land. Then came strangers from across the Great Water. No land had they; we gave them of our land. No food had they; we gave them of our corn. The strangers are become many and they fill all the country. They dig gold—from my mountains; they build houses—of the trees of my forests; they rear cities—of my stones and rocks; they make fine garments—from the hides and wool of animals that eat my grass. None of the things that make their riches did they bring with them from beyond the Great Water; all comes from my land, the land the Great Mystery gave unto the Indian.

And when I think upon this I know that it is right, even thus. In the heart of the great Mystery it was meant that stranger-visitors—my friends across the Great Water—should come to my land; that I should bid them welcome; that all men should sit down with me and eat together of my corn. It was meant by the Great Mystery that the Indian should give to all peoples.

But the white man never has known the Indian. It is thus: there are two roads, the white man's road, and the Indian's road. Neither traveller knows the road of the other. Thus ever has it been, from the long ago, even unto to-day. May this book help to make the Indian truly known in the time to come.

The Indian wise-speakers in this book are of the best men of their tribes. Only what is true is within this book. I want all Indians and white men to read and learn how the Indians lived and thought in the olden time, and may it bring holy-good upon the younger Indians to know of their fathers. A little while, and the old Indians will no longer be, and the young will be even as white men. When I think, I know that it is the mind of the Great Mystery that white men and Indians who fought together should now be one people.

There are birds of many colors—red, blue, green, yellow—yet it is all one bird. There are horses of many colors—brown, black, yellow, white—yet it is all one horse. So cattle, so all living things—animals, flowers, trees. So men: in this land where once were only Indians are now men of every color—white, black, yellow,   red—yet all one people.   That this should come to pass was in the heart of the Great Mystery. It is right thus.   And everywhere there shall be peace.

The Indians are the authors of this volume.   The songs and stories are theirs; the drawings and title-pages were made by them.

The work of the recorder has been but the collecting, editing, and arranging of the Indians' contributions.

CONTENTS

MUSIC

The songs in this book are written after a new manner in that corresponding musical phrases are placed one beneath another like lines of verse. This system makes the form of the song to flash before the eye like the form of a stanza in poetry. For this idea, the recorder is indebted to Mr. Kurt Schindler.

A general characteristic of Indian singing is a rhythmical pulsation of the voice on sustained notes. This pulsation is expressed in this book *wherever tied notes have vocables or syllables written out beneath them.*

A rhythmical peculiarity of Pueblo music is a sudden holding back of the time during one, two, or more bars. This effect is in no sense a rallentando. It is an abrupt change of tempo with no loss of rhythmical precision. At the end of the slower bars the first tempo is resumed with the original impetus. Such change is merely a leap from one tempo to another and back again. As it was impossible wholly to express this peculiarity in the usual musical symbols, *brackets have been placed over the slower bars,* that the eye may catch at a glance the change of time. The exact tempi are designated by metronome marks. For further details in regard to Indian music, see Introduction, page xxvi.

SONGS

(The left-hand column of figures refers to pages of printed text or of explanatory description, the middle column to pages of music, the right-hand column to pages of text with interlinear translations, in the appendix.)

WABANAKI

DAKOTA

[xiv]

SONGS

THE INDIANS' BOOK

SONGS

DRAWINGS

All drawings in this book are by Indians, and were made free-hand without rule or measure, except that in some instances an inverted basket was used to form a circle. Nearly all represent first efforts to draw on paper with the white man's brush, and many were first attempts at drawing of any kind.

The lettering on the title-pages is by Angel De Cora (Hinook Mahiwi Kilinaka), of the Winnebago tribe.

The title-page, by Angel De Cora (Hinook Mahiwi Kilinaka), has for the motive of its design an adaptation of an old Indian design which represents in highly conventionalized form the Eagle, and the Eagle's Song. The soaring eagle is seen in the green figure whose points are the two out-spread wings, with the tail in the centre. The yellow spot at the top of the figure is the eagle's head; from the beak rises the song—waving lines which broaden out as the song floats on the air. The whole symbol is used in decorative form throughout the page, two eagles being joined together by the tips of wings and tails to form a symmetrical design. In the centre of the page, at the top and bottom, and at the sides, is seen the eagle-symbol, while the page is framed, as it were, in the symbol of the song.

The eagle is loved and revered by the Indians. He is strongest of all birds. He soars aloft, and he may look upon the sun, the giver of life, the celestial emblem of divine force. Therefore has the symbol of the Eagle and the Eagle's Song been chosen for the title-page of "The Indians' Book."

ILLUSTRATIONS

(See also Illustrated Tribal Title-pages.)

WHITE HOUSE.
WASHINGTON.

May 17th 1906

These songs cast a wholly new light on the depth and dignity of Indian thought, the simple beauty and strange charm — the charm of a vanished elder world — of Indian poetry.

Theodore Roosevelt

INTRODUCTION

THIS book reflects the soul of one of the noblest types of primitive man—the North American Indian. It is the direct utterance of the Indians themselves. The red man dictated and the white friend has recorded. Songs, stories, and drawings, all have been purposely contributed by Indians as their separate offerings to a volume that should be their own.

By rail, by wagon, and by horse, over prairie and desert, the white friend journeyed from tribe to tribe, seeking the Indians with open friendship, and everywhere meeting their warm response. In nearly every instance a chief was visited first and the purpose of the book explained to him. Would he and his people join in the making of a book to be the Indians' own—a book which should keep for all time the songs and stories of their race? The olden days were gone; the buffalo had vanished from the plains; even so would there soon be lost forever the songs and stories of the Indian. But there was a way to save them to the life and memory of their children, and that was to write them, even as the white man writes. The white friend had come to be the pencil in the hand of the Indian.

Thus was the book undertaken primarily for the Indians, in the hope that this their own volume, when placed in the hands of their children, might help to revive for the younger generation that sense of the dignity and worth of their race which is the Indians' birthright, and without which no people can progress.

With enthusiasm that was touching in its gladness, the Indians responded to the appeal. Already had one or two old men tried to make some record of the songs, others had sought deeply to engrave the old tales upon the minds of a younger generation. All realized that they walked in the sunset hour of their native life and that the night was soon to come.

The Indians sang the songs directly to the recording pencil. Theirs are the explanations and the tales connected with the songs. Of the drawings, every one is Indian.

At first the noting of the music was, to the recorder, though a musician, a task of no small difficulty. In the beginning the songs were first taken upon a phonograph, but the machine soon was abandoned as inadequate and unnecessary, and note-book and pencil, a camera, and a color-box for the use of the Indians made the sole equipment carried into camp or village. The songs were written down by the light of the tipi fire or under the glare of the desert sun; in adobe houses while the women ground the corn, or in the open camp where after some festival or ceremonial gathering of the people a leader resang for the book a characteristic song.

Many Indian songs are sacred to certain occasions or ceremonies. Respect was always shown, therefore, for the natural and sometimes superstitious reluctance of the people to sing such songs at other than the proper time, or even to consent to the recording of them. When a singer chose such a song for his contribution, it was well, indeed; but no one was ever urged to desecrate anything held sacred, no matter what the motive. This book, it is hoped, may serve as an encouragement to educated Indians to carry on the work of record, for their access to their people's holiest rites, and their understanding of Indian thought, make possible for them, as for no white person, a full exposition of Indian religious life. This hope is augmented by the fact that it has been physically impossible, in this collection, to represent every tribe. [1]

Many of the songs in this book are traditional and of lost origin; some are current songs of the day, still others are quite new, taken down, indeed, from the lips of their own composers. Each con-

---

[1] America owes a debt to Miss Alice C. Fletcher, holder of the Thaw Fellowship Department of Anthropology, Harvard University, who has been the pioneer in the study of Indian song. Her very valuable collaborator has been Mr. Francis La Flesche, an Omaha Indian of education and culture, who many years ago first conceived the idea of writing down the songs of his people.

tributor himself chose what songs or stories he wished to put into the book, sometimes spending hours in deliberation.

Old men and young, mothers and maidens — all types of the people were sought that the collection might reflect as fully as possible the many sides of Indian life. Especially sought out were the very oldest men, the keepers of the ancient lore, and these gave stories and songs often entirely unknown to younger generations, and sometimes in archaic language.

The Indians say that the book "speaks with the straight tongue," for it holds the words of their head men, their wise men and their chiefs. They believe it will be an influence in their own future, and they look to it to tell the white man that " Indians are a good people."

The making of this record has been a consecrated work. Joy in the task has been shadowed by close contact with a struggling people in their need. It was impossible to live near to Indian life without being heart-wrung by the pathos of its tragedy—impossible to be among Indians without crying, " Is there a people more deeply misunderstood ?"

This book reveals the inner life of a primitive race. The Indian looks out with reverence upon the world of nature, to him the only world, while deep in his being thrills the consciousness of a power greater than nature, greater than man, yet eternally manifest throughout all life. This consciousness is so vital to the Indian that almost his every act is linked with it. The Indian is at all times prayerful. Sacred to him is the hour of birth, sacred the hour of death; and in symbol and ceremony he tells his reverence.

Art is one of the earliest of human impulses. It is born of man's instinctive desire to create in beauty the objects of his necessity. The earthen jar, the water-gourd, the woven tunic, all are graced with ornament. And the ornament? It is most often the symbol of a prayer.

The prayer of the Indian is offered in many ways—by the ceremonial smoking of tobacco, which symbolizes the breath of life; by the scattering of holy corn-pollen, emblem of fruitfulness and productiveness; or by the planting of plumed prayer-sticks upon

whose feathers is breathed the supplication, to be wafted by the
wind. Prayer is conveyed in the designs of woven fabrics, in bead-
work, pottery, and decorations of all kinds, in dance, in ceremony,
and in song.

Wellnigh impossible is it for civilized man to conceive of the
importance of song in the life of the Indian. To the Indian, song
is the breath of the spirit that consecrates the acts of life. Not
all songs are religious, but there is scarcely a task, light or grave,
scarcely an event, great or small, but has its fitting song.

In the Hebrew "Genesis" the creating word is *spoken*—" And
God said, Let there be light." In nearly every Indian myth the
creator *sings* things into life. For civilized man, the messages of
truth, the traditions of his ancestors, the history of his race, the
records of his thought have been secured upon the written page
and so transmitted through the years. To the Indian, truth, tradition, history, and thought are preserved in ritual of poetry and song.
The red man's song records the teachings of his wise men, the great
deeds of his heroes, the counsel of his seers, the worship of his God.
If all things Indian must, indeed, pass away under the white man's
ban as being "pagan" and "uncivilized," then will be lost to the
red man not only his whole unwritten literature, but also, and
sadder still, the realm wherein his soul aspires. For to the primitive man of another race, no creed wholly alien to his thought
and environment ever can replace his own entire spiritual world,
which is the heritage of his past and the natural expression of
his soul.

Throughout this book the effort has been made to render truthfully into English the thought in the Indian poetry. Translations
have carefully been worked out with educated Indians as inter-
preters and old men of authority as informants. Indian poetry is
difficult of translation, not only because of the differences in language (for there are Indian words that have no counterpart in
English), but also because of the very nature of the poetry.

Indian poetry, like Indian art, is expressed in symbol. The
cloud-form in Indian design is no copy of a cloud, but a conventionalized image that is a symbol *meaning* cloud, as a wavy line
means water or a cross stands for a star. Even so in poetry. One

word may be the symbol of a complete idea that, in English, would need a whole sentence for its expression. Even those who know the language may not understand the songs unless they know what meaning lies behind the symbolic words.[1] Such poetry is impressionistic, and many may be the interpretations of the same song given by different singers. Again, where the songs belong to sacred ceremonies or to secret societies, the meaning is purposely hidden—a holy mystery enshrined—that only the initiated may hear and understand.

Indians feel that, in the English rendering of their verse, justice is not done to the poetry when there is given only a bare and literal translation of the symbolic word instead of a full expression of the meaning. They say, " It takes many words in English to tell what we say in one. But since you have no one word to tell all we mean, then you must speak our one word in your many." In some of the songs, however, the meaning is fully expressed in words. Yet even such a song cannot wholly be understood without a knowledge of the event which called it into being, the legend with which it is connected, or the ceremony of which it is a part.

The translations are as literal as possible, yet the chief desire has been that the real meaning should truthfully flash through the English words, and that the translation should retain the fragrance, the color, and, above all, the spirit of the original. The translation has been fitted to the music, for only when the meaning of the song is clearly revealed through the intertwining of poetry and melody can there be fully felt the elemental emotion, the nature quality, the forceful sweeping charm of Indian song.

Of the music, how does Indian song differ from that of civilization? Music is a trinity. It is composed of three elements—rhythm, melody, and harmony. The first element is rhythm, for rhythm is in the earliest consciousness of man. It is in the throb of the pulses, the beat of horse-hoofs, the break of waves. All life is rhythmic, for life is vibration, motion. So music in its earliest form consists chiefly in rhythm.

[1] Literal translations of the Indian words are offered in the appendix.

The next element is melody—a succession of sounds of different pitch. The wail of the wind, the laughter of the brook, the mating song of birds, these are melodies of nature. The emotional response is in man. Song becomes the cry of the heart and the transfiguration of the spoken word.

Next comes harmony — the combination of different sounds. Harmony is in the blending, blurring overtones of nature, the melting of many sounds into one. It is the last element of music to evolve, and it has developed with the progress of science—the unfolding to man's comprehension of the universal laws of life. With harmony music becomes an art of greatest dignity and power, a subtle, sensitive reflex of the soul's impressions, a language which expresses thoughts, emotions, and aspirations incapable of utterance in form less spiritual.

The unstudied song of primitive man is as soulful in its purpose as developed art, but it is a simple expression of far simpler things. The music of most primitive people contains the first two elements only—rhythm and melody—and these elements, especially rhythm, are highly developed. Harmony is lacking; but the life and art of the Indian are so linked with nature that it is to be questioned whether the sounds of the nature-world do not supply to these singers of the open a certain unconscious sense of harmonic background. No one who has heard Indian songs in their own environment, under broad skies amid the sweep of wind and grasses, can fail to feel that they are there a note in a nature symphony. Take the Indian from nature, or nature from the Indian, and the Indian's art, if it survive, must undergo the change of supplying from within that which was unconsciously received from without. It must embody the lost nature-world. Thus ever in the growth of civilization are the influences of nature absorbed into the creations of art. Not knowing harmony, it is chiefly on variety of rhythm that primitive man depends for his variety of musical effect. No civilized music has such complex, elaborate, and changing rhythm as has the music of the American Indian.

The songs in this book are written exactly as sung by the Indians, as nearly as musical notation can record. No harmony has been added. The original melodies are absolutely unchanged.

INTRODUCTION

The book thus offers a faithful record of the song of primitive man.

Different Indian tribes differ as widely in their music and in their manner of singing as in their life and customs. Yet there is one characteristic peculiarity of Indian song that is almost universal. This is a rhythmic pulsation of the voice on sustained notes somewhat analogous to the effect produced on the violin when the same note is slightly sounded several times during one stroke of the bow. This pulsating accentuation is expressed in this book *wherever tied notes have vocables or syllables written out beneath them.* The effect must be heard, however, in order adequately to be reproduced. Also it should always be borne in mind that Indian music is essentially for singing. It cannot properly be performed on an instrument of percussion, such as a piano, but must be sung, or at least played on a stringed instrument. Nor can it be too emphatically stated that all notation of Indian music, however accurate, must necessarily be but as a skeleton to the living form. The actual melody can be recorded, with its rhythmic accompaniment of drum or rattle. But the rendering of the song — the vocal embellishment, the strange gutturals, slurs, and accents that make Indian singing so distinctive — all this is altogether too subtle and too much a part of the voice itself to be possible of notation.

The Indians of the Lakes and Plains whose lives in the old days. were exposed to all the severities of weather, and who still sing constantly in the open air and against the wind, have voices more striking for their stirring ring than for actual beauty, as we deem it. The voices of the men extend in range from a sort of falsetto tenor to a bass so deep as scarcely to sound the pitch of any given note. Accents are made by an almost harshly aspirated staccato attack, and sustained notes are often sung with a tightening of the throat that produces a peculiar quaver. The songs frequently begin with high quavering tones, then gradually descend and end with low phrases that break off or die away on open vowel syllables. This is consistent with the sounds of nature and with the cries of animals. Indeed, the Indian can so imitate the call of a bird or the howl of the wolf as to be entirely deceptive.

The singing of the Plains women is less violent in its accent and more legato than that of the men, and its mellow nasal quality suggests the rustic note of the oboe.

The song of the Plains Indian has its fitting surrounding in the fire-lit lodge or the open prairie. The drum-beat, vibrant in the crisp, cold air of a winter night, adds its throb to the life-pulse of this music which is exciting, exhilarating, and inspiring through its spirit and vitality.

Strikingly different is the song of the Pueblo Indian. The shrill coyote cry of the Plains warrior is unknown to the Southwestern tiller of the soil. The song of the Pueblo men is a strong, clear outpouring from full lungs, while the note of the ceremonial chant is deep and solemn. The women of the Rio Grande and Zuñi Pueblos have high and flutelike voices; but the gentle Hopi women sing with veiled tone of peculiar feminine charm, and the long-drawn slurring of their phrases gives to their singing a certain vagueness of quality and intonation that is altogether alluring in its suggestion of the surrounding empty desert.

The sacred songs of the Navajos and Apaches are chanted with low nasal swing, but the dance-songs are sung with lusty vigor, and the call of the shepherd on the mountain-side echoes in clear-cut beauty through cliffs and cañons.

Like all folk-music, the music of the Indian is the spontaneous and sincere expression of the soul of a people. It springs from our own continent, and is thus, of all music, distinctively American. If Indian song be encouraged with Indians, and recognition of it awakened among our own people, America may one day contribute a unique music to the world of art. Not that the musical art of America can ever be founded on Indian melodies; for the art of the Aryan must be Aryan to be the true expression of his race. But the folk-music of any land is a soil from which genius draws sustenance for fresh growth, and the stimulus to the creative mind through contact with this native art should give to America a new and vigorous art impulse.

The drawings in this book are all made by the Indians, many of whom had never held brush before. Teachers in Indian schools say that Indian children in the first grade draw as well as white children in the fifth. With the Indian a sense for form and color is inborn. The hand that has woven for generations the matchless basket, perfect in symmetry and beautiful in design, wields the white man's pencil with delicacy and sweeping certitude. Even when painting for the first time, the untutored draughtsman lays the color on the paper as evenly as though drilled to the task.

The technique of all art handwork is the Indian's by nature. But technique is only the offspring of a larger gift which fashions the imagery of cloud, rain, star, and growing corn into symbol, and of symbols composes decorative designs both beautiful and meaningful. The Indian is artistic by nature. His art is not a luxury of the cultured few, but the unconscious striving of the many to make beautiful the things of daily living.

The child race of a by-gone age has left no written record of its thoughts. Silent through the ages has passed barbaric man. The voices that greeted the sunrise of the race have died away without an echo. A bit of broken pottery, a bone-awl, an arrow-head, a grave-mound, mute testimonies these of the art, the industry, the life, the death of man in the long ago. A footprint only tells of his passing. And of his thoughts? The lips of the past are closed forever on the mystery. Of value, then, to the history of the human race, as well as to the history of America, are the written utterances of this primitive people.

In music, art, and letters, as well as in history and archæology, should The Indians' Book find a place. Here may we look into the mind of a race utterly unlike any other in the world. Indian thought presents material absolutely unique. What other nation has in its midst a like opportunity for inspiration? Let us pause in the stress of our modern life to listen to the ancient lore of our own land. From the heart of the nature-world speaks the voice of man proclaiming deity. The Indian's religious thought, uttered with the simplicity of childhood, is born of his recognition of spirit in every form of life, and his conception of an omnipotent and all-pervading divine power is entirely spiritual and impersonal. The Indian has a message for the seekers after truth who welcome, whatsoever its form, the recognition of God by man. And if there be truth in the theory that the American continent was the first to emerge, then are the Indians, indeed, perhaps the most ancient of peoples and their spiritual conceptions should be of interest and value to the whole human race. The whole civilized world to-day faces the question: Is primitive man to retain his God-given right to evolution, or is he to be swept from off the earth before the imperious needs of civilized powers? The Spartan mother left her weakling on the mountain-side to perish. Now science, with the incubator, preserves the life of the pauper babe prematurely born. Should not this recognition of the sacredness of life be applied to races as well as to individuals? He who can offer most to the development of humanity is now deemed the fittest to survive. The primitive races are child races. Who can tell what may be their contribution to humanity when they are grown? And have they not even now something to give?

What of the type of manhood that the Indian presents, reserved and poised, courageous, enduring, master of eloquence, master of silence, above all, self-controlled—a proud, vanishing figure in a nation of unrest? A hewer of wood and a drawer of water, yes— but what more? What of his talents?—have they not a place to fill in the culture and industry of our country? We are a people of great mechanical and inventive genius, but we are not naturally song-makers, poets, or designers. Can we afford to lose from our country any sincere and spontaneous art impulse, however crude? The undeveloped talents native to the aboriginal American are precisely those in which the Anglo-Saxon American is deficient. Far ahead of Europe are we in labor-saving devices, but far behind in all art industries. Our patterns and designs are largely imported from France. And yet, here among us, down-trodden and by us debauched, is a people of real creative artistic genius—the first Americans and possibly the oldest race on earth. And our interests declare that this proud race must perish? If The Indians' Book proves that the Indians have qualities worthy of a place in civilization, may not the same be true of other primitive peoples also? Would we not do well at least to find out what the people really are before we declare that the natural law of the survival of the fittest pronounces for our progress their doom?

INTRODUCTION

If The Indians' Book can help to a recognition of primitive men as men of latent capabilities; if it can help in ever so small degree to herald the day when adult races wisely shall guide child races, and civilization nourish the genius of every people, then will this utterance of the North American Indians be not for the race alone, but for all humanity.

August, 1905.

NOTE

For the benefit of the white reader it may be well to state in brief the present conditions of Indian life. With the advance of the white man the Indian has been pushed from place to place, until the several tribes have finally been located on reservations—that is, land set apart for them. The Indians are considered wards of the nation and are ruled by the Federal government. Each reservation is controlled by a government officer appointed by the Commissioner of Indian Affairs. On nearly every agency is a government Indian school; there are also several non-reservation boarding-schools.

The reservation system is now gradually being abolished, principally on account of the white man's ever-increasing demand for land. The Indians receive a stated number of acres in severalty, and the rest of the reservation is sold for white settlement.

The national policy of the past for the civilization and education of the Indian has been to abolish tribal relations, native religion, customs, art, language, and dress. This form of racial suicide expected of the red man has not added happiness to his lot. Of late years there has been a desire on the part of many earnest people to see this policy modified, and the present Indian Commissioner, Hon. Francis E. Leupp is the friend of intelligent effort along these lines.

Mr. Leupp came into office after this book was undertaken. Since his administration two important reforms in Indian education have been instituted: the official encouragement of native music in the schools, and the appointment of Angel De Cora, a Winnebago Indian, as art instructor at Carlisle Indian School.

No claim is made that all work in this book is without error.

The short sketches of the tribes have been compiled by the recorder with the help of standard authorities, but the migrations and early history of Indians form a subject that is still largely conjectural. Though great care has been taken in the preparation of this material, years might still be spent with advantage in further comparing it with the work of students who have made particular Indian tribes the subject of valuable and exhaustive research. Nevertheless, in view of the eagerness of the Indians for their book, it is deemed desirable to publish the collection as it is, without further delay.

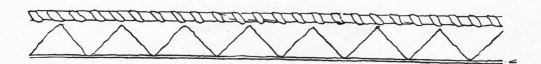

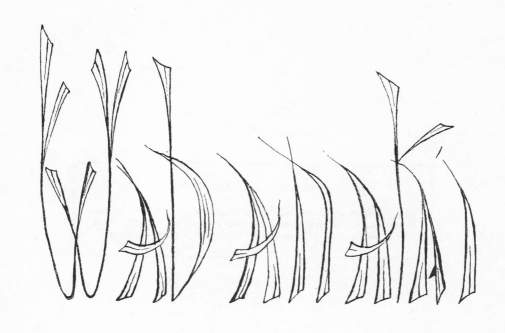

WABANAKI TITLE-PAGE

The design is a picture cut in birch-bark by a Penobscot Indian.
It represents the cow moose, the bull moose, and the wild duck.
The lettering is by Hinook Mahiwi Kilinaka (Angel De Cora).

THE INDIANS' BOOK

THE WABANAKIS [1]

Told by Bedagi (Big Thunder)

WE are the Wabanakis [1]—"Children of the Dawn Country," "People of the East." Five tribes made up our nation —Passamaquoddy, Penobscot, Micmac, Maliseet, and a tribe now gone that lived on the Kennebec River. Some of the tribes had almost the same speech, others a different one. Long have the white men been among us, yet though we have forgotten many of the old songs and stories, we have never lost our language. It is only nowadays that the children use less and less the speech of their fathers.

Long have the white men been among us. Yet some of us still remember the time when our lives were spent in hunting and fishing, and our villages were of wigwams instead of houses.

In the olden time our garments were of moose-skin and fur, our pouches were the skins of animals, our dishes were of wood and bark. Before the coming of white men, our knives and tomahawks and all our tools were of stone. With a stone knife we cut open the moose and with a tool of stone we skinned him. We fished with a bait of stone, well greased with moose-tallow, on a line of moose-sinew. Our lives were simple and glad, and our marriages were happy. Man and woman made their vow to the

NOTE FOR PRONUNCIATION OF WABANAKI TEXT

Unless otherwise indicated, vowels have the Continental sound and consonants the English. Where no translation appears, the song-words are meaningless vocables.

[1] The Wabanakis are of Algonquian stock.

Great Spirit. In our old religion we believed that the Great Spirit who made all things is in everything, and that with every breath of air we drew in the life of the Great Spirit.

THE STORY OF THE FIRST MOTHER

Joseph Nicolar, a Penobscot Indian, compiled and wrote the legends of his people, and published them himself in the year 1893, in a small volume entitled *The Red Man*. " The Story of the First Mother," is adapted from the book and is here contributed by Nicolar's wife, who is still living at Oldtown, Maine. The same story as told to the compiler by Big Thunder differs somewhat in detail, but is essentially the same.

LONG ago, when Kloskurbeh, the great teacher, lived in the land, and there were as yet no other men, there came to him one day at noon a youth; and the youth stood before Kloskurbeh and called him " mother's brother," and said: " I was born of the foam of the waters; for the wind blew, and the waves quickened into foam, and the sun shone on the foam and warmed it, and the warmth made life, and that life is I. See, I am young and swift, and I have come to abide with you and be your help in all things."

Again on a day at noon there came a maiden and stood before the two and called them " my children," and the maiden said: " I have come to abide with you, and I have brought with me love. I will give it to you, and if you will love me and grant my wish, all the world will love me well, even the very beasts. Strength is mine, and I give it to whosoever may get me; comfort also; for though I am young my strength shall be felt over all the earth. I was born of the beautiful plant of the earth; for the dew fell on the leaf, and the sun warmed the dew, and the warmth was life, and that life is I."

Then Kloskurbeh lifted up his hands towards the sun and praised the Great Spirit, and afterwards the young man and the maid were man and wife, and she became the first mother. Kloskurbeh taught their children and did great works for them, and when his works were finished he went away to live in the Northland until it should be time for him to come again. But the people increased until they were very many, and there came a famine among them; and then the first mother grew more and more sorrowful. Every day at noon she left her husband's lodge and stayed from him until the shadows were long. And her husband that dearly loved her was sad because of her sorrow, and one day he followed her trail as far as the ford of the river, and there he waited for her to return. When she came, she sang as she began to ford the river, and as long as her feet were in the water she seemed glad, and the man saw something that trailed behind her right foot, like a long green blade. But when she came out of the water she stooped and cast off the blade, and then she appeared sorrowful.

The husband followed her home as the sun was going down, and he bade her come out and look at the beautiful sun. And while they stood side by side, there came seven little children that stood in front of them and looked into the woman's face, saying, " We are hungry, and the night will soon be here. Where is the food ?" Then the woman's tears ran down, and she said, " Be quiet, little ones; in seven moons you shall be filled, and shall hunger no more."

The husband reached out his hand and wiped away her tears and said, " My wife, what can I do to make you happy ?" And she answered, " Take my life."

" I cannot take your life," said the man; " will nothing else make you happy ?"

" Nothing else," she answered. " Nothing else will make me happy."

Then the husband went away to the Northland to take counsel with Kloskurbeh, and with the rising of the seventh sun he came again and said, " O wife, Kloskurbeh has told me to do the thing you wish." Then the woman was glad and said: " When you have slain me, let two men lay hold of my hair and draw my body all around a field, and when they have come to the middle of the field, there let them bury my bones. Then they must come away; but when seven moons have passed let them go again to the field and gather all that they find, and eat; it is my flesh; but you must save a part of it to put in the ground again. My bones you cannot eat, but you may burn them, and the smoke will bring peace to you and to your children."

[5]

On the morrow when the sun was rising the man slew his wife; and, as she had bidden, men drew her body all about an open field, until the flesh was worn away, and in the middle of the field they buried her bones. But when seven moons had gone by, and the husband came again to that place, he saw it all filled with beautiful tall plants; and he tasted the fruit of the plants and found it sweet, and he called it " Skar-mu-nal," corn. And on the place where her bones were buried he saw a plant with broad leaves, bitter to the taste, and he called it " Utar-Mur-wa-yeh," tobacco.

Then the people were glad in their hearts, and they came to his harvest; but when it was all gathered in, the man did not know how they should divide it, and he sent to Kloskurbeh for counsel. When Kloskurbeh came and saw the great harvest, he gave thanks to the Great Spirit and said, " Now have the first words of the first mother come to pass, for she said she was born of the leaf of the beautiful plant, and that her power should be felt over the whole world, and that all men should love her. And now that she is gone into this substance, take care that this, the second seed of the first mother, be always with you, for it is her flesh. Her bones also have been given for your good; burn them, and the smoke will bring freshness to the mind. And since these things came from the goodness of a woman's heart, see that you hold her always in memory; remember her when you eat, remember her when the smoke of her bones rises before you. And because you are all brothers, divide among you her flesh and her bones—let all shares be alike — for so will the love of the first mother have been fulfilled."

WABANAKI

N'SKAWEWINTUAGUNUL

Songs of Greeting

Sung and told by Blamswe-Zozep Tene (Francis Joseph Dana), Lincoln, Maine, and Asawhis
(John Salis), Eastport, Maine

WHENEVER we saw a canoe rounding the point, flying a white flag, we knew that strangers were coming to visit us. Then we gathered on the shore, men, women, and children, like a great procession, waiting to welcome them. In those days the Wabanaki tribes had each their chief (sagam), lieutenant-chief (mehchichiket, or leptahnit), and five or six head warriors or captains (s'moganis). The stranger (s'moganis) first sprang to land and sang the N'Skawewintuagunul (song of greeting), stepping slowly towards our chief, in time to the song, while all the people sang "hega, hega." At the end of the song the stranger had drawn close to the chief, and holding out his hand said, "I greet you, chief of the Passamaquoddy." Then the people gave a great shout and fired off their guns. In the same way the stranger greeted the lieutenant-chief and the captains. Then we in our turn performed the same ceremony, singing the song of welcome, and shaking hands with the visiting chief and his men.

Then the visitors and all the people went up together to the village, and there the guests were feasted.

These are the songs of greeting of the olden days.

THE GAME OF BARTER

Sung and told by Bedagi (Big Thunder)

WINTER is the season for story-telling and games. One of our amusements in the old days was the game of barter. Two companies would gather in separate wigwams and each dress one of their men in comic dress as a *nolmihigon*, or clown. The first nolmihigon and his company would go to the second wigwam with some article to be offered

[7]

for exchange. Then the nolmihigon would dance and sing so comically and praise the article with so much wit that often he would receive in exchange for it something of far greater value. For instance, he would take an old wooden spoon, and stroking it would say how fair it was, how useful, singing, " If you will keep him well, he will serve you your life long."

The people of the opposite company then would offer him their things in exchange, and if the nolmihigon were clever he might obtain a good canoe for his old spoon. Snow-shoes, moose-skin garments, axes, all things were bartered in this merry way. When the exchange had been made, the first nolmihigon and his company would go back to their own wigwam, and then the nolmihigon and people of the second wigwam would visit them with their wares. But great was the fun if the people of the second wigwam ran very fast and arrived at the first wigwam before their hosts had returned. Of course, the party with the wittiest nolmihigon were winners in the end. So we joked and played on long winter evenings in the olden days.

PENOBSCOT BARTER DANCE-SONG

Ko na wa ya ti ge
Ko na wa ya ti ge
Ko cha ba la chich a
Ni ta ge si za

(Meaning of words unknown)

PENOBSCOT WAR-DANCE SONG

Kwa ha hi-a
Kwa nu kwa nu de he no
Kwa nu de kwa nu de
He no

These are no real words, but the meaning of the song as given by Big Thunder might be, " I wish that you were dancing, too."

PENOBSCOT DANCE-SONG

LIKE most Indian dance-songs, this song may be repeated an indefinite number of times, sometimes varying the form by repeating certain parts instead of singing the song straight through. The beat of the rattle, also, varies. Sometimes the long rattle-shake or the short rattle-beats occur in one place, sometimes in another.

The rattle used is of horn, beautifully carved, and filled with pebbles or shot. The mouth of the horn is stopped with wood.

With the Maliseet Indians, "Kwe-hiu-wha-ni-ho" is a greeting, like "how are you?" It is not used in speech, but only in singing.

PENOBSCOT MEDICINE-SONG

BLAMSWE-ZOZEP TENE used to hear his grandfather sing this song, and in those old days the song had words. But it has not been sung by the people for forty or fifty years, and now Blamswe knows only the vocables used in the refrain. The song is thought to be an old medicine-song of the Penobscots, but some of the Wabanakis say it is a social song.

DANCE-SONGS

Now used at Weddings

Told by Maliseet Indians

WHEN a youth wishes to marry, he sends wampum to the father of the maid by the hand of one of the old men of the tribe. The old man delivers the wampum and speaks in praise of the youth; then he goes away. If the father send the wampum back to the youth, it is a sign that the suit is rejected, but if the wampum be kept, the youth knows that he is accepted. When the wedding-day comes, the maid and her lover each prepare a great feast in the open air, and then a messenger

goes through the village, calling, " Your dishes!"   This is the signal
that the feast is ready, and all the people gather to it, men, women,
and children, bringing bowls and platters; every one is bidden.

These are all that are still kept of the ancient marriage customs,
and it is only at weddings that we still dance the old Indian dances.
We dance half the evening in the French or American manner and
then the other half in the old Indian way.   To keep time in our
dances, we use a rattle made of horn, filled with pebbles or shot, and
stopped with wood.   At the end of the song we call out quickly,
twa, twa, twa, twa, like a summons to others to come and dance
with us.   Sometimes the whole song is sung with only " twa, twa "
for words.   The old people still love the Indian dance, and for
the wedding merry - making wear all their ancient Indian ornaments of silver, shell, or fur.

MALISEET DANCE-SONG

Kwe-hiu-wha-ni-ho	Hey, ho, dance away,
Ya hi ye	Dance away!
Kwe-hiu-wha-ni-yo	Hey, ho, dance away,
Ya hi ye	Dance away!
Ya hi ye	Dance away!
Kshi-te-ka-mo-tik 'lo	Harder, faster let us go.
Ya hi ye	Dance away!
Ya hi ye	Dance away!
Pilsh-kwe-sis-tok 'lo	Youths and maidens, be gay.
Ya hi ye	Dance away!
Ski-no-sis-tok 'lo	Youths and maidens, be gay.
Ya hi ye	Dance away!
Kshi-te-ka-mo-tik 'lo	Fast and faster let us go.
Ya hi ye	Dance away!
Twa, twa, twa, twa! (etc.)	Come, come, come, come!

PASSAMAQUODDY DANCE-SONG

Wagad-alo	He is coming, our grandfather,[1]
N'Musums sanow	Great Blamswe-Zozep,
Kchi Blamswe-Zozep	With a string of fish!
Ha-ba-mes-ba-na	We ho (etc.)
We ho (etc.)	

[1] " Grandfather " is a title of respect or reverence for any old man.

HUNTING THE MOOSE

Told by Bedagi (Big Thunder)

THE Great Spirit made all things; all men are his children. He made the Indians last of all, and so, since they are his youngest children, they are not as wise as the white men. But the Great Spirit said, "In time you shall know me." And he placed in the hands of the Indian the bow and said, "This shall find for you both food and clothing."

The Great Spirit is in all things; he is in the air we breathe. The Great Spirit is our father, but the earth is our mother. She nourishes us; that which we put into the ground she returns to us, and healing plants she gives us likewise. If we are wounded, we go to our mother and seek to lay the wounded part against her, to be healed. Animals, too, do thus, they lay their wounds to the earth. When we go hunting, it is not our arrow that kills the moose, however powerful be the bow; it is nature that kills him. The arrow sticks in his hide; and, like all living things, the moose goes to our mother to be healed. He seeks to lay his wound against the earth, and thus he drives the arrow farther in. Meanwhile I follow. He is out of sight, but I put my ear to a tree in the forest, and that brings me the sound, and I hear when the moose makes his next leap, and I follow. The moose stops again for the pain of the arrow, and he rubs his side upon the earth and drives the arrow farther in. I follow always, listening now and then with my ear against a tree. Every time he stops to rub his side he drives the arrow farther in, till at last when he is nearly exhausted and I come up with him, the arrow may be driven clean through his body. Then I can kill him easily with my knife.

The moose comes when he is called. We call him with a horn made of bark; or we stand in the water and scoop it up and then let it slowly drip as if a moose were drinking. The moose comes to the sound because he thinks to find his mate.

Now follows the story of the moose:

STORY OF THE MOOSE

In olden days the moose was so large that he used to browse on the tops of trees; also he destroyed the people. So the Great Spirit sent Ksiwhambeh[1] to the people, and when he had come he called us all together and said, " I have come to change that animal, the moose, so that you can take comfort in him."

Then Ksiwhambeh called for a strip of birch-bark, three hands long, and when it was brought him he set one hand upon an end of it, and two fingers upon the other end, and he rolled the bark into a horn and began to call the moose. The first time he called, the people could only faintly hear the sound of the answer far in the distance; then he called again, and the answer was nearer and nearer till at last a moose appeared. And Ksiwhambeh spoke to the moose and said: " I have come to make you smaller so that my children can take comfort in you. Come here to me."

The moose came and held down his head, and Ksiwhambeh took him between the horns and pushed him down to the size that he now has. Then Ksiwhambeh said to him, " Henceforth look that you never come till you are called."

Thus Ksiwhambeh changed the moose; and to this day the hunter calls him with a horn of birch-bark.

MALISEET LOVE-SONG

This song comes from St. John, New Brunswick. It is a hunter's farewell song. In the autumn the youth sets out for the long winter hunt, and parts from his love, telling her to watch for him at the breaking of the ice in the spring, that she may see him coming down the river in his canoe.

The Wabanakis have many such songs. They call them " Songs of Loneliness."

[1] Culture hero of the Eastern Algonquins, known among the Penobscots as Ksiwhambeh, Kloskurbeh (Kluskabe). Among the Passamaquoddys the name is Kuloscap or Glooscop.

WABANAKI

LOVE-SONG

(In the Indian text certain syllables are interpolated, changed, or prolonged for euphony)

Boskiu ta-la-bin
Elmi na-lamwouik
Elmi siguak-lo
Tabegi-lok-lo
Chipduk knamihi
Sakwelagweyan
    Ku we nu de nu
    Ku we nu de nu

Look oft up the river, look oft and oft.
In spring at the breaking of the ice,
    look oft;
You may see me coming down in my
    canoe.
Look oft up the river, look anew, anew.

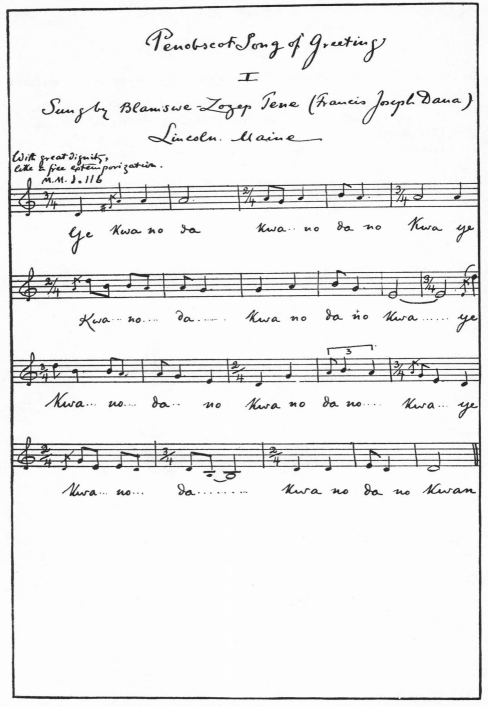

Penobscot Song of Greeting

I

Sung by Blamswe-Zozep Tene (Francis Joseph Dana)
Lincoln. Maine

With great dignity,
like a free extemporization.
M.M. ♩ = 116

Ye Kwa no da   Kwa no da no Kwa ye

Kwa no da   Kwa no da no Kwa ye

Kwa no da no Kwa no da no Kwa ye

Kwa no da   Kwa no da no Kwan

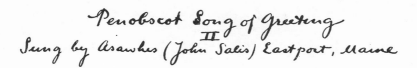

Penobscot Song of Greeting
II
Sung by Asawkes (John Salis) Eastport, Maine

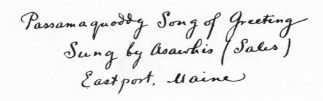

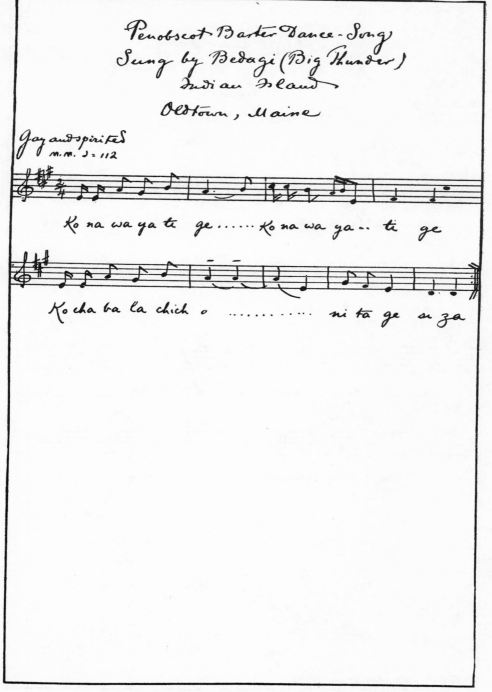

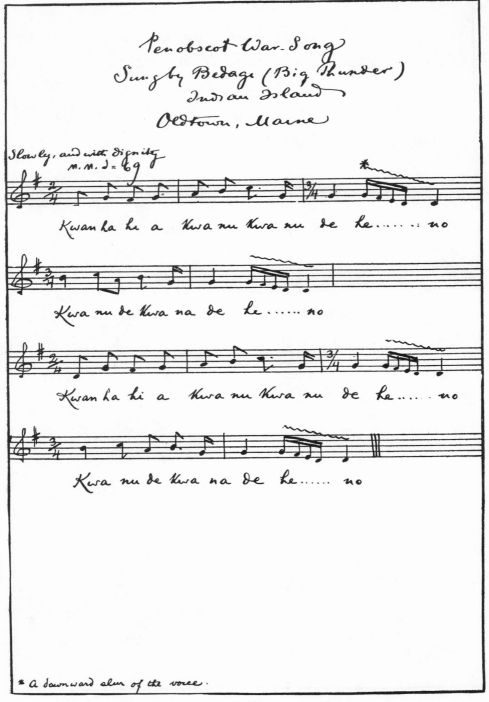

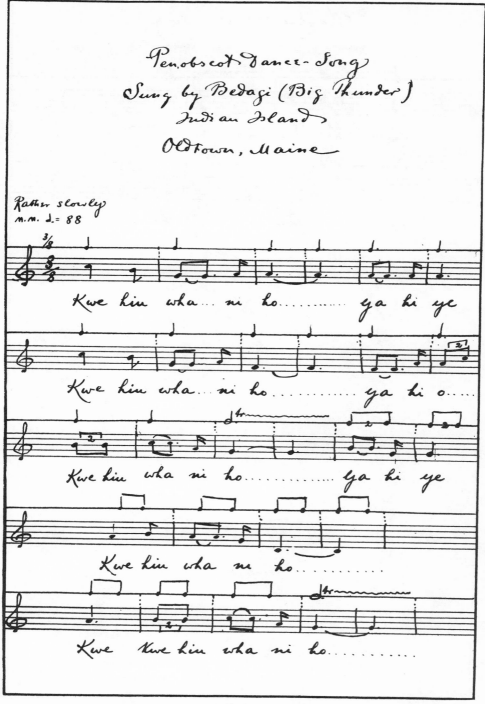

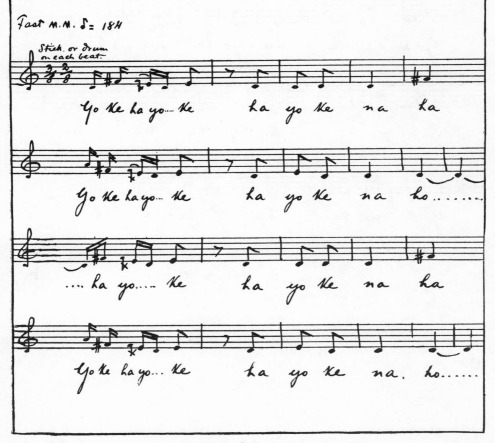

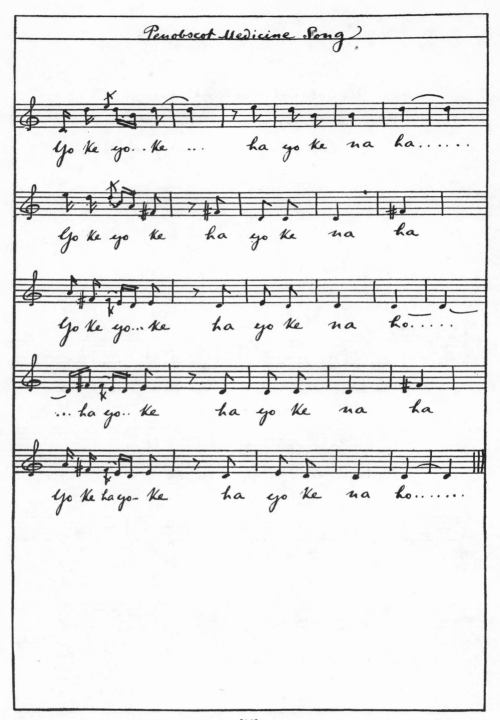

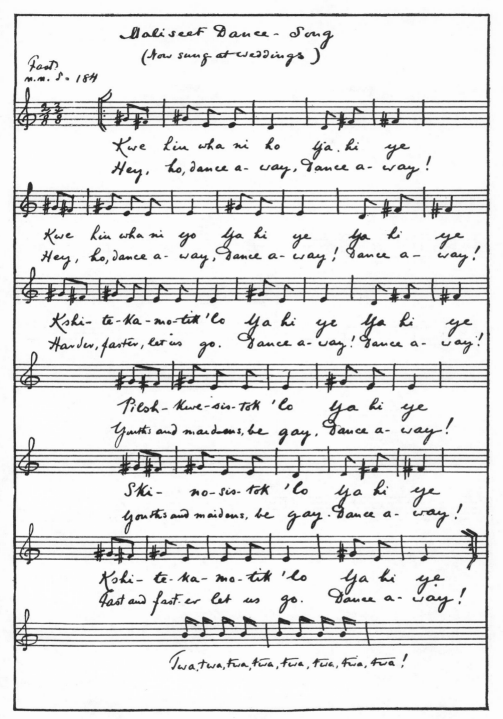

Maliseet Dance-Song
(Now sung at weddings)

Kwe lin wha ni ho   Ya hi ye
Hey, ho, dance a-way, Dance a-way!

Kwe lin wha ni yo   Ya hi ye   Ya hi ye
Hey, ho, dance a-way, dance a-way! Dance a-way!

Kshi-te-ka-mo-tik 'lo   Ya hi ye   Ya hi ye
Harder, faster, let us go. Dance a-way! Dance a-way!

Pilsh-kwe-sis-tok 'lo   Ya hi ye
Youths and maidens, be gay, Dance a-way!

Ski-no-sis-tok 'lo   Ya hi ye
Youths and maidens, be gay. Dance a-way!

Kshi-te-ka-mo-tik 'lo   Ya hi ye
Fast and fast-er let us go. Dance a-way!

Twa, twa, twa, twa, twa, twa, twa, twa!

[23]

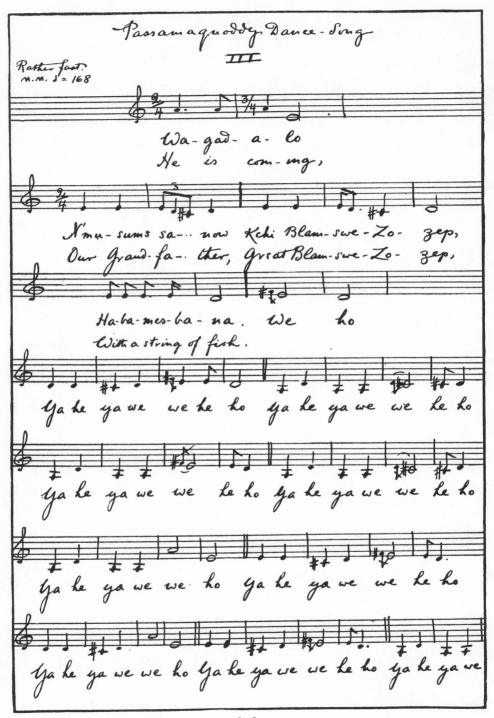

Passamaquoddy Dance-Song

III

Rather fast.
m.m. ♩ = 168

Wa - gad - a - lo
He is com - ing,

N'mu - sums sa - - now Kchi Blam - swe - Zo - zep,
Our Grand-fa - - ther, Great Blam - swe - Zo - zep,

Ha - ba - mes - ba - na. We ho
With a string of fish.

Ya he ya we we he ho Ya he ya we we he ho

Ya he ya we we he ho Ya he ya we we he ho

Ya he ya we we ho Ya he ya we we he ho

Ya he ya we we ho Ya he ya we we he ho Ya he ya we

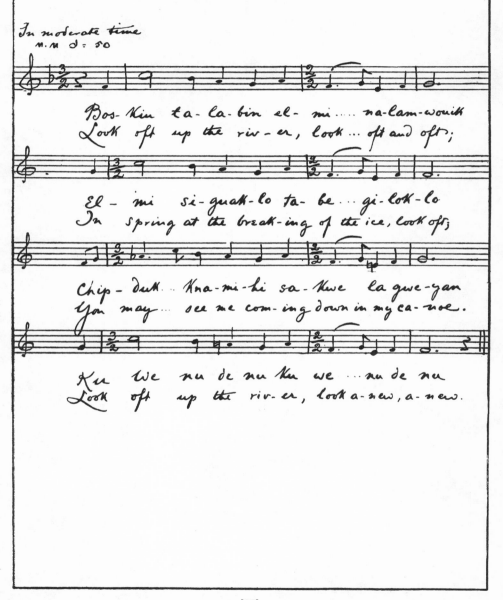

PLAINS

INDIANS

PLAINS INDIANS TITLE-PAGE

The buffalo is painted by Hiamovi (High Chief), of the Cheyenne
tribe. The buffalo is chosen to represent the Plains people, to
whose life in former days it was all important.
The lettering is by Hinook Mahiwi Kilinaka (Angel De Cora).
The letters are formed of the horns of the buffalo.

ORGANIZATIONS OF THE PLAINS INDIANS [1]

AMONG the Indians of the plains there are societies to which the men of the tribe belong according to age or achievement. These societies are religious, military, or social, and some are very old, while others are modern. The military organizations are old, and are commonly called warrior societies. In old times the different societies had their several peculiar functions in warfare, in the hunt, and in camp discipline. Where the organizations are regulated by age, a man passes through successive societies and graduates from the lower to the higher.

Among some tribes the highest is the Chiefs' Society, composed entirely of chiefs; the Fox Men are usually young, while the Dog Soldiers are older warriors of high standing.

Again, a society may have for the nucleus of its being a dream or supernatural revelation common to all its members; or it may be the guardian of some wisdom revealed in vision by a spirit—often the emblematic spirit-animal.[2] Thus an organization may bear the name of some animal whose virtue or psychic power it incorporates.

Each society has its own songs and ceremonies, and in some cases its members carry the peculiar staff or badge of office belonging to the society, such as a lance, a club, or a crook.

[1] The Plains Indians are those who live between the Mississippi River and the Rocky Mountains, and who used to hunt the buffalo in days gone by.

[2] See "Songs of the Dakotas," page 60, and "Introduction to Pawnee Songs," page 96.

THE HOLY MAN, OR "MEDICINE-MAN"

T HE English word "medicine" has come to be applied to what the Dakota Indian calls *wakan*. Wakan means both mystery and holiness, and is used by the Indian to designate all that is sacred, mysterious, spiritual, or supernatural.

The Supreme Being of the Dakotas is called Wakan-Tanka. In English this name is commonly rendered "The Great Spirit," but it would be translated more correctly as "The Great Holy-Mystery."

Wakan-Tanka is an omniscient force. This conception of an impersonal, spiritual, and life-giving power is held by many Indian tribes as well as by the Dakotas, and would seem in no way to be a product of early missionary teaching, but rather an intense and integral part of the Indian's nature. Besides the Great Mystery, the Indians recognize lesser spiritual beings who are personifications of certain elements in nature, in animals, and in man; but these, like all else, owe their existence and their power to the Supreme One.

The Wicasa-Wakan, Holy Men, or Men of Mystery, are the prophets, soothsayers, moral leaders, and healers of the tribe. On account of their service as healers they were called by the early French traders *médecins*, or doctors, and the word "médecin" came to be applied to everything pertaining to the Holy Man and to all that is sacred or supernatural to the Indian. Anglicized, the word became *medicine*, and thus the Holy Man is known everywhere in English as the "Medicine-Man." [1] Catlin says, "The Indians do not use the word medicine, however, but in each tribe they have a word of their own construction, synonymous with mystery or mystery-men."

Healing plants and herbs, manipulation, and the sweat-bath are curative agents long understood by the Indian. In case of wound,

---

[1] A remarkable exposition of the true character of the medicine-man is given in an address by Mr. Francis La Flesche, entitled "Who was the Medicine-Man?" printed in the Thirty-second Annual Report of the Fairmount Park Art Association, Philadelphia, 1904.

the poison is first sucked out by the medicine-man and then healing drugs are applied. The sweat-bath is a means of purification and is connected with the Indian's religion, having its place in many ceremonies.

Broadly speaking, the character and functions of the Holy Man are the same in most Indian tribes. The Indian conception of healing is through divine power; and be the healing agent some supernatural charm, or be it medicine in the ordinary sense of the word, the act of cure is usually accomplished amid song, ceremony, and prayer.

DAKOTA TITLE-PAGE

A Dakota brave and Medicine - Man, painted by a Dakota
Indian, Tatanka-Ptecila (Short Bull). The warrior wears the
horned head-dress emblematic of divine power, the insignia of
the Holy Man, or Man of Medicine.
The lettering is by Hinook Mahiwi Kilinaka (Angel De Cora).

THE DAKOTAS

WITH the possible exception of the Ojibwas, the Dakotas (or Sioux) are the most numerous of any Indian tribe within the United States. The name Sioux is the ending of the word *Nadowessioux,* said to be, in its original form, an Algonquian word signifying "snakes"—that is, enemies—but the Sioux call themselves "Dakota," or "Lakota," a name meaning "allied," or "many in one." Although the Dakotas have come to be associated almost exclusively with the West, there is a theory to the effect that their home was originally east of the Alleghanies. When first known to the French, the main body of the Dakota nation had already migrated to the most westerly regions of the Great Lakes, in northwestern Wisconsin, eastern Minnesota, and about the headwaters of the Mississippi. From this country they were driven by the French and the Ojibwas, who possessed fire-arms, of which the Dakotas were at that time ignorant.. They then established themselves in the Black Hills and Platte country. In the course of their migrations they lost entirely the agricultural

NOTE FOR PRONUNCIATION OF DAKOTA TEXT

(Adapted from Riggs's Dakota-English Dictionary)

The five vowels have each one uniform sound—the Continental.
The following consonants are peculiar to the Dakota language :
c is an aspirate with the sound of English ch, as in *chin.*
ç is an emphatic " c," pronounced like a vigorous " c " and followed by sudden expulsion of the breath.
ġ is a deep sonant guttural like Arabic *ghain.*
h is a strong surd guttural like Arabic *kha.*
n in italic has the nasal sound of " n " in the French word *bon.*
q represents a sound bearing the same relation to " k " that " ç " does to " c."
ś has the sound of sh, as in *shine.*
ż has the value of " s " in *pleasure.*

[37]

habits that had characterized them in their more easterly homes, and with the exception of the Eastern and Santee branches, who remained sedentary and agricultural, the tribe, with the acquisition of the horse, adopted the roving life of the Plains hunters.

About the year 1875, when the Dakota and Ojibwa struggle came to a close, the Dakotas were in undisputed possession of territory that stretched from Devil's Lake to Sioux City, and from the east bank of the Mississippi River almost to the Rocky Mountains. Little by little these Indians were forced to yield to the United States government one tract after another of this country. Yet in the face of suffering, and, it must be admitted, of great provocation to violence, the Dakotas have shown themselves capable of superb loyalty, truth, and heroism. When forced to fight in defence of their hunting-grounds, the warriors proved themselves brave and skilful in battle; while the warlike ability of their chiefs won the admiration of those who fought against them. Nor can the massacres and depredations perpetrated by minorities of the tribe counterbalance the uprightness of the majority and the honor of the leaders.

The Dakota songs in this book were contributed by members of the Ogallalla and Brule bands, belonging to the Teton branch of the Dakota family, and now living in the reservations of Pine Ridge and Rosebud, South Dakota.

A HOLY STORY

Told by Chief Maza Blaska (Flat-Iron, meaning a piece of flat iron). Maza Blaska is one of the oldest living chiefs of the Ogallalla band

FROM Wakan-Tanka, the Great Mystery, comes all power. It is from Wakan-Tanka that the Holy Man has wisdom and the power to heal and to make holy charms. Man knows that all healing plants are given by Wakan-Tanka; therefore are they holy. So too is the buffalo holy, because it is the gift of Wakan-Tanka. The Great Mystery gave to men all things for their food, their clothing, and their welfare. And to man he gave also the knowledge how to use these gifts—how to find the holy healing plants, how to hunt and surround the buffalo, how to know wisdom. For all comes from Wakan-Tanka—all.

To the Holy Man comes in youth the knowledge that he will be holy. The Great Mystery makes him to know this. Sometimes it is the Spirits who tell him. The Spirits come not in sleep always, but also when man is awake. When a Spirit comes it would seem as though a man stood there, but when this man has spoken and goes forth again, none may see whither he goes. Thus the Spirits. With the Spirits the Holy Man may commune always, and they teach him holy things.

The Holy Man goes apart to a lone tipi and fasts and prays. Or he goes into the hills in solitude. When he returns to men, he teaches them and tells them what the Great Mystery has bidden him to tell. He counsels, he heals, and he makes holy charms to protect the people from all evil. Great is his power and greatly is he revered; his place in the tipi is an honored one.

Now I will tell the story of how a Holy Man, the greatest in the tribe, made mystery-power in the olden days.

The people were encamped in a circle[1] with the opening towards the east. In the middle of the circle they set up a great tipi[2] made of several tipis put together. On one side of the tipi sat the women, on the other side the men. And they made ready a great feast. Beyond the central fire, opposite the doorway, the Holy Man made mystery. With a stick like an arrow he made a line of holes in the ground a finger's-length deep. Then he touched the ground[3] in front of all the people and came back to the door-

[1] From the writings of Mr. Francis La Flesche we learn that with the Omaha tribe the tribal circle typified the cosmos, the dwelling-place of the Great Spirit. The circle was divided in half, one section representing the heavens, the other the earth—a symbolic division embodying the idea that the Great Spirit pervades the heavens and the earth. Mr. La Flesche says, further, " Each of the two great divisions of the tribe had its particular symbol, representing a cosmic force, or one of the various forms of life on the earth. The name of the clan, and the personal names of its members, all have reference to its symbol. The personal name was ceremonially bestowed upon the child; so within the tribe we have clan names that refer to the sun, moon, stars, clouds, rain, and wind; the earth, hills, lakes, rivers, and all animals from birds to insects. In this manner the Indian recognized that all things were created by the Great Spirit."

[2] Tipi is the Dakota word for the native dwelling of the Plains Indians—a conical tent, formerly made of buffalo-hide, and frequently ornamented and painted with symbols.

[3] An act of consecration.

way and sat down. And he bade the people hasten to prepare
the mystery. So they took clay and filled the holes with it and
covered the holes with earth. When they had done this the Holy
Man touched the ground. Then he came back to the doorway and
was about to sing. And the people watched the ground where the
clay was buried, and behold, young plants began to sprout. Then,
before he sang, the Holy Man said:

> "Far to the west,
> Far by the sky
> Stands a blue[1] Elk.
> That Elk standing yonder
> Watches o'er all the females
> On the earth.

> "Far to the east,
> Far by the sky
> Stands a blue Elk.
> That Elk standing yonder
> Watches o'er all the females
> On the earth."[2]

Thus he spoke; then he said, "Now I will sing," and beating on his
drum he sang a holy song. When he had sung he bade the people
pull up the sprouts, and they did so; one by one they pulled them
up. And behold, the roots were holy mystery-power. And the
people took the mystery-power and laid it on sprigs of sage, for sage
is holy because it will heal. This mystery would protect the warriors
in war. No arrow could pierce them, no arrow could strike them,
unharmed would they pass through every danger.

So have I told of how a Holy Man made mystery to help the
people. Now may Wakan-Tanka help me, because I have spoken
truly of how Wakan-Tanka bade the Indians to do in the olden
times.

---

[1] The Dakotas call "blue" what the white man calls gray.

[2] The Elk is said to have power to guard females. Thus the Holy Man has invoked the power
of the Elk to watch over the women, and has made mystery-power to help the men in battle.

THE HISTORY OF THE SPIRIT-DANCE [1]

TO understand the so-called "Ghost-Dance Movement" among the Indians, the white reader will find it necessary to understand the causes that inspired it.

It is hard for the white man to realize the suffering of the red man in the first sharp crisis of adjustment to the new life. The span of one generation brought to the Indian of the plains change such as the white man experienced only through long centuries of evolution—the change from the life of primitive man to that of civilization. Nor did the white man in his wholesale slaughter of the buffalo for hides realize, perhaps, what the extinction of the animal would mean to the people of the prairies, to whom the buffalo supplied nearly every physical want—food, clothing, and even lodging, for of buffalo-hides were made the portable skin lodges of the prairie tribes.

In the white man's invasion of the plains and in the advent of the railroad, the red man saw his own doom. All effort of the Indian to stem the stream of settlement pouring through his territory was as a straw against the tide. The railroad brought more white men; the buffalo vanished, and with it passed forever from the Indian the old life—the only life he had ever known.

The change was swift and cruel. "The earth is our mother," had declared the Indian. But now no longer was the Indian the free child of the prairie. Confined in reservations and fed on rations, or transported to another clime where he fevered and died; swept by disease, bewildered amid conflicting change, crushed in spirit and broken of heart, the Plains Indian at this period presents to the calm eye of history a tragic picture of the workings of a seemingly relentless destiny.

In about the year 1888, perhaps at a time when, to the prairie tribes, their utter subjugation had become a vivid and despairing

[1] A very full and valuable study of the religion of the Ghost-Dance, as it is usually called, has been made by Mr. James Mooney, of the Bureau of American Ethnology, Washington, D. C. The work is contained in the fourteenth annual report of the bureau.

truth, there arose in western Nevada an Indian prophet. He was a simple Paiute, and his teachings were simple. He announced that he had been with God, of God was his wisdom, and from God were the messages he brought. First, there should be no fighting; all men should love one another. A great change was to come over the earth—a day when there would be no misery and no sickness. The dead would return from the spirit-world, and all Indians would be united in deathless happiness upon a rejuvenated earth. The Indians should make themselves worthy of the change. "Harm no man, do right always," taught the prophet. As a holy rite, all people should dance a holy dance which the prophet gave to his followers. The Indians should be honest and industrious, should quietly do their work and remain at peace with the whites. For by God alone would be wrought the change, and earthquakes would herald its approach. It was soon to come, even with the spring.

Word flashed from tribe to tribe—"A savior has arisen for the Indians." Delegates from different tribes were sent to the prophet and returned convinced. Then followed unconscious distortions of the messages. Some Indians, influenced by missionary teachings, cried: "Jesus is on earth. He came once long ago beyond the waters, and the white people killed him. Now he is come to the Indians, who never did him harm." The Plains Indians believed that the race would be reinforced by the spirits of the dead, that the old days would come again, the buffalo return, the white man be swept back across the sea or buried beneath the new earth which would cover the land. In the country of their fathers again would the Indians be powerful and free. Men wise and less despairing than these hopeless Indians have known religious revivals scarcely less fanatic.

The new religion developed into an answer to the longing of the Indian's heart. Some tribes laid aside fire-arms and everything of metal, that they might be as they were before the coming of the white man. Many were drawn to the new faith by the word that those who danced in the holy dance "died" (fell in a trance) and went to the spirit-world, where they saw their dead loved ones. Any one familiar with the inner life of the Indians knows that, to this people, the trance condition is not uncommon.

DAKOTAS

The dancers moved in a circle, with clasped hands and slow, dragging step, singing with rhythmic swing the songs of the Spirit-Dance. Round and round went the circle, while every now and then a dancer staggered from the ring and fell swooning in a trance. On awakening, the "dreamer" described his vision of the spirit-world. Then the experience of the trance was embodied in a spontaneous song, to be thereafter used in the dance. The passionate attachment of Indians to their children and to chosen friends made this religion, with its hope and its communion with the spirit-world, seize upon the people with twofold intensity. The new faith spread from tribe to tribe like prairie-fire. It was as though a sudden breath of hope had blown into one last flame the dying embers of the native spirit. The flame flared for a moment on the Indian's night, then sank with the hideous tragedy, the battle at "Wounded Knee" in South Dakota.

News that the Indians were meeting and dancing spread alarm among the whites. Those who knew the Indians vainly counselled, "This is a religious movement; do not oppose it and it will pass." Commands to the Indians to cease dancing met with the response: "We harm no one. The Father has bidden us to dance. We will defend our religion, if need be, with our lives."

The agent in charge of the Dakota Indians at Pine Ridge was unable to check the dance among his people. Thoroughly frightened, he telegraphed for troops. At sight of the soldiers, the warlike Dakotas were in arms. "We will die, but we will not give up our religion," they cried. Broken promises of the government, insufficient rations, ravages of disease, had rendered these Indians wellnigh desperate. An attempt to disarm them in the effort to bring them amicably to the agency was misunderstood by the Indians, who feared massacre. An Indian fired his rifle. The shot was answered by a volley from the troops. Machine guns at close range mowed down the entire camp, blowing the victims to pieces. Wellnigh three hundred Dakotas, men, women, and children, fell in what is now called the massacre of Wounded Knee. Brave Roman Catholic missionaries succored the few wounded Indians who escaped. Throughout the trouble, their loyalty to their duty met with answering loyalty from the Indians. The torn, frozen bodies of the dead were thrown by the whites into an open trench one upon another. Around the trench the Indians have since placed posts decorated with red paint, the holy emblem of the Spirit-Dance. There is probably throughout the country no more pathetic burial-ground. All silently it tells of the struggle of a desperate people.

Thus perished among the Dakota Indians the so-called " Ghost-Dance Movement." With some other tribes the dance is still continued, but not with the old significance. The religion of which the dance is the embodiment has undergone this change—the hope contained in it is now a spiritual one. The old days never came again, but the prophet's moral teachings still endure. Since the message of the Paiute, all thought of strife has ceased.

May another prophet tell a future of happy adjustment to the new life! For with the slaughtered Indians in the trench at Wounded Knee lies buried the hope of the people of the plains for the happiness of vanished days.

Short Bull (Tatanka-Ptecila), a Dakota medicine-man, had been a leader in the new religion. He was revered among his people as a great medicine-man, a prophet, and a worker of miracles. He was one of those who first sought " the Father," as the Indians called the Paiute prophet. He had brought back to his people the messages and the dance, and had given them many songs. He had made the charmed " ghost-shirts " which should render the Indians invulnerable to the white man's bullet. He had taught, had prophesied, had led.

Short Bull is low of stature (hence his name, " Short-Buffalo-Bull "), but he bears himself with the dignity of the Indian of the past generation. His face is full of distinction, diplomacy, and power; but it is marked with wistful dreaminess. It is the face of the seer—visionary, intellectual, and idealistic. Most striking of all is the expression of profound sadness.

Short Bull saw the old life pass, he saw the new hope killed at a blow. The noble sorrow of his race is graven on his face.

From Short Bull's own lips The Indians' Book receives the story of his visit to " the Father " and his message to his people.

[44]

Tatanka-Ptecila (Short Bull)

SHORT BULL'S NARRATIVE

Note.—The white reader should bear in mind that this is the narrative of a
seer. As is usual with Indians, the language is often figurative. In the English
rendering, the attempt has been made to reflect the rhythmic dignity and simplicity
of the Dakota. The narrated visit to the spirit-camp was probably a vision, or
was made in a trance. To the Indian, such a vision is as real as a waking event.
The visit to the other camp was a reality. The Paiute Indians wear blankets or
robes of rabbit-skin. He who is referred to as " this one of the rabbit-robe " is
the prophet, known to the people as " the Father." " The land where the sun sets "
is Nevada, the home of the prophet. " Rosebud " is an Indian reservation in
South Dakota.

WHO would have thought that dancing could make such
trouble? We had no wish to make trouble, nor did we
cause it of ourselves. There was trouble, but it was
not of my making. We had no thought of fighting;
if we had meant to fight, would we not have carried arms? We
went unarmed to the dance. How could we have held weapons?
For thus we danced, in a circle, hand in hand, each man's fingers
linked in those of his neighbor.

Who would have thought that dancing could make such trouble?
For the message that I brought was peace. And the message was
given by the Father to all the tribes. Thus it happened:

I journeyed to the land where the sun sets; and then I went
to the spirit-land, where I saw the spirit-encampment. I drew
near and stood outside a spirit-tipi. A spirit-man came out and
stood beside me. He spoke to me and said:

" Behold, I give you something holy!" Then he said, " Whence
come you?"

And I answered, " I come from Rosebud."

Then said the spirit-man, " Go we together in a cloud, upward,
to the Father."

So we rose in a cloud to where were other camps, and there we
saw those who wear the blanket of rabbit-skin. As we passed
through the camp of these, there came towards us a man and his
wife. Said this one of the rabbit-robe:

"I would speak with you now. Behold, I tell you something for you to tell to all the people! Give this dance to all the different tribes of Indians. White people and Indians shall all dance together. But first they shall sing. There shall be no more fighting. No man shall kill another. If any man should be killed it would be a grievous thing. No man shall lie. Love one another. Help one another. Revile not one another. Hear me, for I will give you water to drink. Thus I tell you, this is why I have called you. My meaning, have you understood it?"

Thus spoke he of the rabbit-blanket, and holy red paint he gave to me. In the spirit-camp I had seen those who had died, and when I came homeward there came with me two spirit-companions, invisible to all but me. These journeyed with me and stayed ever with me. I heard their counsel.

Alone in my tipi I dreamed, and saw visions, and communed with the spirits. And I went forth and taught the people and told them of the Father's word and of the help that should come to the Indians. There were others who taught as well as I. The Father had commanded all the world to dance, and we gave the dance to the people as we had been bidden. When they danced they fell dead and went to the spirit-camp and saw those who had died, those whom they loved — their fathers, their mothers, and their little children. Then came trouble. Yet in our dance we harmed no one, nor meant we ill to any man. As the Father had commanded, so did we.

It is true, all men should love one another. It is true, all men should live as brothers. Is it we who do not thus? What others demand of us, should they not themselves give? Is it just to expect one friend to give all the friendship? We are glad to live with white men as brothers. But we ask that they expect not the brotherhood and the love to come from the Indian alone.

In this world the Great Father has given to the white man everything and to the Indian nothing. But it will not always be thus. In another world the Indian shall be as the white man and the white man as the Indian. To the Indian will be given wisdom and power, and the white man shall be helpless and unknowing with only the bow and arrow. For ere long this world will be consumed in flame and pass away. Then, in the life after this, to the Indian shall all be given.

With clasped hands stood the Indian narrator and the white recorder, and then the white friend spoke:

"I leave you with this word: Be of good heart. Even though the old days are gone, never to come again, still be of good heart. A better day will dawn for your people. The old days will never be again, even as a man will never again be a child. Those days were the happy childhood of your race. Manhood brings sorrow and sorrow wisdom. Wise through sorrow will be your people, and the days of full maturity will be warm with sunshine. You journeyed to the west for tidings of hope. You sought the Father in the land of the sinking sun. The hope you brought of the old life was not as the dawn-light, but as the after-glow of sunset skies. Now look for the new day. In the land where the sun rises the Indians have friends. Not westward, but eastward seek the coming of the light."

May The Indians' Book echo to every Indian the message, " Look for the new day!"

WANAĠI WACIPI OLOWAN

Songs of the Spirit-Dance (Ghost-Dance Songs)

Sung and told by Tataŋka-Ptecila (Short Bull)

I

WANAĠI WACIPI OLOWAN	SONG OF THE SPIRIT-DANCE
Ateyapi kiŋ	Thus the Father saith,
Maka owancaya	Lo, he now commandeth
Lowaŋ nisipe-lo	All on earth to sing,
Heya-po,	To sing now.
Heya-po,	Thus he hath spoken,
Oyakapo—he !	Thus he hath spoken.
Oyakapo—he !	Tell afar his message,
	Tell afar his message !

II

In this song the dancer calls to the dead mother to come back, for the little brother is always crying, always crying. The song was much sung in the time of the Spirit-Dance. Many of the songs of the Spirit-Dance end with the words, "Saith the Father," like a final benediction.

WANAĠI WACIPI OLOWAN

Ina, hekuye,
Ina, hekuye,
Misunkala ceya-ya omani,
Misunkala ceya-ya omani
Ina, hekuye,
Ina, hekuye !
Ate heye-lo,
Ate heye-lo !

SONG OF THE SPIRIT-DANCE

Mother, oh come back,
Mother, oh come back,
Little brother calls as he seeks
    thee, weeping,
Little brother calls as he seeks
    thee, weeping.
Mother, oh come back,
Mother, oh come back !
Saith the Father,
Saith the Father.

III

This song tells how the dancer has been, in trance, to the spirit-world, and there has feasted with his friends upon the old-time Indian dish of pemmican, made of dried buffalo-meat, pounded fine, with tallow, wild-cherries, and spices.[1]

WANAĠI WACIPI OLOWAN

He, he, wanna wawate,
He, he, wanna wawate ;
Wasna watinkte,
Wasna watinkte !

SONG OF THE SPIRIT-DANCE

Hey, hey, joyous feast we now,
Hey, hey, joyous feast we now ;
    Eating pemmican,
    Eating pemmican !

[1] According to the teaching of the prophets the dancer who in a trance feasted on pemmican in the spirit-world would find upon awakening in this world a piece of pemmican in his hand. The song is also prophetic of the time when through a miracle the white men should be swept back across the Big Waters, the buffalo would return, and the Indian would feast as of old on buffalo meat.

DAKOTAS

WICAŚA-ATAWAN OLOWAN

Song of the Seer

Sung and told by Tatanka-Ptecila (Short Bull), a Holy Man, Prophet, or "Medicine-Man."

THE tribe always camped in a circle, and in the middle of the circle was a place called Hocoka, the centre.

Before the people set out to war, the prophet, or holy man, made a tipi for himself and sat in it alone, looking into the future and seeing in vision all that would befall. The people brought him offerings of gifts, and he made holy emblems and charms to protect them in battle.

Then, before sending out the scouts, the warriors assembled in the centre of the camp and sat in a circle awaiting the prophet. He came forth, singing a holy song, and bestowed upon the warriors the charms that he had made, and told to every man his fate.

This is the song of prophecy that he sang. In the last part of the song, where now there are only sounds of no meaning, he sang words which foretold to each warrior the fate that would befall him in the strife.

This song is sung when the tribe is going to war, just before the scouts set out to find the enemy.

WICAŚA-ATAWAN OLOWAN

    Hocoka wan cicuqon
    Yutonkal nunwe

SONG OF THE SEER

    In this circle,
    O ye warriors,
    Lo, I tell you
    Each his future.
    All shall be
    As I now reveal it
    In this circle;
          Hear ye!

SUNKA OLOWAN

Song of the Dog Society[1]

IN old times when the hosts were drawn up for battle, it was the duty of certain of the Dog Soldiers to dismount in front of the hosts and drive their lances into the ground. To these lances they tied themselves with a buckskin thong. Every man's heart grew strong when the Dog Soldiers drove down the lance.[2] There they stood at the front of the battle, shaking their rattles and singing. Howsoever the battle might go, the hosts might not turn back until the Dog Soldiers gave the signal. Even then the Dog Soldiers would not themselves leave their posts until one of their own society should pull up the lance and whip them away. If the flying warriors forgot to release them, the Dog Soldiers died where they stood. For death is as nothing, and pain is as nothing; but cowardice is crime, and disgrace is the greatest punishment.

TASUNKE-SKA OLOWAN

Song of the White-Horse Society[3]

Sung by Matoisto-Nakipin (Bear-Arm-Necklace, meaning necklace of claws from the forefeet of the bear).

TASUNKE-SKA OLOWAN	SONG OF THE WHITE-HORSE SOCIETY
Kola, taku	Friend, whatever hardships threaten,
Otehika	If thou call me,
Imakuwapi-lo	I'll befriend thee;
Hena kowokipi sni	All enduring fearlessly,
Waon welo !	I'll befriend thee.

[1] See " Organizations of the Plains Indians," page 31.
[2] The Dog Soldiers were human emblems of courage, and their presence inspired their followers with desperate zeal.
[3] Often sung while on the war-path. See "The War-Path," page 154.

TOKALA OLOWA*N*

Songs of the Fox Society

Sung and told by Wicapi (Star)

THE Dakotas tell how, a few years ago, a party of young men went over into Montana to hunt. They were unjustly arrested by the local sheriff, and Agna-Iyanke (Runs Beside) was shot. Though mortally wounded, he lived two days, and, being a Fox warrior, he sang on his homeward journey a song of the Fox Society. His song is the first of the two Fox songs here recorded. The melody is old, but the words are Agna-Iyanke's own.

The second song was sung by the men of the Fox Society at their next dance in honor of their dead companion.

TOKALA OLOWA*N*

Tokalaka miye ca,
Nakenula wao*n* welo.

SONG OF THE FOX SOCIETY

Lo, the Fox, the Fox am I!
Still the Fox a moment yet,
Then the Fox shall be no more.

TOKALA WACIPI OLOWA*N*

Omani ki*n* nayapapi, ca
Agna-Iyanke hena yunke-lo!

DANCE-SONG OF THE FOX SOCIETY

Ha, you hunters,
All you hunters fled,
Yea, but the Fox fled not,
There, behold, he lay!
Ha, you fled,
But there, behold, he lay!

WAKAN OLOWAN

Holy Song (Medicine-Song)

Sung and told by Wambli-Waśte (Good-Eagle), a Holy Man.

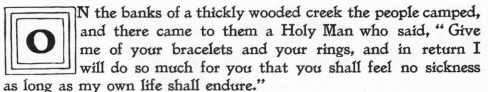

ON the banks of a thickly wooded creek the people camped, and there came to them a Holy Man who said, " Give me of your bracelets and your rings, and in return I will do so much for you that you shall feel no sickness as long as my own life shall endure."

They gave him bracelets and rings, both of buffalo-hide and of silver, and then the Holy Man told them to make for him a sweat-lodge, such as the people call " new life," because the man that comes out of it feels as if made anew. So when he had purified himself in solitude he set up a pole in the earth, and bound upon it a buffalo-calf's hide painted red. Then the crier went throughout the camp and called for all the sick to come close to the pole, and when they were gathered there they cut off strips of skin from their arms for an offering and laid them at the foot of the pole. Then came forth the Holy Man, and he set a wooden cup at the foot of the pole, and began to sing this song:

> " O ye people, be ye healed;
> Life anew I bring unto ye.
> Through the Father over all
> Do I thus.
> Life anew I bring unto ye."

While he sang, water trickled down the pole until it filled the cup. He gave the cup to the sick, and they all drank of the water and were healed, yet the cup was never empty. And when they had all drunk, he sent them to their tipis and bade them rest until evening. When the sun was down they gathered again about the pole, and the Holy Man cleared a space upon the ground and sang again and drew with his finger in the dust. No man could tell the meaning of that which he had drawn, until the Holy Man spread his hand above the characters, and looked upon the ground and said, " The spirits of the fathers tell me that to-morrow you shall see buffalo in plenty, and every man of you shall kill three." Also he said, " You shall cut off the legs and cut out the tongues and hearts of all those that you kill, and leave them for an offering to the Great Mystery; but you shall bring to me forty hides."

All happened as he had said, and he took the hides and made of them forty holy shirts for the people. Then he told them to bring him clay and straw and charcoal, and with these he made gunpowder, caps, and wads, and gave to all men. So when he had provided thus for the people, he called them all and ranged them in a line, and then he stood at the end of the line holding a wooden pipe in his hands, and he filled the pipe and lit it from the rays of the sun,[1] and then passing it from hand to hand each man blew out a few whiffs to symbolize the breath of life. Then said the Holy Man: " This people is good. I have healed their sickness. I have renewed their life. Now shall I go back to my own place." After that the people saw him no more.

WAKAN OLOWAN	HOLY SONG
Oyate wan waśte ca	O ye people, be ye healed;
Wanna piyawakaǧe-lo !	Life anew I bring unto ye.
Wankanta Tunkanśila heya ca	O ye people, be ye healed;
Wanna piyawakaǧe-lo !	Life anew I bring unto ye.
	Through the Father over all
	Do I thus.
	Life anew I bring unto ye.

[1] The Navajo Indians light their ceremonial cigarettes by the sun by means of a crystal.

SUNGMANITU OLOWAN

Wolf Song

Sung and told by Chief Tasunke-Hinto (Blue Horse)[1]

O other man may sing this song but Tasunke-Hinto. He only has the right, for it is his own song, learned by him of the wolves. So long as the wolves shall live, so long shall Tasunke-Hinto live; and when they die, he too will die.

This is how he learned the song:

When he was a young man of twenty-seven winters, he set out on the war-path[2] with twelve other warriors. Just as the dawn grew yellow he heard the wolves begin to sing, and one of them broke into this song. Tasunke-Hinto listened to the wolf's song and learned it and took it for his own. It is in very truth the song that the wolf sang at dawn. Tasunke-Hinto then sang it to his comrades—and lo! on that same day they met a war-party of Pawnees, and killed them, every man.[3]

Tasunke-Hinto is now very old, but he still sings the Song of the Wolf. Before he sings he turns to the west, and, holding up his hand, calls aloud: " O West Wind, and ye, my old comrades, if any be there, listen, listen to my song!" For he says: " The East is the white man's country, but the West is where we belong, I and the wolves, and my old friends now long dead. Perhaps I shall soon be with them!"

[1] The Dakotas call " blue " what the white man calls gray.
[2] See " The War-Path," page 154.
[3] The wolf, as an animal, is a symbol of war. Also, the Pawnees are known as Wolves; they are hereditary foes of the Dakotas.

A Chief of the Olden Time (Chief Yellow-Hair)

Tasunke-Ciqala (Little Horse)

DAKOTA

OLOWAN

Song

Sung and told by Tasunke-Ciqala (Little Horse)

HIS song tells how an aged warrior sees the young men setting out to war, and as he thinks of his own by-gone glory, he sadly realizes that he is now only an old man with the toothache. When the people are gathered for a dance or festival, this song may be sung in honor of some old warrior, who then makes gifts of garments or horses to the singers.

OLOWAN	SONG
Okicize iyotan micilaqon, Miye sni se, iyotiyewakiye-lo !	Mighty, mighty, great in war, So was I honored ; Now behold me old and wretched !

OMAHA WACIPI OLOWAN

Omaha Dance-Songs

Sung by Tasunke Ciqala (Little Horse)

HE Omaha Dance[1] came from the Omahas. It is an occasion when men narrate the tales of great deeds and make gifts to one another; it has now become also a social gathering of the people.

I

OMAHA WACIPI OLOWAN	OMAHA DANCE-SONG
Natanhiwan winyan wakage	Charged the foe, But I made a woman of him !

[1] See " Winnebago He-lush-ka Na-wan."

II

At the end of the Omaha dance a feast is held, the food being first consecrated by ceremony. This song is sung during the consecration, as a summons to the people to partake of the feast.

OMAHA WACIPI OLOWA*N*

Ho, leciya nicopi !

OMAHA DANCE-SONG

Come hither, hither, ho !
Hither now we summon ye !
Come hither, ho !
Hither, ho !

WIOŚTE OLOWA*N*

Love-Songs

These love-songs are modern; they are current Indian songs of the day.

I

Sung by Capa-Ta*n*ka (Big Beaver, Frank Goings)

WIOŚTE OLOWA*N*

Tokiya amayaleso?
Tokiya amayaleso?
Hignawaya cin na
Temahilaqon,
Eśa wagnikte!
Eśa wagnikte!

LOVE-SONG

Nay, love, but whither are you leading me?
Nay, love, but whither are you leading me?
My own husband loves me,
He whom I have left.
Leave me, for he loves me,
Leave me, let me go.
O leave me !

II

Sung by Capa-Ta*n*ka (Big Beaver)

WIOŚTE OLOWA*N*

Inkpataya nawaźin
Na śina çiçoze
Ma-ya, Ma-ya,
Leciya ku wanna !

LOVE-SONG

Up the creek I stand and wave ;
See, all alone I wave !
Ah, hither,
Ah, hither,
Haste thee to me !

[56]

DAKOTA

III

Sung by Tašunke-Ciqala (Little Horse)

WIOŚTE OLOWAN	LOVE-SONG
Koškalaka otapi tka,	Many are the youths, many youths :
Nišna iyokipi mayaye.	Thou alone art he who pleaseth me.
Iyotan cilaqon,	Over all I love thee.
Wankiciyake šni unqonkte !	Long shall be the years of parting !

IV

Sung by Tatanka-Hinapawi (Buffalo-Appearing) wife of Tašunke-Ciqala

WIOŚTE OLOWAN	LOVE-SONG
Eyaš hececa ye lakaš,	Know the reason of our parting :
Awanicigla waonqon.	I have watched thee well, faithless one !
He-ye, he-ye,	He-ye, he-ye,
Nape-mayuza !	Clasp my hand and part !

V

Sung by Wicapi-Wakan (Holy Star, Julia Yellow-Hair)

In the present state of transition from the old life to the new, Indian children often are educated by the government at a distant boarding-school, where they must remain for five years without returning home.[1] Not infrequently the pupil stays in school for a longer period than the five years, and on going home finds the life of his people completely strange to him.   It is not at all uncommon for the Indian child to have forgotten his own language during the school period, and so, on his return, to be unable to speak with his parents. The going away to boarding-school, with its parting from parents and friends, is a distinct era in the life of the Indian. The following song shows how throughout the changing conditions of his life the Indian retains the instinct to embody experience in song. It is supposed to be sung by a young maid just setting out for school.

[1] See page xxxiii.

Holy Star (Julia Yellow-Hair) is in boarding-school, and that is why she has chosen this song for her contribution to The Indians' Book. She is granddaughter of the aged chief, Yellow-Hair, renowned among the Dakotas.

WIOŚTE OLOWAN	LOVE-SONG
Ehake wanmayakuwe,	For the last time, come greet me again,
Ehake wanmayakuwe.	For the last time, come greet me again,
Sice tecihilaqon !	Dear friend, I loved thee alone !
Wanna waya wamanikte.	Now to school I'm going away ;
Ehake wanmayakuwe,	For the last time, come greet me again,
Ehake nape-mayuza !	For the last time, come take my hand !

ŚUNKA OLOWAN

Song of the Dog-Feast

Sung and told by Chief Maza-Blaska (Flat-Iron, meaning a piece of flat iron)

BEHOLD, it was thus. Once long ago in the season of falling leaves the Dakotas went hunting at the edge of the Black Hills. The people were starving and great was their need of meat, So they vowed,[1] "If only we find buffalo we will give all our dogs a feast." Thus they vowed.

Lo, soon afterwards they saw a herd and killed many buffaloes, and came back to their camp, weary but rejoicing. Then, true to their vow, they made a great feast for their dogs; in the centre of the camp they piled all the tallow from the buffaloes and amid this they scattered the tongues. So they did, giving to the dogs the choicest morsels. Then the men took their dogs and painted them for the feast. With a stripe of red down the back and red on the side of the jaw they painted them. Then they led them to the pile of tallow in the centre of the camp and held them in a circle while all sang, "May you feast well, O dog!" Three times they sang this song, while the dogs strained and growled and yelped. Then a man cried out, "Hold well your dogs! Once more shall the song be sung."

[1] To the spirit-animals: perhaps to the Dog. See introduction to Pawnee songs.

Wicapi-Wakan (Holy Star)

So yet again the people sang, while the dogs strained harder; then at the last of the song—away! The dogs flew at the meat and devoured it eagerly, every morsel. Lo, they as well as their masters had hungered long.

Thus came about the custom of the Dog-Feast. It was the grandfather of Maza-Blaska who originated it. It has great mystery-power; through it the Dog is honored, and the secrets of the Dog, in mystery and in hunting, are revealed to the men of the feast.

ŚUNKA OLOWAN	SONG OF THE DOG-FEAST
Śunka wayatanin!	May you feast well, O dog!

OKICIZE OLOWAN

War-Song

Sung by Tasunke-Hinsa (Sorrel Horse), Mahpiya-Tatanka (Sky Bull, meaning buffalo-bull), and Mato-Wankantuya (High Bear)

THIS is a war-song well-known among the Dakotas. It is an old song and was sung by the Dakotas when fighting for their land. It is now sung by chiefs on various occasions, sometimes at the opening of ceremonies or of councils.

The melody is also used with different words as Wopila Olowan, a song of thanksgiving. A gathering of the people for social festival or ceremonial dance is an occasion for the giving of presents.[1] At some time during the dance or ceremony a herald announces that a gift is to be made, and summons by name him who is to receive it. This one goes forward and accepts his present, or, if the present be a pony or other animal, he may receive at the moment only the promise of the gift. He expresses his thanks with quiet solemnity and passes his hand in blessing over the giver. Many may give presents one after the other on the same occasion.

If blankets or robes are given at a dance, it is customary some-

---

[1] Strangers or visitors from other tribes receive at such times gifts of horses, money, food, and clothing. This hospitality is reciprocated when the visit is returned.

times for parents to make the gift through their child, dressed for the occasion in fairest apparel. The parent spreads the gift upon the ground, and the child, shod in finest moccasins, dances upon it in consecration while appropriate songs are sung. Sometimes the child is a young maiden in buckskin dress ornamented with elk-teeth, who dances shyly with drooping head and downcast eyes. Sometimes it is a little lad in costume of the olden time, with painted face and jangling ornaments. The boy is led by his father to the blanket, and, in imitation of his elders, right manfully dances a little war-dance to the rhythmic beat of the drum.

The recipients return thanks with song, and visitors from another tribe sing in thank-offering the songs of their people.

This song is frequently sung on such occasions; it is used in many bands of the Dakotas, and has come to be known to other tribes as well:

OKICIZE OLOWAN

Kolapila takuyakapi-lo !
Maka kin mitawa yelo !
Epinahan blehemiciye-lo !

WAR-SONG

Comrades, kinsmen,
　　Now have ye spoken thus,
The earth is mine,
　　'Tis my domain.
'Tis said, and now anew I exert me !

THE SONGS OF THE DAKOTAS[1]

Told by Huhuseca-ska (White Bone), Zintkala Maza (Iron Bird), and Mato-Nažin
(Standing-Bear)

TWO are the kinds of songs: songs made by man, and songs that come in dreams or in visions through the spirits from Wakan-Tanka.

Of the first kind there are songs made by the mind of man to please the ear. Then there are songs to express feelings, and to rouse feelings—songs to stir men to brave deeds, to give

---

[1] Dakota musical instruments are flute, rattle, drum, and whistle of eagle-bone.

strength in battle, and songs to make strong the heart to meet danger, grief, and death.

War - songs, victory - songs, songs sung in Omaha dances — all these are of this first kind. So also are the songs of the different societies, such as the White-Horse Society, the Fox Society, and many others. Love-songs, gaming-songs, more kinds of songs than can be named are made by man for his feeling, and his pleasure. All such songs may be sung by any one.

Songs of the second kind come from Wakan-Tanka and are *wakan*—holy, apart. No man has the right to sing such a song save him to whom the song came in dream or in vision. But this man may teach the song to others and give to them the right to sing it.[1]

All songs that are holy, that belong to sacred rites and ceremonies, that have power to work wonders, that go with healing, are of this kind: for holy rites, wisdom, and healing are from Wakan-Tanka.

Everything that has life has spirit as well as fleshly form. All things have *nagi*—soul. Rocks and animals have the power to appear in the form of man, and to speak to man in dream or in vision.[2] It is from Wakan - Tanka that they have power and wisdom.[3]

Spirits come to man in dreams and in waking visions. When the spirit comes to man in a dream, it may be thus: a song is heard on the air, then a form appears. This form is of a man, often dressed or painted in some particular or strange way. It is a spirit, who gives to the man a message, a teaching, or a song. When he turns to go, he takes, in disappearing, whatsoever form may be his own, —if he be animal, he will take the form of bear, buffalo, or bird— whatever his nature.

When the spirit comes in waking vision, it may be in this way: A man wants to gain some power, or to learn some holy practice. Into the wilderness he goes alone, and seeks the mountain-top. There without food or drink he stays, three days, three nights, and cries for power to come to him, whether from bear or snake or rock.

---

[1] The spirit may give a man a song of great power. If this man give the holy song with its power to another, the recipient will make a gift to the donor in token of his gratitude. But the Dakotas do not *sell* their songs, as some white people have supposed.

[2] Rocks, or trees may also appear in animal form.

[3] Thus the Indian learns from nature, from the animals, and from elemental forces, whose power to teach him is from the Supreme Being.

Then in the darkness will appear to him some animal in the form of man. This spirit talks to the fasting man as one man to another and teaches him to gain that power for which he cries. Thus the spirits come to man in solitude.

So are the songs of two kinds: songs made by man, and songs given from Wakan-Tanka, the Great Power that is not to be understood.

Note: Rarely it may happen that when many men are gathered in a holy work they may all hear a holy song on the air. But the song thus heard is sent to some one man of the number alone and the others may not own it or its power. In sacred ceremony when many voices are needed to sing a holy song, others may sing the song as well as the man to whom it belongs. But the others may not own the song nor have they the right to give it to others. Only in the Spirit Dance (the "Ghost-Dance") were holy songs first freely given to all the people: everyone may sing the songs of the Spirit Dance.

Wanaǧi-Wacipi Olowaṇ
Songs of the Spirit-Dance
(Ghost-Dance Songs)
Sung by Tataṇka-Ptecila (Short Bull)
Pine Ridge, South Dakota

I

With spirit, in moderate time. M.M. ♩ = 144

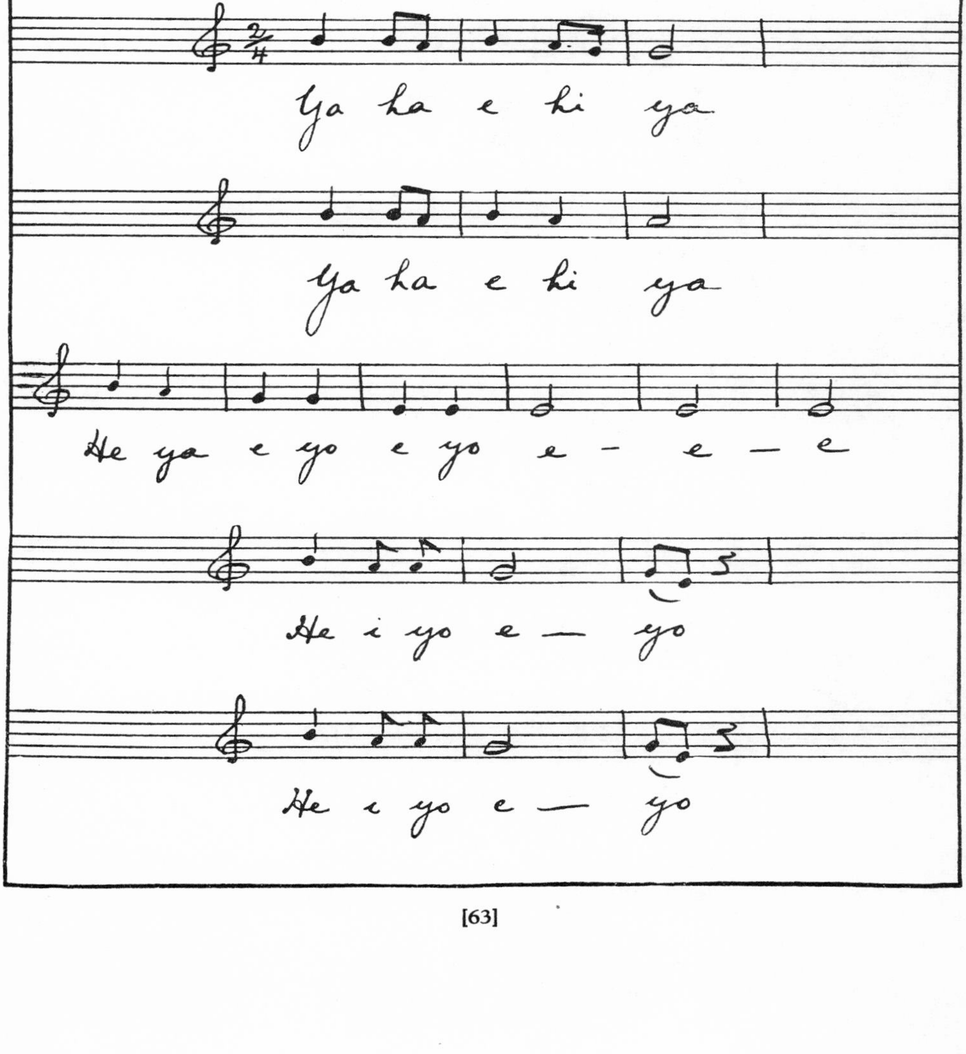

Ya ha e hi ya

Ya ha e hi ya

He ya e yo e yo e — e — e

He i yo e — yo

He i yo e — yo

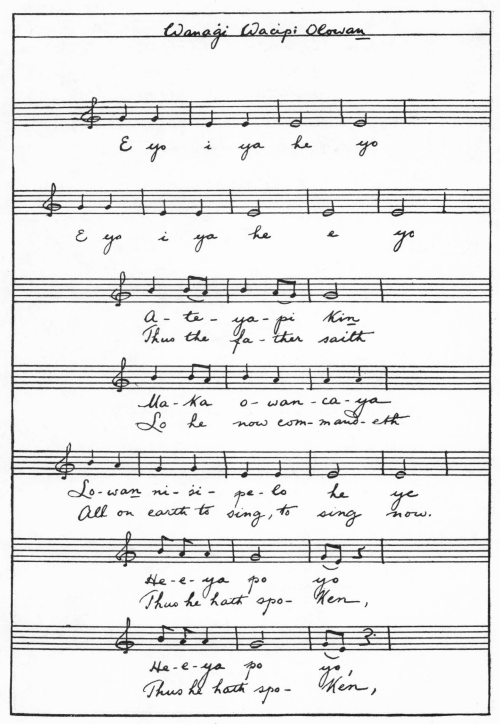

Wanagi Wacipi Olowan

E yo i ya he yo

E yo i ya he e yo

A - te - ya - pi Kin
Thus the fa - ther saith

Ma - Ka o - wan - ca - ya
Lo he now com - mand - eth

Lo - wan ni - si - pe - lo he ye
All on earth to sing, to sing now.

He - e - ya po yo
Thus he hath spo - Ken,

He - e - ya po yo
Thus he hath spo - Ken,

Wanagi Wacipi Olowan

O- ya- ka- po he - e
Tell a - far his mes.- sage

O- ya- ka- po he e yo
Tell a - far his mes.- sage, yo!

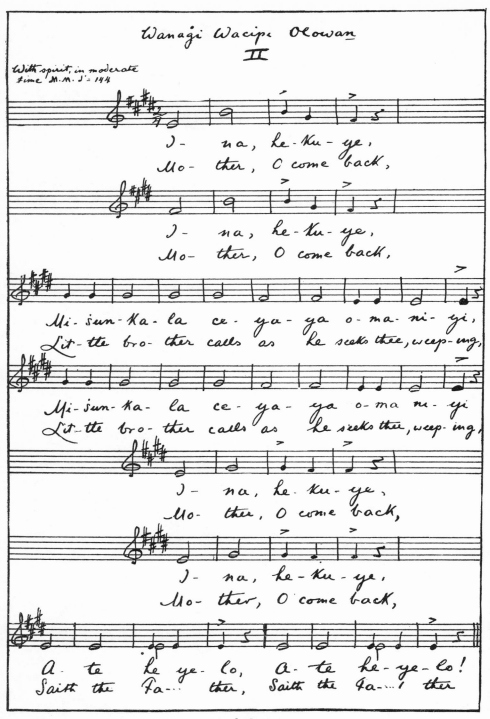

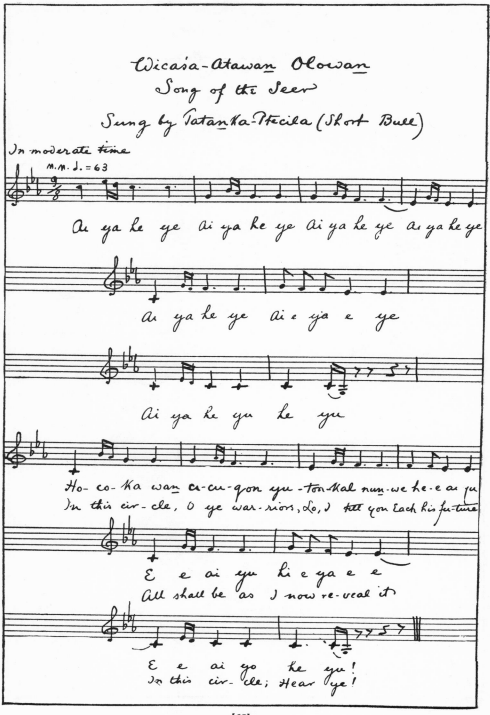

Wicasa-Atawan Olowan
Song of the Seer
Sung by Tatanka-Ptecila (Short Bull)

In moderate time
m.m. ♩. = 63

Ai ya he ye Ai ya he ye Ai ya he ye Ai ya he ye

Ai ya he ye Ai e ya e ye

Ai ya he yu he yu

Ho-co-ka wan ca-cu-qon yu-ton-kal num-we he-e ai yu
In this cir-cle, O ye war-riors, Lo, I tell you each his fu-ture

E e ai yu he ya e e
All shall be as I now re-veal it

E e ai yo he yu!
In this cir-cle; Hear ye!

[68]

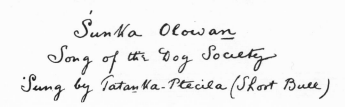

Sunka Olowan
Song of the Dog Society
Sung by Tatanka-Ptecila (Short Bull)

In moderate time
M.M. ♩ = 144.

Ya o... yo o yo

O. ya he ya

O..... ya o. ya he. ya he ... ya

He e ..... ya he ha

E e. ... ya he o e... yo

[69]

Śunka Olowan

Ya ha.... i ya he . e yo . o

he . e   e - e   yo!

Tasunke-ska Olowan
Song of the White-Horse Society
Sung by Matoisto-Nakipin (Bear-Arm-Necklace)
Pine Ridge

Not too fast
m.m. ♩ = 96

Tasunke-ska Olowan

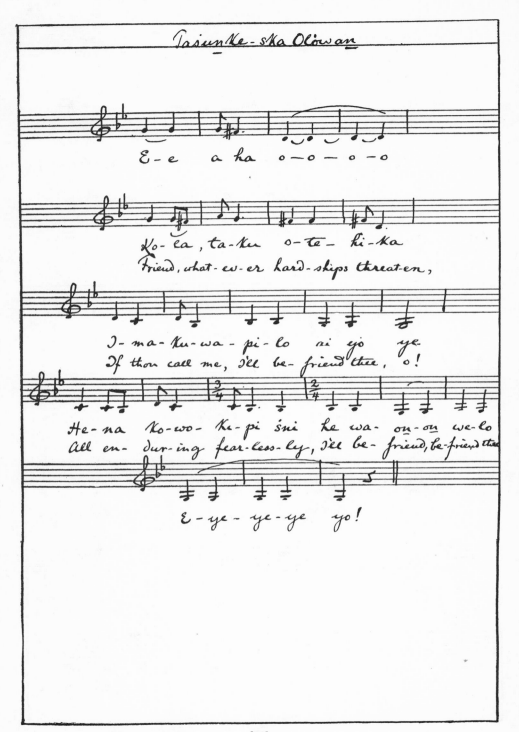

E-e a ha o—o—o—o

Ko-la, ta-ku o-te-hi-ka
Friend, what-ev-er hard-ships threat-en,

I-ma-ku-wa-pi-lo ni yo ye
If thou call me, I'll be-friend thee, o!

He-na ko-wo-ki-pi śni he wa-on-on we-lo
All en-dur-ing fear-less-ly, I'll be-friend, be-friend thee

E-ye-ye-ye yo!

Tokala Wacipi Olowan

O ma-ni Kin na-ya-pa-pi, ca
Ha, you hunt-ers, All you hunt-ers fled,

A-ga-na-I-yan Ke
Yea, but the Fox fled not,

He-na yun-Ke-lo
There, be-hold, he lay!

Hi he he ha e yo e ya he-e-e
Ha, you fled, But there,-be-hold, he lay, he lay!

He-e he-e he no!

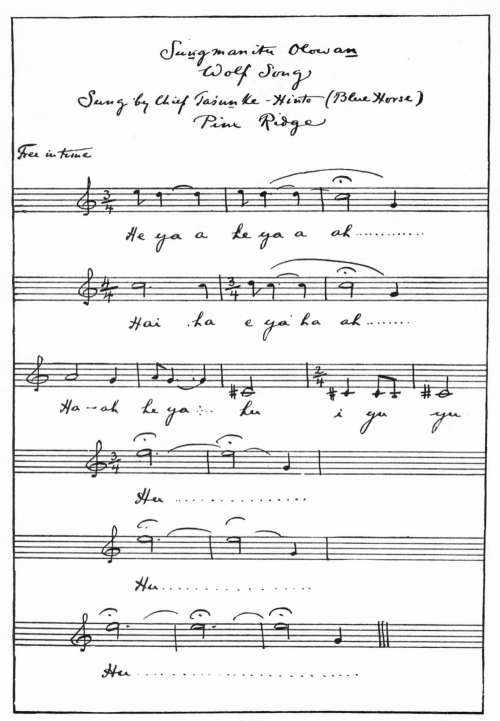

Omaha Wacipi Olowaŋ
Omaha Dance-Song)
Sung by Tašuŋke-Ciqala (Little Horse)

Fast and rhythmic.
M.M. ♩ = 88

E a- a- a- a he ya he yo-o

E a- a- a a he ya he yo-oi

E a- a- a- a he ya he yo-oi

E a- a- a wi-ya-a he- e- e- e- e!

A he ya- a ta-tan-hi-waŋ win-yan wa-ka-ge-e!
Charged the foe,   But I made a wo-man of him! wi-ya-he-e!

E a- a- a- a he ya he yo-oi

E ha-a-a wi-ya-a he-e- e- e- yo!

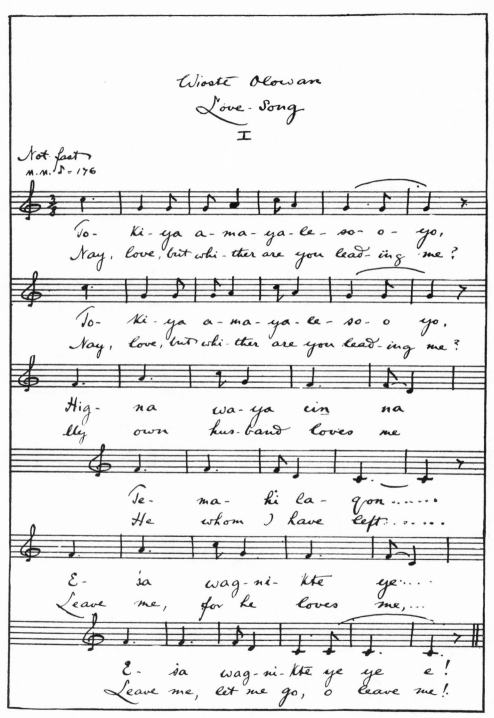

Wioste Olowan
Love-Song

II

Not fast
M.M. ♪ = 140

Inkpata ya nawa žin
Up the creek I stand and wave;

Na sina ci co ze.... e
See, all a-lone I wave......!

Maya, Maya,....
Ah, hither. Ah, hither,

Le ciya ku: wan na!.........
Haste.... thee to me!.........

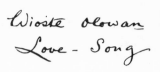

Wioste olowan
Love - Song

III

Moderately slow
m.m. ♪ = 126

Koś-ka- la-ka o- ta-pi tka,.......
Ma-ny are the youths, ma-ny youths:....

Nis-na i-yo-ki-pi ma-ya- ye.......
Thou a-lone art he who pleas-eth me.........

I-yo- tan ci-la- qon,.......
O-ver all I love thee.........,

Wan-ki-ci-ya- ke........śni un-qon-kte...........!
Long shall be the years....... of part- ing.......!

Wióšte Olowan
Love-Song
V

Sung by Wićapi Wakaŋ, Holy Star & Rosebud, South Dakota.

In moderate time
M.M. ♩ = 76

E- ha- ke waŋ- ma- ya-ku- we ye ye,
For the last time, come greet me a- gain, a-gain,

E ha- ke waŋ- ma- ya-ku- we ye ye,
For the last time, come greet me a- gain, a-gain,

E- ha- ke waŋ-ma-ya-ku- we ye ye,
For the last time, come greet me a- gain, a-gain,

E- ha- ke waŋ- ma- ya-ku we ye ye.
For the last time, come greet me a- gain, a-gain!

Si ce te- ce- hi- la- go' yo-yoŋ
Dear friend, I loved thee a- lone, a-lone,

Waŋ na. wa- ya wa-ma-ni- kte ye- ye
Now to school I'm go-ing a-way, a-way;

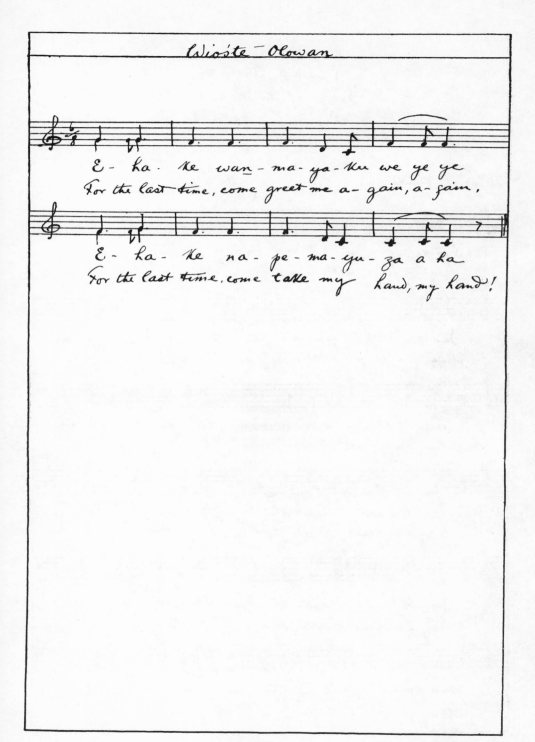

Wioste-Olowan

E - ka - ke wan - ma - ya - ku we ye ye
For the last time, come greet me a- gain, a- gain,

E - ka - ke na - pe - ma - yu - za a ka
For the last time, come take my hand, my hand!

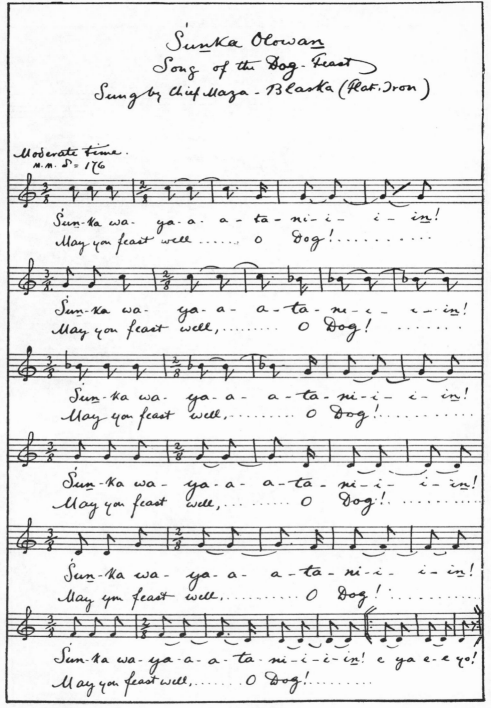

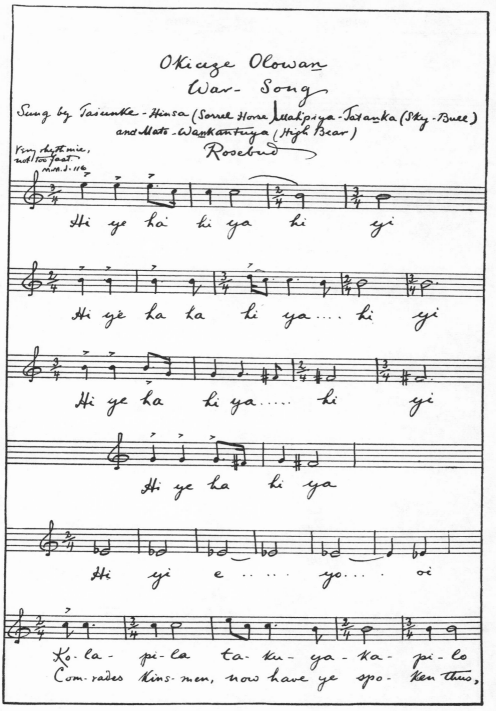

Okicize Olowan

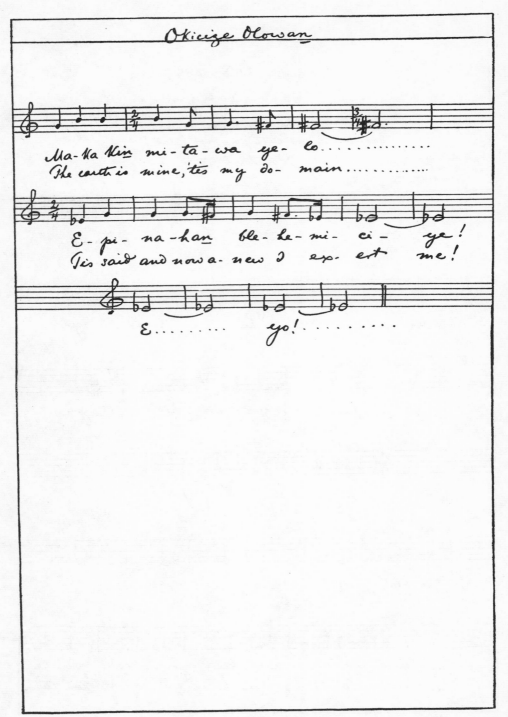

Ma-ka kin mi-ta-wa ye-lo..............
The earth is mine, 'tis my do-main..............

E-pi-na-han ble-he-mi ci-ye!
'Tis said and now a-new I ex-ert me!

E......... yo!.........

PAWNEE TITLE-PAGE

The design represents a Pawnee tipi, and is painted by a Pawnee girl.   The tipi is decorated with symbols of the buffalo, giver of life; the eagle, Tirawa's bird; the sun; the ceremonial pipe; the dome of heaven; the rainbow; the moon-mother; the morning star; horse and corn, emblems of plenty; the eagle and the evening star.

The lettering is by Hinook Mahiwi Kilinaka (Angel De Cora). From the border, in the centre, hangs the star, an emblem of Pawnee religious thought.

THE PAWNEES

THE Pawnees are one of the most famed tribes of the West. Though they form a group of the Plains Indians, yet are the Pawnees a distinct linguistic stock, allied to the Wichitas, Caddos, Arikarees, Waces, Keechis, and Tawacumers. The name Pawnee (Pa'ni) is generally conceded to mean "Wolf," and was probably given to the Pawnees because of their method of warfare, their skill as scouts, their custom of simulating wolves while on the war-path, and their tireless endurance. The Pawnees, however, have their own legend regarding the origin of their name.

Until recent years the home of the Pawnees was in southern Nebraska and northern Kansas. But it is generally believed that the tribe came originally from the Southwest, some say even from Mexico. Customs are said to have been found among them closely resembling those of the Aztecs when first discovered by the Spaniards. Their mythology as well as their traditions would help to bear out the theory of their southern origin, for their religion shows an observance of the stars and a reverence for the heavenly bodies which, to a people of deep religious thought, would be the natural result of life in a dry climate and clear atmosphere. The Morning Star

NOTE FOR PRONUNCIATION OF PAWNEE TEXT

Unless otherwise indicated, vowels have the Continental sound and consonants the English.

Ch, in italic, is a guttural, like ch in German.

The Pawnee songs are spelled according to the pronunciation of the Skidi band. The Skidi dialect differs from that of the three other bands in that what is pronounced as an *l* in the others is pronounced as an *r* in Skidi.

Acknowledgment is made to Sakuruta (Coming Sun, James R. Murie) for his help in the gathering and in the translation of these songs of his people.

and the Evening Star, the Sun and the Moon, are deeply revered by
the Pawnees, and the myths relating to the two stars are of peculiar
beauty. But highest of all, the Pawnees hold the Ruler, Atius
Tirawa, the Father Above, him whom they have always known
and recognized — a being omniscient, spiritual, supreme. Tirawa
made the Morning Star and the Evening Star, and he made all
lesser spiritual beings to carry out his commands. Say the
Pawnees, "Of Tirawa himself we know only that he made all
things, that he is everywhere and in everything, and that he is
almighty."

Another argument in favor of the southern origin of this people
is the fact that the Pawnees were perhaps more distinctly agricultural than most of the Plains Indians, and possessed permanent villages like the people of the Southwest, in addition to the portable
skin lodges common to the prairie tribes. Though in olden days
they were skilled hunters, and spent many months each year upon
the buffalo chase to provide the people with meat and skins, yet
their agricultural life was of great importance, and they returned
regularly to their villages at certain seasons to work in their fields.
Like almost all Indians, they have cultivated corn since earliest
times, and crops of beans, pumpkins, and squash rewarded their
toil as well.

The permanent dwellings of the Pawnees were earth lodges,
almost conical in shape, whose entrance was a covered passage.
The earth was laid on a frame-work of poles, and the structure was
supported within by stout posts ranged in a circle. The hearth
was in the centre of the lodge, and the smoke passed out through
a hole in the roof. The simple dwelling is full of beauty to him
who knows its meaning. There is no part of it that is not symbolic.
The entrance must always face the rising sun, the round, domed
roof is a symbol of the sky, and each post represents a star which
tells the Pawnee of some divine being. So whether within his walls
or upon the open prairie the Pawnee lived in conscious recognition
of the universe about him, ever in the presence of Tirawa, the
One Above.

The Pawnees were intrepid warriors, known to their enemies
as strong and courageous fighters. Yet they have always been

the friends of the United States government, and their loyal valor as government scouts is widely known.

In 1874 the pressure of white interests forced the Pawnees from their homes on the Platte River to Oklahoma, then known as the Indian Territory. Since their removal the people have suffered great sickness and loss. Scarcely had they time to become adjusted to the change of climate and conditions before their new home was thrown open to white settlement. The up-springing of the pioneer town and the close proximity of the frontiersman brought to the Pawnees disease, discouragement, and vice. From a tribe eight thousand strong they have dwindled to a scant six hundred.

Yet these Indians have splendid qualities of manhood. They are truly worthy of life, evolution, and development. They are, as a tribe, brave, loyal, self-controlled, lofty of thought, and fine of feeling. May these sons of our continent be better known to the race that now must dominate their lives. The warriors of yesterday must make their hardest fight to-day—a fight in the name of peace against degradation and extinction. Better to understand them will mean better to help them in their struggle.

These are their songs, sung and explained by the Pawnees themselves. There are here not enough of the songs to give more than the merest glimpse into the Pawnee mind. But even this glimpse may help to reveal something of that which to the red man is more vital than material possessions—his inner world of thought and feeling, an appreciation of which alone makes possible to the white man a knowledge of the real Indian.

INTRODUCTION TO THE PAWNEE SONGS

By Letakots-Lesa (Eagle Chief)

Letakots-Lesa is chief of the Pita-hau-erat band, one of the four divisions of the Pawnees. As part of his ceremonial dress he wears a necklace of bear-claws, for he is one of the Bear Society, a turban of otter-skin, and two eagle-feathers in his hair

IN the beginning of all things, wisdom and knowledge were with the animals,[1] for Tirawa, the One Above, did not speak directly to man. He sent certain animals to tell men that he showed himself through the beasts, and that from them, and from the stars and the sun and the moon should man learn. Tirawa spoke to man through his works, and the Pawnee understands the heavens, the beasts, and the plants. For all things tell of Tirawa.

When man sought to know how he should live, he went into solitude and cried until in vision some animal brought wisdom to him. It was Tirawa, in truth, who sent his message through the animal. He never spoke to man himself, but gave his command to beast or bird, and this one came to some chosen man and taught him holy things. Thus were the sacred songs and ceremonial dances given the Pawnees through the animals.

So it was in the beginning.

In the beginning Tirawa gave to man the corn. The corn told man that she is mother—almighty, like Tirawa. If a grain of corn be split, within it will be found a juice like mother's milk. So the corn is mother, because she nourishes.

Some animals are spiritual beings with deified attributes, each one possessing a psychic quality peculiar to itself. The actual animals upon earth are the diminutive earthly image of these divine ones, and are placed here for the good of man. The spiritual animals are often symbolic of forces in nature. The Pawnees say that the Bear—the divine, generic Bear—is hard to kill, and this not only because of his thick hide but because of the psychic quality of ever-renewing life within him. The man who has learned of the Bear, or upon whom the Bear has bestowed power, has attained something of the nature of the Bear; he has become like the Bear, hard to kill because of the miraculous life force within him. The Bear has his power from the Sun, and the Bear himself is oftentimes the symbol of the Sun. The Sun is recognized by man throughout the world as the ever-renewing life principle. This knowledge of the power of the Bear is the secret of the Bear Society, a secret never lightly told.

That is why, long ago, woman had all the work of planting. We might, indeed, call all women " mother." Men might call their wives " mother," for women grow the corn and cook for men; they nourish men, and give them food.

The corn is mother, but the bow and arrow is father, for the father always protects. So man must wield the bow and arrow. Thus it was long ago.

The Pawnees hold the Bear in reverence. He has wonderful power. A chosen man once saw the Bear. The Bear came to him and revealed to him a dance, and gave him all the Bear Songs. The Bear had been commanded of Tirawa thus to instruct the man, and to tell him that Tirawa had said that certain beasts would give man wisdom and power.

But the animal supreme for the Pawnees is the Otter. His is a message of wisdom, for of all beasts the Otter is the wisest. No other people than the Pawnees has deeper knowledge of medicines, roots, and herbs, and of all that lives upon the earth, in the air, and under the ground.

The Eagle is Tirawa's bird. Of all birds Tirawa loves this one the most. For the Eagle has two eggs, and only two, and this tells the story. All things in the world are two—man and woman. This is true whether of men, of animals, of trees, of flowers. All things have children of two kinds in order that life may be. Look well upon the eagle-feathers worn by Letakots-Lesa: the one on the right side is tall and fair and decorated with a tuft. This is man. The one on the left is short and unadorned. This is woman. So do the feathers tell the story—man and woman.[1]

All things in the world are two. Man himself is two in everything. Two eyes, two ears, two nostrils, two hands, two feet—one for man and one for woman.[2] Stand in the sunshine and behold how man is two—substance and shadow, body and spirit. Even

---

[1] The feathers are in accordance with the law of nature that makes the male creature, whether bird or animal, to be the larger, the stronger, and the more beautiful.

[2] The idea evidently is that the human form is in itself symbolic of all created life, in that it is two in everything, typifying the male and female principles. Indeed, it would seem that to the Pawnees the right side typifies man, the left side woman. See the above description of the wearing of the eagle-feathers. Also compare Tawi'-Kuruks, Song of the Bear Society, page 107, where the warrior wears the Father-Hawk on the right side and the Mother-Corn on the left.

so there are sun and moon, and in moonlight as in sunlight man is two, always two.

All things in the world are two, the Eagle's eggs tell us this story. But behold, the Eagle's feather tells the story also, for the feather in itself is two—half dark, half light. So we see upon it daylight and darkness, summer and winter. The white tells of the summer when the earth is fair, the dark of the winter when the skies are gloomy. Even in a single day we may see weather that is two—cloud and sunshine.

All things in the world are two. In our minds we are two—good and evil. With our eyes we see two things—things that are fair and things that are ugly. Through our nostrils we smell two things—things that are good, things that are bad. With our ears we hear two things—things that fill us with joy, things that fill us with sorrow. We have the right hand that strikes and makes for evil, and the left hand full of kindness, near the heart. One foot may lead us to an evil way, the other foot may lead us to a good. So are all things two, all two.

This is the Eagle's story, known to the fathers of Eagle Chief, and handed down from son to son. Thus did the Pawnees learn of the wisest bird, and thus did they learn of the Otter and of the Bear. Even so came the messages of Tirawa to man.

All this will make clear the songs, and will tell why Letakots-Lesa wears the necklace of bear-claws, the turban of otter-skin, and two eagle-feathers in his hair.

Letakots-Lesa (Eagle Chief) owns a modern frame house, cattle, and horses. He is thrifty and well to do. Upon the side of his American house, at the top, beneath the gable, is painted a white star on a blue ground. Thus he explained the decoration:

"Once I saw in a trance the white star—the Evening Star. It told me that it stood there to watch over the people and give them plenty. I took the star for my emblem, and painted it on my house, and branded all my animals with it."

To infuse into the new life of labor something of the old Indian poetry is an ideal for the future Indian working-man, unconsciously set before him by the thoughtful chief of the Pita-hau-erat.

Letakots-Lesa (Eagle Chief)

THE MORNING STAR AND THE EVENING STAR

Told by Sakuruta (Coming Sun)

Sakuruta is a Pawnee of the Skidi band, and belongs to the Morning-Star Clan. He is one of the four Kurahus (priests) who own the right to tell this story. Also he is one of the heirs to the Morning-Star Bundle.

Indian thought finds sublime expression in this myth, and in the Introduction to the Pawnee Songs, by Eagle Chief. Over all is the supreme, impersonal Being, Tirawa, the infinite Creator. After Tirawa, the Pawnee sees duality in all life. The very universe is divided into two great elements, male and female, finding their natural counterpart in day and night. Humanity is not the direct child of Tirawa, but the offspring of dual elements in the cosmic world. It is not the part of the recorder to point out beauties in song and story. When questioned deeply as to the meaning of a myth, the Indian sometimes replies, "That is for each to think out for himself."

O VER all is Tirawa, the One Above, changeless and supreme. From Tirawa come all things: Tirawa made the heavens and the stars.

The Pathway of Departed Spirits[1] parts the heavens. In the beginning, east of the path was Man: west of the path was Woman.[2] In the east was creation planned: in the west was creation fulfilled.[3] All that the stars[4] did in the heavens foretold what would befall upon the earth, for as yet was the earth not made.

In the west dwelt the White Star Woman, the Evening Star, who must be sought and overcome that creation might be achieved. From the east went forth the Great Star, the Morning Star, to find and overcome the Evening Star, that creation might be achieved. The Morning Star called to his younger brother:[5] "Take the Sacred Bundle,[6] bear it over thy shoulder and follow." And the Morning

---

[1] The Milky Way is called by the Pawnees "The Pathway of Departed Spirits," because after death the spirit passes on this pathway to the Southern Star, the abiding place of the dead. A star that stands in the north first receives the spirit and sends it onward to the Southern Star. This is the sacred belief, known to the priests, but the common people say that the Milky Way is the dust of the Buffalo (the Spirit-Buffalo). The Southern Star is not always seen. At a certain time in summer, just at dusk, it rises like fire for a moment, and then disappears. When the star rises thus, it means that a great man will die.

[2] Man, meaning the male principle: woman, meaning the female principle.

[3] Even as the creative impulse is in man, and the power of fruition in woman.

[4] The stars are divine beings.

[5] A small star just above the horizon.

[6] The Sacred Bundles contain certain symbols of cosmic forces, or symbols representing the psychological or elemental attributes of the divinity to whom they are consecrated. The Pawnees say that these Bundles came from Tirawa. Different clans among the Pawnees keep different Bundles. The Morning-Star Bundle is kept by the Morning-Star Clan. See page 107.

Star journeyed to the west. And ever as he journeyed, the Evening Star moved, came, and drew him towards her. (For men may see how the Evening Star moves nightly. One night she is low in the heavens, another night she is high in the heavens. Even so she moved and drew the Morning Star.) Yet when the Evening Star beheld the Morning Star draw near, she placed in his path Hard Things to hinder his approach. Thus, even as the Morning Star first saw the Evening Star, she rose and looked on him and beckoned him. He started towards her, but the earth opened and waters swept down, and in the waters was a serpent with mouth wide opened to devour.

The Morning Star sang,[1] and drew from his pouch a ball of fire[2] and threw it at the serpent; and straightway the monster vanished, the waters dried, the ground was level, and the Morning Star passed on.

Even so, each time the Evening Star placed in the path of the Morning Star Hard Things to hinder his approach, the Morning Star sang, and drew from his pouch a ball of fire and threw it at the hinderance; and straightway the hinderance vanished and the Morning Star passed on. After each triumph he spoke, saying, " I have overcome my Grandfather," or, " I have overcome my Grandmother," and again, " I have overcome my Father," " I have overcome my Mother," and again, " I have overcome my Brother," " I have overcome my Sister."

Ten were the hinderances, and ten times spake he thus, each time naming a kinship, in prophecy of kinships on the earth: for of human kinships is the number ten.[3] Cactus, thorns, and thick woods, monsters, and evil animals—of such forms were the hinderances;[4] so were they the prophecy of what should be Hard Things for man upon the earth.

[1] In olden times a maiden was ceremonially slain in sacrifice to the Morning Star. This song sung by the Morning Star was the prophecy of the song that the people should sing when they captured the maiden for the sacrifice. Also the song was to be sung by Pawnee warriors of the Morning-Star Clan before setting out on the war-path.

[2] In another version the younger brother each time draws a war-club from the Sacred Bundle and gives it to the Morning Star.

[3] The Pawnees say that even so have the Pawnee songs ten steps. A stanza is perhaps the nearest English equivalent to what the Pawnee calls a " step." The idea would seem to be that the stanzas of the song are as kinsmen in a family, or that they typify, by their number, the human relationships. Of course the songs alluded to are sacred, ritualistic songs.

[4] The hinderances were also symbolic of dangers and of forces of nature.

So passed the Morning Star in victory, and journeyed westward ever, and reached the lodge of the Evening Star.

To the Evening Star had Tirawa given the Powers of the West. Also had he placed, to guard her, four beasts—Black Bear, Mountain Lion, Wild-Cat, and Wolf. These Beasts, placed by Tirawa in the heavens, were stars—Black Star, Yellow Star, White Star, Red Star. They were beings who should send to earth beasts like themselves. They were the prophecy of animals to be upon the earth. Also were they Autumn, Spring, Winter, Summer; thunder, lightning, clouds, winds; and they betokened four kinds of wood to be upon the earth—cottonwood, elm, willow, box-elder; and four kinds of corn—black, yellow, white, red. Great was the power of the four beasts: great was their power to guard the Evening Star; yet were they vanquished by the Morning Star.

And the Morning Star spoke and said, " I have conquered, and ye shall obey my command. Thou, Black Star, shalt stand in the northeast, whence cometh night. Thou art Autumn. Thou, Yellow Star, shalt stand in the northwest, where is the golden setting of the sun. Thou art Spring. Thou, White Star, shalt stand in the south, facing north, whence cometh the snow. Thou art Winter. Thou, Red Star, shalt stand in the southeast. Thou art Summer."[1]

Now are the four stars known as the four World-Quarter Gods. At the four world-points they stand to hold up the heavens, and they obey the Morning Star.

Then the Morning Star approached the Evening Star to overcome her. Yet might the Evening Star not yield until the Morning Star should bring to her the cradle-board for the child that was to be born.[2] The board should be of the cottonwood; the covering, a speckled wild-cat-skin, emblem of the starry heavens. With strips of otter-skin should the child be bound upon the board; for the otter lives in the water, and betokens the rain-storms.

---

[1] The Pawnees say that the Yellow Star faces to the south, and the White Star faces to the north, and the Yellow Star and the White Star change places. For the Yellow Star stands to the north in winter, and the White Star stands to the north in summer. Thus the stars of the west change places, even as the change of seasons comes in the west. The east is plan; the west is fulfilment, movement, achievement.

[2] Among the Pawnees the husband brings to his wife the cradle-board. This is ceremonially cut from a tree by the husband's kinsmen, and decorated with symbolic emblems. See illustration, Pawnee cradle-board.

Above the board, over the head of the child, should be stretched a hoop, cut from the willow-tree. This too betokens the rain-storm, also the Arch-Above-the-Earth—the Rainbow.

The Morning Star went forth to seek the cradle-board.[1] The Star Beasts helped him,[2] and the Morning Star found, and won, and brought the cradle-board to the Evening Star. But still, ere she yielded, the Evening Star bade the Morning Star seek and bring to her a mat for the child to lie upon. And the Morning Star went to the south and killed a buffalo, and brought the softest part of the hide to be a mat for the child to lie upon.

Then said the Evening Star, " Yet must thou seek and bring to me water wherewith to bathe the child." And the Morning Star sought and won and brought to the Evening Star water wherewith to bathe the child.[3] The water was sweet and fragrant, for it came from a spring around which grew sweet-smelling grasses. The water was the rain, and it was part of the garden of the Evening Star— her garden, ever growing and ever green. This water, brought by the Morning Star to the Evening Star, was that rain which from henceforth should go to the people of the earth.

Now could the Morning Star approach the Evening Star and overcome her. And when the Morning Star overcame the Evening Star, he gave to her all that he had. And when the Evening Star

---

[1] There is a detailed legend of how the Morning Star won the cradle-board, which hung with many other cradle-boards upon posts within a lodge in the heavens. These cradle-boards were decorated with emblematic designs, which the people of earth now use to decorate their cradle-boards. Thus the Pawnees say that their designs came from the stars.

[2] Probably a prophecy of how on earth the kinsmen of the husband should procure the cradle-board.

[3] There is also a detailed legend of how the Morning Star got the water through the help of a woman. The Evening Star herself controlled the waters. But the woman knew how to find the water for the Morning Star. As she started forth she said to her children, " Sing, for I go to fetch water for the Morning Star." And the children helped her through their singing. The woman came to a hollow around which grew sweet grasses, and within the hollow was the spring. She thrust a stick into the hollow, and water gushed forth; and she caught the water in a sack made from the covering of the buffalo's heart, and gave it to the Morning Star.

The woman is probably emblematic of the midwife. " And so to-day," say the Pawnees, " when a child is born, the midwife takes a wooden bowl and goes to a running stream and fetches water to bathe the child."

The incident of the singing of the children draws attention to the Indians' belief in the power of thought directed by one person or group of persons towards another. The thought, will-power, or prayer sent out for another is often uttered in song. The absence of the one to whom the thought is directed does not interfere with the helpful power of the thought. See *Indian Story and Song*, by Alice C. Fletcher, page 81. Also compare Gomda Daakia, page 223, and Tuari's song, page 463.

CRADLE-BOARD FOR THE MORNING STAR CLAN

Painted by Pawnee Women. Upon this cradle-board have been bound the children of Sakuruta and his wife. Above the head of the child, at the top of the board, are painted the morning star, flint arrow-heads, and the rainbow. This design tells that the child is under the protection of the morning star and is watched over by the Powers of the West, because of the rainbow. On each side of the drawing of the cradle-board is a bead-work design, painted by Pawnee women.

yielded to the Morning Star, she gave to him all that she had: each gave unto the other of their Power for the sake of the people; for all that they gave should henceforth go to men upon the earth. The Power of the Morning Star is in the bed of flint on which he stands. And the Morning Star gave to the Evening Star his Power. To the Evening Star belong the Powers of the West: the Power of the Storms is hers. But into the Storms the Morning Star put his Power of Flint, and placed it in the clouds to strike as lightning from the rainstorms. This Power of Flint from the Morning Star would give knives, axes, and weapons to the people of the earth.[1]

Now when the Morning Star had overcome the Evening Star, he received from her a pebble, and he let fall the pebble into great waters. After a long time (so tell the songs) the pebble became the earth. Then the Morning Star threw into the air his ball of fire, and said, " Stand there, and give light to the earth!" And the ball of fire became the Sun. The Power of the Sun is from the Morning Star.

Now when the pebble under the waters had become the earth, the four World-Quarter Gods struck downward, with closed hands, and on each side of the waters the earth rose up. (Thus in the Bundle of each World-Quarter God is a war-club to mean the downward stroke that made the earth to rise up on each side of the waters.)

The Evening Star bore a daughter. And she placed the little maiden on a cloud to send her to the earth. Now in the garden of the Evening Star were seeds of all kinds that should go to the people of earth. Here grew the Mother-Corn.[2] And the Evening

---

[1] The Morning Star typifies the masculine principle. The part of man in ancient times was to hunt the game that was his food, to protect himself from beast or foe, and to fight his enemies. Man's power was in the strength and skill of his weaponed arm. All sharp weapons were of flint. It is natural, therefore, that the power of the Morning Star should be the Power of Flint. In ancient times arrow-heads were of flint. Flint generates fire. With many tribes it is connected with lightning, and the flint-tipped arrows of the Indian correspond to the lightning arrows shot to earth by higher powers. In Navajo mythology the war-god, Nayenezrani, is clad all in flint, and from the joints of his flint armor flash the four lightnings, hurling his enemies down into the earth (see pages 351, 362). Pueblo Indian designs also show the zigzag lightning, tipped with arrow-heads. It is of interest to note that the Power of the Morning Star is the fire-impelling *stone*. (Compare Pima creation myth, page 315.)

The Evening Star typifies the female principle. Rain makes the earth to bring forth, and so this fructifying element is part of the Power of the Evening Star.

[2] The Mother-Corn is a small and very beautiful corn-ear, symbolic of fruitfulness and of the female principle.

Star gave to the maiden the Mother-Corn and said, " Plant this upon the earth!" Then she sent her daughter downward.

The maiden dropped from the cloud upon the earth like rain, and to this day the name for maiden in the Pawnee tongue is " Standing Rain." The little maiden knew not where she was. She turned her ear this way and that, listening, till at last there came towards her a boy, child of the Sun and the Moon, even as was the maiden child of the Morning Star and the Evening Star. From the union of these two sprang the people of the earth.

To the Stars did Tirawa give power to watch over the people. If the people were evil, the Stars might send storms to destroy them. But Tirawa himself is ever without anger. He is feared by none. Tirawa is changeless.

TAWI' KURUKS

Song of the Bear Society [1]

Sung and told by Letakots-Lesa (Eagle Chief)

THE men of the Bear Society are called Bear Warriors. The Bear, the great Spirit-Bear, receives his power from the sun, and so it was through the sun that the Bear Warriors had been victorious. In this song they are returning from war just as the sun rises. The women go forth with song to meet the victors, who are coming all splendidly decked and painted. One of the women, seeing the warriors thus beautiful in their triumph, cries:

" If Atius Tirawa, the Father Above, had but made me man, I too might be like these! But alas! women may never achieve greatness. They must remain ever in the same station. Great deeds are not for them. But had I been a man, I might have done even what these have done!"

The rays of the rising sun now touch the earth and speed swiftly over the ground until they shine upon the victors. The hidden meaning of the song is the victorious power of the sun.

[1] See "Organizations of the Plains Indians," page 31.

A Daughter of the Prairie

PAWNEE

In the first stanza, the "many coming" are the warriors: in the second, the sunbeams. This is a very old song, and is sung in ceremonies of the Bear Society just as the sun is about to rise.

TAWI' KURUKS

Rerawha-a
Rerawha-a
Rerawha-a rera e
        Yo!

Para riku ratutah
Rerawha-a rera e
        Yo!

Hi tzapat rakuwaka kuatutah
  Iriritah
  Rerawha-a
  Rerawha-a
Rerawha-a rera e
        Yo!

Para riku ratutah
Rerawha-a rera e
        Yo!

Rasakura rukuksa rerawha-a
  Rerawha-a
  Rerawha-a
  Rerawha-a
Rerawha-a rera e
        Yo!

Rasakura rura whia
Rerawha-a rera e
        Yo!

SONG OF THE BEAR SOCIETY
(Literal translation)

Yonder coming,
Yonder coming,
Lo, the many yonder, he—
        Yo!

Mine, too, might have been a triumph
Like the many yonder, he—
        Yo!

Cried the woman,
  Would that I were like to these,
    The many coming,
    Yonder coming,
    Yonder coming,
Lo, the many yonder, he—
        Yo!

Mine, too, might have been a triumph
Like the many yonder, he—
        Yo!

Now the rising sun hath sent his rays
  to earth,
    A many coming,
    Yonder coming,
    Yonder coming,
Lo, the many yonder, he—
        Yo!

Sunbeams o'er the ground are speeding,
  Lo. the many yonder, he—
        Yo!

SONG OF THE BEAR SOCIETY

(Free metrical translation—the hidden meaning revealed)

They are coming,
They are coming
Lo, the victor hosts, ya he—
　　　　　Yo!

Forth to meet them go the women
With the rising sun, ya he—
　　　　　Yo!

Cries a maid,
Had but the Father made me man,
Oh then might I have been like these
Who now are coming,
With the rising sun, ya he—
　　　　　Yo!

Like to these who now are coming
With the rising sun, ya he—
　　　　　Yo!

Now the sun
Hath sent to earth his hosts of sunbeams
Swiftly speeding
Who are coming,
Who are coming
With the rising sun, ya he—
　　　　　Yo!

Radiant now the warriors' triumph
In the rising sun, ya he—
　　　　　Yo!

TAWI' KURUKS

Song of the Bear Society

Sung and told by Sakuruta (Coming Sun)

THE Sacred Bundles are bundles containing holy symbols. These bundles came to the Pawnees long ago through the power of Tirawa.

Once a warrior of the Bear Society borrowed from a Sacred Bundle the Mother-Corn[1] and the Father-Hawk, and wore them upon his back forth to war—the Father-Hawk on the right side where is the power to smite, for the Father-Hawk strikes with his wing and kills his prey; the Mother-Corn on the left side, near the heart, where is kindness, for the Mother-Corn harms no thing, but protects only.

Mother-Corn and Father-Hawk brought victory to the warrior, for Tirawa watched over the man because he wore these holy things, and, because of the bundle, Tirawa sent storms of wind and rain to protect him from his enemies. For this Sacred Bundle was known as the Rains-Enfolded, and when it was opened at the time of the first thunder, and certain songs were sung, the clouds opened and the rains fell.

So, because of his triumph the warrior made this song, that when he came with the sacred symbols upon his back the people might sing, " Yonder come the Mother-Corn and the Father-Hawk," for it was through these, and through the power of Tirawa, that the man had been victorious. No man may succeed except it be through Tirawa's aid.

The warrior was afterwards made the leader of the Bear Society, and this his song may be sung in ceremony by night or day :

---

[1] The Mother-Corn and the Father-Hawk are sacred symbols, representing the female principle and the male principle. They also stand for the Evening Star and the Morning Star. The one is an ear of corn symbolically decorated and painted, the other is a stuffed hawk. A full description of the Mother-Corn is given in *The Hako, a Pawnee Ceremony*, by Miss Alice C. Fletcher, published by the Bureau of American Ethnology, 1904.

TAWI' KURUKS

SONG OF THE BEAR SOCIETY

(Literal translation)

Nawa Atira,	Hither the Mother—
Nawa Atira,	Hither the Mother—
Nawa Atira,	Hither the Mother—
Ha we-ra	Now she cometh,
Nawa Atira,	Hither the Mother!
He yo!	He yo!

Nawa Atius,	Hither the Father—
Nawa Atius,	Hither the Father—
Nawa Atius,	Hither the Father—
Ha we-ra	Now he cometh,
Nawa Atius,	Hither the Father!
He yo!	He yo!

(Translation with full meaning revealed)

Hither the Mother-Corn—
Greet we the Mother-Corn—
Thanks to the Mother-Corn—
Now she cometh,
Hither the Mother-Corn!
He yo!

Hither the Father-Hawk—
Greet we the Father-Hawk—
Thanks to the Father-Hawk—
Now he cometh,
Hither the Father-Hawk!
He yo!

PAWNEE

IRUSKA

Songs of the "Iruska"—warriors who have won war honors[1]

I

Sung and told by Lesa-Kipiliru (Young Chief)

A CERTAIN man had a loved son. This son had a fine spotted horse of which he thought highly. The son died and the father cherished the horse. Of all his many horses he loved the spotted horse the most. Then the father, too, died, and the horse went from one person to another. But of the many masters, none gave it the love of the owners of old. So was it, in very truth, an orphaned steed.

Once while Young Chief lay sleeping, he heard in dream as from afar some one singing. He could not see the singer, but the song was plain upon the air. Then, still dreaming, he saw four men seated about a drum. Beside them stood the old man who had died, dressed even as in life, around him his blanket and on his head a wide hat decked with a feather from the eagle's breast. Then the men struck the drum and broke into the song which had come from the unknown voice upon the air.

Young Chief awoke and sang aloud the song. His wife heard him, and she, too, caught up the song and learned it. For hours after waking it seemed to Young Chief as though the song still hovered in the air around him.

The song became a favorite among the people and was used in the Iruska dances.

IRUSKA	SONG OF THE IRUSKA
Narutitawe—he-re !	Orphaned, lone, forsaken !
Narutitawe—he-re !	Orphaned, lone, forsaken !
Narutitawe—he-re !	Orphaned, lone, forsaken !
Atius tiwaku,	Father saith
Asawaki ratawe ;	In your midst
Narutitawe—he !	A spotted horse
	Is ownerless ;
	Orphaned, lone, forsaken !

[1] See "Omaha Dance-Songs of the Dakotas," page 55, and "He-lush-ka Songs of Winnebagos," page 257.

II

Sung by Sakuruta (Coming Sun)

IRUSKA	SONG OF THE IRUSKA
Hawa Atira, E-yo! Atira tziksu weta tariruta Hawa Atira, E-yo!	Again, O Mother-Moon, E-yo! In thy power, Mother-Moon, I put my faith again, Again, O Mother-Moon, E-yo!

III

WAR-DANCE SONG OF THE IRUSKA

Sung by Letakots-Lesa (Eagle Chief)

IRUSKA	SONG OF THE IRUSKA
Atius si tus kitawi', Atius si tus kitawi', Atius si tus kitawi', Karaku ukitawiu He-hi! Atius si taku ruski Taku tus kitawi', Atius si, Karaku ukitawiu He-yo!	O Father, thou dost rule supreme, O Father, thou dost rule supreme, O Father, thou dost rule supreme, None greater, thou dost rule supreme. Can there be any over thee? O Father, can there greater be than thou? None greater, thou dost rule supreme.

IV

IRUSKA SONG OF THE CORN-OFFERING

Sung and told by Sakuruta (Coming Sun)

The corn is upheld and offered to Tirawa, and he is implored to look down while the people sing, " Partake we together," for while we offer the corn we eat in symbol with the Father.

IRUSKA	SONG OF THE IRUSKA
Atius, Ha, is-tewat Askururit Weta tsihakawatsista	Father, thou, Look upon us, Now partake we Of the corn with thee.

PAWNEE

SKIRIKI

Coyote Warrior-Song

Sung and told by Lukitawika-wari (Rider-Around-the-Great-Heaven-Domed-Lodge)

THIS is a Coyote warrior-song, belonging to the Chawi band of Pawnees. A man upon the war-path[1] strays from his companions, roaming the prairie alone. He thinks of home, of those whom he loves, and is lonely and sad. Then he looks up at the heavens and knows that ever present is Tirawa, the One Above, in whom he puts his trust. So he sings:

> "O great expanse of the blue sky,
>   See me roaming here
> Again on the war-path, lonely;
> I trust in you, protect me!"

This song belonged first to Tirirak-tawirus. The friend of Tirirak-tawirus was Lukitawika-wari. These two were brothers in the Indian manner—that is, brothers by mutual adoption, and such brotherhood is stronger than blood.

Tirirak-tawirus was older than Lukitawika-wari. He was a man when the other was but a boy. When the elder brother was grown old, indeed, he gave to the youth this, his own song, bidding him sing it when he needed help or protection. While singing it Lukitawika-wari would remember his brother.

The song is a prayer to Tirawa for guidance and protection. As such, Lukitawika-wari sang it when far from home. He sang it, too, while on the water for the first time. Tirirak-tawirus is long dead, but Lukitawika-wari still lives and cherishes the song.

The names of the two brothers are very beautiful. Tirirak-tawirus means the Rescuer, or the good one who comes forward in time of need. The significance is twofold. It may mean him who

---

[1] See "The War-Path," page 154.

saved the life of a friend in battle, or him who went to kill a buffalo as a consecrated and necessary offering to Tirawa in religious ceremony.

Lukitawika-wari means: He who rides his horse around in the lodge. But the lodge here meant is not such as the Pawnees used to build of earth with a domed roof supported by posts; the lodge is the world—the open prairie, roofed with the blue vault of the sky.

SKIRIKI	COYOTE WARRIOR-SONG
Ah! Tirus takawaha Tiratpari—ho! Tatara kita-wira Hawa re-rawira—he-yo!	O great expanse of the blue sky, See me roaming here Again on the war-path, lonely; I trust in you, protect me!

SAKIPIRIRU

Young Dog Dance-Song

Sung and told by Letakots-Lesa (Eagle Chief)

IN olden times the Pawnee would dream of the protection of Tirawa. He would see in vision the war-bonnet, for this may be worn only by those who have achieved greatness, and thus the war-bonnet is a symbol of Tirawa. So in dream or trance might the Pawnees see the Father[1] wearing the war-bonnet. Such was the vision of Eagle Chief.

The music of this song is a "Young Dog Dance-Song," an old song of the Dog Society. But the words are those heard by Eagle Chief in a trance. The song as here written is sometimes sung at the opening of the Pawnee Spirit-Dance ceremonies, when the dancers stand in a circle before beginning the dance.

SAKIPIRIRU	YOUNG DOG DANCE-SONG
Atius esa ruka ratu teriku	The Father, him I saw Wearing bonnet of war, Wearing emblem of power— Father, him I saw, Yea, 'twas the Father I saw.

[1] In this particular song it is the prophet of the Spirit-Dance religion who is alluded to as "the Father." See "History of the Spirit-Dance," page 41.

PAWNEE

KISAKA

Song of Rejoicing and Thanksgiving

Explained by Lesa-Kipiliru (Young Chief)

WHEN a man receives presents from another, he may sing this song, remembering that all things come through the power of Tirawa, and asking of the Father, while giving thanks, a renewal of his gifts—long life, good health, and plenty in the fields.

The man who receives prays for a blessing on the man who gives. Thus thanks he the giver. Well is it to give to the poor and to the helpless, for they are heeded of the Father. Their prayers will be heard, and more surely than those of all others will their blessings be fulfilled upon the giver. Worth more than all the prayers of the prosperous and strong are the thankful prayers of the feeble, the aged, and the poor.

KISAKA	SONG OF THANKSGIVING
Nawa Atius,	Now, O Father,
Iri ta-titska,	Our thanks be unto thee,
Iri asuta hawa,	Our thanks ! Renew our plenty !
Iri rurahe !	Our thanks !
	Renew these thy gifts to us !

KITZICHTA

Song of the Lance Ceremony

Sung and told by Letakots-Lesa (Eagle Chief)

THE men of the Lance Society are all brave warriors who never turn back for fear of death. One day while they were holding their ceremonial dance in the village a boy-child was born. Said the mother to her dearly loved babe, " When you are grown, join not that Society lest you be killed; for those men fear not death." One of the braves heard the woman speaking thus to the boy, and told the other warriors of her words. Said one of these:

"Where will the woman send her son that he will not meet death? All men must die; every man must one day meet with death."

So the Lance Warriors made this song which is sung in their ceremonies. The woman's words of warning to her son were indeed proof that all knew the Lance Warriors feared not death. But the inner meaning of the song is the reply: "Where will the woman send her son that he will not meet death? All men must die."

KITZICHTA	SONG OF THE LANCE CEREMONY
Nari-ru-rit riwaka	This the word there overheard,
Nari-ru-rit riwaka	This the word there overheard;
Tzapat tiwaku	'Twas a woman spoke:
Taku kaki nariksha	"Heed not you the men who dance,
Kitzichta ra huriwi	Never, my son, for you the Lance!"
Nari-ru-rit riwaka.	This the word there overheard.

KEHARE KATZARU [1]

Songs of the Spirit-Dance (Ghost-Dance Songs)

I

Sung and told by Letakots-Lesa (Eagle Chief)

In a dream, Eagle Chief saw spread out above him the heaven with all its stars, like the many stars upon the American flag; so in this song, which he heard in his dream, he sings of the heavens as of the flag.

KEHARE KATZARU	SONG OF THE SPIRIT-DANCE
Irittatu terit,	I saw it, yea, I saw it,
Irittatu terit,	I saw it, yea, I saw it,
Na-rittatu terit,	In very truth I saw it,
Na-rittatu terit.	In very truth I saw it.
Nawiru-tzawhio rhurhera,	'Twas the starry banner beautiful,
Nawiru-tzawhio rhurhera.	'Twas the starry banner beautiful.

[1] See "The History of the Spirit-Dance," page 41. Compare songs of the Spirit-Dance, Dakota, and Arapaho.

PAWNEE

II

Explained by Sakuruta (Coming Sun)

Once the spirit of Tirawa touched a woman as she lay in trance during the Spirit-Dance. So afterwards when Spirit-Dances were held, the people would call the woman to join them, singing this song:

KEHARE KATZARU	SONG OF THE SPIRIT-DANCE
Ah, heru tzu-ut,	Ah, beloved sister,
Ah, heru tzu-ut,	Ah, beloved sister,
Atius,	He above,
We ta-ita Atius,	He the Father knoweth thee,
Atius,	He above,
We ta-ita Atius.	He the Father knoweth thee.

III

Explained by Sakuruta (Coming Sun)

The dancers in the Spirit-Dance gather at sundown and dance all night until the rising of the morning star. The Pawnees are a people of deep feeling. Sometimes the spirit of man is touched and stirred with the coming of night. In this song the dancer is impelled to utter his feeling, and gives the cry of the crow, the sacred bird of the Spirit-Dance.

KEHARE KATZARU	SONG OF THE SPIRIT-DANCE
Ah, tziksu rutatiku	Ah, now my spirit stirreth
We raku retkaha ra,	With the coming of the nightfall,
Kaw-kaw, rakuwak-tahu,	Caw-caw, like the crow I cry,
Kaw-kaw, rakuwak-tahu,	Caw-caw, like the crow I cry.
Operit we ra ti kuhruri,	All the night we shall wait for the star
Operit ti ra-hu.	Till the star riseth here.

IV

Explained and translated by Lesa-Kipiliru (Young Chief)

In singing this song, whenever the dancers, through weariness, begin to flag and make as though they would cease at the end of the round, some one starts another verse to the song. So long as new verses are started, the dance continues, round on round.

KEHARE KATZARU

Ruwerera, ruwerera,
Operit ruwerera,
Operit ruwerera.

Rerawha-a, rerawha-a,
Operit rerawha-a,
Operit rerawha-a.

Ruwerera, ruwerera,
Atira ruwerera,
Atira ruwerera.

Ruwerera, ruwerera,
Operit ruwerera,
Operit ruwerera.

Ruwerera, ruwerera,
Atius ruwerera,
Atius ruwerera.

SONG OF THE SPIRIT-DANCE

Star of Evening, Star of Evening,
Look, where yonder she cometh,
Look, where yonder she cometh.

Stars of heaven, stars of heaven,
Lo, the many are coming,
Lo, the many are coming.

Mother-Moon, Mother-Moon,
Look, where yonder she cometh,
Look, where yonder she cometh.

Star of Morning, Star of Morning,
Look, where yonder he cometh,
Look, where yonder he cometh.

Father-Sun, Father-Sun,
Look, where yonder he cometh,
Look, where yonder he cometh.

Tawi' Kuruks
Song of the Bear Society
Sung by LetaKots-Lesa (Eagle Chief)

Not too fast.
M.M. ♩ = 76

I

Re - ra - wha - a - a   Re - ra - wha - a - a
They are com - - ing, They are com - - ing,

Re - ra - wha - a - a   Re - ra - wha - a
They are com - - ing, They are com - ing,

Re - ra - wha - a - a   Re - ra   e - e - e - e   yo!
Lo, the vic - tor hosts, ya he - e - e - e yo!

Pa - ra ri - ku ra - tu - ta o
Forth to meet them go the wo - men

Re - ra - wha - a - a   Re - ra   e - e - e - e   yo!
With the ris - ing sun, ya he - e - e - e yo!

[117]

Tawi' Kuruko

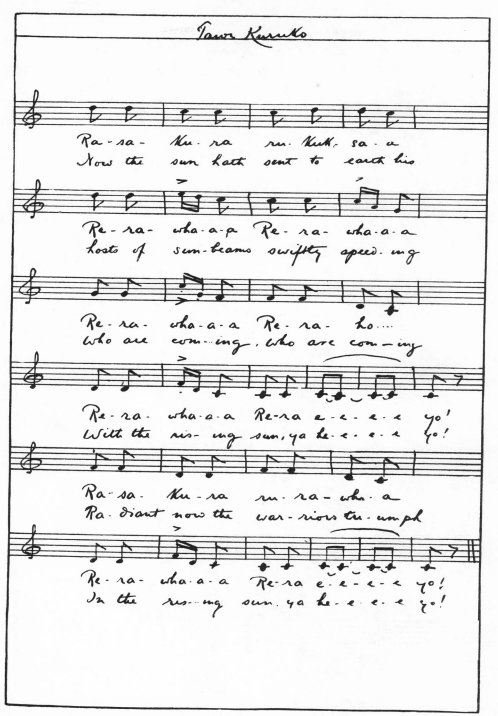

Tawi Kuruks

Ra-sa-   Ku-ra   ru-Kukk-sa-a
Now the   sun hath   sent to   earth his

Re-ra-   wha-a-p   Re-ra-   wha-a-a
hosts of   sun-beams swiftly speed-ing

Re-ra-   wha-a-a   Re-ra-   ho....
Who are   com-ing, who are   com——ing

Re-ra-   wha-a-a   Re-ra e-e-e-e   yo'
With the   ris-ing sun, ya he-e-e-e   yo!

Ra-sa-   Ku-ra   ru-ra-wha-a
Ra-diant now the   war-riors tri-umph

Re-ra-   wha-a-a   Re-ra e-e-e-e   yo!
In the   ris-ing sun, ya he-e-e-e   yo!

[119]

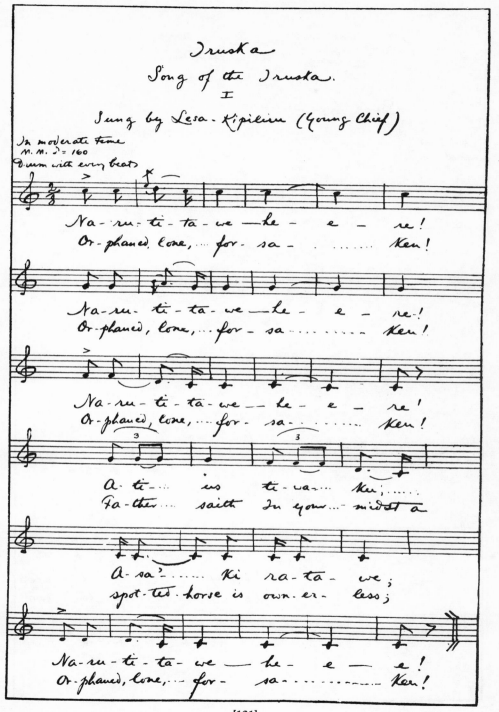

Iruska

Ta-ku tus Ki-ta-wi; a-ti-us si,
O Fa-ther can there great-er be than thou?

Ka-ra-ku u-Ki-ta-wi-u
None great-er, thou dost rule su-preme.

He-e-e-e ye-e-e-e Yo!

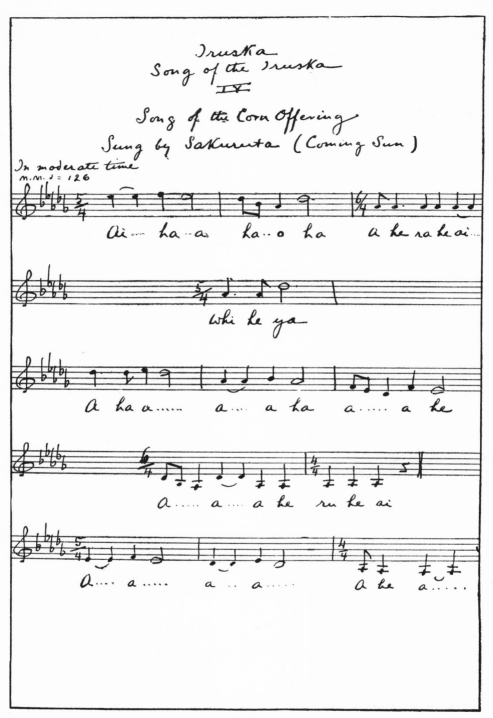

Iruska

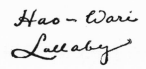

Hao-Wari
Lullaby

Not too fast
m.m ♩ = 80

Ha u - o   ha - u - o......   Ha - u - o......

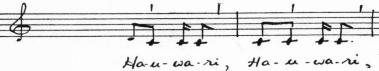

Ha-u-wa-ri,   Ha-u-wa-ri,

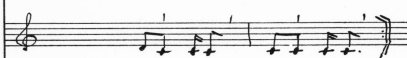

Ha-u-wa-ri,   Ha-u-wa-ri,

Hao means sleep, and Wari signifies the moving of the child to and fro. The baby is usually bound upon a board for slumber. This cradle-board is held on the arms of the parent, and the child is rocked up and down during the first three bars of the song, the motion occurring with each beat. From the fourth bar on, the baby is swayed from side to side, horizontally, the motion not occurring with the first beat of the bar but in syncopation with the rhythm, on the second half of the first and second beats. The motions are indicated by perpendicular marks over the notes.

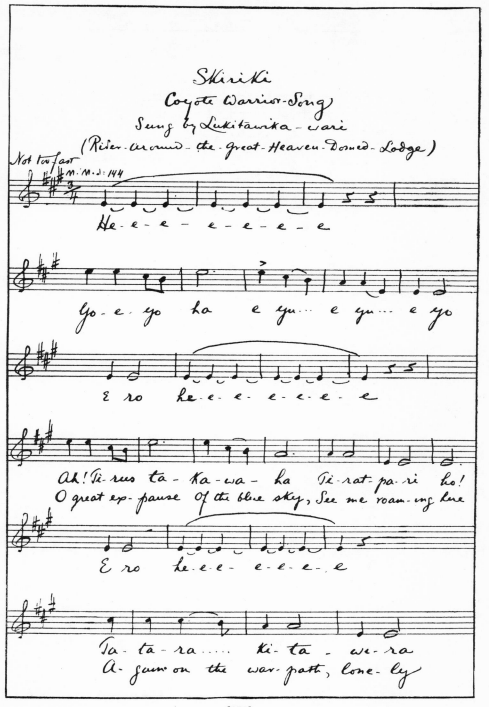

Skiriki.

Ha-wa.... re- ra- wi-ra
I trust in you, pro- tect me!

He-e-e- e-e-e yo!

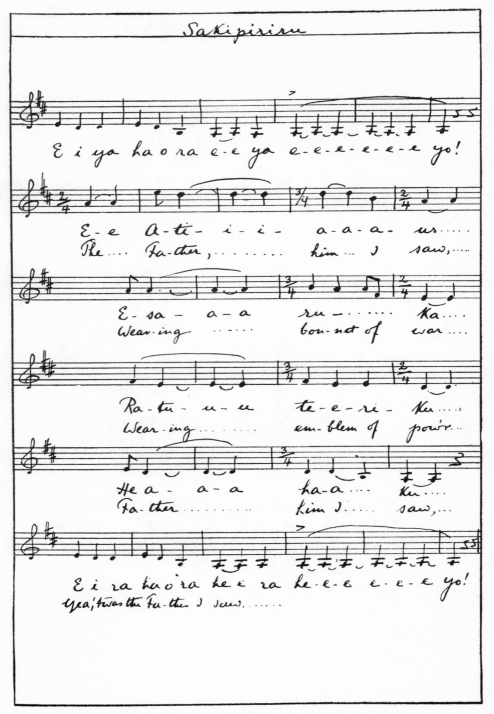

Sakipiriru

E i ya ha o ra e-e ya e-e-e-e-e-e yo!

E-e A-ti- i- i- a-a-a- us.....
The.... Fa-ther,........ him... I saw,.....

E-sa- a-a ru-..... Ka....
Wear-ing ...... bon-net of war....

Ra-tu-u-u te-e-ri- Ku.....
Wear-ing........ em-blem of pow'r...

He a- a-a ha-a.... Ku....
Fa-ther.......... him I..... saw,...

E i ra ha o ra he i ra he-e-e e-e-e yo!
Yea, 'twas the Fa-ther I saw.......

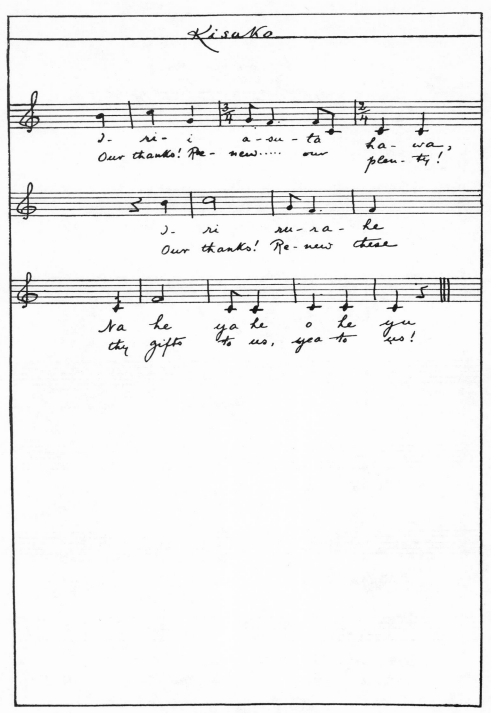

Kitzichta

Ki-zich-ta ra hu-ri-wi......
Ne-ver, my son, for you the Lance!..."

Na-ri-ru-rit ri-wa-ka..
This the word there o-ver-heard,

Na-ri-ru-rit ri-wa-ka..
This the word there o-ver-heard,

Na-ri-ru-rit ri-wa-ka...
This the word there o-ver-heard,

Na-ri-ru-rit ri-wa-ka....
This the word there o-ver-heard,

Na-ri-ru-rit.. ri-wa-ka
This the word there o-ver-heard,

Na-ri-ru-rit ri-wa-ka
This the word there o-ver-heard,

Kitzichta

Tza-pat te-wa-ku   Ta-ku Ka-ki na-rit-sha
'Twas a wo-man spoke: "Heed not you the. men who dance,

Ki-tzich-ta na   hu-ri- we ...
Ne-ver, my son, for you the Lance! "

Na - ri - ru - rit   ri-wa-Ka .
This the word there o - ver- heard,

Na - ri-ru- rit   ri-wa- Ka...
This the word there o- ver- heard,

Na - ri - ru- rit   ri-wa- Ka...
This- the word there o-ver- heard,

Na- ri - ru-rit   ri-wa- Ka...
This the word there o-ver- heard,

Na - ri - ru-rit   ri-wa-. Ka.
This the word there o- ver- heard.

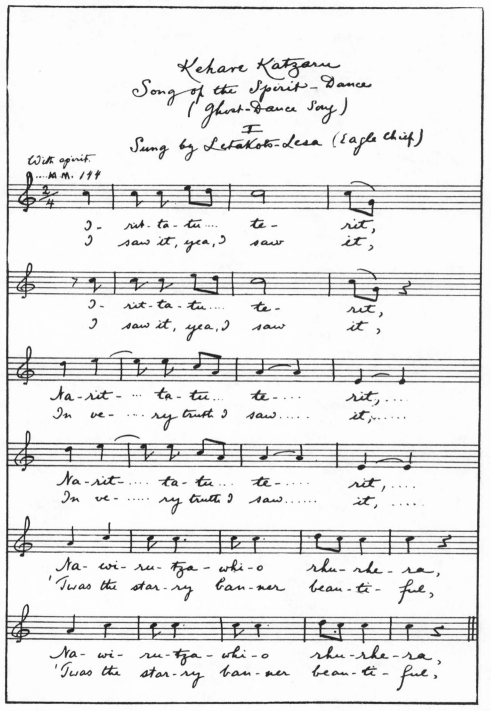

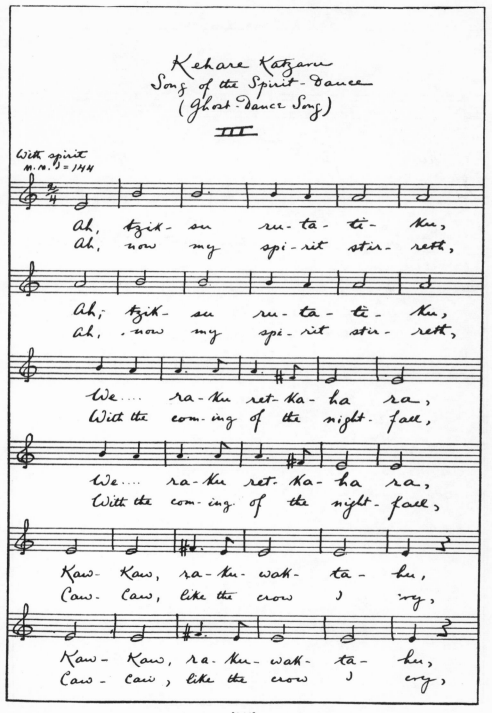

Kehare Katzaru
Song of the Spirit-Dance
(Ghost-Dance Song)

III

With spirit
M.M. ♩ = 144

Ah, tzik- su ru-ta- ti- ku,
Ah, now my spi-rit stir-reth,

Ah, tzik- su ru-ta- ti- ku,
ah, now my spi-rit stir-reth,

We.... ra-ku ret-Ka-ha ra,
With the com-ing of the night-fall,

We.... ra-ku ret-Ka-ha ra,
With the com-ing of the night-fall,

Kaw- Kaw, ra-ku-wak- ta- hu,
Caw- Caw, like the crow   cry,

Kaw- Kaw, ra-ku-wak- ta- hu,
Caw- Caw, like the crow   cry,

[141]

Kehare Katzarn

O- pe- rit we ra te ku- hru- ri,
All the night we shall wait for the star,

O- pe- rit we ra te ku- hru- re,
all the night we shall wait for the star,

O- pe- rit te ra- hu,
Till the star ri- seth here,

O pe- rit te ra- hu.
Till the star ri- seth here.

Kehare Katzare
Song of the Spirit Dance
(Ghost Dance Song.)

IV

With spirit
M.M. ♩ = 144

Ru— we - re—— ra,
Star of Eve—— ning,

Ru— we - re—— ra,
Star of Eve—— ning,

O— pe - rit ru—— we - re - ra,
Look where yon-der—— she com——eth

O— pe - rit ru—— we - re - ra.
Look where yon-der—— she com—eth.

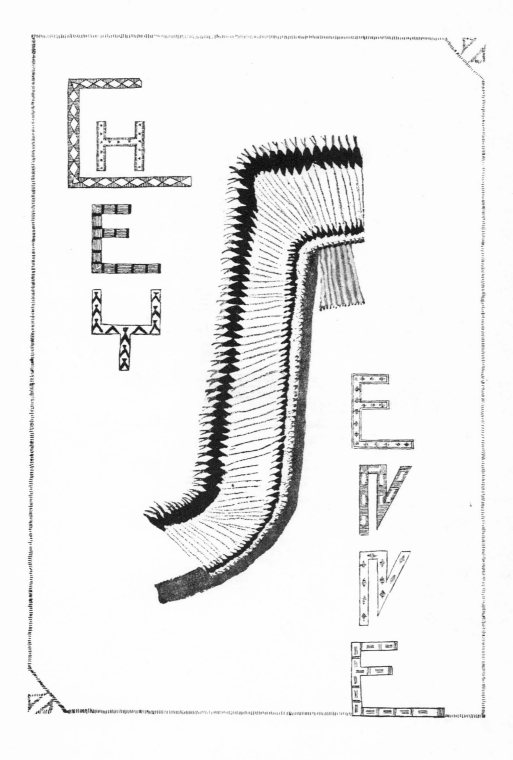

CHEYENNE TITLE-PAGE

The war-bonnet is painted by a Cheyenne Indian, Hotuwasu
(Little Buffalo Bull).
The lettering is by Hinook Mahiwi Kilinaka (Angel De Cora).

THE CHEYENNES

T HE Cheyennes belong, linguistically, to the wide-spread Algonquian family, and are one of its northwestern outposts. Their original home was probably in Minnesota along the river that now bears their name, but they had migrated westward of the Missouri, and were found by Lewis and Clark in the Black Hills region of the Dakota and Wyoming States. The name " Cheyenne " is of Dakota origin, and means " red," or " alien." In their own tongue the Cheyennes call themselves " our people."

Early in the last century there occurred a division in the tribe— one band went southward to the Arkansas River with the Arapahos, while the rest remained in the neighborhood of the Dakotas. Thus originated the northern and southern bands of the Cheyenne.

Before the coming of the white man brought them change, these Indians were a sturdy, prosperous folk, fighting their enemies lustily, trading with friendly neighbors over a vast territory, and themselves supplying all the needs of their self-respecting and vigorous community life. To them, as to all of the Indians of the plains, the buffalo was the giver and sustainer of earthly life. It was small wonder, indeed, that the buffalo, like the sun, should have been revered as a glorified and visible emblem of the source of life and power.

None of the plains tribes was more skilful in the chase, and none more daring on horseback, than the Cheyenne. Nor were

NOTE FOR PRONUNCIATION OF CHEYENNE TEXT

Unless otherwise indicated, vowels have the Continental sound, and consonants the English.

Ch, in italic, is a guttural, like ch in German.

any Indians more thrifty than they in acquiring the ponies and buffalo-robes that constituted wealth.

White men who knew the Cheyennes in those early days have left indisputable testimony of their virtue and endurance. Crime was scarcely known among them. Their family government, like that of many other tribes, was admirable, and even beautiful. Old age everywhere received the veneration and respect that are its due; the child rendered complete obedience to the parent, yet harsh punishment was scarcely ever practised, and child-whipping, it is said, was quite unknown. The Cheyennes were truthful, invariably brave, and devout in peace and in war.

When the westward-bound emigrant began to cross the Cheyenne country it was such a people whom he found. Though the white man slaughtered the Indians' game and burned their grass, the Cheyennes at first contented themselves with urging that their possessions be protected, if need be, by a military guard, and that the tribe be compensated for the right of way through its territory. It was only later, when whiskey and plunder in the name of trade had done their work—only when misunderstandings, betrayals, starvation, and massacre had destroyed his faith and exhausted human endurance—that the Cheyenne turned aggressor. Then it was that he repaid in deeds of obvious cruelty and horror the unseen suffering he had borne from youth almost to old age.

History tells of no finer effort at loyalty than that made by the Cheyenne and allied tribes after the treaty at Fort Laramie was signed. Nor did ever a more heroic and desperate attempt at self-preservation thrill the records of a people than the tragic effort of the little band of Northern Cheyennes to escape from the Indian Territory and return to their homes—the country of their ancient freedom and manhood.[1]

The Cheyenne songs in The Indians' Book were contributed by the Southern Cheyennes, who, with their neighbors the Arapahos, have received lands in severalty in Oklahoma. They are still a valiant, vigorous people, temperate, keen-sighted, and intelligent. Indeed, if human nature be measured by qualities of loyalty and

[1] See pamphlet entitled " The Case of Dull Knife's Band," Court of Claims, Government Printing-Office, Washington, 1901.

courage, by scorn of death and scorn of falsehood, even by spirited uprisings against oppression and injustice, then is there, perhaps, in all America no finer stock than that embodied in the Cheyenne people. Nor is there a truer man of any race than High Chief, the noble Indian who has helped so greatly in the making of this book.

WIHU-HWAIHU-O-USZ, OR HIAMOVI

High Chief, or High Wolf

IGH CHIEF is the great son of great parents. His father was a famed Dakota chief. His aged mother is a Cheyenne woman of high standing. The forceful qualities of both tribes have united to make in High Chief a striking expression of all that is best in Indian character. He is a chief among both the Dakotas and Cheyennes, and is cousin to Apiatan, the head-chief of the Kiowas. He has travelled widely, and is known throughout the Indian country. Of late he has been employed by the government as Indian policeman, and his fidelity to duty, whether he be observed or unobserved, makes his service a lesson in loyalty.

With entire devotion he has given himself to the making of this book, going with the white friends from camp to camp, telling other Indians of the purpose of the book, everywhere hallowing the undertaking through his interest and enthusiasm. It is his wish that the collection of Cheyenne songs should open with the Sun-Dance Song, "because," he said, "it is a prayer." Then should follow the Song of the Buffalo-Dance, because this song belongs to the society composed entirely of chiefs.

The drawings that High Chief has made for this book are faithful pictures of things of the olden time, made by his own desire. He has drawn nothing which he has not himself seen. Every picture is the "straight truth," not one is "a lie."[1]

To the loving enthusiasm of this Indian chief The Indians' Book owes more than can ever be told.

[1] Of the many illustrations made by High Chief, it has been possible to reproduce only a few.

CHEYENNE LIFE IN THE OLDEN TIME

Told by Chief Hiamovi (High Chief)

IN the beginning our Father made the earth and gave to us all things. We had no such clothes as now, nor had we any metals. We wore the skins of beasts, for the Father gave to us the buffalo and all kinds of animals to meet our wants.

The bow we made ourselves, and arrows, too, pointed with sharp stone. When we had made the bow and arrow we began to hunt, and when we saw the buffalo we would creep up to him on hands and knees, softly, softly, until within a hundred paces of him. Then we would rise on one knee and shoot him dead. We had knives made of the ribs of the buffalo or of sharpened stones, and with these we skinned the buffalo and cut off the meat and carried it home on our backs. The women sliced the meat and then set up long poles supported on notched sticks, and on these poles they hung the meat to dry. They dried the hides, too, and then scraped them with sharp stones until they grew soft, and of these they made shirts and leggings.

We had no horses, but used big, shaggy dogs. When we journeyed we packed the dried meat in satchels of painted hide. These were carried by the dogs. Two poles were bound together by a strip of hide and fastened to the neck of the dog, and the bundles were tied upon the poles. Each family had its own dogs. Sometimes on a long journey the dogs would grow tired and begin to droop and flag. Then the people would call to the dogs, "Hiya, go on, go on!" But no matter how we called, the dogs would hang their tongues and lag slower and slower.

Then some one would cry, "Buffalo ahead; fresh meat in plenty!" and then the dogs would bound forward as though they had just set out.

When we came to a camping-ground the women untied the bundles and put the meat in pots to boil. These pots were made of fine earth hardened in the fire.

Híamoví (High Chief)

When any one wanted to kindle a fire he would hold a piece of dry, rotten wood against a stone, and then strike the stone with flint so that the sparks would light upon the dry wood. Or he would take the stalk of the soapweed plant and rest one end in a socket bored in a stone. Then he would twirl the stalk between his hands, and twirl and twirl till at last smoke and fire came at the end. All this was long ago, before our people ever had seen the white man.

But one time a man was far away in Texas and there he saw a horse. He was frightened at first because he thought it must be a creature that would kill men and devour them. But he caught the horse and tied him fast and patted him, and when he found the horse did not bite he was glad and tried to tame him. When he had tamed him he harnessed him with poles, like a dog, and put his children on the horse's back and seated himself on the poles behind. Afterwards the people found other horses, and these had colts. So we came to have many horses. Nobody now remembers the time when we had no horses. Only the old people tell of it.

My mother told me all these things. She is over a hundred years old, and she learned these stories from her grandmother. This was the way we lived in the old, old time when all that we had was given to us by the Father or made by us ourselves.

OHWIWI NO-OTZ

Song of the Offering Ceremony (Sun-Dance Song)

Sung and told by Chief Hiamovi (High Chief, or High Wolf)

THE Sun-Dance is the name the white man has given to what the Cheyenne calls *The Offering*. This is an ancient religious ceremony, and through it is worshipped Macha-Mahaiyu, the Great Mystery, who rules the day by the sun and the night by the moon. The ceremony is also for the healing of the sick.

This song is the first in the ceremony. It is a prayer, sung slowly four times while the dancers stand in a circle, with out-stretched hands, gazing upward. Sometimes tears will stream from the upturned eyes in the intensity of prayer. Thus the people pray that all evil may be lifted from them. At the end of the fourth singing of the song the drum is struck, the time of the song changes, and the dance begins. The dancers, looking ever upward, blow on whistles made from the eagle's wing. The song is then sung in quick dance-time, while the whistle and drum are sounded with each beat.

This is only one of the wellnigh countless Sun-Dance songs. But it is an old song hallowed by sacred use.

MAHOEVA[1] NO-OTZ

Buffalo-Dance Song

Sung and told by Chief Hiamovi (High Chief)

THE Buffalo-Dance, or Red Shields' Dance, belonged to the Red Shields Society. Nearly every society has its own songs. But the Chiefs' Society, which is composed only of chiefs, has no songs, and, therefore, uses those of the Red Shields. Thus the Buffalo-Dance Song belongs to the Chiefs' Society as well as to the Red Shields. This is an old song of high importance.

WU*CH*TCHSE ETAN NO-OTZ

Song of the Red Fox Society

Sung and told by Chief Hiamovi (High Chief)

THE men of the Red Fox Society are the bravest young warriors of the tribe. To them death is as nothing. Their thought is only of great deeds and war honors. So the young Red Fox sings that the aching tooth and bent back of age are not for him; rather would he die gloriously in the strength of young manhood than creep through the camp feeble and old.

[1] Mahoevas, "Red Shields"

Hiamovi (High Chief). With War-Bonnet and Lance

So while adorning himself for battle he sings this song; at the same time may be heard the sound of women's wailing and lamenting that one so young and comely must so soon meet his death. Then, armed and mounted, splendid in paint and eagle-feathers, with holy emblems fixed upon himself and his horse, the warrior goes forth to dash along the line of his enemies, shooting into the midst of them as he rides through the storm of their bullets and arrows. If he pass the line unscathed, he turns his horse and rides back again braving the same storm; but now perhaps the power of his protecting emblems no longer holds, and horse and man roll to the earth, shot through and through.

The fight is done. All have left the field. There lies the young warrior, wounded or hopelessly crippled. How long will he lie alone on the prairie ? Perhaps the wolves will come with the stars. But the Red Fox warrior shows no pain. Sitting up and awaiting his death, he rocks softly to and fro, singing this song :

Ma-achis hevisa   Nay, I fear the aching tooth of age !
Naehio !

HOHIOTSITSI NO-OTZ

Morning Song

Sung and told by Chief Honihi-Wotoma (Wolf-Robe)

This is one of the oldest Cheyenne melodies. Different words have been put to it from time to time. It is sung by old men, often from the summit of the hills at dawn.

HOHIOTSITSI NO-OTZ   MORNING SONG

Ehani nah-hiwatama.   He, our Father,
Napave vihnivo.   He hath shown His mercy unto me.
                        In peace I walk the straight road.

THE WAR-PATH

THE war-path might bring to a man honor and glory, or disgrace and death, but in the olden time it was the life of every man.[1]

A war-party was usually led by a tried warrior, wise through experience and consecrated to his trust. He was known as the Leader, and the other warriors swore allegiance to his command. Great was his honor if he always brought back his men unharmed.

The war-party might be large, or it might number but a few. Sometimes two men only would set out together. Often a warrior would go on the war-path entirely alone; in some rare case a woman might accompany her husband. But in time of intertribal strife the whole tribe would go forth. No one knew how long the warriors would be gone. Life upon the war-path was full of danger, privation, and indescribable hardship.

No important task is undertaken by the Indian without preparation, consecration, and prayer. If the Indian prays in common acts of life, how serious and devout is he upon the war-path, when life and more than life—renown and honor—are at stake.

Before setting out on the war-path religious ceremonies are performed and the protection of the Supreme Being is invoked. Every night upon the war-path prayers are made, and every morning each warrior renews his supplication and his consecration. Many of the so-called war-songs are religious in character, many again are expressions of grief for slain comrades, or songs in praise of the valiant dead. Others are outbursts of longing for loved ones at home, or weary sighs of loneliness. Still others tell more directly of the deeds of war.

The Songs of Victory are usually sung on return of the victors,

---

[1] An Indian went upon the war-path in somewhat the spirit of a knight-errant setting out in search of adventure and glory. Every Indian was a warrior, as every nobleman was a knight. Chivalry and ideality of purpose were not the cause of the Indian's warfare. But like the knight, the Indian went out to fight from personal motives and through the desire for great deeds. The war-path was most often the path of individual adventure, not necessarily a general conflict of one tribe with another.

and are filled with praise, flings of sarcasm, bits of high-spirited humor, and triumphant taunts of victory. Yet many of these victory-songs are religious also in character and speak the profound belief that great deeds are achieved through a power that is greater than man.

AOTZI NO-OTZ

Song of Victory

I

Sung and told by Chief Honihi-Wotoma (Wolf-Robe)

This song tells how the triumphant Cheyennes have left their slain enemies to the wolves. It is also descriptive of the Cheyenne himself, who on the war-path must be as the wolf, often hungry, lone, and enduring.[1]

AOTZI NO-OTZ	SONG OF VICTORY
Honih-hio	Ho ye ! hear ye ! Come ye ! Feast ye !
Tsi-wona-atz	O wolves !
Imio-missi-yo !	Feast, be ye merry,
	Yo, ho, gather
	At the dawn.

AOTZI NO-OTZ [2]

Song of Victory

II

Sung by Chief Honihi-Wotoma (Wolf-Robe)

WAR-PARTY is returning in triumph. The faces of the warriors are blackened with ashes as a sign of victory, for to the Cheyenne black is the symbol of good.

Among the watching people are men who stayed behind when the war-party set out, and these all wear on their faces the usual red paint.

[1] See "Hache-hi Naad, Arapaho," page 199.
[2] The story of this song was told by an aged Cheyenne warrior.

Now the warriors had not gone forth stealthily, nor by night, but by open day in view of all. The men who had stayed at home could have joined them had they wished.

So, as they come, the warriors fling a triumphant taunt at those with the red paint thick upon them, while on their own faces is the black of victory.

The song is a very old one, and is sung in time of victory or rejoicing.

AOTZI NO-OTZ

Tsivais siyo tsitonitoyus
Maitorn tsihotonihos.
Tahta nanias-sini !

SONG OF VICTORY

Who are these
Who stand and gaze at us ?
Who are these
With red paint thick upon them ?
By day
In the sight of all men
Went we forth to war !

AOTZI NO-OTZ

III

Song of Victory

Sung and told by Chief Nahios-si (Three Fingers)

THE song tells of the Sacred Bow which came to the people through the Great Mystery.[1] This was made of box-wood, and was so holy that it never was allowed to touch the ground. When the people encamped, it was hung upon the branch of a tree, or, if there were no timber, it was laid upon buffalo-dung, for the buffalo is revered by the Cheyenne. No one was allowed to touch the Bow except the man appointed as its bearer. Once it happened that just before the warriors set out on the war-path the young man who bore the Bow went to speak to the maiden whom he loved, and as he came he warned her, saying, " Come not near, for I carry the Sacred Bow." Then he joined the warriors and was foremost in the attack when they

[1] Cheyenne name for the Supreme Being.

[156]

galloped upon the enemy, but in the midst of the charge his courage failed him, and he turned his horse to one side. When the war-party returned successful, they celebrated their victory with a dance.

But the young man's beloved had heard of his cowardice, and she called out to the dancers, "Wait, let me sing you a song." Then in scornful mockery of her lover she sang:

> " Bearer of the Sacred Bow,
>   You should carry a bow of elm!"

The young man stood apart, because as bearer of the Bow he might not mingle with others lest some one accidentally touch the sacred charge. When he heard the reproach in this song he felt such bitter sorrow and shame that he went away to a high hill and there wept like a child.

There were but two or three of these bows in the whole tribe, and now there is none at all among the Southern Cheyennes, though there is one man still living who in his younger days carried a Sacred Bow.

No one knows how old is this song. The people sang it when they had been victorious over their enemies or successful on the buffalo-hunt. Nahios-si knows that his great-grandfather sang the song, and that it was sung by the grandfathers of those who now are old men.

AOTZI NO-OTZ	SONG OF VICTORY
Hetanu dzinimat 'tu,	Bearer of the Sacred Bow,
Hetanu dzinimat 'tu,	Bearer of the Sacred Bow,
Hitu hominu nimadzi!	You should carry a bow of elm,
Hitu hominu nimadzi!	You should carry a bow of elm!

AN OLD TALE

Told by Mochta-Wontz-tz (Starving Elk)

ONCE on a time the people were encamped in a circle, and in the centre of the camp they held a game. But the people were hungry; they had nothing to eat.

Now there were two medicine-men, holy men, men of mystery, who had dressed themselves in great beauty to go to the game. The first holy man wore a buffalo-robe, the second wore one also. The two medicine-men looked at each other. They were dressed exactly alike, their faces were painted alike, and their feathers were arranged in the same way.

Said the first holy man, " Have you aught against me that you imitate my dress? Are you mocking me?"

And the second answered, " It seems that you are mocking me. Where did you learn to dress like this?"

Then the first said, " In a dream I went to the clear spring that is near the camp, and there in the spring I learned this dress."

And the second said, " I too went to the spring in a dream, and there I learned this dress."

Then they argued, and at last they said, " Go we together to the spring by open day and let us prove which has the better right to wear this dress."

So they set out and all the people followed.

When they came to the spring, each one said defiantly to the other, " Dare you go in?"

So they stepped in together and sank to the very bottom. There at the bottom they saw an old woman who lived in the spring, and she asked of them, " What want you here?"

Now they both were hungry, and they answered, " Our people have nothing to eat."

So the woman gave to each a bowl of food to take back with him; in the one bowl she put corn, and in the other pemmican.

So the two holy men went back to their people and gave them the food, and they all ate of it, the whole tribe, even the little children. Yet, however much they ate of it, the two bowls never were empty.

This is an old tale, often told, and many a Cheyenne knows how thus there first came to his people the food on which they live —meat and corn.

NAI NO-OTZ

Song of Healing (Medicine-Song)

Sung and told by Chief Nahios-si (Three Fingers)

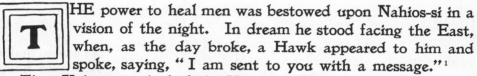

THE power to heal men was bestowed upon Nahios-si in a vision of the night. In dream he stood facing the East, when, as the day broke, a Hawk appeared to him and spoke, saying, " I am sent to you with a message."[1]
Then Nahios-si asked of the Hawk, " Who are you ? "

And the Hawk said, " Macha-Mahaiyu, the Great Mystery, has sent me to tell you that henceforth you shall have power to heal all kinds of sickness among white men and black, as well as among your own people and the animals."

Thus through the Hawk came power and knowledge to Nahios-si, also this song which the Hawk sang, and which henceforth Nahios-si should sing in making his cures.

In this wise Nahios-si became a man of medicine. To cure the sick he brews a drink from juniper and the root of wild anise, according to the knowledge revealed to him through the Hawk. This drink has great healing power. Nahios-si stays beside the sick all night and sings his healing song until just before the sun rises.

And now, even as the Hawk foretold, do white men and black, as well as his own people, come to Nahios-si to be healed, and for all men and animals he sings his holy song.

Often still in sleep the Hawk appears to him, teaching him wisdom, and giving him anew the power to heal.

So long as Nahios-si shall live will he cherish the message of the Hawk, and this story of his vision will he never lightly tell to any man.

---

[1] See " Songs of the Dakotas," page 60, and " Introduction to Pawnee Songs," page 96.

NAI NO-OTZ

Taeva nama-eyoni,
Tze-ihutzittu nama-eyoni.

SONG OF HEALING

By night I go on my way unseen.
Then am I holy,
Then have I power to heal men.

WAWAHI NO-OTZ

Swinging-Song (a very old song)

Sung and told by Chief Nahios-si (Three Fingers)

IN olden times, long, long ago, the Cheyennes used to make swings of strips of buffalo-hide which they would hang from the boughs of trees. Men, women, and children would swing in pairs, standing face to face in the swing, each with his feet braced against those of the other. The on-lookers sat around them, and all the people sang while the swings moved to and fro. They sang to the wood-rats, bidding them come; for in those days the Cheyennes used to eat the wood-rats, and they were hard to catch. They called the rats " timber-men," and so they sang:

WAWAHI NO-OTZ

Huchdjeho niochdzi'!
Huchdjeho niochdzi'!
Mata-etanio-o
Ini-stoni-wahno-tziyo,
Ehenowe, h'm-h'm-h'm !

SWINGING-SONG

Come, ye wood-rats, here to me !
Come, ye wood-rats, here to me !
Now the timber-men draw near,
Hither stealing, creeping hither,
Now I hear them, h'm-h'm-h'm !

MESHIVOTZI NO-OTZ

Baby-Song (Lullaby)

Sung by Wihunahe (Chief Woman)

MESHIVOTZI NO-OTZ

Meshivotzis-o—
          he-ye,
Naotziyo tsiso
          A-ha, h'm.

BABY-SONG

Little good baby,
          he-ye,
Sleepy little baby.
          A-ha, h'm.

The Pipe of Friendship
(Hiamovi: High Chief)

CHEYENNE

NU-U-SINIM NO-OTZ

Hand-Game Songs

IN winter the Cheyennes often meet in little companies to play the "hand-game." The game is held in a tipi, which is lit by a central fire constantly replenished with fresh logs. The company sit on the ground, with four or five leaders of the singing grouped around a drum and the rest lined about the circular wall. The game opens with a prayer, delivered by the one who may be, for the night, the leader in the game. In some tribes the hand-game is itself a religious ceremony, but this is not the case among the Cheyennes. With the Cheyennes, the details of the game may change with each night of the playing, so there is always a leader to direct the game. This leader has usually beheld in a dream the arrangement of the game—the placing of the tally-sticks, and other details—or he has been taught by some spirit how the game is to be played on the night of his leadership, for, with the Indian, even sports are divinely directed. Said an educated half-breed : " I have been to school, and I have lived among white men, but I never saw any people so religious as my own. My people begin all things, even their games, with prayer."

The opening hand-game prayer asks that the game may be played as divinely revealed, and that to the people may be given happiness, good luck, health, welfare, and old age. With simple dignity, the leader tells of his dream, and gives his directions for the game. In making the preparations for the game, he accompanies his acts with the saying, "So was it seen by me," or, "So I heard it commanded," or, again, "According to the Spirit."

In a general way, the game is played as follows : The players are divided into two sides, the object being for one side to guess in whose hands, on the opposite side, are held certain little sticks or counters.[1] The counters are often carved in the form of a little black bird, probably a crow, symbol of good. If all the guesses in one round have been right, the hiding side must give over the

[1] See " Arapaho Hand-Game Song," page 201.

counters to the guessing side, and the guessers now become the hiders. With the winning of the counters from one side to the other, there comes a cry of triumph from the men, a trilling halloo of victory from the women, and laughter from all. The drum-beat changes, a dance-song is struck up, and then the tipi is filled with the rhythm of dancing feet and jangling ornaments.

During the whole game the hand-game songs are sung, while all the players wave their closed hands to and fro in time to the song. The hands are often thrown out or crossed in the air, while mystic motions are made to confuse the guesser, or to blight his power of divination.

At the close of the game there is a dance, and then the feast is brought in by the women. Before eating, the company is silent while a man rises and delivers a long prayer for the welfare of the people. When the feasting is over, the guests quietly disperse without formality, disappearing through the tipi-flap. In a few short moments the gay hand-game company has melted away into the darkness.

THE MESCAL RELIGION

THE pellote (peyote), or "mescal-button" is the top of a cactus that grows in Mexico and in the southwestern borderland of the United States. In shape it is a disk from an inch to an inch and a half in diameter, and perhaps a quarter of an inch thick. When eaten in sufficient quantity the mescal has an effect which, though quite distinct, is more like that of hashish than of anything else known. It produces a strange feeling of lightness, dispels pain and fatigue, and causes visions of marvellous beauty and grandeur.

The religion that has the mescal for its principal symbol is a very ancient Indian faith that probably had its origin with the Indians of Mexico. In the United States it was formerly known only to the southern plains tribes, but it has spread from the Comanches and Kiowas to the Arapahos and Cheyennes, and on up through Oklahoma till now the mescal rites are performed as far north as Winnebago, in Nebraska. The ancient faith has undergone change, and the mescal religion, as it is practised to-day, may almost be called a modern cult. Its leaders are mostly the younger men who have never known the old life of the buffalo-hunting days. Many are drawn to this faith through the belief that its followers are cured of consumption[1] and drunkenness—the two dread enemies of the Indian, which were unknown till the coming of the white man.

In the ancient faith the mescal-button was the symbol of the sun, which is the manifestation of the source of life. Indeed, the button itself resembles the sun, for it has a circle in the centre which is surrounded with white spots like sun-rays.

Like many Indian rites, the mescal ceremony begins at night and lasts until daybreak.[2] As performed among the Southern Cheyennes, it is held in a tipi, which is consecrated to this use, and must always be scrupulously clean. In the centre is a crescent of earth some six inches high, which curves around a fire built of sticks so arranged that the ashes as they fall form a second crescent within the other. A man tends this sacred fire all night. At the centre of the earth-crescent, upon a little cross of sage-twigs,[3] lies the vision-impelling mescal, the symbol of the rite. The leader of the ceremony sits opposite this, in the place of honor, facing the opening of the tipi. In his hands he holds the emblems of his office, a rattle, a wand, and a fan of eagle-plumes. All around the tipi sit motionless blanketed forms. Four is the sacred number in this religion, and four mescal-buttons are ceremonially eaten during the rite. Each ritualist brings with him his own supply, and it is often customary to take more of the mescal-buttons than the ceremonial four. There is a solemnity in the atmosphere that awes the on-looker. Intense consecration seems to burn like a holy fire. Some sit with heads bowed, but most of the devotees gaze fixedly upon the mescal. Every now and then a man

---

[1] Indeed, it has been claimed by a medical authority, S. F. Landry, that the mescal is a very powerful cardiac and respiratory stimulant, especially useful in cases of asthma.
[2] The recorder has made no exhaustive study of the mescal religion, and describes only that which she has seen.
[3] The cross is an ancient Indian symbol, in this case meaning a star. For the significance of sage, see "A Holy Story," page 38.

will slowly draw his blanket over his head and sink back to receive the vision.

All night they sing, each one in his turn, the singer shaking his rattle, while the man next to him beats upon a small buckskin drum. Each song is sung four times. At the close of the ceremony, the worshippers go down to the river and bathe; for cleanliness is enjoined by the mescal faith. The rest of the day is passed in sleep.

The mescal songs are all esoteric. They contain no words, the meaning usually being known only to the members of the same lodge or fraternity, or sometimes only to the singer or to the man who made the song. Many men have their own songs, inspired by some spiritual experience. The mescal-songs are invocations that the truths of the universe may be revealed. The poetry and mysticism of this cult supply to the modern Indian the spiritual uplift known in the old days to those who went apart to fast and learn of the spirits what should be their guiding "medicine" through life.[1] But it is possible that the physical effect of the mescal may in time fulfil the forebodings of the older Indians who fear that visions thus produced can bring to their people little good.

MATA NO-OTZ

Song of the Mescal Rite

Sung and told by Mowihaiz (Magpie), nephew of High Chief and of Wolf-Robe, and leader of the mescal religion among the Southern Cheyennes

OTHER religions teach men what to believe, but in this religion each man learns truth for himself. God has given the mescal to man that through it man might know. There is a word that comes at the end of mescal-songs and that word means "the road." Each man's road is shown to him within his own heart. When he eats the mescal he sees the road; he knows; he sees all the truths of life and of the spirit.

---

[1] See "Songs of the Dakotas," page 60, and Winnebago "Song to the Earth-Maker," "Medicine-Song," and "A True Story," pages 253. 256, 262.

You have seen the mescal lodge. The round tipi is the sun, and the half-circle of earth is the moon. The star of sage on which the mescal rests is woman, for the earth is woman, mother of all things. The fire of sticks is man, and the flame and smoke are the spirit.

You ask why I wear purple. Purple is my color. I choose it because it means the spirit, it means the breath. The breath of man and of every living thing is purple. You can see it in the cold. So is smoke purple. Breath and smoke are the spirit. That is why I have taken purple for my color. So will another man take green, to mean the green earth. All things in the mescal ceremony have their meaning. The gourd-rattle is the sun; the tuft of red feathers at the end of the rattle is flame, spirit; the handle is "the road"; the beaded decoration on the handle of each rattle is different, because each man's road is different, and what the man wears or uses must speak of himself and of what he has himself seen or heard.

The mescal takes from us sickness and pain. It purifies us. Through it we may come to know all. We eat the mescal because we want to see—we want to know—we want to know God.

The song that I have sung for you is the one that I sing last in the ceremony, just before dawn. It means the eagle who spreads his wings and soars aloft and breathes deep with the joy of well-being. The eagle is myself. God has given me that bird. I have taken the eagle for my bird because he is greatest of all birds. He is the father, and all little birds are his children. He is strong, for he flies where no man can reach him. He is clean, for he spreads his wings when he eats that no dirt may fall upon his food, and he washes his claws in the mud of streams. In his feathers, white and black, we see day and night. That is why I carry the fan of eagle-feathers. So this song is the eagle, breathing deep, rejoicing in his strength. I sing it just at sunrise.

Ohwiwi Na-otz.

Mahoeva No-otz
Buffalo-Dance Song
Sung by Chief Hiamovi (High Chief)

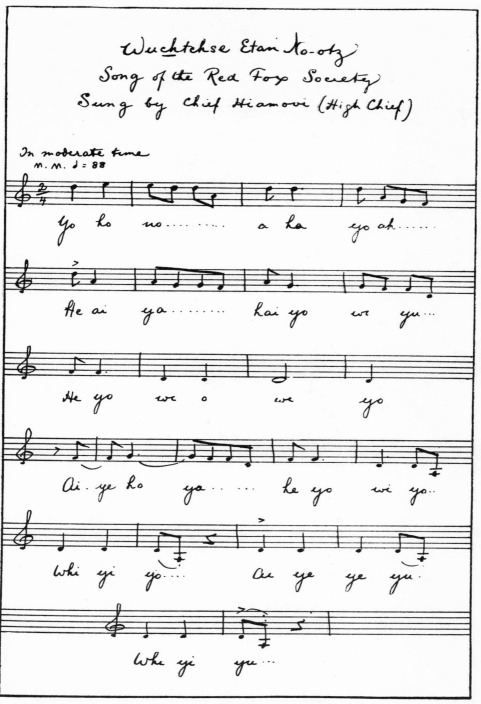

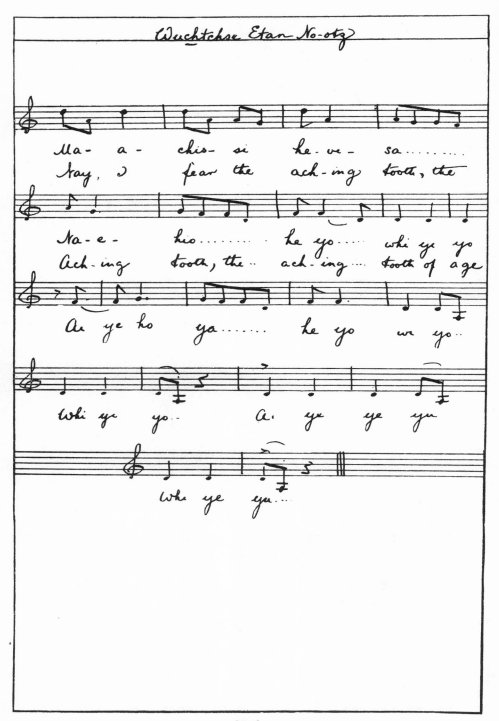

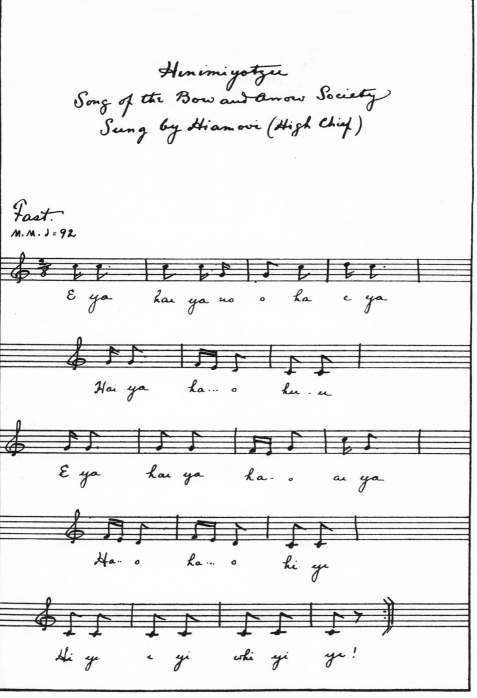

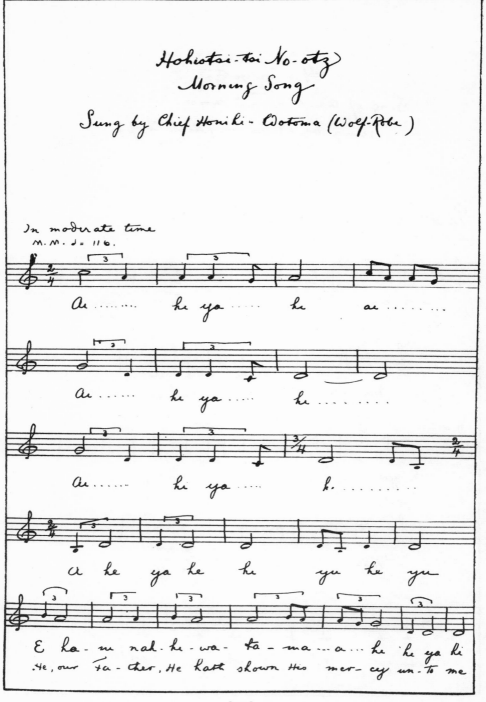

Hohiotsi-tsi No-otz

Na pa - ve - ve vih-ni- vo.
In peace I walk the straight road

A he   a he.... hi   yu hi   yu!

[173]

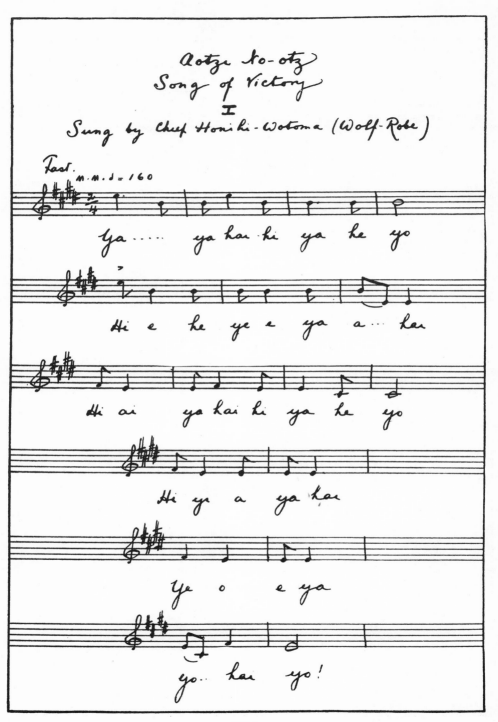

Aotzi No-otz

Ho-nih----- hi- o .
Ho ye, hear ye,

Tsi wo-- na- atz tsi- i ye
Come ye, feast ye, O ..... wolves!

I- mi-o - mis-si-
Feast, be ye mer-ry,

Yo lo e ya
Yo, ho, ga-ther

yo hai iyo!
At the dawn

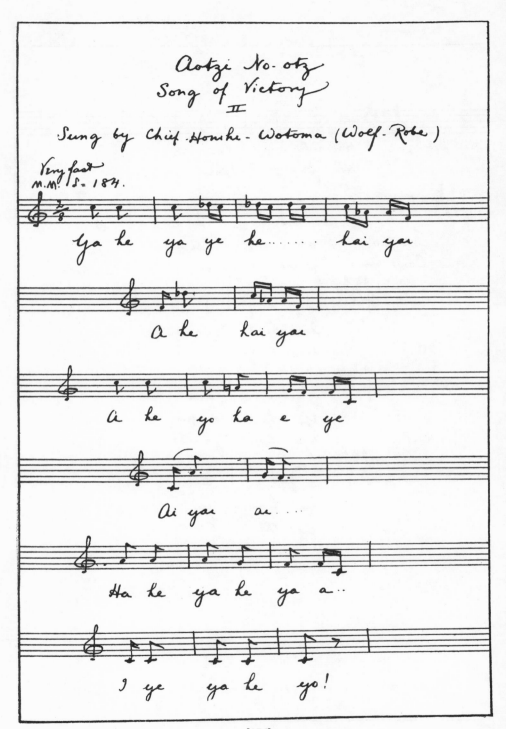

Aotzi Na-otzi

Tsi-vais   si-yo tsi- to- ni- to- yus
Who are   these who stand and gaze at us?

Ma-i-   to- ma
who are   these with

Tsi- ho- ti- ni- hos-si
Red paint thick up- on them

Tah-   ta......
By......   day....

Na-ni- as-si- ni eyi
In the   sight of all men

I hai   yu hai yu!
Went we   forth to war!

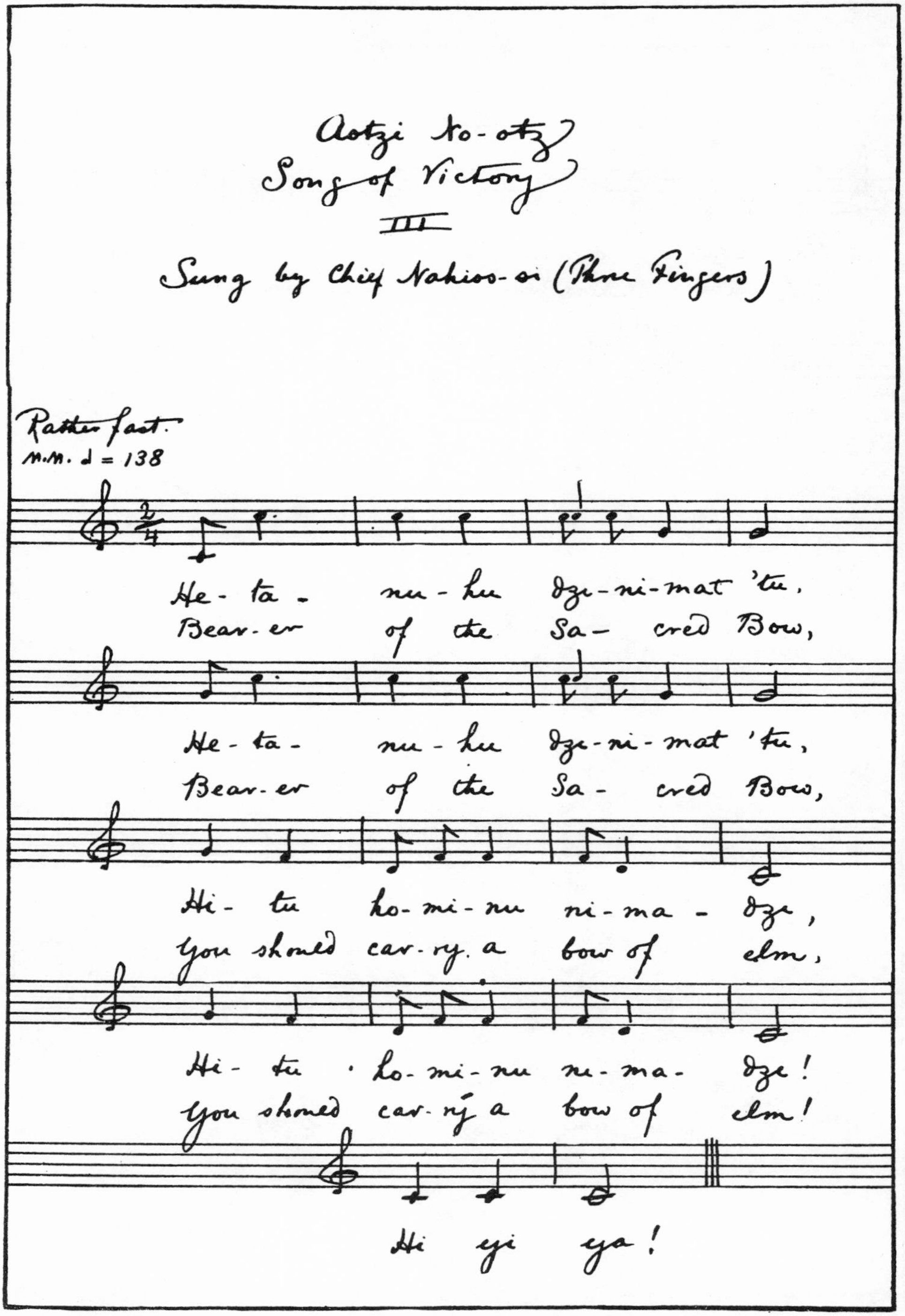

Aotzi No-otz
Song of Victory

III

Sung by Chief Nahioo-si (Three Fingers)

Rather fast.
m.m. ♩ = 138

He - ta - nu - hu dzi - ni - mat 'tu,
Bear - er of the Sa - cred Bow,

He - ta - nu - hu dzi - ni - mat 'tu,
Bear - er of the Sa - cred Bow,

Hi - tu ho - mi - nu ni - ma - dze,
You should car - ry a bow of elm,

Hi - tu ho - mi - nu ni - ma - dze!
You should car - ry a bow of elm!

Hi yi ya!

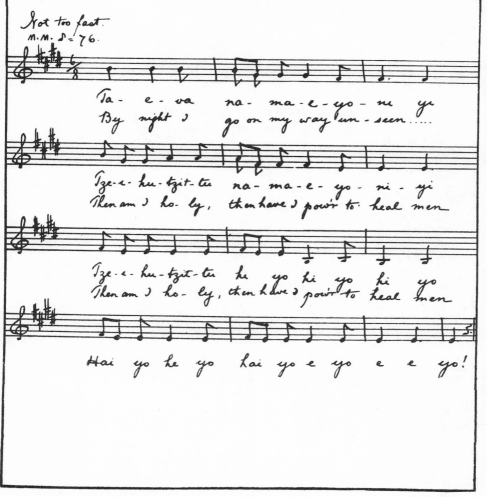

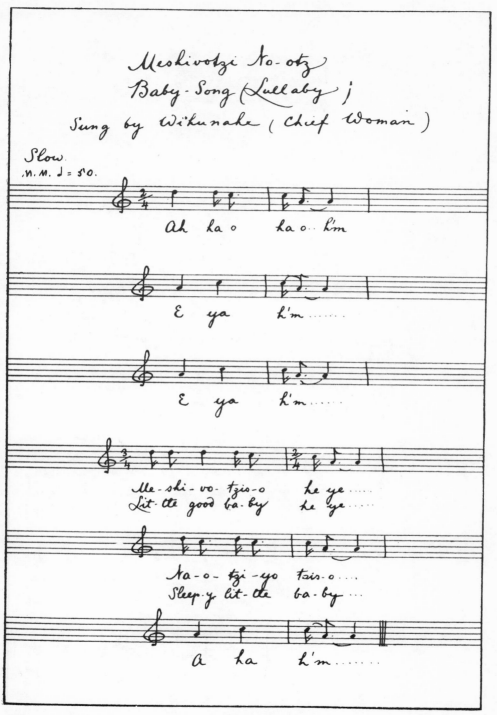

Meshivotzi No-otz
Baby-Song (Lullaby);
Sung by Wikunahe (Chief Woman)

Slow.
M.M. ♩ = 50.

Ah ha o ha o h'm

E ya h'm......

E ya h'm......

Me-shi-vo-tzis-o he ye......
Lit-tle good ba-by he ye......

Na-o-tzi-yo tzis-o.....
Sleep-y lit-tle ba-by...

a ha h'm......

[182]

[186]

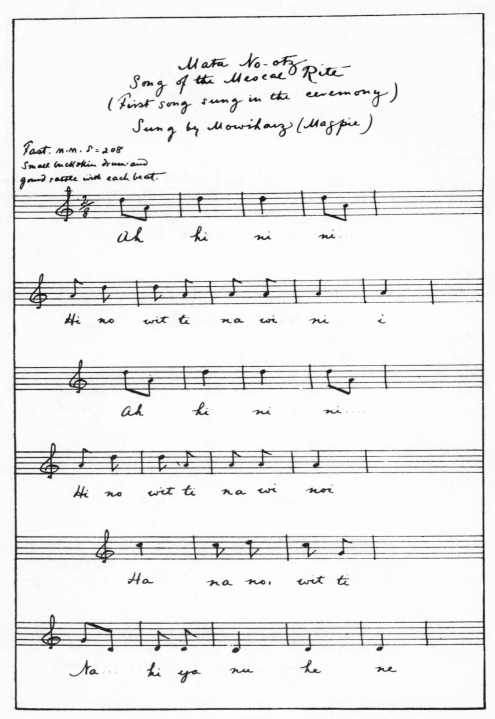

Mata No-otz
Song of the Mescal Rite
(First song sung in the ceremony)
Sung by Mowihaiz (Magpie)

Fast. m.m. ♪ = 208
Small buckskin drum and
gourd rattle with each beat.

Ah hi ni ni....

Hi no wit ti na wi ni i

Ah hi ni ni....

Hi no wit ti na wi noi

Ha na noi wit ti

Na.... hi ya nu he ne

Mata No-otz

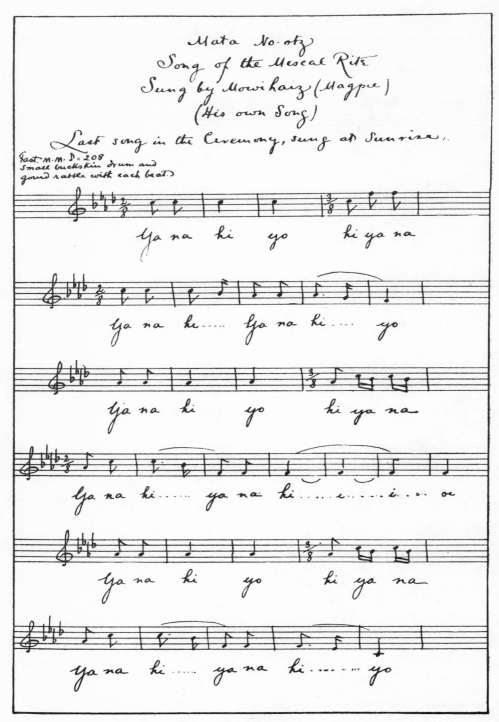

Mata No-otz
Song of the Mescal Rite
Sung by Mowihaiz (Magpie)
(His own Song)
Last song in the Ceremony, sung at Sunrise.

Fast. M. M. ♪ = 208
Small buckskin drum and
gourd rattle with each beat.

Ya na hi yo hi ya na

Ya na hi...... Ya na hi..... yo

Ya na hi yo hi ya na

Ya na hi...... ya na hi.........i.... oe

Ya na hi yo hi ya na

ya na hi...... ya na hi......... yo

Mata to-otz

ARAPAHO TITLE-PAGE

The drawing of the bow and arrows is by an Arapaho Indian, Waatina Bichut (Black Shirt).
The lettering is by Hinook Mahiwi Kilinaka (Angel De Cora).

THE ARAPAHOS

THE Arapahos are allies of the Cheyennes, and, like the Cheyennes, are a northern Algonquian tribe. Early in the last century, about the year 1800, both tribes were living in the Black Hills region. The Arapahos had probably pushed their way through alien peoples east of the Missouri and continued their migrations on into Wyoming until they reached and occupied the lands about the head-waters of the Arkansas and Platte rivers. Their range practically extended from the Rio Grande to the Yellowstone.

The Arapaho tribe falls properly into five divisions, each of which is recognized by the others as an integral part of the nation. The Gros Ventres are reckoned as the fifth of these sub-tribes. Originally these divisions were separate entities, though they always were allied and sometimes closely associated, but gradually all were absorbed by the Hinanatina, or Arapaho people proper.

As with the Cheyenne, the Arapaho nation underwent a distinct cleavage into a Northern and a Southern branch, a division which, according to ethnologists, seems to have occurred before the tribe was placed on reservations. The Northern Arapahos share their reservation in Wyoming with the Shoshones, while the Southern Arapahos are affiliated with the Southern Cheyennes, with whom they have received land in severalty in Oklahoma.

In olden times the Arapahos lived altogether in tipis of buffalo-skin, and depended upon the buffalo almost exclusively for the

NOTE FOR PRONUNCIATION OF ARAPAHO TEXT

Unless otherwise indicated, vowels have the Continental sound, and consonants the English.

ch, in italic, is a guttural, like ch in German.

ä has the sound of the same character in German.

necessities of life. Unlike many of the plains tribes, they practised little or no agriculture, and accordingly had no fixed settlements to which to return for planting or harvesting.

Though in the border warfare with white settlers, their neighbors the Cheyennes and Kiowas were classed as hostiles, the Arapahos remained for the most part neutral and unaggressive. They are an imaginative and very devoutly religious people. The religion of the Spirit-Dance (Ghost-Dance) was received by them with particular fervor, and the Arapahos are to-day among the few tribes who still perform the ancient and deeply emblematic religious ceremonial known to white men as the Sun-Dance.

Said a young Arapaho, "Our fathers and mothers knew religion, even though not the same as what the white people teach."

HASSE-HI NAAD

Song of the Buffalo-Hide Ceremony (Sun-Dance Song)

I

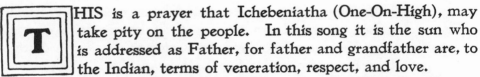

THIS is a prayer that Ichebeniatha (One-On-High), may take pity on the people. In this song it is the sun who is addressed as Father, for father and grandfather are, to the Indian, terms of veneration, respect, and love.

The ceremony is commonly called by the whites the Sun-Dance. The Arapaho word, "Hasse," means rawhide, and refers to the buffalo - hide, which is an important part of the ceremony. According to Dr. George A. Dorsey, of the Field Columbian Museum, Chicago, the ceremony is known as "Hassehawu," the Ceremony of the Offerings' Lodge.[1]

HASSE-HI NAAD	SONG OF THE BUFFALO-HIDE CEREMONY
Hedawunaneina Hishish nisana !	O may he take pity on us, Father Sun, O my Father !

[1] See page 151 for songs of the same ceremony among the Cheyennes.

ARAPAHO

HASSE-HI NAAD

Song of the Buffalo-Hide Ceremony

II

Sung by Chief Nakos (Sage)

This is the last song in the ceremony. While it is sung the people run hither and thither in symbol of dispersing to the four ends of the earth. At the close of the song they shake their blankets and garments to symbolize the casting from themselves of all evil.

HACHE-HI NAAD, JACHU NAAD[1]

Wolf-Song, or Comanche-Song

Sung by Chief Nakos (Sage)

I is the duty of certain warriors to go ahead of the war-party and spy on the enemy, and then to return and give the signal for the attack. These warriors are called wolves, for they are like wolves, prowling about the enemy's camp, moving by night, and falling on the foe unawares. This is one of the oldest songs of the Wolf warriors. Such songs are also called Jachu-naad, Comanche-Songs, because in former days the Comanches were the foes of the Arapahos, and "Comanche" came to be a common word for enemy.

HACHE-HI NAAD

Nah'ni cl.ita-ini,
Hitha bäbian niyihana;
Hani hätinahawuni,
Haka nihin.

WOLF-SONG

Look, O maid, behold me,
  I am going far away
Upon the war-path roaming;
And your words have caused the parting,
Long shall be the time
Ere again you see me.

[1] See "Cheyenne Songs of Victory," page 155.
[199]

KAINAWAD NAAD [1]

Song of the Spirit-Dance (Ghost-Dance Song)

Sung by many Arapahos, and explained by Chief Nakos (Sage)

LONG ago all was water, and the Turtle went to the bottom of the water and brought up a bit of clay. Out of this clay the world was made, and thereafter the Turtle became a symbol of the earth. The ridge on his back is the mountain-line, and the marks are streams and rivers. He himself is like a bit of land in the midst of water.

The Turtle Waters are yellow, and through these must the spirit pass to enter the spirit-world. The man who falls entranced during the Spirit-Dance knows nothing until he finds himself upon the brink of the yellow waters. In this song the dreamer tells how he waded through the Turtle Lake even to the spirit-world.

The song was composed by Hänächä-thiak (Sitting Buffalo-Bull), an Arapaho leader in the Spirit-Dance.

KAINAWAD NAAD	SONG OF THE SPIRIT-DANCE
Seniesäna	Wading passed I through
Niha-nawu,	Yellow waters,
Seniesäna	Wading passed I through
Niha-nawu,	Yellow waters,
Nänäi bäeno nidjieh-hi,	Ah, 'twas e'en, e'en the Turtle Lake—
Niha-nawu,	Yellow waters—
Nänäi bäeno nidjieh-hi,	Ah, 'twas e'en, e'en the Turtle Lake—
Niha-nawu.	Yellow waters.

[1] See " History of the Spirit-Dance," page 41. Compare songs of the Spirit-Dance, Dakota, and Pawnee, pages 47–48, 114–116.

ARAPAHO

HO NAWAD NAAD[1]

Crow-Dance Song

The Crow-Dance is a ceremony that the Arapahos hold in con-
nection with the Spirit-Dance. The crow is the messenger of the
Father.[2] As black paint is symbolic of good, so is the black crow
a symbol of good. For the crow is a harmless bird; he kills nothing:
even little birds can drive him away. In this song the crow is the
symbol of the Father.

HO NAWAD NAAD	CROW-DANCE SONG
Hesunani' ho-hu	Oh, the Crow, our Father,
Băhinahnit-ti,	He is all in all,
Hesunani' no!	Oh, our Father Crow!
A e-yo he-ye he-ye yo!	A e-yo he-ye he-ye yo!

NAKAHU NAAD

Lullaby

Sung by Wageoh (Maud Shawnee), Nawadek (Susie Sage), Nabilase (Jessie Sage), Gelbini
(Cappie Webster)

NAKAHU NAAD	LULLABY
Cheda-e,	Go to sleep,
Nakahu-kahu,	Baby dear, slumber,
Be-be!	Baby!

GOCHOTI NAAD[3]

Hand-Game Song

THE Indian turns his horses loose to graze where they
may find pasture. When he wants to use his horses
he must hunt them up and drive them home. Sometimes the horses wander far away and the man must be
up before daylight to bring them in for a day's work, or else hunt

[1] See "Pawnee Song of the Spirit-Dance," page 115.
[2] In this particular song it is the prophet of the Spirit-Dance religion who is alluded
to as "the Father."
[3] See "Cheyenne Hand-Game Songs," page 161.

them the day before. White men, too, who cannot afford to buy feed, turn their horses loose in this way.

This Hand-Game Song refers to the search for the sticks hidden in the hands of the players.

GOCHOTI NAAD

Natinachabena,
Ni nananaechana !
Ni nananaechana !
Natinachabena,

HAND-GAME SONG

Now I go to seek my horses !
So here I stand and look about me !
So here I stand and look about me !
Now I go to seek my horses !

HICHAÄCHUTHI [1]

Song of the Club Society

Sung and told by a member of the society

The melody of this song is old, and it is used by the Cheyennes as well as by the Arapahos with some slight changes to fit the Cheyenne words. But these words were heard in sleep by an Arapaho brave of the Club Society. In dream there appeared to him two Arapaho warriors, White-Horn and Running-Whirlwind,[2] who had both been killed by the Pawnees, and they sang this song:

HICHAÄCHUTHI

Nanänina Nanakunithäna
Nanänina Neyachat-Chawaat
Chä änitana.

SONG OF THE CLUB SOCIETY

Behold, I am White-Horn,
Behold, I am Running-Whirlwind,
We live, we live,
Behold us !

[1] See " Organizations of the Plains Indians," page 31.
[2] The whirlwind, the thunder, the sun, and other forces of nature are personifications of divine power. As such they are spirits, and the name Running-Whirlwind might hold much significance to the Indian. Most Indian names have deeper meaning than is conveyed by the actual word.

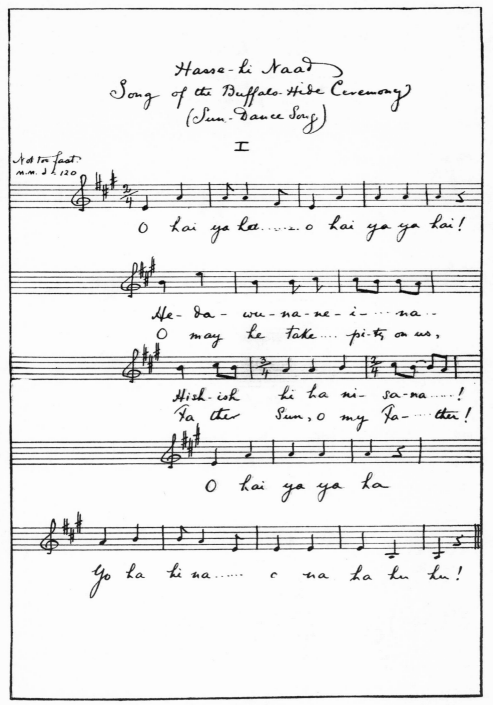

Hasse-hi Naad

He ya he ya ya he ya he hi ya ho

A he ya he ho o he ye ye ye

A he ya he ho o he ye ye!

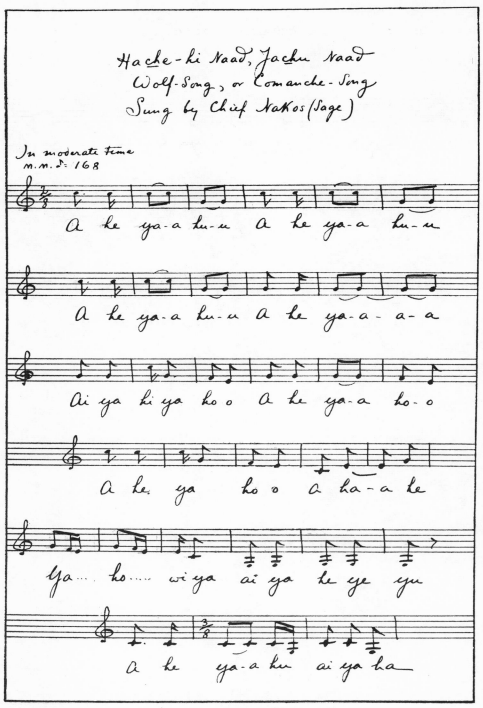

Hache-hi Naad

A he   ya-a hu   ai ya a he ya-a hu!

Nah'ni chi-ta-i-ni,
Look, O maid, be-hold me,

Hi-tha bä-bi-an-ni ni-yi-ha-na-a ni yi i yi
I am go-ing far a- way.... up-on the war-path roaming;

Ha-ni ka-ti-na-ha-wu-ni
And your words have caused the part-ing,

Ya ho Ha-ka ni-hi-ni ya ho wi ya
Long shall be the time ...... ere a- gain you see me.

[208]

Ho Nawad Naad
Crow-Dance Song

Ho Nawað Naad

Nakalu Naad
Lullaby
Sung by Wageah (Maud Shawnee) Nawadek (Susie Sage)
Nabilase (Jessie Sage) Gilbini (Cappie Webster)

In moderate time
M.M. ♩ = 92.

Che - da - e Na - Ka - hu - Ka - hu, Be - he - be, ... --.
Go to sleep, Ba - by dear, slum - ber, Ba - by .... sleep ......

E - Be - he - be, ... --.
Sleep, Ba - by sleep ......

Na - Ka - hu - Ka - hu, Be - he - be, ...
Ba - by dear, slum - ber, Ba - by .... sleep ......

Be be - he - be - he - be, ...
Sleep, sleep .... Ba - by sleep ......

E - Be - he - be, ...
Sleep, Ba - by .... sleep

Na - Ka - hu - Ka - hu, Be - he - be! .....
Ba - by dear, slum - ber Ba - by .... sleep ......

[211]

Gochoti-Naad

a hi ye...... he

a hi ye...... he

Na-ti-na-cha-be-na, he-e-e!
Now I go to seek my hor-ses.........!

Na-ti-na-cha-be-na, he-e-e!
Now I go to seek my hor-ses.........—!

Hichaächuthi
Song of the Club Society
Sung by a Member of the Society

Not too slow.
m.m. ♩ = 168

E ha e ye he ye

Ai ya ai ya...... kai ha

Ai ya e ye a he ya he...... hu hi yi......

A he he yu he ye...... hu

Ai ya e ye a he ya he...... hu...... hu wi

A he a he ya he he ye...... yu

[215]

Hichaächutti

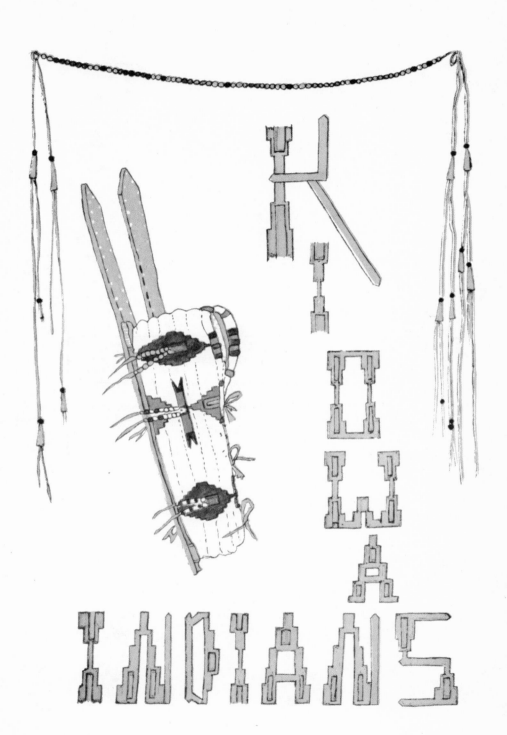

KIOWA INDIANS

KIOWA TITLE-PAGE

The design is of a Kiowa cradle-board with covering of bead-work.
The lettering and decorations are by Hinook Mahiwi Kilinaka
(Angel De Cora). The string of beads is such as children wear,
and is here used to typify childhood.

THE KIOWAS

OF all the plains tribes, perhaps none is more obscure of origin than the Kiowa, or "Gaigwu," as they call themselves. Although, according to some ethnologists, their language bears a certain resemblance to those of the Athapascan and Shoshonean groups, the similarity is not sufficient to justify the identification of the Kiowas with these tribes. For the present these Indians stand apart in a family by themselves.

The Kiowas have lived on the southwestern plains for more than half a century, but their earliest home of which there is historic evidence was around the sources of the Missouri and the Yellowstone rivers. Here they seem to have led a nomadic life, depending upon game, great and small, for their livelihood.

The Kiowas have a tradition of an ancient division of the tribe. A quarrel arose between two chiefs over an antelope, which resulted in the migration of part of the tribe from the river country to the Black Hills, where they came into relation with the Crow Indians and settled near them. Then they pushed southward again, raiding and wandering and frequently entering what was

NOTE FOR PRONUNCIATION OF KIOWA TEXT

Unless otherwise indicated, vowels have the Continental sound, and consonants the English.

The inverted apostrophe after a consonant signifies an explosive sound, sharper than an asperated consonant.

ä has the sound of the same character in German.

n has the nasal sound, as in French.

ain has the vowel-sound of the French word, " main."

Since words are sometimes changed and distorted to fit the rhythm of a song, and vowel-sounds modified for euphony, the ear has been the sole guide in writing the Kiowa song-words. The spelling here adopted is an attempt of the recorder to reproduce the sounds as sung.

then Spanish territory. The migrators were the ancestors of the Kiowas. But these Indians believe that descendants of the other ancient branch still dwell in the ancestral home about the head-waters of the two great rivers.

The Kiowas were known in the old days as strong fighters, and were among the fiercest of the plains warriors. Their roving life brought them into contact with other tribes to a marked degree, and alien blood was frequently absorbed into the tribe through the adoption of captives.

In 1867 they forsook the free life of the plains and entered upon the reservation in Indian Territory which, in common with the Comanches, they have since occupied. They are now citizens, having received allotments of land in severalty in what is now Oklahoma. Their life has undergone great change. Ill-ventilated frame-houses have replaced the tipi with its leaping fire and its open flap and smoke-hole, and the Kiowas have suffered the ravages of that foe to Indians in the transition state—consumption. But these people are industrious and for the most part hardy, and it is to be hoped that discrimination in their absorption of new ways may help them to bring something of the old vigor into their new life.

APIATAN

APIATAN is the head chief of the Kiowas. He is the cousin of High Chief, the Cheyenne,[1] and High Chief it was who brought his white friends to the Kiowa country and led them to Apiatan. The Kiowa chief received his guests with Indian dignity and courtesy. The purpose of the visit and the mission of the book were explained to him, and he was asked to contribute something to represent the Kiowa people. He sang the oldest song he knew, an ancient lay with archaic words, and then some of his Indian guests also offered songs. It is owing to High Chief's full explanation to the Kiowas of the purpose of the book, and to the interest of Apiatan, that all the songs contrib-

---

[1] See Wihu-Hwaihu-o-usz, or Hiamovi (High Chief, or High Wolf), page 149.

Apiatan (Wooden Lance), Head Chief of the Kiowas

uted then and afterwards by the Kiowas are some of the oldest now remembered by the tribe. At the mid-day meal the white visitors were given the place of honor facing the opening of the tent, and were treated with the marked courtesy typical of Indian hospitality. Afterwards Apiatan complied with the wish of his new friends and prepared himself to be photographed. He voluntarily put on the dress worn in the ceremony of the mescal religion, of which he is a leader—a beautiful costume of buckskin decorated with fine bead-work designs symbolic of the mescal faith. In his hand he carried a fan of eagle-feathers, an emblem of his high office. Thus clothed he was an imposing figure, the earthly chief of his people and their spiritual leader.

Apiatan is a man of intelligence and strong personality. At the time when the Ghost-Dance movement[1] reached the Kiowas, Apiatan was stricken with grief at the loss of a dearly loved son. Hearing that this religion promised communion with the dead, the Kiowa chief determined to see the Prophet and learn more of the new faith. Apiatan found the Father, but only to be disappointed, and to return to his people unconvinced. This checked the ardor of the Ghost-Dance movement among the Kiowas, in whose lives the mescal religion, long known to them, is now the strongest spiritual influence.[2] As mescal leader, Apiatan receives a loyalty from his people that is second only to their faith in his judgment and in his ability to guard their welfare.

GOMDA DAAGYA

Wind-Songs

Told by Owik'uyain (The Home-Comer)

THERE are different kinds of war-songs. Gomda Daagya (Wind-Songs) are war-songs made while the men are on the war-path, and are sung by those at home who think of the distant warriors, or by the men on the war-path who think of their loved ones at home. As a mother sings a lullaby to the child in her arms, even so she sings to the absent son far

[1] See "History of the Spirit-Dance," page 41.
[2] See "The Mescal Religion" and "Song of the Mescal Rite," pages 162–165.

away. "Ah, my poor boy!" might she croon, "Alone on the prairie
—how hard are thy days!" So might the maiden sing, thinking of
her lover; so might the young warrior sing, thinking of the maid.[1]

Such songs are called Wind-Songs because they are songs of
loneliness and longing like the open prairie where there is only the
sweep of the wind.[2]

GOMDA DAAGYA

Wind-Song

Very ancient song; words archaic

I

Sung by Apiatan (Wooden Lance)

GOMDA DAAGYA	WIND-SONG
A-doguonko do-peya kuyo,	Idlers and cowards are here at home now,
O a-doguonko do-peya kuyo,	Whenever they wish, they see their be-
Kionte-go-k'ian etbonholgon.	loved ones.
Ayi-ya on-pali, on-dekia.	Oh, idlers and cowards are here at home
	now,
	Idlers and cowards are here at home now,
	But the youth I love is gone to war, far
	hence.
	Weary, lonely, for me he longs.

GOMDA DAAGYA

Wind-Song

II

Sung by T'e-ne-t'e (Eagle Chief)

GOMDA DAAGYA	WIND-SONG
Pako e'k'ianda,	I have but one love,
Pako e'k'ianda,	I have but one love,
Pako e'k'ianda,	I have but one love,
Ayi apo	And he is far away,
Hayi ankom oyom giie.	On the war-path, e-ye, e-ye!
	Lonely are the days and weary.

[1] See foot-note No. 3, page 102, also page 453.
[2] See " The War-Path," page 154.

KIOWA

GOMDA DAAGYA
Wind-Song

A very old song; some words archaic.

III

Sung and told by Sah-mount (Samon)

A group of young men are on the war-path. They are well-born, rich in love and in the goods of the world. Yet they are pining, silent, and forlorn, overcome with homesick longing. Then one of the war-party, a poor young man with never a sweetheart to mark his absence, upbraids the drooping warriors, saying that he should be the one to pine, for no one misses him. But these others who have loved ones thinking of them—they should sing and be glad!

GOMDA DAAGYA

Agulkide dogul-ongu,
Ambonpoya, ambonpoya
  Dogya-hi !
Agulkide dogul-ongu,
Ambonpoya, dogya-hi !
Nokon honde imp'oya tont'-o-no
Yai-dahe-ba kuyo !

WIND-SONG

O you warriors, you have loved ones
  Longing for you, longing for you ;
    Rich are ye.
O you lovers, you have maidens
  Longing for you ; none have I.
Wherefore droop ye in silence, so down-
    cast ?
  Cheer your hearts with song, ho !

KOALDA DAAGYA
Begging-Song

Sung and told by Potine (White Beaver)

Sometimes twenty or thirty children go at night to the tipi of some people who have one dearly loved child. They stand outside the tipi and make songs about the child, begging that for love of the little one the parents will throw them something to eat.

KOALDA DAAGYA

Inhote to sai tălyi
K'anhoton atzeyuda
Hondeta al ahanda
  Goa-ain,
Ak'ainkot'na giat'akwot !

BEGGING-SONG

Give us food we beg of you,
For the love of your only child,
And his little spider-pet.
  For their sake,
Give, oh give us something,
  Give !

T'ÄPK'O DAAGYA

Song of the Antelope Ceremony

Sung and told by T'e-ne-t'e (Eagle Chief)

THERE was once a little boy who lived with his old grandmother. One day he happened to lose her spoon—a wooden spoon—for this was long ago, when the people had no iron or other metals. His grandmother was angry and whipped him, and so the boy threw himself upon the ground, crying, beside the wall of the tipi. There he lay, sobbing, until he fell asleep; and in his sleep he dreamed a wonderful dream which gave him mysterious power, so that he would always be able to kill game in plenty.

Time passed, and at length there came a famine upon the people; for many days they could get no meat, and they were hungry. The boy had grown to be a man, yet had he not forgotten the secret power that he had learned in a dream. So he spoke to his grandmother and said: "Call all the people to my tipi. Bid them all come."

"Why," said the grandmother, "we are poor, and we have neither wisdom nor power. The people will be angry if we call them here, for there is no help in us."

The young man himself went out and summoned all the people, and when they were come he took his seat opposite the door of the tipi, and the people sat around in a circle, as many as could find room within the tipi, and the rest waited outside. The man made two arrows, one of wild-cherry, and the other of plum-tree wood.[1]

[1] The wild-cherry tree and the plum-tree are symbols of spring and autumn fruitfulness, and are thus symbols of plenty. Other details of the ceremony also are probably emblematic.

When they were finished he stood them in the ground before him and began to sing:

> "My grandmother punished me,
> I wept until I fell asleep,
> In dream came a holy power, wonderful,
> Mighty to win food."

He waved the arrows in time to the song, and at the end of each verse he shook them, and blew upon his whistle of eagle-bone, "Whew!" Down from the arrows fell a shower of antelope-fur! He did this wonder in order to prove to the people his power. When he had finished singing he took his bow in his hands and reached down to the edge of the tipi wall where he had thrown himself when a child. There was nothing there that any man could see, yet the wonderful power that had visited the sleeping boy was still present; and so when he drew back his bow, behold an antelope was caught in it by the horns, and the man dragged him forth into the light of the fire and showed him to the astonished people. All night long they sat in the tipi, singing together in mystic ceremony.

When morning came the man went out on the prairie and walked to the top of a high hill. There he sat down, and the people sat on each side of him, forming a circle as before; and those who had come on horseback gathered outside the circle. The man planted his arrows in the ground and sang again and did his mystic work. Then he gave the two arrows to the two men who sat opposite to him, and they set off in opposite directions, carrying the arrows. The people followed them on foot, gradually separating from one another until they had formed the half of a large circle. Then the two leaders stopped and delivered the arrows to two horsemen, and the horsemen rode on, and other horsemen followed them, gradually separating from one another just as the people afoot had done until they had completed the great circle. And when the arrow-bearers met at the far side of the circle they turned and rode back through the centre of the circle till they came again to the starting-point and delivered up their mystic arrows. Then all the horsemen forming the farther side of the great circle began to gallop here and there, whooping and shouting, to rouse the game; and the horsemen gradually drew nearer, driving the game towards the men on foot; and when the animals were gathered together the people on foot closed in around them, and kept closing in until the circle was small enough for the people to join hands. The frightened antelopes ran around inside the circle until they became dizzy and exhausted; then the people killed them easily with tomahawks and knives, or if any broke through the circle the horsemen outside caught and killed them.

So the people had meat in plenty through the miraculous wisdom taught the boy in a dream. Thus originated this rite, which was performed only when the people were in great need. It came down from father to son for many years—none know how many. It is now no longer used, for all is changed, and there is little game to hunt. But some of the old men saw the ceremony in their youth, and it is well remembered by the aged Eagle Chief.

| T'APK'Ö DAAGYA | SONG OF THE ANTELOPE CEREMONY |
| | (Antelope-Song) |

Ton-k'an giapowitzep no	My grandmother punished me,
Tainkyowitte tain hol	I wept until I fell asleep,
Komdombe tonok'o	In dream came a holy power, wonderful,
Tsainiya ode domgya	Mighty to win food.

OKUM DAAGYA

Lullabies

Sung and told by Owik'uyain (The Home-Comer)

The Holy Man[1] has performed the ceremony to gather in the game, and the mother has gone to kill an antelope. She has left her baby to the care of an old woman, who soothes the crying child with this song:

I

OKUM DAAGYA	LULLABY
A-go-go	Hush thee, child—
T'oph'o goan-kontono,	Mother bringeth an antelope,
T'anba ok'un-balita.	And the tid-bit shall be thine.

[1] See "The Holy Man," page 32.

KIOWA

II

Nonsense-Rhyme

OKUM DAAGYA

I'pagy'mainte koain-ko,
Zotom tonsäd'l,
Tsainyi tonsäd'l,
Polainyi tonsäd'l.

LULLABY

Baby swimming down the river,
Driftwood leggies, rabbit leggies,
Little rabbit leggies.

GWU DAAGYA [1]

War-Path Song

Sung and told by T'e-ne-t'e (Eagle Chief)

WHEN a young man woos a maiden he brings gifts of horses to her father. The maid in this song is thinking of her first lover whose playful word she never can forget. For the man who now seeks to marry her, offering her father his sore-backed ponies, she has only scorn. So she waits for her first lover.

This is a very old war-path song, and the words are not all in the Kiowa language of to-day. It was often sung before the war-party set out. The war-leader would start the song, and those young men who wanted to follow him would join in the singing.

GWU DAAGYA

Ameyaidonhonme
Ain honya mopoiko
Anti ya'wut hoyano
Tsainko gompaomk'o
Eyamkom

WAR-PATH SONG

Ah, I never, never can forget
The playful word you spoke long since.
This man who seeks to marry me,
He with his sore-backed ponies,
What's he to me!

See " The War-Path," page 154.

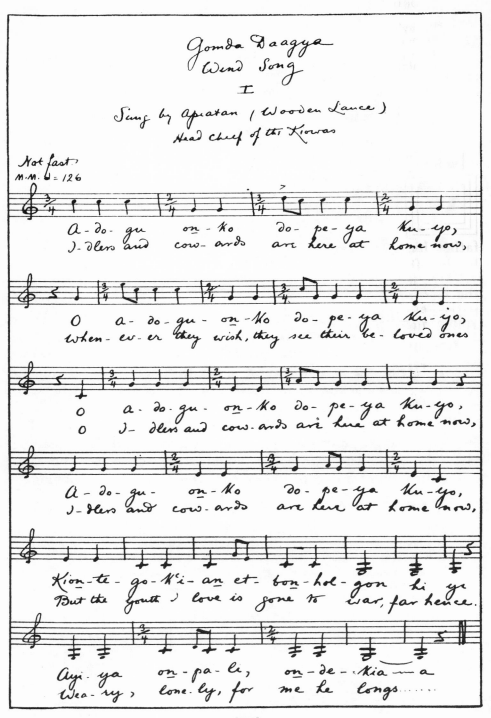

[231]

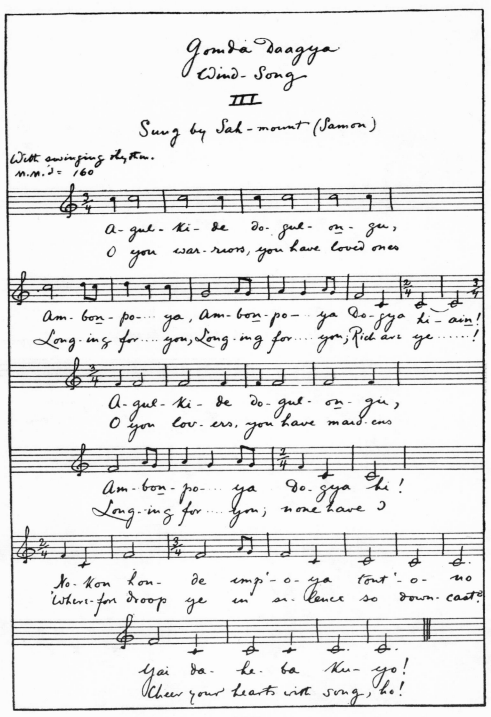

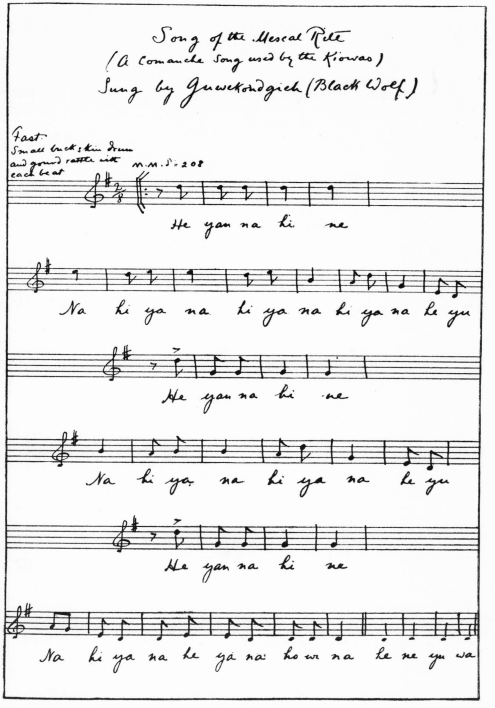

Song of the Mescal Rite

He yan na he ne ya na he ya

He yan na he ne

Na hi ya na hi ya na he yu

He yan na hi ne

Na hi ye na he ya na ho wr na

He ne yu wa

The Mescal Songs of one verse are sung four times. This song, containing two verses, is sung but twice.

[234]

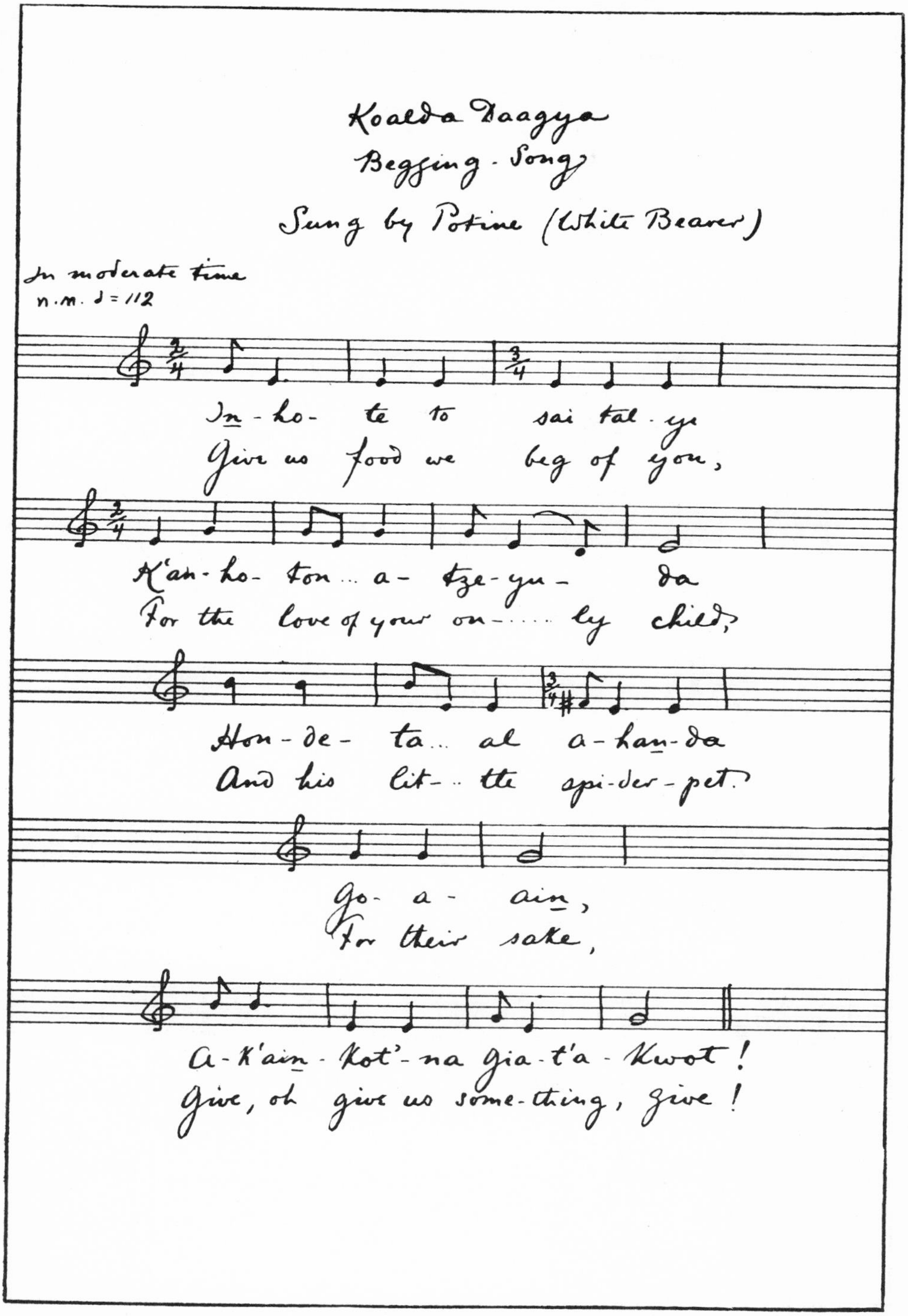

Koalda Daagya
Begging-Song

Sung by Potine (White Beaver)

In moderate time
n.m. ♩ = 112

In - ho- te to sai tal-ye
Give us food we beg of you,

K'an-ho- ton ... a- tze-yu- da
For the love of your on----ly child,

Hon - de- ta... al a-han-da
And his lit----tle spi-der-pet,

Go- a- ain,
For their sake,

A-K'ain-Kot'-na gia-t'a-Kwot!
Give, oh give us some-thing, give!

T'äpk'o Daagya

A hai ya he ya.... ya

A.... hai... ya.... he ya... ya

T'on-k'an giap-o-witz ep no
My grand-mo-ther pun-ished me, and

Tain-kyo-wit-te tain-yi hol....
I wept un-til I fell a-sleep......

Kom-dom-be ton- o... k'o.... Tain-i-ya
In dream came a ho-... ly.... powr.... Won-der-ful

O-de.... do-om-gya he ye ye
Might-y... to win food.

[237]

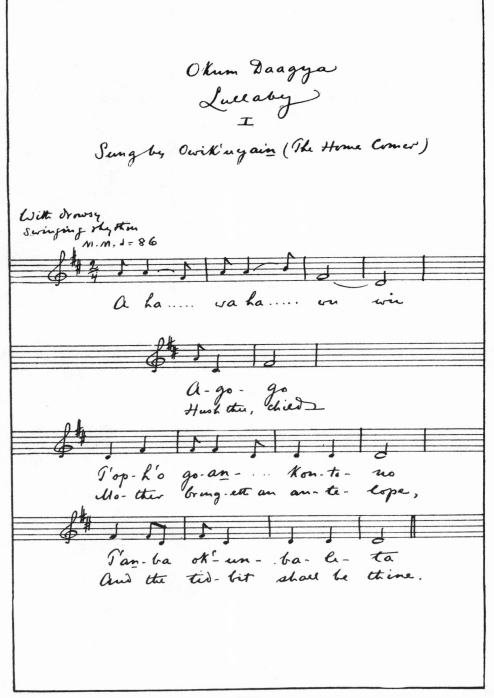

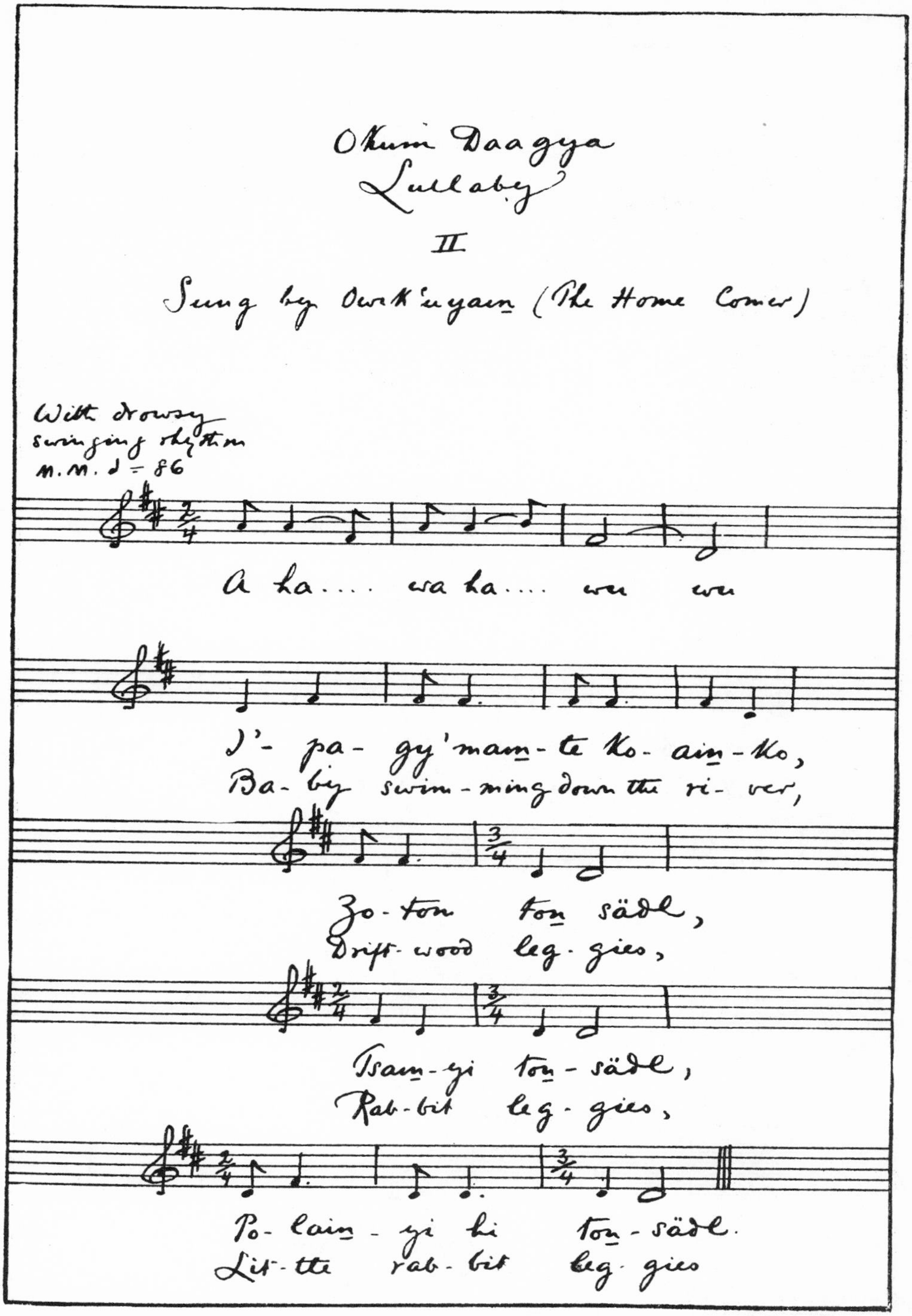

Okun Daagya
Lullaby

II

Sung by Ourk'uyain (The Home Comer)

With drowsy
swinging rhythm
M.M. ♩ = 86

A ha.... wa ha.... wu   wu

J'- pa- gy'mam- te ko- ain- ko,
Ba- by swim- ming down the ri- ver,

Zo - ton   ton sädl,
Drift- wood leg- gies,

Tsam- yi ton- sädl,
Rab- bit leg- gies,

Po- lain- yi hi   ton- sädl.
Lit- tle rab- bit leg- gies

[239]

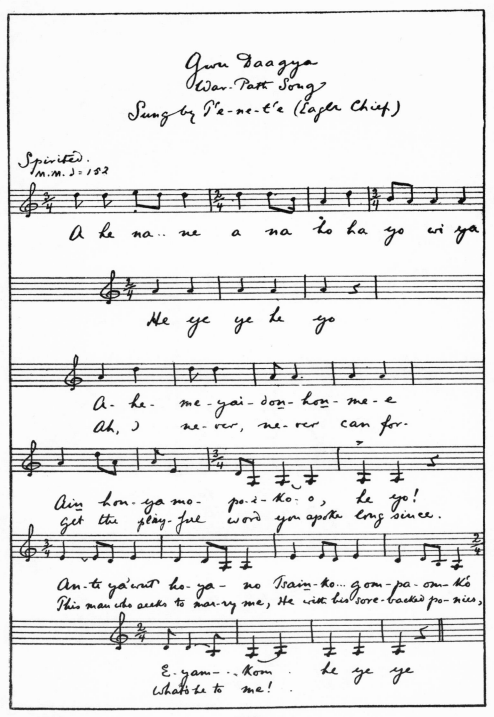

LAKE
INDIANS
WINNEBAGO

WINNEBAGO TITLE-PAGE

The design and the lettering are by Hinook Mahiwi Kilinaka (Angel De Cora), of the Winnebago tribe. The design represents a piece of Winnebago bead-work. The Winnebagos are skilled in bead and quill work.

THE WINNEBAGOS

T HE Winnebagos are a branch of the great Siouan family, yet they never have affiliated with its more warlike divisions. Though now in Nebraska, in the early days when these Indians first became known to white men they were living in a fertile and beautiful country on the shores of Lake Michigan. Early travellers have told of the almost idyllic conditions of the Winnebago life in this lake country. The Indians were hospitable and temperate, "remarkably provident" and industrious, raising crops of corn, beans, squash, and pumpkins, and fishing in lake or stream. As white settlement increased, the pressure was such that in the year 1832 the Winnebagos ceded a large tract of country to the United States, receiving in exchange land to the west of the Mississippi. This was but the first of a series of cessions and removals which entailed great hardships to the Indians, and which culminated when the Winnebagos were moved against their will and at their own expense from prosperous homes in Minnesota to a desolate Dakota agency, where, because of their fidelity to the whites, they were in peril from bands of desperate Dakotas, and where the conditions of the country were such that it was impossible for them to sustain themselves either by farming or by the chase. Such was their suffering that within a year over a thousand of them escaped in canoes to the Omaha reservation in

NOTE FOR PRONUNCIATION OF WINNEBAGO TEXT

Unless otherwise indicated, vowels have the Continental sound, and consonants the English.

n has the nasal sound, as in French.

ch, in italic, is a guttural, like ch in German.

The use of the hyphen, in Winnebago words, is by the advice of an educated member of the tribe.

Nebraska, where they were fed and sheltered. They preferred to be shot by the United States troops, if detected, than to die of starvation, disease, and cold. The friendly Omahas allowed them to settle upon their land. The Winnebagos started farming, and in 1889 they received land in allotments; but since this, their last resting-place, was thrown open to white settlement, their deterioration has been rapid. It is now to be hoped that an awakened interest in the Indians may help to revivify this exhausted and discouraged tribe, and that the happy memories of past days, deep-planted in the hearts of the old people, may be to younger Winnebagos as seeds for growth in character and endurance that shall bring to their future the strength and virtue of their old lake life.

STORIES OF WAK-CHUNG-KAKA AND WASH-CHING-GEKA

Told by Chash-chunk-a (Wave), Nek-hu-wi-ka (South Wind), and other Winnebagos of Nebraska and Wisconsin

MA-O-NA, the Earth-Maker, made the earth and everything on it. He made a man, but the man was not good. Ma-o-na did not want to burn him up, so he tossed him to one side and went on with his work. This man became Wa-cho-pi-ni-Shi-shik, an evil spirit. He watched Ma-o-na at work, and everything that Ma-o-na made he copied; but whereas Ma-o-na's works were all good, those of Wa-cho-pi-ni-Shi-shik were evil. Ma-o-na made the deer and elk and buffalo; Wa-cho-pi-ni-Shi-shik made the huge animals, the monsters that devoured men. All bad things, evil spirits and the like, are the work of Wa-cho-pi-ni-Shi-shik.

Ma-o-na sent his son, Wak-chung-kaka, the Foolish One, to kill the monsters and make the earth fit for man. But Wak-chung-kaka could not destroy all the works of the evil spirit. Then Ma-o-na sent another son, Ke-chung-geka, the Tortoise, but he was too fond of war. So, too, was Wuh-te-huk, the third son. Last of all Ma-o-na sent his youngest son, Wash-ching-geka, the Little Hare.

These are stories of Wak-chung-kaka and Wash-ching-geka.

WINNEBAGO

STORIES OF WAK-CHUNG-KAKA, THE FOOLISH ONE

I

ONE day Wak-chung-kaka was walking over a hill and he looked down into a hollow where reeds grew tall, and he thought he saw a throng of people with feathers on their heads. The wind blew through the reeds, and Wak-chung-kaka thought that the people danced and hallooed "Wu-wu-wu!" So he put a feather on his head and went in among the people and danced and shouted "Wu-wu-wu!" He danced all day long, till at evening the wind dropped and everything was still; and then Wak-chung-kaka looked around him and found himself alone among the reeds.

II

Wak-chung-kaka was walking one day beside the water when he saw a chief standing there dressed all in black with a shining disk on his breast, and the chief was pointing across the water. He stood quite still, and always pointed steadily across the water. Wak-chung-kaka spoke to him, but the chief never moved or answered; he still pointed steadily across the water. Wak-chung-kaka spoke to him again, and still there was no answer. Four times he spoke to him, and then at last Wak-chung-kaka grew angry and said, "I can point, too, and I can point longer than you."

So Wak-chung-kaka set down his bundle and opened it and dressed himself all in black like the chief, and hung a disk on his breast and stood there beside the chief, pointing across the water. But when he had stood thus for a great time without moving, Wak-chung-kaka began to be weary of this, and he looked around at the chief, and, behold! it was only the blackened stump of a burned tree with a white spot that the fire had not touched.

III

Another time Wak-chung-kaka was walking along the sandy shore of a lake, and when he came to a point of the shore he heard a cry, "Wu-wu-wu!" He looked over the point, but could see nobody, so he walked on till he heard the cry, "Wu-wu-wu!" and saw a little cloud of flies fly up into the air. There was an elk's head lying on the shore, and a swarm of flies flew in at the neck-hole behind, and then flew out again all at once. Wak-chung-kaka stood and looked at them. "That must be good sport," he thought. "I wish I could do that too."

A little fly looked up at him and said, "Wak-chung-kaka, you can!"

At once Wak-chung-kaka felt himself growing smaller and smaller, till he was no bigger than a fly, and then he easily went in at the hole in the head and flew out again, crying, "Wu-wu-wu!" He thought it was fine sport to fly in and out, in and out, with the swarm of flies. So the flies let him play with them for a while, till all at once, when Wak-chung-kaka was just starting to go in, he grew to his own natural size, and as he already had his head within the elk's head, the neck-hole fitted him so closely that he could not get his head out again.

Wak-chung-kaka walked on, wearing the elk's head; and as he could not see very well, he walked into the lake. The water came up to the eye-holes of the head, and Wak-chung-kaka swam until he came near a village that stood beside the lake, and when the people saw the elk-horns moving along the water they said, "It is a water-spirit; let us offer him gifts." For there are spirits in the ground, under the water, and in great springs of the hills, and the spirits often look like elk or buffalo.

So the people brought tobacco and beads and laid them on the shore before Wak-chung-kaka, and he stayed in the water; and the young people prayed to him, "Spirit, grant us long life!" and the old people prayed, "Long life for our children!" and to every prayer Wak-chung-kaka answered, "Ho!" (yes). At length, when all the people were gathered before him, he said: "My nephews and nieces, I will grant your prayers if you will do what I tell you. Let two strong men take hold of my horns, one on each side, and let another one split my head down the middle, carefully, carefully —he must be careful not to cut too deep."

So two strong men took hold of his horns, one on each side, and pulled with all their might, while a third took a stone axe and very carefully chopped the elk's head down the middle, till, crack! the skull fell apart and there stood Wak-chung-kaka, and laughed, "Haw, haw, haw!"

STORIES OF WASH-CHING-GEKA, THE LITTLE HARE

Youngest son of Ma-o-na (Earth-Maker)

I

ASH-CHING-GEKA lived with his grandmother while doing his works. His grandmother was the earth, and she was very wise. She cooked for the Little Hare and nourished him and took care of him.

Now among the other evil things then in the world were eight blind men who lived in a wood; they went about with the help of long cords and spread webs among the trees, in which they caught people and killed them.

One day when the blind men were cooking their dinner of bear's meat, Wash-ching-geka went in among them. There was a piece of meat for each. Now the men could not see Wash-ching-geka, and he stepped softly to the pot and took out one portion of meat. When the blind men began to eat they quarrelled with one another over the missing portion, because each one thought another had taken his meat. As they were quarrelling, Wash-ching-geka slapped one of them, and then that one slapped his neighbor, and he slapped the next, and so they all fell to fighting.

Meanwhile, Wash-ching-geka ran home to his wise grandmother and took counsel with her.

Next day he went again to the blind men, and while they were cooking he took out the meat and put poison on it. So the blind men ate of the poisoned meat and were killed. They would never again spread webs among the trees to destroy the people. And now when they were dead, behold, Wash-ching-geka saw that really they were spiders.

II

In the early days there was a great hill that used to open and shut like a pair of jaws and devour men and animals. The hill would open in the middle and the sides would fall back till they lay flat upon the ground, and all the land looked like good smooth prairie.

Then herds of elk and deer and buffalo would come to graze, and when the place was full, the jaws of the hill would close, and, crack! all the animals would be crushed and killed. This hill killed so much game that the Earth-Maker feared that all the people would starve. So he sent his son, Wash-ching-geka, to destroy the hill.

When the Little Hare came there the hill opened and all the ground was smooth; and Wash-ching-geka made himself like a small stone and lay quite still. Then the elk and deer and buffalo came to graze, but as soon as the mouth began to close on them, see! Wash-ching-geka quickly changed himself into a great stone, and so, when the hill shut on him, hoo! the jaws were broken all to pieces. The hill lay shattered and never could devour men or animals any more.

III

There was a great, great elephant [1] that used to devour people by reaching out for them with his long tongue [2] and swallowing them. This elephant looked like a large hill all covered with grass. Wash-ching-geka went out to kill the elephant because he devoured so many of the people. First he sprinkled himself all over with little pieces of flint, and then he sat down in front of the elephant and sang this song:

> " You, who reach with your tongue,
> Great One, you draw them in,
> So have I heard it told.
> Gather me in, gather me in !"

[1] The Indians have many legends to account for the remains of prehistoric animals.
[2] "Tongue" is of course his "trunk."

The elephant saw Wash-ching-geka's ears sticking up in the grass, and he thought they were feathers on somebody's head, so he reached out his tongue and swallowed the Little Hare. Inside the elephant all was dark and vast; there were starving people here, some dead and some dying, for they had no wood to cook with.

Then Wash-ching-geka said to a young woman that was inside, "Look in my fur and see if you can find a piece of flint."

The woman searched through his fur and found a little piece of flint. Wash-ching-geka struck his hand upon the flint and said, "Grow bigger!" and it was bigger. Four times he struck thus, and each time the flint grew bigger. Then he struck it again and said, "Be a knife!" and it was a knife. Then he struck yet again and said, "Be a big knife!" and it was a great big knife.

Wash-ching-geka felt along the ribs of the elephant till he found a soft place between two rib-bones, and there he cut a hole like a door and sent out all the people. Then he ran forward to the elephant's heart, and with one blow of his knife he split the heart in two. Then he also jumped out through the hole. But on his way he caught up the elephant's young, and when he came outside he threw the little elephants clear across the water. That is why the elephant now lives only on the other side of the water.

WASH-CHING-GEKA NA-WA' NI-NA

Wa-le ki-zi-na-nap,
Chun-ka, wa-lai-na-nap,
Sa-ah-zhe ai-le-la,
    Hin-gi na-nap !
    Hin-gi na-nap !

SONG OF THE HARE

You, who reach with your tongue,
Great One, you draw them in,
So have I heard it told.
    Gather me in !
    Gather me in !

IV

While running here and there over the earth to see what work was still to do, Wash-ching-geka found a pass or trail where some huge thing had gone by.

"I must find out what this is," said he; "maybe it is some great animal that will run over the people and kill them."

So he blocked up the pass with trees and stones; but when he came there again, lo! the big thing had burst through them.

Then he went to his grandmother and told her about it, and she made a net which he spread across the pass. Next day he heard some one crying aloud and singing this song:

"Wash-ching-ge, let me loose, I cry,
Wash-ching-ge, let me loose, I cry!
Your uncles and your aunts,
Oh, whatever will they do,
Whatever, whatever will they do!
Wash-ching-ge, let me loose, I cry,
Wash-ching-ge, let me loose, I cry!"

Who was it that Wash-ching-geka had caught—who but the sun! For the sun used to go through that pass every day, and now he was fast in Wash-ching-geka's net!

"Go you and set him loose!" cried the grandmother, and she scolded the Little Hare and beat him over the head with her cane. "What will all your little-fathers and your little-mothers[1] do without the sun? Go, set him loose!"

So Wash-ching-geka tried to untie the net. But the sun was so hot that the Little Hare could not face him. He could only back up, turning away his head; and so his hinder parts were so scorched that, to this day, the skin of the hare's hind-quarters is tender and easily broken.

WI-LA NA-WA' NI-NA

Wash-ching-ge, hin-khu lush-ka-le,
Wash-ching-ge, hin-khu lush-ka-le!
Hi-tek-nik wa-la-ka,
Hi-u-ni-nik wa-la-ka,
Cha-ku ki-shkan hi-la-ni-he kche-zhe!
Wash-ching-ge, hin-khu lush-ka-le,
Wash-ching-ge, hin-khu lush-ka-le!

SONG OF THE SUN

Wash-ching-ge, let me loose, I cry,
Wash-ching-ge, let me loose, I cry!
Your uncles and your aunts,
Oh, whatever will they do,
Whatever, whatever will they do!
Wash-ching-ge, let me loose, I cry,
Wash-ching-ge, let me loose, I cry!

[1] Literal translation of aunts and uncles. Aunt and uncle are terms of respect or reverence. An older person, or a person of importance, will address a younger one as "my nephew" or "my niece." "Your uncles and your aunts" means here, of course, all the people in the world.

V

La-ga-ka-nan-shke was a monster shaped like a flying ant, with a big body and legs, but very, very small in the middle. He lived behind a hill and never came out. But he carried a great tree and pounded with it on the ground while he sang a song, and when the elk and other animals came near he threw down his tree upon them and killed them. This ant-man was scarcely thicker at the waist than a hair. Wash-ching-geka thought that he could blow him in two, so he blew—"Soo! soo!" But instead of blowing La-ga-ka-nan-shke in two, Wash-ching-geka himself got killed, for the ant-man threw his tree and crushed the Little Hare.

When La-ga-ka-nan-shke lifted up his tree he found only a very small and flattened thing. He picked it up by the ears. "No good to eat," he thought, so he threw the Little Hare away.

That evening when Wash-ching-geka did not come home his grandmother said, "My little nephew is killed." For though Wash-ching-geka ran over the whole earth in the daytime, he always came back at night; so when he did not return his grandmother knew that he had been killed.

Next morning she rose up and ate and girt her dress above her knees so that she could run faster, and she took an elk-horn club of Wash-ching-geka's and started out to find him. The old grandmother could run fast like Wash-ching-geka, and she ran over the whole earth till she heard the noise of the huge ant-man pounding and singing. La-ga-ka-nan-shke lifted up his tree to throw it on her, but the grandmother said, "Brother, better not do that!" So he stayed his hand and talked with her.

Said the grandmother: "Brother, I fear my little nephew has been killed. Perhaps he came here and annoyed you and you killed him."

Said the ant-man, "Well, sister, what kind of nephew was it, big or little?"

"Oh," she said, "very little."

Then said he: "Well, sister, maybe I did kill him. I killed something very small yesterday. It was no good for eating, so I threw it away. Go you down there and look at it. Maybe it was the little nephew."

So the grandmother went down and looked, and there lay the Little Hare. Then she said: "Brother, it was my little nephew you killed yesterday. He is here now, dead."

Then she picked up the Little Hare by the ears and said, "You sleep here too long; wake up and go to work!"

She threw him to one side, and just as he touched the ground he jumped and ran a little, as hares do, and sat up and said, "Grandmother, I was asleep here, and you wakened me."

"No, nephew," said the grandmother, "you were not asleep. You were killed by the grandfather that walks and walks up there on the hill. You came here yesterday and annoyed him, and he killed you. I made you alive again."

The Little Hare said: "Oh, that is so. I remember now. I will go to see him again and set that right."

So the Hare went home with his grandmother. Next morning after he had eaten he started out. La-ga-ka-nan-shke had a big fir-tree, so the Little Hare went away to the very edge of the earth where the biggest pine-trees grow, and there he spoke to Wa-zi-chunk, the tallest tree in the world.

"Big tree," said he, "I have come for you; I am going to use you. I will pull you out of the ground, but when I have finished with you I will set you back again."

So he laid hold of the tree and pulled it out, and then went to the place where he had been killed. He climbed the hill at one end; La-ga-ka-nan-shke was at the other end, and he began to sing and pound with his tree. Wash-ching-geka did the same, and they danced towards each other, singing and pounding. But soon the big ant-man walked slower, and could hardly keep on his feet, because the Hare made the ground shake with the pounding of the tallest tree in the world.

La-ga-ka-nan-shke came slowly, growing more and more frightened, and at last when they were close to each other he cried out, "Ka-lo-quaw!" And the Hare answered, "Ka-lo-quaw!" The Little Hare heard where the ant-man was, and he took his tall tree and crushed the monster—"Boom!" and a swarm of flying ants came out of the monster's body. And the wise grandmother, far away, when she heard the noise of that blow, cried, "Oh, little nephew has killed his grandfather!" Then Wash-ching-geka said, "You big flying ant can never kill anything more, and you little ants will have to creep on the ground, but sometimes you may fly." And then he carried the tall tree to the edge of the earth and set it back in its place.

WAI-KUN

Fable

Sung and told by Chash-chunk-a (Wave, Peter Sampson)

Once there were some mice under a crooked log and they believed they were the only people in the whole world. One of them standing up and stretching his little arms could just touch the under side of the log. He thought that he was very tall and that he touched the sky. So he danced and sang this song:

WAI-KUN	FABLE
Mo-zhun-na-le,	Throughout the world
Pe-zhe ya-ki-ske shun-non-nink	Who is there like little me!
na-gi-kche!	Who is like me!
Mo-zhun-na-le,	I can touch the sky,
Pe-zhe ya-ki-ske shun-non-nink	I touch the sky indeed!
na-gi-kche!	
Ne-sha-na ma-chi-nik-gla ya-ki-o-o!	

MA-O-NA

Song to the Earth-Maker

Sung and told by Chash-chunk-a (Wave, Peter Sampson)

IN olden times it was customary for a young man often to blacken his face and go into solitude to fast. Then while his body lay sleeping his soul went away to the spirits. Spirits often have the form of animals,[1] and so the young man might see in dream the Elk Chief or the Buffalo Chief.

[1] See "The Songs of the Dakotas," page 60, and "Introduction to the Pawnee Songs," page 96.

[253]

The thunder is a spirit, and it is the emblem of war; it is winged, mighty, and awful, and it is called the Thunder-Bird. Great is he to whom the thunder appears in vision, for he will become war-chief.

So this man who fasted would see and talk with the spirits and they would teach him wisdom. From some one of them, perhaps from his own guiding spirit, would he learn a song. So did a man long ago learn of the spirits this song. Thereafter it was sung as a consecration before going to war.

MA-O-NA	SONG TO THE EARTH-MAKER
Ma-o-na	Earth-Maker,
Wai-kan-chunk hi kche, hing-ge !	Holy shall I be,—holy !

MUN-KUN NA-WAN

Holy Song (Medicine Song)

Sung and told by Nek-hu-wi-ka (South Wind, Jacob Russell)

I

ONCE long ago, before the Winnebagos left their old home by the Great Water in Wisconsin, there went a young man into the hills to fast.[1] He fasted for twelve days, and then a spirit came to him in a vision and talked with him. Ma-o-na, the Earth-Maker, had sent the spirit to teach the man; and the spirit gave him knowledge and taught him wonderful words that brought health, welfare, and long life. Wise was the young man when he left the hills, for he brought with him the teachings of the spirit and the power of the holy words. When he came back to his people he sang this song, and this was the beginning of one kind of medicine ceremony. The words he had learned of the spirit were so holy that the man lived long without any sickness, nor did he die of any ill. At the last all the joints of his body fell apart from mere old age, and of old age alone he died.

So the song that he made containing the wonderful words has always been cherished by the Winnebagos because of its great power.

[1] See "The Holy Man," page 32; "The Songs of the Dakotas," page 60; and "Introduction to the Pawnee Songs," page 96.

WINNEBAGO

All this was long ago when the language of the Winnebagos was different from what it is to-day. Now the people no longer use such words in common speech. Indeed, no one knows the exact meaning of the wonderful words. The song is still used in some of the medicine ceremonies, but only the Medicine-Men, the Holy Men, understand its meaning.

The medicine ceremony of the Winnebagos lasts four days and nights. Holy songs are sung, and there is spoken ritual, when the Holy Man gives commandments and teaches the people the ways of goodness. Now and again, that the people may not become tired and drowsy, the ceremony is enlivened by dancing. So the slow part of this holy song is followed by a quick part which is the music of the dance. The medicine ceremony used to be very solemn and sacred in the olden times, and its mysteries were known only to the initiated. The white people called it the "medicine religion" of the Winnebagos.

MUN-KUN NA-WAN

Ni hai na wi nu hu
   Ha ha ti hi
   Hi na wi hi na
Ma-na-gle he
   Na ha wha
   Han gle he
   Ha ha ti hi
   Hi na wi hi na
Shi-ke hai na wi na-a
   Ha ha ti hi
   Hi na wi hi na
Shi-ke hai na wi na-a
   Ha ha ti hi
   Hi na wi hi na

HOLY SONG

(Saith the Spirit,
  "Dream, oh, dream again,
And tell of me,
   Dream thou !")
Into solitude went I
And wisdom was revealed to me.
  (Saith the Spirit,
  "Dream, oh, dream again,
And tell of me,
   Dream thou !")
Let the whole world hear me,
Wise am I !
  (Now saith the Spirit,
  "Tell of me,
   Dream thou !")
All was revealed to me;
From the beginning
Know I all, hear me !
All was revealed to me !
  (Now saith the Spirit,
  "Tell of me,
   Dream thou !")

HI-WA-SHI-DA	DANCE

Ma-na-gle wu-hi-ni-gi-gi-na,
Ma-na-gle wu-hi-ni-gi-gi-na,
Ha-chi-je-na !
	I have won the world,
	  The world is won,
	I have won the world,
	  The world is won,
	I am come,
	I am come here now !

Chi-na-gla wu-hi-ni-gi-gi-na,
Chi-na-gla wu-hi-ni-gi-gi-na,
Ha-chi-je-na !
	I have won the village,
	  Yea, 'tis won,
	I have won the village,
	  Yea, 'tis won,
	I am come,
	I am come here now !

MUN-KUN NA-WAN

Holy Song (Medicine Song)

II

THE wisdom of the otter[1] is known to the Men of Medicine. In pouches made of otter-skin, or of the skin of some other emblematic animal, the Men of Medicine put their mystic "medicine" and charms. During a Medicine-Dance the Medicine-Men hold their skin-pouches in their hands, and suddenly shoot them out at arm's-length towards some man, when the mysterious power that is inside the pouch flies out like an arrow and strikes the man dead. He falls on his face, and lies motionless until the Men of Medicine, through their mysterious power, bring him to life again. Women, too, are pierced by the unseen arrows.

MUN-KUN NA-WAN	HOLY SONG
Ma-ni-na, le-ha-no, Ma-ni-na, le-ha-no, Wunk-i-wi-zha le-ha-no, Ma-ni-na, le-ha-no !	Let it fly—the arrow, Let it fly—the arrow, Pierce with a spell the man, oh ! Let it fly—the arrow.

[1] See "Introduction to the Pawnee Songs," page 96.

Ma-ní-na, le-ha-no,	Let it fly—the arrow,
Ma-ní-na, le-ha-no,	Let it fly—the arrow,
Hí-nuk-í-zha le-ha-no,	Pierce with a spell the woman !
Ma-ní-na, le-ha-no !	Let it fly—the arrow.

HE-LUSH-KA NA-WA*N*[1]

Warrior-Songs

THE Winnebago ceremony of the He-lush-ka is of Omaha origin, and corresponds to the "Omaha Dance" of the Dakotas. It has come to be a purely sociable dance, but the recitals, in song and story, of great deeds or of events in the tribe form still an important part of the ceremony.

The dance is an occasion of general gift-making, and any one who gives may be called "He-lush-ka."

HE-LUSH-KA NA-WA*N*

Three Warrior-Songs

Sung and told by Chash-chunk-a (Wave, Peter Sampson)

THESE three warrior-songs tell the story of the last fighting done by the Winnebagos. Some of the tribe were employed in the year 1864 as government scouts. They were looking for the Arapahos, when they came suddenly upon a party of Pawnees and charged them, mistaking them for the enemy. The Pawnees, who were themselves friends of the government, did not wish to fight the government scouts, so they fled in haste, dropping their bundles to lighten their ponies as they galloped away. Now, among the pursuing Winnebagos was a Pawnee who had married into the Winnebago tribe, so when the Pawnee chief lifted his hand and cried out, "Friends!" this man recognized the flying braves as his own people, and the Winnebagos, seeing their mistake, ceased their pursuit. But in the excitement

[1] See Dakota "Omaha Dance-Songs," page 55.

one of the Winnebagos fired a shot and wounded the horse of a Pawnee; and the owner afterwards came to the Winnebagos and claimed payment for damages. But the Winnebago refused to pay, and, with Winnebago wit, put in a counter-claim for his lost bullet, which, he said, had been intended for an Arapaho. This man was called by the whites George Eaton, but after this incident he was known to the Winnebagos as "Pawnee Shooter."

The first song describes the pursuit of the Pawnees by the Winnebagos. The next is an exclamation of derisive triumph at the trail the Pawnees have left, all strewn with their bundles. The last tells of the mutual recognition of the pursuers and pursued: "Winnebagos,[1] these, you say! Pawnees, these, you say! Friends, halloo, you say!" These three songs are well liked by the Winnebagos and are still sung at the He-lush-ka dances.

I

HE-LUSH-KA NA-WAN

Shun-ke wo-djin wi-ne !
Shun-ke wo-djin wi-ne !
   Ko-la-wi-la,
Pa-ni ka-lai-la-dju-ka !
Shun-ke wo-djin wi-ne !

Shun-ke wa-na-ma-ne !
Shun-ke wa-na-ma-ne !
Pa-ni guch-la,
Pa-ni ka-lai-la-dju-ka !
Shun-ke wa-na-ma-ne !

WARRIOR-SONG

Ho, friend, whip up your horse !
Now they fly fast—Pawnees—see
   how they fly !
Ho, friend, whip up your horse !

Ho, friend, prick up your horse !
Pawnee Shooter, ride fast, for
   they are gone !
Ho, friend, prick up your horse !

II

HE-LUSH-KA NA-WAN

Wa-we-la ha-dja-le !
Wa-we-la ha-dja-le !
Hi-cha-ko-lo,
Pa-ni-na wa-cha-la !
Wa-we-la ga-ske-na !
Wa-we-la ha-dja-le !

WARRIOR-SONG

See the trail they've left here !
Comrades, hearken—Pawnee braves,
   I saw them.
What a trail they've left here !

[1] It was not possible to make an absolutely literal translation to fit the music.

WINNEBAGO

III

HE-LUSH-KA NA-WAN

WARRIOR-SONG

Ho-chunk-gi-le, hi-she-na !
Ho-chunk-gi-le, hi-she-na !
Pa-ni-na, hi-she-na !
Hi-ta-lo, hi-she-na !
Ho-chunk-gi-le, hi-she-na !

Ho, they are Winnebagos !
Pawnee braves, they hailed us;
" Friends ! Halloo !" they hailed us.
Ho, they are Winnebagos !

HE-LUSH-KA NA-WAN

Warrior-Song

IV

Sung and told by Wa-che-li-man-iga (Surly Walker, of the Bear Clan, James Mallory)

MAN-CHO-SEP-KA (Black Bear) was one of the leaders of the Winnebago scouts in the United States service during the Civil War. In the Black Hills he fought alone against forty Dakota braves and received many wounds. This song was sung in honor of him. Eagle-feathers are worn by braves, and each feather is a war honor given for some valorous deed.

HE-LUSH-KA NA-WAN

WARRIOR-SONG

Ho-wi lo-ki-wa-wi-le !
Lo-han tt'eh-hi-ga,
Ma-shon o-ni je-na !
Ho-wi lo-ki-wa-wi-le !

Follow him, mount your horses !
He killed many,
He hunts eagle-feathers now !
Follow him, mount your horses !

HE-LUSH-KA NA-WAN

Warrior-Song

V

Sung and told by Wa-che-li-man-iga (Surly Walker, of the Bear Clan, James Mallory)

Some Winnebagos went to visit the Dakota chief, " Yellow-Hair "[1] and his people. While there they sang this song:

[1] See illustration, facing page 54.

HE-LUSH-KA	WARRIOR-SONG
Ya-tt'-eh-la hamb-la pi*n*-na,	When I talk, 'tis fair weather,
Ya-tt'-eh-la hamb-la pi*n*-na,	When I talk, 'tis fair weather,
Hi-he-la na-na*ch*-kon-je,	So say I, you hear me,
Ya-tt'-eh-la hamb-la pi*n*-na !	When I talk, 'tis fair weather !
Na-ju-zi-la,	Yellow-Hair, ho,
Ho-chunk-la zhe-skai-le,	Thus are all Winnebagos,
Hi-he-la na-na*ch*-kon-je,	So say I, you hear me,
Ya-tt'-eh-la hamb-la pi*n*-na !	When I talk, 'tis fair weather !

WA-GI-TT'EH NA-WA*N*

Wailing-Song

Sung and told by Chash-chunk-a (Wave, Peter Sampson)

MAN was riding homeward in a wagon with an old woman whom he called grandmother, for aged people of kin, or even aged friends, may always be known as grandmother or as grandfather to those who are younger. On the way the grandmother suddenly died. So as he came near home the man began to sing this wailing-song with sobbing voice to let the people know that she was dead.

WA-GI-TT'EH NA-WA*N*	WAILING-SONG
Pe-zhe-ga ko-ni-ka ya-ge-kche-ne-zhe !	Whom, oh, whom shall I now call grandmother !

WAK-JE NA-WA*N*[1]

Victory-Song

Pajoka is the Winnebago name for Comanche. In this song the triumphant Winnebago has shot a Pajoka.

WAK-JE NA-WA*N*	VICTORY-SONG
Pa-jo-ka nik-la, Hi-zhuk ha-ni-na Na*n*-na-ke-we-no !	Ah, my little Pajoka, Do you fear my gun, Pajoka ?

[1] See "Victory-Songs of the Cheyennes," pages 155–157.

WINNEBAGO

WUNK-HI NA-WAN

Love-Song

Sung and told by Winnebago women

I

IN the summer of the olden time there might often be heard at eventide the call of flutes. It was the youths upon the hill-side piping love-songs. Every one may know a love-song when he hears it, for the flute-tones are long and languorous, and are filled with a soft tremor. When a maiden heard the flute-music of her lover without, she always found it necessary to leave the tipi to draw water or to visit some neighbor.

In this song the maid asks leave of her mother to go to see her uncle, but the music tells that it is really her lover to whom she is going. The old people were not often deceived when the flute-music sounded.

WUNK-HI NA-WAN	LOVE-SONG
Na-ni, dega-go	Mother, let me go to my uncle!
E-dja wa-de-kjela!	

WUNK-HI NA-WAN

Love-Song

II

A WINNEBAGO maiden dreamed of a mythical Dakota woman famed for her many lovers and for her great power of inspiring love. On awakening, the maiden felt herself impelled to lead the same kind of life. At once she composed this song, in which she tells another woman of the miraculous power that has come upon her. This song is only a few years old.

WUNK-HI NA-WAN

Hi-zhan ho-do-chuch-ka,
   Zhe-ske shu-nu-na;
Hi-zhan wa-ki-tt'-eh-ka,
   Zhe-ske shu-nu-na;
Hi-zhan wai-zhi-zhi-ka,
   Zhe-ske shu-nu-na;
Hi-cha-ko-lo, hi-nuk lo-in-na-gle
      wi-do-kan-na-na;
Hi-zhan do-mai-ku-ka,
   Zhe-ske shu-nu-na.

LOVE-SONG

Whomsoe'er look I upon,
   He becomes love-crazed;
Whomsoever speak I unto,
   He becomes love-crazed;
Whomsoever whisper I to,
   He becomes love-crazed;
All men who love women,
Them I rule, them I rule,
   My friend;
Whom I touch, whom I touch,
He becomes love-crazed.

A TRUE STORY

THERE was once a young man who was about to enter upon a fast, and nothing less would satisfy him than that he must dream of Ma-o-na, the Earth-Maker. He blackened his face, as was the custom, and fasted four days or more, and dreamed of many things; then he ate a little food, and fasted again. So he persevered until he had dreamed of everything on the earth, or under the earth, or in the air; he dreamed of the whole world, but he never saw Ma-o-na. The spirits said to him, "You have dreamed of Ma-o-na because you have dreamed of all his works." But the man was not satisfied. He blackened his face and lay down again, and again he dreamed of the whole world, yet still he wished to dream of Ma-o-na, but could not. But after four nights he dreamed again, and now at last he dreamed of Ma-o-na. And Ma-o-na said: "I am the Earth-Maker. You will see me to-morrow at noon. But it is not well; you wish too much."

So the next morning the man rose up and made himself ready and took some tobacco for an offering, and before noon he set out for the place where Ma-o-na had said that he could meet him, a place where mighty oak-trees grew to a vast height. There he stood still, and watched and listened, till just at noon he saw a large flag drop down to the earth and hang suspended before him. The man looked up and saw that Ma-o-na was there, among the tall oaks; he saw only the face of Ma-o-na, a long face with good eyes, for the flag covered all the rest. Then the face spoke to him and said: "Nephew, you said that if you could not dream of me you would die. Nephew, you never can die. You never can die, because you are like me. You have dreamed of all my works, you know them all, and so you are like me. The spirits told you this, but you would not believe. You wanted to see me. Now you see me here to-day."

The man thought that he saw Ma-o-na, and he looked long at the face and never turned his eyes away, till at last the creature before him grew tired and drew back his wing; and then the man saw that it was only a chicken-hawk, one of the evil spirit's birds, that had flown down into a low oak close in front of him; and the chicken-hawk's wing had seemed to be the flag. The man cried for sorrow, and he lay four nights more, and then the spirits came and talked with him and took his soul away with them and said to him: "Cease trying to dream of Ma-o-na. There are many more little birds and creatures of the evil spirit that may deceive you. You can dream no more, for you have seen all things."

So the man ceased his fast and no longer tried to dream of Ma-o-na. He never saw Ma-o-na, nor he nor any one upon this earth. It is not possible to see Ma-o-na.

Note.—This story was told to the recorder as the actual experience of an Indian in his youth. It gives a deep insight into Indian thought. Maona is no personified deity to be seen with fleshly eye. He who would thus seek to look upon the Earth-Maker is but deceived by trivial things. Maona, to the Indian, is seen in all his works, and the whole world of nature tells of spiritual life. Maona is reflected in the mind of man himself, for man is like Maona when he has seen and understood Maona's works—the universe about him.

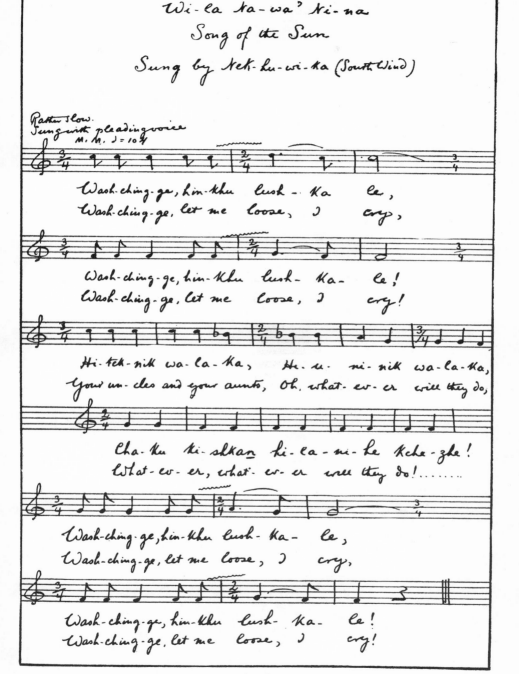

Wi-la Na-wa' Ni-na
Song of the Sun
Sung by Neh-hu-wi-ka (South Wind)

Wash-ching-ge, hin-khu lush-ka le,
Wash-ching-ge, let me loose, I cry,

Wash-ching-ge, hin-khu lush-ka le!
Wash-ching-ge, let me loose, I cry!

Hi-teh-nik wa-la-ka, He-u-ni-nik wa-la-ka,
Your un-cles and your aunts, Oh, what-ev-er will they do,

Cha-ku hi-sikan hi-la-ni-he Kche-zhe!
What-ev-er, what-ev-er will they do!........

Wash-ching-ge, hin-khu lush-ka le,
Wash-ching-ge, let me loose, I cry,

Wash-ching-ge, hin-khu lush-ka le!
Wash-ching-ge, let me loose, I cry!

[265]

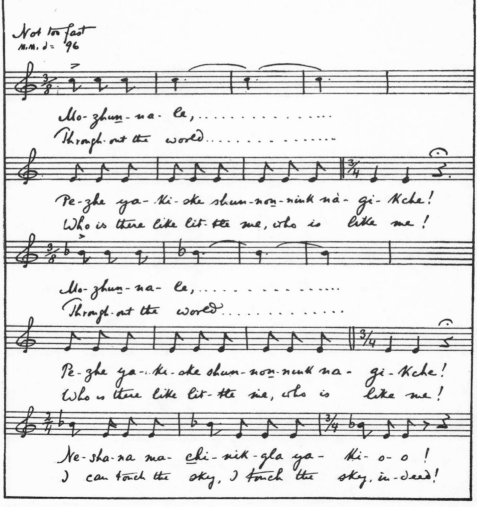

Wai-Kun
Fable

Sung by Chash-chunk-a (Wave)

Not too fast
M.M. ♩ = 96

Mo-zhun-na-le,...........
Through-out the world...........

Pe-zhe ya-ki-ske shun-non-nink nà-gi-Kche!
Who is there like lit-tle me, who is like me!

Mo-zhun-na-le,...........
Through-out the world...........

Pe-zhe ya-ki-ske shun-non-nink na-gi-Kche!
Who is there like lit-tle me, who is like me!

Ne-sha-na ma-chi-sik-gla ya-ki-o-o!
I can touch the sky, I touch the sky, in-deed!

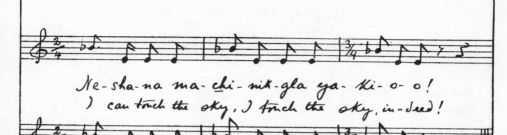

Ne-sha-na ma-chi-nik-gla ya-ki-o-o!
I can touch the sky, I touch the sky, in-deed!

Ne-sha-na ma-chi-na ma-chi-nik-gla ya-ki-o-o!
I can touch the sky, I touch the sky, in-deed!

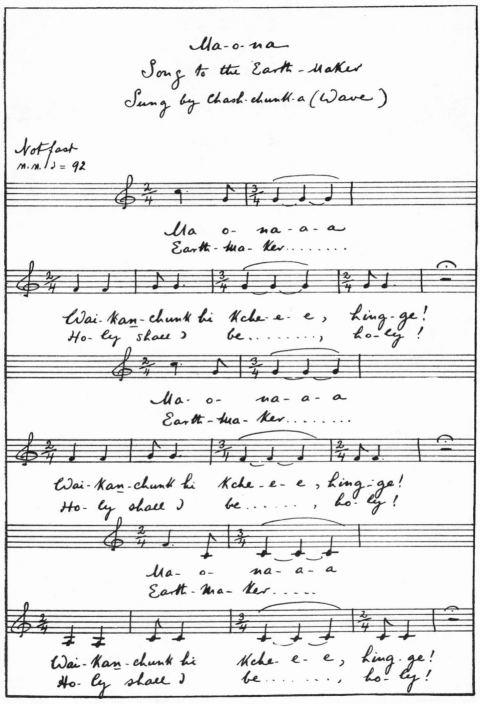

Ma-o-na

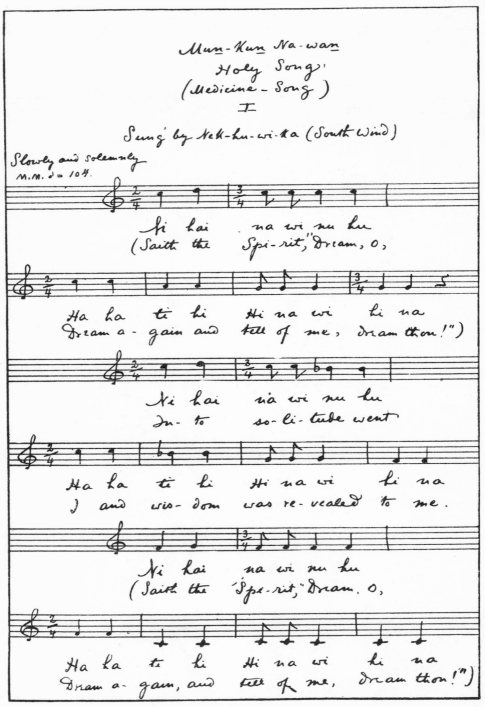

Ai-hai na wi nu hu
In- to so-li-tude went

Ha ha ti hi Hi na wi hi na
) and wis-dom was re-vealed to me.

Ni hai na wi nu hu
(Saith the Spi-rit, Dream, O;

Ti. hi Hi na wi hi na
Dream and tell of me, Dream thou!")

Ma-na-gle he Na ha wha Han gle he
Let the whole world hear me, Wise am I! (Now

Ha ha ti hi Hi na wi hi na
saith the Spe-rit "Tell of me, dream thou!")

Shi he hai na wi na-a
All was re- vealed to me; from

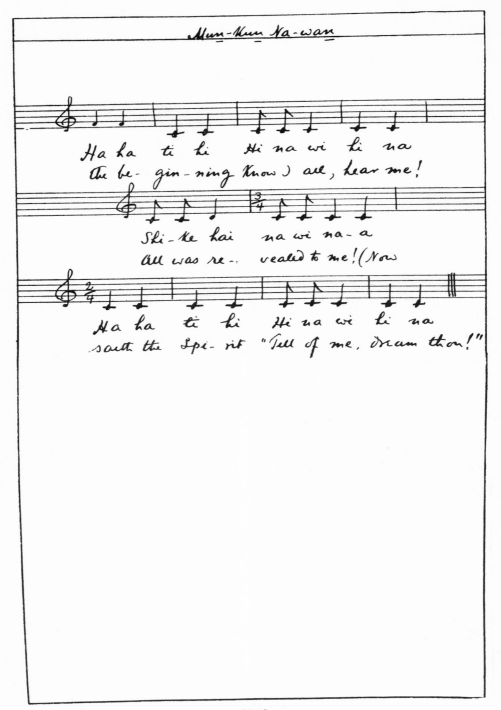

Mun-Hun Na-wan

Ha ha ti hi   Hi na wi hi na
the be- gin- ning Know) all, hear me!

Shi- ke hai   na wi na- a
All was re- vealed to me! (Now

Ha ha ti hi   Hi na wi hi na
saith the Spi- rit "Tell of me, dream thou!"

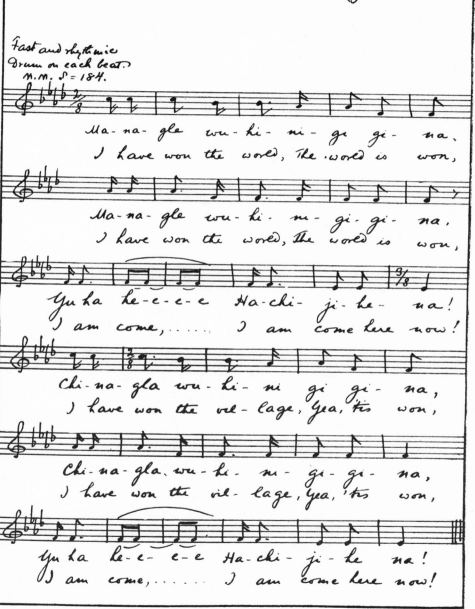

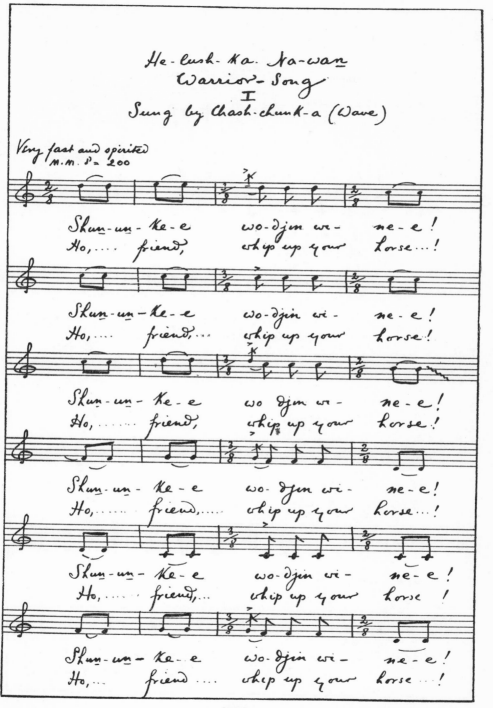

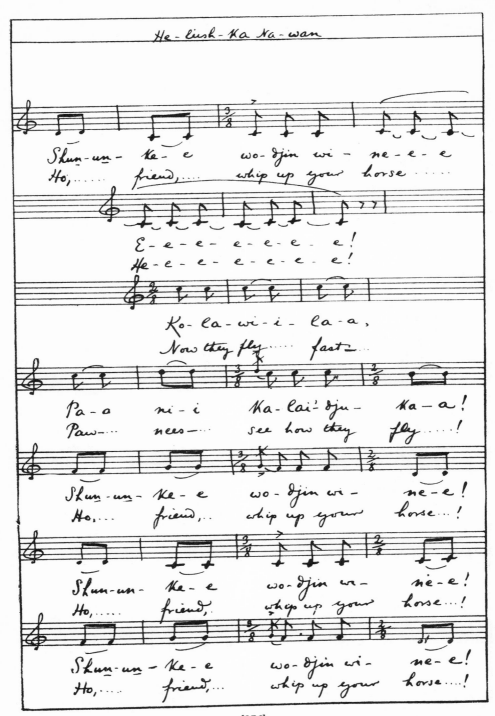

He-lush-Ka Na-wan

Shun-un-Ke-e wo-djin wi-ne-e-e
Ho, friend, whip up your horse

E-e-e-e-e-e-e!
He-e-e-e-e-e-e!

Ko-la-wi-i-la-a,
Now they fly fast

Pa-a ni-i Ka-lai-dju-Ka-a!
Paw- nees- see how they fly!

Shun-un-Ke-e wo-djin wi-ne-e!
Ho, friend, whip up your horse!

Shun-un-Ke-e wo-djin wi-ne-e!
Ho, friend, whip up your horse!

Shun-un-Ke-e wo-djin wi-ne-e!
Ho, friend, whip up your horse!

Shun-un-Ke-e   wo-djin wi   ne-e e
Ho,...... friend,...... whip up your horse......

E-e-e- e-e-e-e!
He-e-e- e-e-e-e!

Second Verse

Shun-Ke wa-na-ma-ne!   Ho, friend, prick up your horse!
Shun-Ke wa-na-ma-ne!   Ho, friend, prick up your horse!
   Pa-ni guch-la,   Pawnee - Shooter,
Pa-ni Ka-lai-la-dju-Ka!   Ride fast, for they are gone!
Shun-Ke wa-na-ma-ne!   Ho, friend, prick up your horse!

He-lush-ka Na-wan

He-cha-ko-lo,
Com-rades, hear-ken —

Pa-a- ni-i- na-a wa-a-cha-a- la-a!
Paw- nee.... braves. I..... saw... them!

Wa-a- we-e- la-a ga-a-ske-e- na-a!
What... a .... trail.. they've. left .. here !

Wa-a-we-e- la-a ha-a-dja-a- le-e!
See.... the.... trail.... they've. left.... here !

Wa-a- we-e- la-a ha-a-dja-a- le-e!
See.... the..... trail... they've.. left.... here ..!

He-e-e- e-e-e-e- e-e-e-e!

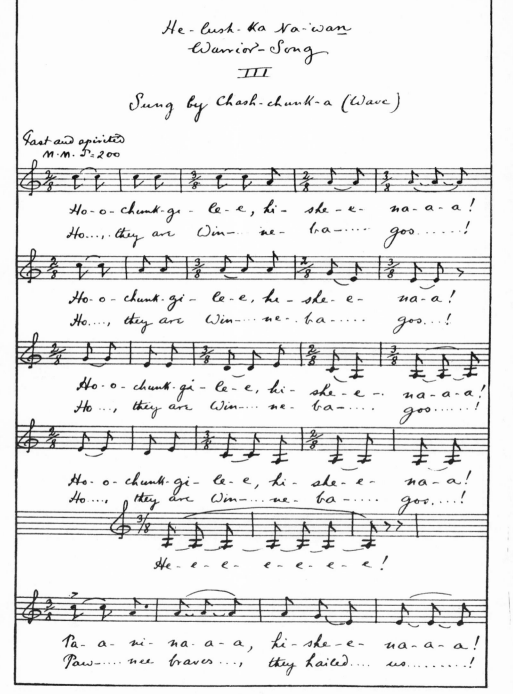

He-lush-ka Na-wan

Hi-i-ta lo-o-o, hi-she-e - na-a-a!
"Friendo! Hal-loo.......!" they hailed... us.........

Ho-o- chunk-gi- le- e, hi- she-e- na-a-a!
Ho..., they are Win--- ne- ba--- gos.....!

He-e-e- e-e- e-e!

[281]

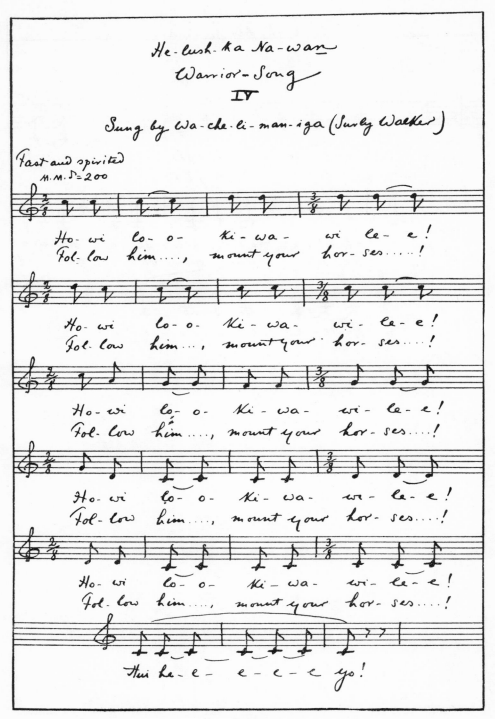

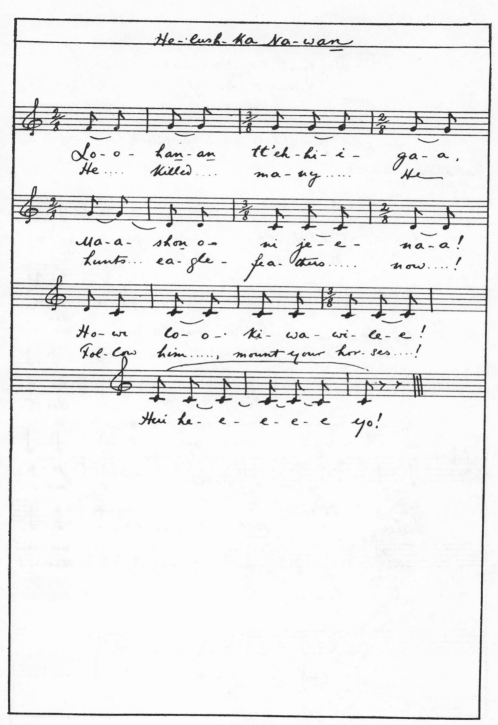
He-lush-Ka Na-wan

[283]

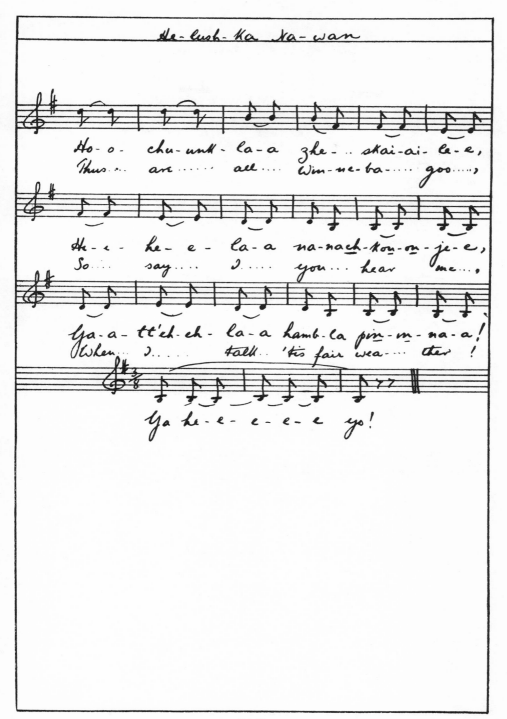

He-lush-ka Na-wan

Ho-o- chu-unk-la-a zhe-- skai-ai-le-e,
Thus-- are...... all.... Win-ne-ba---goo...,

He-e- he-e-la-a na-nach-kou-on-je-e,
So..... say.... I..... you... hear me...,

Ya-a-tt'ch-ch- la-a hamb-la pin-in-na-a!
When I..... fall 'tis fair wea---ther!

Ya he-e- e- e-e yo!

He-lush-Ka Na-wan

Ha hi o ho we ye he-e-e-e yo

Whi ya he ya whi ya he ya

Whi ya he-ya whi ya he-ya

A ha e ya he-e-e-e

Whi ya he ya whi ya he ya

Ha hi o ho wi e

He-e-e-e-yo!

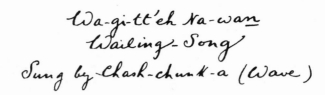

Wa-gi-tt'eh Na-wan
Wailing-Song
Sung by Chash-chunk-a (Wave)

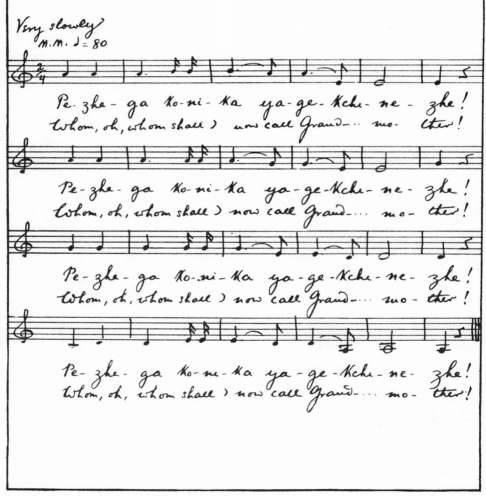

Very slowly
M.M. ♩ = 80

Pe-zhe-ga Ko-ni-ka ya-ge-Kche-ne-zhe!
Whom, oh, whom shall I now call Grand—mo-ther!

Pe-zhe-ga Ko-ni-ka ya-ge-Kche-ne-zhe!
Whom, oh, whom shall I now call Grand—mo-ther!

Pe-zhe-ga Ko-ni-ka ya-ge-Kche-ne-zhe!
Whom, oh, whom shall I now call Grand—mo-ther!

Pe-zhe-ga Ko-ne-ka ya-ge-Kche-ne-zhe!
Whom, oh, whom shall I now call Grand—mo-ther!

Wak-je" Na-wan

Ha-re na nan na ke- we- no!
Do you fear my gun, Pa-jo- Ka!

E ya he e ya he e ya

E ya he... e ya he yu he yu!

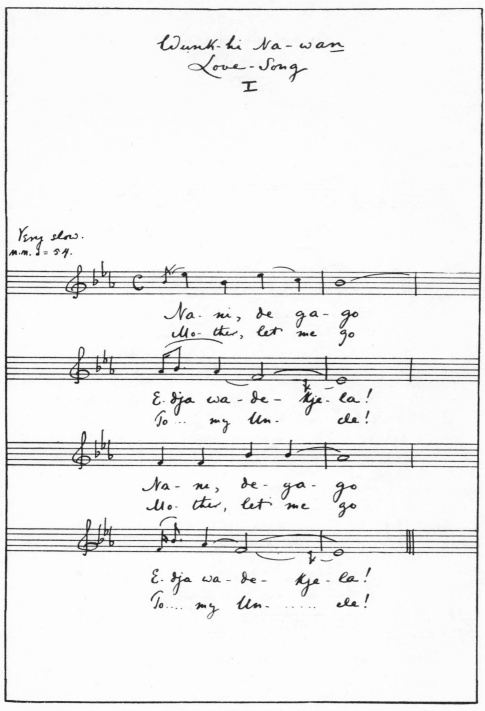

Wunk-hi Na-wan
Love-Song
II

Not too slow
M.M. ♩ = 104

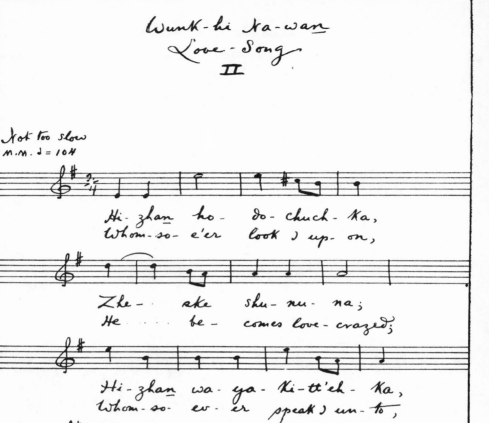

Hi-zhan ho- do-chuch-Ka,
Whom-so- e'er look I up- on,

Zhe- ske shu- nu- na;
He be- comes love-crazed;

Hi-zhan wa- ya- Ki-tt'eh- Ka,
Whom-so- ev- er speak I un-to,

Zhe- ske shu-nu- na,
He be- comes love-crazed;

Hi-zhan wai-ya-zhi-zhi- Ka,
Whom-so- ev- er whis-per I to,

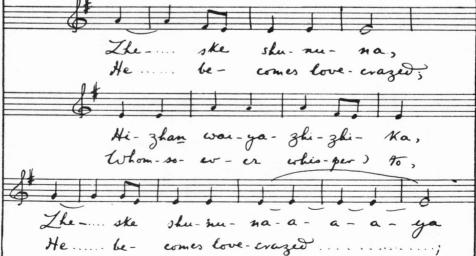

Zhe- ske shu-nu- na-a- a- a- ya
He be- comes love-crazed . . . . ;

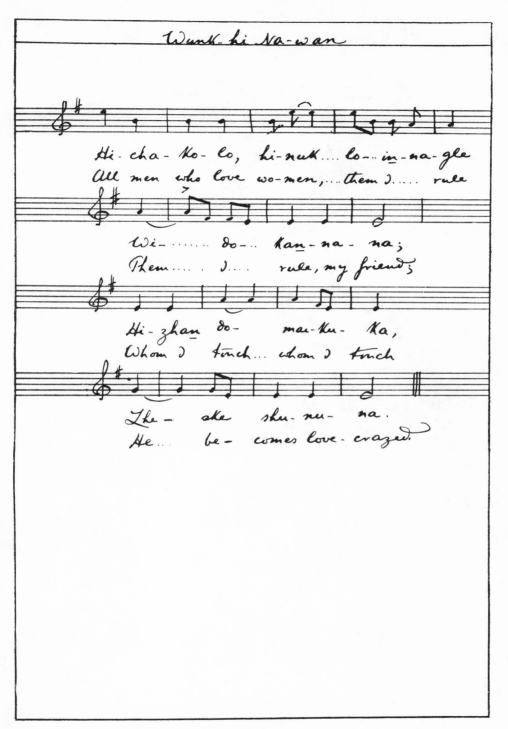

Wunk-hi Na-wan

Hi-cha-ko-lo, hi-nuk.....lo--in-na-gle
All men who love wo-men,....them I.....rule

Wi-.......do--- kan-na- na;
Them.... I.... rule, my friend;

Hi-zhan do- mai-ku- Ka,
Whom I touch... whom I touch

Lhe- ske shu-nu- na.
He... be- comes love- crazed.

KWAKIUTL

KWAKIUTL TITLE-PAGE

The design at the top of the page represents the grizzly bear;
that at the bottom the "killer-whale." These drawings are by
Kialish (Charles James Nowell), a Kwakiutl Indian.
The lettering is by Hinook Mahiwi Kilinaka (Angel De Cora).
The letters are composed of motives peculiar to Kwakiutl de-
sign: the tail and fin of the whale, the hawk, and the eye-joint.

THE KWAKIUTLS

THE Indians of the Northwest coast, between Juan de Fuca Strait and Yakutat Bay, are classed by ethnologists as a single culture family, subdivided into many linguistic and physical groupings, but a unit in point of general development. Of the linguistic branches, the Wakashan is among the most important, and to this division the Kwakiutl Indians belong.

Physically the Kwakiutl is different from the other Indians of the North Pacific group. While his neighbors all have low faces with broad, flat noses, the Kwakiutl has an unusually long face and a high, arched nose. The social organization, too, of these Indians is different in some important respects from that of the surrounding groups.

The singers here represented have their home on Vancouver Island. Like all the Northwest coast tribes, these Indians are great fishermen. The deep fiords and inlets which cut into the mainland of British Columbia and the shores of Vancouver Island yield quantities of salmon, sea-lions, and even whales. The women also gather mussels. The coast tribes are dexterous seamen, and make a variety of strong canoes hewn sometimes from a single great log and decorated with strange emblematic signs and figures. Similar emblems appear upon the carved wooden house-posts and

NOTE FOR PRONUNCIATION OF KWAKIUTL TEXT

While in many Indian languages there are sounds not exactly the same as the corresponding ones of European tongues, in the Kwakiutl occur sounds that have no counterpart at all in European languages. Such sounds, therefore, can be expressed by the Roman alphabet approximately only.

Unless otherwise indicated, vowels have the Continental sound, and consonants the English.

ch, in italic, is a guttural, like ch in German.

totem - poles. Such emblems often represent to the Indian a long and sacred narrative of his ancestors; they are, as it were, family or tribal coats of arms. Each clan among the Kwakiutls is derived from a mythical ancestor who acquired a crest in the course of some phenomenal adventure, and whose privileges descend from generation to generation.[1]

The Kwakiutls make a variety of beautiful things, and unlike many other tribes they set great value upon their possessions. Their arts and art industries reflect a wealth of barbaric imagination in design and show power and accuracy in execution. The superb grotesques of the giant totem-poles and carved canoes are wrought with the same skill as are the delicate and symmetrical tracings upon stone and silver, and the easy curves on painted boxes and other articles of use and decoration.

These Indians live in wooden houses on which are often painted animal forms both decorative and emblematic. The totem-pole, carved from a great tree, rises at the front of the house; the entrance is often a doorway cut through the pole. The native life is rich in ceremonial and symbolic functions which are frequently accompanied by song. "Everything has its song," say the Kwakiutls; "Every person, every animal, and everything has its song and its story." Even objects have songs either connected directly with the object itself or through the association of song and object in ceremonial. So there is a song belonging to each totem-pole. Certain songs belong to certain families, and are as much a part of the family inheritance as are the crest and the clan emblems.

The Kwakiutl music, with its sharp and rugged rhythm, suggests to the imagination the steady yet broken beat of the sea, while in the melodies we seem to hear the cry of the sea-gull or the shriek of the Hu-huk, the mythical bird of prey. To the white man there hovers over this music a spirit of the wilder elements of nature, sublime, sometimes destructive, mysterious, and awful, like the whir of the Thunder-Bird's wings. Yet the music is often as full of beauty as the white gull on the blue sky.

The Kwakiutls are sinewy, strong, and of keen and fearless im-

---

[1] The ethnological facts regarding the Kwakiutl Indians are derived from the works of Dr. Franz Boas, the authority on this subject.

agination. Though their carved canoes seek no new lands, yet well might the Indians of the Northwest coast be called the sea-kings of America.

THE STORY OF WAKIASH AND THE FIRST TOTEM-POLE

Told by Klalish (Charles James Nowell)

T HERE was once a chief named Wakiash, and he was named after the river Wakiash because he was open-handed, flowing with gifts even as the river flowed with fish. It happened on a time that all the tribe were having a big dance. Wakiash had never had any kind of dance of his own, and he was unhappy because all the other chiefs of the tribe had fine dances. So he thought to himself, "I will go up into the mountains to fast." And he made himself ready, and went up into the mountains and stayed there four days, fasting and bathing. On the fourth day, early in the morning, he grew so weary that he lay upon his back and fell asleep; and then he felt something that came upon his breast and woke him. It was a little green frog. The frog said, "Wake up, that you may see where you are going."

Wakiash opened his eyes and saw that the frog was on his breast. The frog said, "Lie still as you are, because you are on the back of a raven that is going to fly with you around the

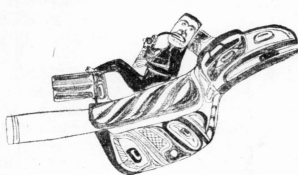

This drawing by a Kwakiutl Indian represents the carved rattle used in the Klawulacha dance and song. It shows Wakiash on the raven's back with the frog upon his breast. The line from the mouth of the frog to that of Wakiash indicates that the frog is talking to the man.

world, so that you may see what you want, and take it." And the frog said that he would stay with the man till they came back again to the same place. Then the frog told the man to get ready, and bade the raven to start.

The raven flew and carried the man around the world and showed him all the things of the world. They flew four days, and when they were on their way back Wakiash saw a house with a beautiful totem-pole in front, and heard a noise of singing inside the house. He thought to himself that these were fine things, and he wished that he might take them with him. Now the frog knew his thoughts and told the raven to stop. So the raven stopped and the frog told the man to hide himself behind the door. The man did as the frog told him, and the frog said, "Stay here, and when they begin to dance, leap out into the room."

The people tried to begin a dance, but could do nothing—they could neither dance nor sing. One of them stood up and said, "There is something the matter with us; there must be something near us that makes us feel like this." And the chief said, "Let one of us, who can run faster than the flames of the fire, go around the house and see." So the little mouse came and said that she would go, for she could go anywhere, even into a box, and if any one were hiding she could find him. The mouse was in the form of a woman, because she had taken off her mouse-skin clothes; indeed, all the people in the house were animals, and their chief was the beaver, but they had taken off their animal-skin clothes to dance, and so they looked like men.

The mouse ran out, and Wakiash caught her and said, "Ha, my friend, wait here and I will make you a gift." And he gave the mouse a piece of mountain-goat's fat. Now this mouse was so pleased with Wakiash that she talked with him and asked him what he wanted, and Wakiash said that he wanted the totem-pole, the house, and the kind of dances and songs that belonged to them. The mouse said, "Stay here, and wait till I come again."

Wakiash stayed, and the mouse went in and said to the people, "I have been everywhere to find if there were a man about, but I could find nobody." And the chief said, "Now let us try again to dance." They tried three times before they could do anything, and they sent out the mouse each time to see what she could find. But each time the mouse was sent out she talked with Wakiash;

A Kwakiutl Chief Standing before His Canoe, Holding Carved
Dance Rattle

Klalish in Ceremonial Costume

and the third time that she went out she said, "Now make ready, and when they begin to dance, leap into the room."

Then the mouse went back to the animals and told them that she could find no one, and so they began to dance, and just then Wakiash sprang in. At once the dancers dropped their heads for shame, because a man had seen them looking like men, whereas they were really animals. And they stood silent for some time, till at last the mouse began to speak and said: "Let us not wait thus; let us ask our friend what he wants. He must want something or he would not come here." So they all lifted up their heads, and the chief asked the man what he wanted. Wakiash thought to himself that he would like to have the dance, because he had never had one of his own, though all the other chiefs had dances. Also he wanted the house, and the totem-pole that he had seen outside. Though the man did not speak, the mouse heard his thoughts and told the people. And the chief said, "Let our friend sit down and we will show him how we dance, and he can pick out whatsoever kind of dance he wants."

So they began to dance, and when they had ended the chief asked Wakiash what kind of dance he would like. They were using all sorts of masks. Wakiash wanted most of all the Echo mask, and the mask of the Little Man that goes about the house talking, talking, and trying to quarrel with others. Wakiash only thought to himself; the mouse told the chief his thoughts. So the animals taught Wakiash all their dances, and the chief told him that he might take as many dances and masks as he wished, also the house and the totem-pole. The chief said to Wakiash that these things would all go with him when he went home, and that he should use them all in one dance; also that he should thenceforth have, for his own, the name of the totem-pole, Kalakuyuwish, meaning sky-pole, because the pole was so tall. So the chief took the house and folded it up in a little bundle. He put it in the headdress of one of the dancers, and this he gave to Wakiash, saying, "When you reach home, throw down this bundle; the house will become as it was when you first saw it, and then you can begin to give a dance."

Wakiash went back to the raven, and the raven flew away with him towards the mountain from which they had set out; but before they arrived there Wakiash fell asleep, and when he awoke the raven and the frog were gone and he was all alone. Then he started for home, and when he got there it was night, and he threw down the bundle that was in the head-dress, and there was the house with its totem-pole! The whale painted on the house was blowing, the animals carved on the totem-pole were making their noises, and all the masks inside the house were talking and crying aloud. At once Wakiash's people awoke and came out to see what was happening, and Wakiash found that instead of four days he had been away four years. They went into the house, and Wakiash began to make a dance; he taught the people the songs, and they sang, and Wakiash danced, and then the Echo came, and whosoever made a noise the Echo made the same, changing its mouths[1]. When they had finished dancing the house was gone; it went back to the animals. And all the chiefs were ashamed because Wakiash now had the best dance.

Then Wakiash made, out of wood, a house and masks and a totem-pole; and when the totem-pole was finished the people made a song for it. This totem-pole was the first that this tribe had ever had; the animals had named it *Kalakuyuwish*, "the pole that holds up the sky," and they said that it made a creaking noise because the sky was so heavy. And Wakiash took for his own the name of the totem-pole, Kalakuyuwish.

KLAWULACHA

Song of the Totem-Pole. In praise of Wakiash Kalakuyuwish

Sung by Klalish (Charles James Nowell)

KLAWULACHA	SONG OF THE TOTEM-POLE
Waw haw le	Now doth it rise, our river;
Pulnakwila kiash ila koi	Our river is Wakiash, good is he.
Wakiash kiash o wa	
Ya choi	

[1] Alluding to different mouth-pieces that fit into the echo-mask.

[302]

KWAKIUTL

Waw haw le
Hitlpalkwala kyilish
   Kiash ila koi
Kalakuyuwish kiash o wa
Lachnahkwulla
   Ya choi

Now doth it creak, this totem-pole;
   Clouds rest on its top.
Kalakuyuwish, great as the sky-pole is he !

CRADLE-SONG

THE Kwakiutl baby hangs in his cradle from a cross-beam in a corner of the house. A cord is attached to the cradle, and the mother rocks her baby by pulling on the cord. To and fro swings the cradle, to and fro, while the mother sings a lullaby.

Sometimes the cradle is hung from a long pole, one end of which is fixed aslant in the ground while the middle rests on a forked stick set upright in the earth. The cradle hangs from the free, flexible end of the pole, and instead of swinging to and fro, it springs up and down with the mother's touch upon the cord—up and down, up and down, while the mother sings a lullaby.

Klawulacha

Ya choi ya ha wi ha ha ha

Wu ah hi........ ha hi

Wo he ha wo o ha ha

Wo ha ha ha wo ha ha ha

O wa........ hoi ye

Ya-a he e ah yi

Waw-aw haw le Hitt-pal-kwa-la-kyi-lish-kiash-i-la-koi
tow..... Doth it creak this to tem-pole; Clouds rest on its top

Klawulacha

Ka- la- ku- yu- wish Kiash o wa Lach-na- kwul- la
Ka- la- ku- yu- wish, great as the sky- pole is he!

Ya choi ya ha wu ha ha ha

Wa ah hi..... ha ha wo he!

Cradle-Song

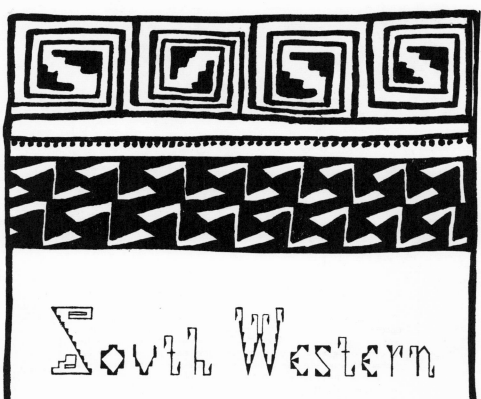

South Western Indians

SOUTHWESTERN INDIANS TITLE-PAGE

The designs are copies of decorations on Southwestern prehistoric pottery. These copies were painted free-hand by Pueblo Indians of Laguna, New Mexico. The uppermost design has for its central figure a cloud-form; the dots on the line below are grains of corn, and the design immediately beneath represents the young corn-shoots. At the bottom of the page is seen the corn-stalk with its joints. Corn might almost be called a symbol of the life of the Southwestern Indians, who are, before all else, agriculturalists.

The lettering is by Hinook Mahiwi Kilinaka (Angel De Cora).

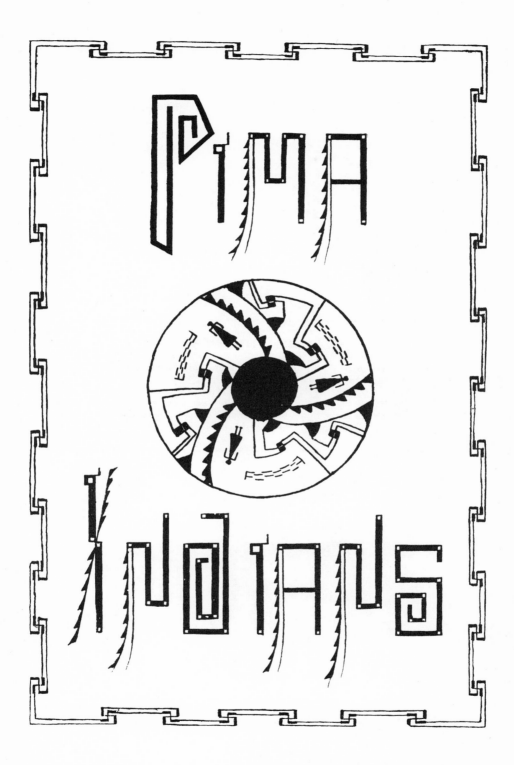

PIMA TITLE-PAGE

The design is a copy of a typical Pima basket, and was drawn free-hand by Ataloya, a Pima Indian girl.
The lettering is by Hinook Mahiwi Kilinaka (Angel De Cora). The letters suggest the motives in the basket design; the border of the page is the figure of the running swastika, seen also in the basket.   The Pimas are skilled basket-makers.

THE PIMAS

I N the deserts of southern Arizona the Pima Indians have their home. Though brave, the Pimas never were aggressive fighters.   So far as known, the life of this ancient people always has been one of agriculture and simple industry. Through a native system of irrigation, they raise the crops that are their sustenance. Formerly they grew cotton also, which they wove and dyed. This industry is now abandoned, but the beautiful art of basket-weaving still survives.

It is thought that in olden times the people lived in villages of adobe with strongholds of defence.   Indeed, it is said that the ruins of Casa Grande and other similar ones in Arizona are those of ancient Pima buildings.

Because of their gentle and submissive disposition, the Pimas never have offered much resistance to the white man. Though to-day the dwellings still are native houses of adobe and woven saplings; though, as of old, the life is that of agriculture, yet all trace of native dress has vanished, and of the old customs little is left—dances and ceremonies are gone, and to the younger generation the songs are wellnigh utterly lost.   Yet Pima mythology is full of beauty and poetry, and the music has plaintive individuality.

That The Indians' Book might hold some record of the fast-vanishing Pima lore, an aged Pima chief was sought out for a contribution.

His face and mien had the grave sadness, the retrospective melancholy of the old Indian.

"We are glad, indeed, to sing our songs for you," said the chief,

NOTE FOR PRONUNCIATION OF PIMA TEXT

Unless otherwise indicated, vowels have the Continental sound and consonants the English.

"for thus we can hear them again ourselves. On our reservation no man dares to sing. It is as you say—soon all the songs will be forgotten. White people do not like us to sing Indian songs. They think our songs are bad. We are glad you say they are good."

"And how did you make your songs?" the chief was asked.

"We dreamed them," was the answer. "When a man would go away by himself—off into solitude—then he would dream a song."

"And do the men still dream songs?"

"If they do, they do not tell. White people do not like it. But if a man has dreamed a song, he may take another man quietly aside and teach the song to him. His song will not so soon be forgotten if one other has it as well as he himself. But he dares not sing for many. White people say our dances and our songs are not good. We are glad that you say it is no harm for us to sing."

"It is no harm, but good for you to sing. When a man sings, we know his heart is happy."

"It is well that you have come to do this thing for us, but we have not much money to offer you in return. The white people living up above us on the river have taken all the water, so that our fields are dry. We are poor."

"A task that is done in friendship asks only friendship in return. Do not be sad. When the songs are written, perhaps white people will no longer think them bad."

The chief dropped his head in thought. "I will sing," he said, "an old, old song—a song sung by the Creator at the beginning of the world. I am a medicine-man,[1] and I know all the stories and songs of my people. I will tell you the story of how the world was made. The story tells of the beginning of all things, and there are many songs in the story. To tell it rightly and to sing all the songs would take all night and longer. So I will only tell you, shortly, just a part of it, and sing you the one song. I am glad to tell this now to you. It will keep me from forgetting it. Leave me now, and come back when I have thought more over it."

Later, in the shadow of afternoon, the old chief told the story of the beginning of the world.

See "The Holy Man," page 32.

PIMA

CHUHWUHT

Song of the World

Sung and told by Chief Visak-Vo-o-yim (Hovering Hawk)

IN the beginning there was only darkness everywhere—darkness and water. And the darkness gathered thick in places, crowding together and then separating, crowding and separating until at last out of one of the places where the darkness had crowded there came forth a man. This man wandered through the darkness until he began to think; then he knew himself and that he was a man; he knew that he was there for some purpose.

He put his hand over his heart and drew forth a large stick. He used the stick to help him through the darkness, and when he was weary he rested upon it. Then he made for himself little ants; he brought them from his body and put them on the stick. Everything that he made he drew from his own body even as he had drawn the stick from his heart. The stick was of grease-wood, and of the gum of the wood the ants made a round ball upon the stick. Then the man took the ball from the stick and put it down in the darkness under his foot, and as he stood upon the ball he rolled it under his foot and sang:

> "I make the world, and lo!
> The world is finished.
> Thus I make the world, and lo!
> The world is finished."

So he sang, calling himself the maker of the world.[1] He sang slowly, and all the while the ball grew larger as he rolled it, till at the end of his song, behold, it was the world. Then he sang more quickly:

> "Let it go, let it go,
> Let it go, start it forth!"

[1] The story is striking because of the conception of the world as a *round ball, rolled* beneath the foot of the Creator and then started going. Also because the heavenly bodies are conceived to be made of *rock*.

So the world was made, and now the man brought from himself a rock and divided it into little pieces. Of these he made stars, and put them in the sky to light the darkness. But the stars were not bright enough.

So he made Tau-muk, the milky-way. Yet Tau-muk was not bright enough. Then he made the moon. All these he made of rocks drawn forth from himself. But even the moon was not bright enough. So he began to wonder what next he could do. He could bring nothing from himself that could lighten the darkness.

Then he thought. And from himself he made two large bowls, and he filled the one with water and covered it with the other. He sat and watched the bowls, and while he watched he wished that what he wanted to make in very truth would come to be. And it was even as he wished. For the water in the bowl turned into the sun and shone out in rays through the cracks where the bowls joined.

When the sun was made, the man lifted off the top bowl and took out the sun and threw it to the east. But the sun did not touch the ground; it stayed in the sky where he threw it and never moved. Then in the same way he threw the sun to the north and to the west and to the south. But each time it only stayed in the sky, motionless, for it never touched the ground. Then he threw it once more to the east, and this time it touched the ground and bounced and started upward. Since then the sun has never ceased to move. It goes around the world in a day, but every morning it must bounce anew in the east.

CHUHWUHT

Chuhwuht-tuh maka-i,
Chuhwuht-tuh nato—
Chuhwuht-tuh maka-i
Chuhwuht-tuh nato—
　Himalo, himalo,
　Himalo, himicho !

SONG OF THE WORLD

I make the world, and lo !
The world is finished.
Thus I make the world, and lo !
The world is finished.
　Let it go, let it go,
　Let it go, start it forth !

[316]

A Daughter of the Desert

PIMA

CHUHTEK-OHOHIK NIEH

Bluebird Song

Sung by Katarina Valenzuela

This is a dance-song. It is the lament of a bluebird for his lost song. Nearly all the Pima dance-songs are named after birds.

CHUHTEK-OHOHIK NIEH

Hai-ya, hai-ya—hai-ya, hai-ya—
Nieh ha nieh va yo-hu-ka
Cheh wahl ohi nieh-nieh
Va ha maw-haw va yu-ka
Cheh wahl ohi nieh-nieh
Va ha maw-haw va yu-ka.

BLUEBIRD SONG

Hai-ya, hai-ya—hai-ya, hai-ya—
All my song is lost and gone.
Sad at heart is the bluebird,
All my song is lost and gone,
Woe is me, alas! alas!
All my song is lost and gone!

HUHWUHLI NIEH

Wind - Song (Medicine - Song)

Sung by Hal Antonio

HUHWUHLI NIEH

Hanam-a yo-osik-a
Ya-hai huh-wurt
Kani-hu-va muh-muhk
Ka-cho-wuch-chi kano ya ki-moi

WIND-SONG

Far on the desert ridges
    Stands the cactus;
Lo, the blossoms swaying
To and fro, the blossoms swaying, swaying.

Chuhwuht
Song of the World.
Sung by Chief Visak Vo-o-yim (Hovering Hawk)

Chuh-wuht tuh na-Ka-i, chuh-wuht tuh na- to
) make the world, and lo, the world is fin- ished

Chuh-wuht tuh ma-Ka-i, chuh-wuht tuh na- a- to
Thus) make the world, and lo, the world is... fin- ished.

Hi- ma- lo, hi- ma- lo,
Let it go, let it go,

Hi- ma- lo, hi- ma- cho!
Let it go, start it forth!

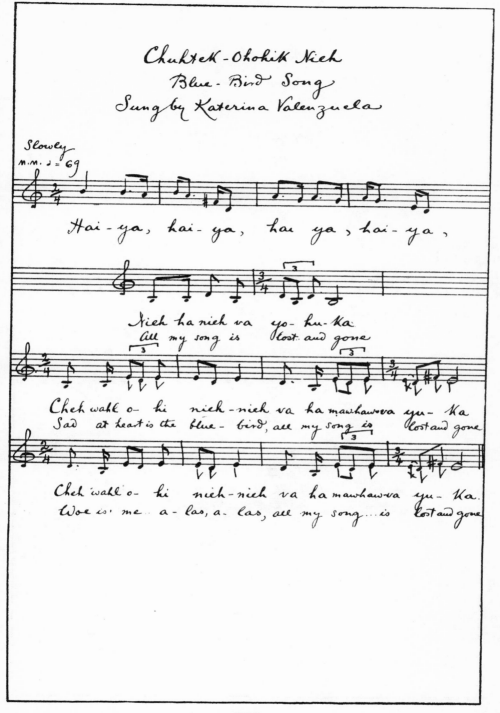

Chuktek-Ohohitk Nich
Blue-Bird Song
Sung by Katerina Valenzuela

Slowly
M.M. ♩ = 69

Hai-ya, hai-ya, hai ya, hai-ya,

Nich ha nich va yo-hu-Ka
All my song is lost and gone

Cheh wahl o- hi nich-nich va ha mawhawva yu-Ka
Sad at heart is the blue-bird, all my song is lost and gone

Cheh wahl o- hi nich-nich va ha mawhawva yu-Ka.
Woe is me a-las, a-las, all my song...is lost and gone

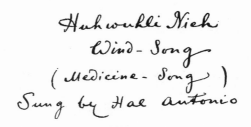

Huhwuhli Nieh
Wind-Song
(Medicine-Song)
Sung by Hal Antonio

Slowly
m.m. ♩ = 94.

Ha- nam'a yo- o- sik- a ya hai huh- wurt.....
Far on the des- ert rid- ges stand the cac- tus; .....

Ka- m- hu- va muh- mahk
Lo, the blos- soms sway- ing

Ka- cho- wuch- chi Ka- no ya Ki- moi
To and fro the blos- soms sway- ing, sway- ing.

APACHE TITLE-PAGE

The design shows an Apache dancer, painted by an Apache
Indian, Gumanchiä (Rivers Lavender). The dancer is in ceremonial dress, and wears a symbolic head-dress, and a black
mask of buckskin.
The lettering is by Hinook Mahiwi Kilinaka (Angel De Cora).

THE APACHES

THE Apaches, a tribe of Athapascan stock, have their home in New Mexico and Arizona. They are related to the Navajos and speak a similar tongue. The name "Apache" is a Yuma Indian word meaning "fighting-men," and was probably given to the Apaches by neighboring tribes of Yuman stock.

The acquisition by the United States of new territory at the close of the Mexican War, and the discovery of gold in California in the year 1849, brought more and more white emigrants through New Mexico and Arizona. The fierce, intrepid Apaches resisted with open hostility the encroachment of the whites, and for a long period of years there were bloody clashings. The Indian war leaders and warriors showed not only daring and cruelty, but also extraordinary skill and strategy in warfare, and endurance that seemed inexhaustible. The tribe was finally subdued, and has been placed on reservations, but the old invincible spirit is still shown to-day by an energy and fire which should make of the Apaches a people strong and hardy in the new life of industry.

GERONIMO

GERONIMO is perhaps the most famous of Apache war-leaders. He and his followers long withstood and evaded the United States troops, and were captured at the last only by the aid of other Indians—scouts employed in the army. Geronimo is now between seventy and eighty years of age, but he bears himself with the erectness of the Indian warrior,

NOTE FOR PRONUNCIATION OF APACHE TEXT

Unless otherwise indicated, vowels have the Continental sound, and consonants the English.

ch, in italic, is a guttural, like ch in German.

and in his eye is still the tiger-flash.[1] Among his people he is famed as Chief and Holy Man (Man of Medicine).[2]

Said Geronimo: "The song that I will sing is an old song, so old that none knows who made it. It has been handed down through generations and was taught to me when I was but a little lad. It is now my own song. It belongs to me.

"This is a holy song (medicine-song), and great is its power. The song tells how, as I sing, I go through the air to a holy place where Yusun[3] will give me power to do wonderful things. I am surrounded by little clouds, and as I go through the air I change, becoming spirit only."

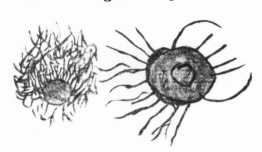

Geronimo drew an illustration of his song, showing himself passing through the sky to the holy place. His changed form is symbolized by a circle, and this is surrounded by a "kind of air"—a mystic aureole. The holy place is symbolized by the sun, which is decorated with a horned head-dress emblematic of divine power. Such head-dress is the insignia of the Holy Man.

MEDICINE-SONG

Sung by Geronimo

O, ha le	O, ha le
O, ha le !	O, ha le !
Awbizhaye	Through the air
Shichl hadahiyago niniya	I fly upon a cloud
O, ha le	Towards the sky, far, far, far,
O, ha le !	O, ha le
Tsago degi naleya	O, ha le !
Ah—yu whi ye !	There to find the holy place,
O, ha le	Ah, now the change comes o'er me !
O, ha le !	O, ha le
	O, ha le !

---

[1] Since contributing to "The Indians' Book," Geronimo has dictated an autobiography, "Geronimo's Story of His Life." Taken down and edited by S. M. Barrett, Superintendent of Education, Lawton, Oklahoma. New York : Duffield & Co., 1906.

[2] See "The Holy Man," page 32.   [3] The Supreme Being.

Geronimo

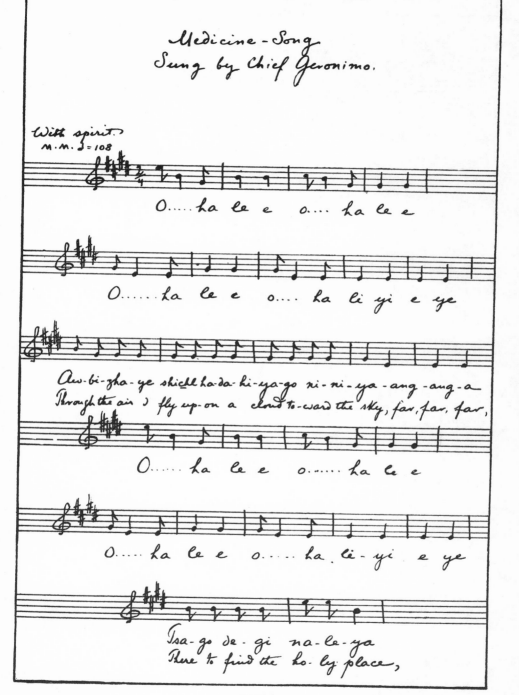

Medicine-Song

Ăh yu whi yu whi ye e

Tsa-go de-gi na-le-ya ..
There to find the ho-ly place,

Ăh yu whi yu whi ne ya
Ah, now the change comes o'er me!

O.....ha le e o......ha le e

O......ha le e o......ha le yi e ye

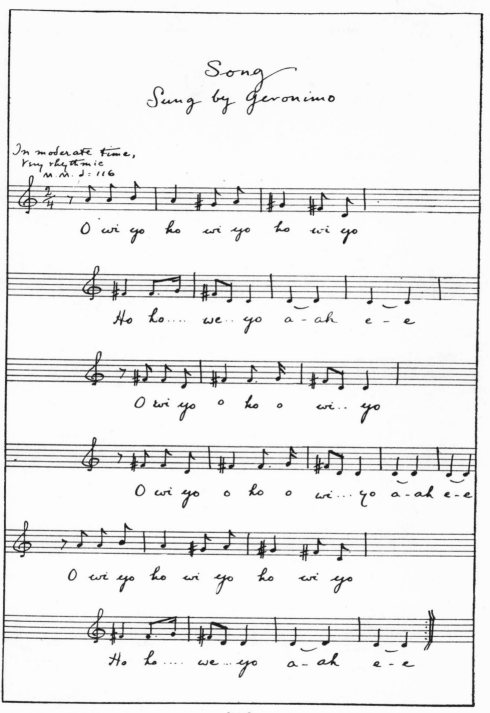

THE MOJAVE-APACHES

THE Mojave-Apaches are a band of Mojave Indians whose original home was in the Verde Valley of Arizona. Like the Apaches, these Indians were hostile to American invasion of their land. In about the year 1874 they were conquered and placed with the Apaches on a reservation in San Carlos County, Arizona, and accordingly are known as Mojave-Apaches.

On their removal to San Carlos, these Indians were promised that if they would remain there peacefully and adopt the white man's ways, they should be allowed, when civilized, to return to their land, there to resume their life of agriculture. The Indians faithfully kept the pledge, but when, after twenty-nine years, they were allowed to leave San Carlos, they found their land in the Verde Valley completely taken up by white settlers. In piteous poverty they waited in the mountains, sending appeal on appeal to Washington. Four years they waited with the natural trust of an Indian that a promise made would be fulfilled. At last help came to them from a private citizen, Mr. Frank Mead, who found them starving, with winter coming on. Mr. Mead brought the matter directly to President Roosevelt, and obtained the power to buy for the Indians, from the settlers, a fertile tract of country in the Verde Valley. So the Mojave-Apaches came into their own again, and on Christmas Day, in the year 1903, the land was divided among them. That night the Indians gave a dance in honor of their "Savior," as they called Mr. Mead, and in thanksgiving for their land. "We have our homes; we are men again," they said. Beneath the moon on the open desert they danced in a wide circle around a fire of blazing logs. The recorder was present at the time, and so two of the dance-songs then sung are preserved in The Indians' Book.[1]

[1] For a more complete description of this incident see "The Winning of an Indian Reservation," by Natalie Curtis, *The Outlook*, June 25, 1919.

THE STORY OF GOMOIDEMA POKOMA-KIAKA

The First Woman who made the Son of God

MANY years ago we lived not here upon this earth but down under the ground. And there came a time when we had no fruit and there was nothing to eat. So we sent the humming-bird to see what he could find. Wherever he might find fruit or food of any kind, there the people would go. He flew up into the sky, and there he saw a grape-vine that had its roots in the underworld and grew up through a hole in the middle of the sky into the upper world. The humming-bird saw the hole in the sky and flew through it, and came to a land where mescal and fruits and flowers of all kinds were growing. It was a good land. It was this world.

So the humming-bird flew back and told the people that he had seen a beautiful country above. "Let us all go up there," he said. So they all went up, climbing on the grape-vine. They climbed without stopping until they had come out through the hole in the sky into the upper world. But they left behind them in the underworld the frog-folk, who were blind. Now when the people had lived for a while in that land they heard a noise, and they wondered at it and sent a man to look down the hole, through which they had come, to see what made the noise. The man looked and saw that waters were rising from the underworld and were already so high that they nearly reached the mouth of the hole. The people said, "The blind frogs below have made this flood, and if it rises out of the hole it will wash us all away." So they took counsel together, and then they hollowed out a tree like a trough and put into it plenty of fruits and blankets. They chose a beautiful maiden and laid her in the trough, and closed it up and said, "Now if the waters come and we are all washed away, she will be saved alive."

The flood came up through the hole, and the people ran to the mountains, but though the mountains were high the waters rose over them.

The trough floated like a boat, and the flood kept rising, till at last it nearly touched the sky. Still the waters rose till the waves dashed the trough against the sky, where it struck with a loud noise. It struck first to the south, then to the west, then to the north, then nearly to the east. Then the flood began to go down.

The people had said to the woman, "If you hear the waters going down, wait till the trough rests on the earth, then make a little opening and look around you."

When the trough rested on the ground the woman opened it and went out. She looked all around her, over all the world, but saw no one. All the people had been drowned. Then the woman thought, "How can I bear children and make a new people?"

She went up into the mountains early, before sunrise, and lay there alone. Then the daylight came and the beams from the sun shone warm upon the woman, and the water dripped from the crag, and in this way she conceived, and bore a daughter. When the child was grown to maidenhood the mother said to her, "Do you know, my daughter, how you came to be?" And the maid said, "No."

"I will show you," said the mother.

So she led her daughter up into the mountains, and bade her lie down as she herself had lain. And the maid lay on the mountain all day. Next morning early, before sunrise, the mother went to her, and she lay down upon her daughter and looked at the sun. Then she quickly sprang up, and in this way the maiden conceived of the sun, and the child that she bore was the Son of God—Sekala Ka-amja, "The-One-Who-Never-Died."

THE DEATHLESS ONE AND THE WIND

THE Son of God, the Deathless One, had a wife, and she was a good woman. One day she went out to gather fruit, and the Hot Wind saw her and stole her away. The Deathless One found the Wind's trail, and knew the footprints; so he went home to his grandmother, the First Woman, and said, "I have seen the trail of the Wind who has stolen my wife, and I am going to follow him." So the Deathless One

THE INDIANS' BOOK

followed the trail until he came upon some people who lived close beside it, and he asked of them, "Have you seen any one pass?"

"Yes," said the people, "the Wind passed by a short time ago, and with him went a beautiful woman." Also they said, "The Wind is a great pole-player.[1] He has beaten every one, and has won all the people. Stop for a while and we will tell you how the Wind plays. If you let him play with his own pole, he will beat you and put you with the rest of the men, women, and children that he has won. But if you will wait we will make you two good poles to play with, and then perhaps you will beat the Wind and win back the people and set them free."

So they made good poles for him, and the Deathless One went on until he came to the Wind's lodge that was made of willow-brush, and there, inside, sitting with the Wind, he saw his wife.

"Ho, friend!" said the Wind, "will you play pole with me?"

"Yes," said the Deathless One. "That is why I have come."

The Deathless One looked at the Wind's pole; it was not made of wood, but of a dead man's thigh-bone. He did not want to play with the bone pole. Then he said to the Wind, "Give me your ring that I may look at it." He took the ring and knew that it was made of a live snake, for he saw the gleam of its eyes. He had pins[2] in his hand, and with these he pierced the eyes of the snake, and gave back the ring to the Wind. The Wind tried to throw the ring, but he could not, because it was dead. He tried again, and then asked of the Son of God, "How did you kill this?"

"I like not your ring nor your bone pole," said the Deathless One; "I have a good ring and good wooden poles." Then he threw away the Wind's ring and pole and made ready to play.

"Where did you get these good poles and this ring?" said the Wind. "I like them. I will play with you and stake half of these people."

They played one game, and the ring leaped over the Wind's pole and fell on the pole of the Deathless One, and so the Deathless One won half the people. The second game went the same way, and the Deathless One won the other half of the people.

[1] Games played with poles and rings are aboriginal Indian games found among many tribes.
[2] The "pins" are possibly cactus thorns.

[332]

Then said the Wind, "Are you a runner?"

"No," said the Deathless One, "I am not a runner, but I mean to run with you to-day."

"Let us race," said the Wind. "Let us start from the south and race all around the earth. The one that first reaches again the south point shall win the other. If I win you, I shall kill you; if you win me, you may kill me."

They started from the south and ran all around the earth, and before noon the Deathless One reached again the starting-point. There he waited until the Wind came. The Wind stepped up close to him and said: "I am ready if you are ready. You may kill me." The Deathless One took up a stick and struck at the Wind's head, but every time he struck the Wind dodged. Then a little fly helped the Deathless One; the fly flew into his ear and said, "Aim at his head, but strike the shadow of his head upon the ground."

So the Deathless One struck downward at the shadow and killed the Wind. Then he said: "I never saw a man such as the Wind. Now I will make him no man, but wind only." So he cut the body into four quarters, and threw them east, west, north, and south. That is why the wind still blows from four directions, but no longer lives in the form of a man.[1] Then the Deathless One released his wife and brought her home.

---

[1] The wife of the Deathless One probably represents the fruitfulness of the earth which was taken away by the hot wind, and upon whose release depended the life of the people.

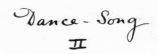

Dance-Song
II

Samadia Suan
Medicine Song
II

Sung by Somurturgigu-a

Fast
M.M. ♩ = 104.

Ya e ya e ya he ye yu

Ya e ya e ya he ya na

Hi .... hi yu

Ya e ya e ya ' he ye yu

Ya e ya e ya he ya na

E ya e ya e ye yu

THE YUMAS

THE word "Yuma" is said to mean "Sons of the River," and this name is given to a southwestern linguistic family comprising several tribes, among them the Cocopas, Havasupais, Maricopas, Cochimis, Walapais, Seris, Mojaves, and the Yumas proper.[1] This last-named tribe is on a reservation on the Colorado River, in the southernmost part of California, near the border-line of California and Arizona.

The Yumas are a quiet peaceable people, yet they are strong and brave, and, like the Apaches, they fought the whites and Mexicans who traversed their territory in the rush of emigration after the discovery of gold in California.

In spite of the proximity of whites and Mexicans, many of the native Yuma customs endure, and the Indians still practise their ancient mode of agriculture.

In spring when the melted snows pour down from the mountains the Colorado River overflows its banks, like the Nile, and in the soil thus fertilized, these "River Indians" plant their crops of corn, wheat, squash and melons.

Among the wisest and most thoughtful of the Yumas, in recent years, was *Ch*iparopai, an aged woman, whose knowledge of Spanish and English had made her a leader among her people. In the year 1905 the Yumas received news that their land was to be irrigated, as part of a great irrigation scheme, one-fifth of the reservation to be left to them and the rest sold for white settlement. Alarmed at

NOTE FOR PRONUNCIATION OF YUMA TEXT

Unless otherwise indicated, vowels have the Continental sound, and consonants the English.

Ch, in italic, is a guttural, like ch in German.

[1] The Yuma Indians call themselves Cochan.

this, they met in council with a government official and *Chiparopai* was chosen as their interpreter. The Indians dreaded the change to come upon them through the proposed transaction, fearing that closer contact with the whites would mean their doom.[1] "Why not knock us on the head and end it at once," they cried; "it would be kinder than the slow agony."

Chiparopai was old and bent, and said that it was only service to her people that kept life within her frail form. "I want to live to help them through the trouble that will come when white settlers are among us," she said. But *Chiparopai* has been spared the sight of the change to come upon her people. She has died consecrated to the good of her tribe.[2]

AROWP

Song of the Mocking-Bird

THIS Song of the Mocking-Bird was sung by *Chiparopai*. It is a song of happiness. The Yuma Indians live beneath rainless desert skies and love the days when thin little clouds veil the blue. The mocking-bird is a voice of melody in the silent desert. Of this song *Chiparopai* said: "I am going my way when I hear the mocking-bird singing. It sings only when it is happy, so I stop to listen. It sings that the world is fair, the clouds are in the sky, and it is glad at heart. Then I, too, am glad at heart and go on my uphill road, the road of goodness and happiness."

The meaning is only implied, not fully expressed, by the words of the song, but the Indian understands all that lies behind the few syllables.

[1] The Yuma reservation still intact as Indian land lies on the opposite side of the river from the town of Yuma and the white settlements. The irrigation scheme has not yet been carried through—1906.

[2] For a further account of this interesting character see Appendix, page 568.

AROWP

SONG OF THE MOCKING-BIRD

'Mai ariwa—
　　'riwa—
'Mai ariwa—
　　'riwa—

" Thin little clouds are spread
　Across the blue of the sky,
　Thin little clouds are spread—
　Oh, happy am I as I sing,
　I sing of the clouds in the sky."

Shakwa tza mi na hi
Shakwa tza mi na

Thus tells the bird,
'Tis the mocking-bird who sings,
And I stop to hear,
For he is glad at heart
And I will list to his message.

Hunya kwa pai va
Hunya kwa hul pa

Then up the hill,
Up the hill I go my straight road,
The road of good—
Up the hill I go my straight road,
The happy road and good.

LITERAL VERSION

"Sky so thinly covered with clouds,
　　With clouds,

Sky so thinly covered with clouds,
　　With clouds!"

The mocking-bird he it is who thus sings,
The mocking-bird he it is who thus sings.

I go up the mesa.
I go up the straight trail.

CREATION MYTH

See Appendix, page 562.

ASH'VAR' HOMAR TASHMATSK

Song for putting child to sleep.
See Appendix, page 571.

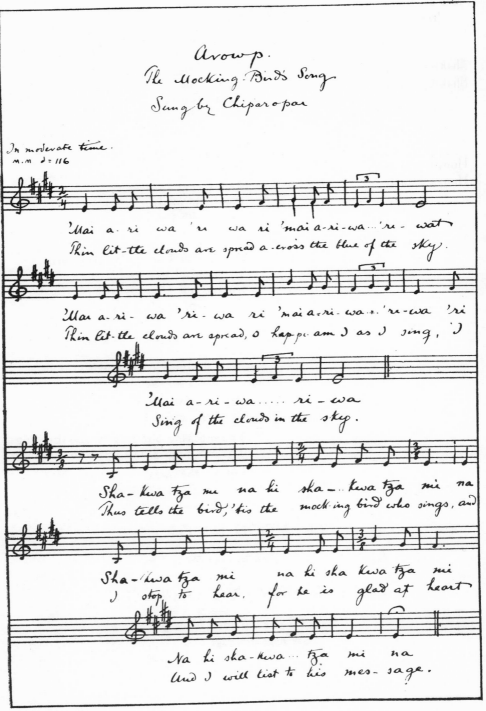

Avowp.
The Mocking-Bird's Song
Sung by Chiparopai

In moderate time.
m.m ♩= 116

'Mai a-ri wa 're wa ri 'mai a-ri-wa....'re- wat
Thin lit-tle clouds are spread a-cross the blue of the sky.

'Mai a-ri- wa 'ri- wa ri 'mai a-ri- wa...'re-wa 'ri
Thin lit-tle clouds are spread, o happe am I as I sing, I

'Mai a-ri-wa..... ri - wa
Sing of the clouds in the sky.

Sha-kwa tza me na hi sha—kwa tza mi na
Thus tells the bird,'tis the mock-ing bird who sings, and

Sha-kwa tza mi na hi sha kwa tza mi
I stop to hear, for he is glad at heart

Na hi sha-kwa....tza mi na
And I will list to his mes-sage.

[342]

Arowp

O nya kwa pai va ku-nya kwa hul..... pa
Then up the hill, up the hill I go my straight road,

Hu-nya kwa pai va ku-nya kwa hul..... pa
The road of good, up the hill I go my straight road,

Hu-nya kwa hul ...pa
The hap-py road and good

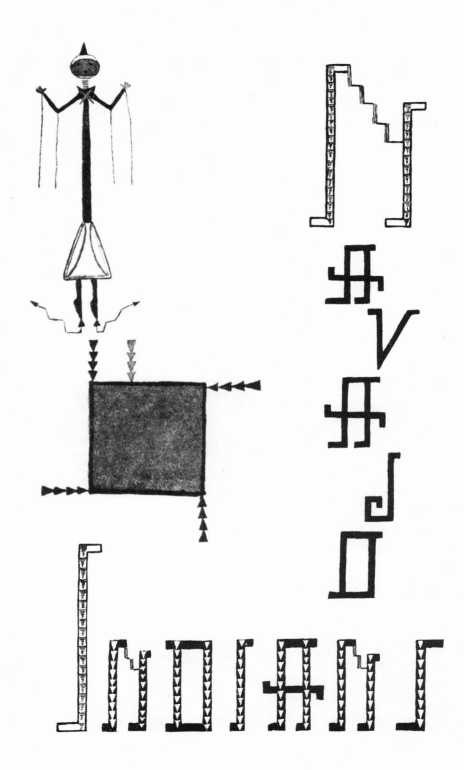

NAVAJO TITLE-PAGE

The design is a copy of a figure from a Navajo ceremonial sand-picture, representing in conventionalized form a Navajo deity standing upon the lightning arrows. The drawing is by a Navajo Indian.

The lettering by Hinook Mahiwi Kilinaka (Angel De Cora), suggests the metal-work for which the Navajos are famed; the characters at the foot of the page hold the corn-symbol, which is seen at the four corners of the square below the Navajo deity.

THE NAVAJOS

T HE Navajos, often and truly called the Bedouins of America, are a large nomad tribe whose home is in the deserts and table-lands of Arizona and New Mexico. Their own name for themselves is "Diné, or the People." They are of Athapascan stock, though in their veins flows the blood of other peoples with whom they have mixed—Pueblo, Zuñi, and Mexican. The lands of the Navajos are arid, and therefore useless to the white man. Accordingly, this tribe has remained, until quite recently, comparatively remote from white intercourse. The conquest of New Mexico by Coronado, in the year 1540, brought domestic animals to the Indians, and since that time the Navajos have been a shepherd folk whose main sustenance is from their flocks of sheep and goats.

NOTE FOR PRONUNCIATION OF NAVAJO TEXT

While in many Indian languages there are sounds not exactly the same as the corresponding ones of European tongues, in the Navajo occur sounds that have no counterpart at all in European languages. Such sounds, therefore, can be expressed by the Roman alphabet approximately only.[1]

Unless otherwise indicated, vowels have the Continental sound, and consonants the English.

n has the nasal sound, as in French.

ch, in italic, is a guttural, like ch in German.

r has a guttural roll.

Navajo songs frequently begin and end with the vocables "Ko-la-ra-ne," and the song-words are often prolonged with vocables interspersed among the syllables or added to the end of the word.

The Navajo legends and stories connected with the songs here given were heard by the recorder with slight variations in different parts of the Navajo country. To insure authenticity, and also to avoid discrepancy, the recorder has consulted the works of the late Washington Matthews and those of the late James Stevenson, to which authorities indebtedness is acknowledged.

[1] The pronunciation of the word for "water," for example, which with its compounds appears in many of the following songs, is indicated by one authority as "T'o," by another as "Tqŏ." For convenience the author's version "Tro" is retained.

The dwelling of the Navajo is a "hogan," or rude hut built of poles and earth when on the level desert, or of stone and timber when on the fir-grown mountain-side. With ceremony and song the hogan is consecrated to the use of the owner; yet it is rarely more than a temporary dwelling, to be abandoned when the flock must seek new pastures.

It is thought that the Navajos acquired the art of weaving from the Pueblo peoples, their close neighbors. To-day the Navajos are famed for the blankets they make from the wool of their sheep. From the Mexicans the Navajos learned smithing; and in their crude forges they make necklaces, buttons, clasps, bridle-ornaments, rings, bracelets, and every sort of silver decoration, using metal obtained from melted coin. The originality of design and the barbaric charm of the workmanship make the handiwork of the Navajos unique of its kind. Of such art industries the Southwest may well be proud.

Like all Indians, the Navajos are intensely religious, and their ceremonies are long, elaborate, poetic, and ritualistic, abounding in long chants, which contain many verses with preludes and refrains. Indeed. the ceremonies themselves are called "hatal," meaning chant, a name which well describes the importance of music in the rite.

The mythology of this tribe contains a wealth of beautiful imagery striking in its originality, and strongly reflecting the nature-world of the Southwest.

The Navajo is industrious, independent, and fearless. He has the strength of the warrior and the simplicity of the shepherd. In his glance is the lightning's flash and the wide freedom of the desert, yet the absent, dreamy look of the herdsman accustomed to gazing off upon a vast horizon gives to the face an almost graven calm. Pastoral yet majestic, the Navajo is the true son of the silence, the awe, the grandeur of the desert.

A Shepherd Leaving His Hogan at Dawn

HOZHONJI SONGS

"T HE Hozhonji songs are holy songs, given to us by the gods," say the Navajos. "They are songs of peace and of blessing. They protect the people against all evil. A man will often sing a Hozhonji song before starting on a journey. Ceremonies are begun sometimes with a Hozhonji song, and always end with one, for the song is a final blessing. It is the parting song before the people scatter at daybreak after a rite which has lasted all night. The Navajo must never make a mistake or miss a word in singing any sacred chant; if he does, the singing must stop, for its good has been blighted. Even a whole ceremony will be given up if a single mistake occur in any part of the ritual. That is why we often close our eyes when we sing, that we may think of the song more clearly. The Navajo sings a Hozhonji song to purify or bless himself or others; or he will sing in order that his flocks and herds may thrive. If he make no mistake, blessings will surely follow and evils will be warded off."

So say the Navajos, and an educated member of the tribe adds: "Our Hozhonji songs are like the Psalms of David. We sing them as a white man says his prayers. Our hero, Nayenezrani, is like the Bible hero.David. By our Holy Ones were the songs made, even as the Bible was made by holy people."

To the white man there is scarcely a more impressive sight than a group of Navajos chanting these ancient traditional songs which have been learned and handed down with the greatest accuracy and care. The quiet, monotonous quality of the chant seems heightened by the concentration of the singers, who, with closed eyes or fixed gaze, bend every thought upon their singing that they may not err in word or sequence of the holy song.

At a healing-ceremony in some hogan where there is sickness, the steady rhythm of the medicine-songs pulses all night long, groups of singers on opposite sides of the fire vying with one another in endurance. Does one group flag, another starts in freshly, and so, like the central pile of burning logs, the song flares unextinguished till the paling of the stars. Then comes a pause—the song changes;

all the voices join in chanting, and then in measured cadence rises a Hozhonji song to end the ceremony of the night and greet the coming day. The singing of a Hozhonji song is at all times an act of consecration.

DSI*CHL* BIYIN

Mountain-Song (Hozhonji Song)

HE singer of this Mountain-Song was an old man of character and great intelligence, who was looked upon as leader by a certain band of Navajos in New Mexico. Said he:

"It is well that our songs should be written, and it is now time, indeed, that this should be done. The young people grow careless of the songs, and mistakes will come into them. Unless the songs are written they will in time be forgotten. I know this; I have long known it. I have tried myself to find a way to record the songs, but I cannot write. Now you will write what I sing.

"I will sing for you the oldest song I know. It was taught to me by my grandfather. He learned it from his father, for it has been taught by fathers to their sons for no one knows how many years. It is true, there were older songs than this sung by an ancient people in days before the coming of the Navajos. But those songs are all lost because the people themselves have perished; they grew wicked, therefore sand-storms and cyclones were sent to destroy them and their villages. There is nothing left of them but the ruins of their dwellings.[1]

"The song that I will sing is a holy song. In olden times it was the first song that a boy learned. It was taught to him by his father, for every boy should know this song before starting into life."

The following narrative explaining the song was told in part by the aged singer, in part by other Navajos:[2]

[1] The ruins and cliff-dwellings of New Mexico and Arizona.
[2] There are other versions of the Navajo story of the Emergence.

There are four worlds, one above another: the first world; the second world, which is the underworld; the third, which is the middle world; and the fourth world, our own world. In the underworld there arose a great flood and the people were driven up by the waters. They planted a hollow reed and came up through it to this world.

First-Man and First-Woman had brought with them earth from the mountains of the world below. With this they made the sacred mountains of the Navajo land.

To the East they placed the sacred mountain Sisnajinni.[1] They adorned it with white shell and fastened it to the earth with a bolt of lightning. They covered it with a sheet of daylight, and put the Dawn Youth and the Dawn Maiden to dwell in it.

To the South they placed Tsodsichl. They adorned it with turquoise and fastened it to the earth with a knife of stone. They covered it with blue sky, and put the Turquoise Youth and the Turquoise Maiden to dwell in it.

To the West they placed Doko-oslid. They adorned it with haliotis-shell and fastened it to the earth with a sunbeam. They covered it with a yellow cloud, and put the Twilight Youth and the Haliotis Maiden to dwell in it.

To the North they placed Depenitsa. They adorned it with cannel coal[2] and fastened it to the earth with a rainbow. They covered it with a covering of darkness, and put the Youth of Cannel Coal and the Darkness Maiden to dwell in it.

In the centre they placed Tsichlnaodichli and adorned it with striped agate. Here were created the first Navajos. The Navajos will never live elsewhere than around this mountain.

So the mountains were placed and decorated; then, before they were named, holy songs were sung which tell of a journey up the mountain. The song here given is the first of these.

[1] The recorder acknowledges indebtedness to the works of Dr. Washington Matthews for some of the details contained in the description of the decoration of the mountains.

[2] This beautiful, lustrous coal is highly prized by the Navajos, who make from it black beads. Turquoise (abundantly found in the Southwest), different kinds of shell, and this variety of coal are gems to the Navajos, who make from them their necklaces and ornaments. Such gems are also used as sacred offerings to the gods. The decorations of the mountains accord with the Navajo color-symbolism—white for the east; blue for the south; yellow for the west; black for the north. " The north skies are dark and the south skies are blue," say the Navajos.

When the Navajo sings "Chief of all mountains," he means something higher and holier than chief. He sings to the mountain as to a god, for the mountain is pure and holy; there is freedom above it, freedom below it, freedom all around it. Happiness and peace are given by the mountain, and the mountain blesses man when in the song it calls him "son."

DSI*CHL* BIYIN	MOUNTAIN-SONG
Piki yo-ye!	Thither go I !
Dsi*chl*-nantaï,	Chief of all mountains,
Piki yo-ye,	Thither go I,
Sa-a naraï,	Living forever,
Piki yo-ye,	Thither go I,
Bike hozhoni,	Blessings bestowing.
Piki yo-ye,	Thither go I,
Tsoya shi*ch* ni-la !	Calling me " Son, my son."
Piki yo-ye!	Thither go I !

DSI*CHL* BIYIN

Mountain-Songs

Sung and told by Navajos near Fort Defiance, Arizona

IN a certain ceremony for healing, holy mountain-songs are sung over the sick man. These songs describe a journey to a holy place beyond the sacred mountains where are everlasting life and blessedness. The Divine Ones who live in and beyond the mountains made the songs, and so they tell of the journey as of a home-coming.

When these songs are sung over a man, the spirit of the man makes the journey that the song describes. Upon the rainbow he moves from mountain to mountain, for it is thus that the gods travel, standing upon the rainbow. The rainbow is swift as lightning. Any man may know this to be true, for he may see clearly where the rainbow touches the ground, and walk to the spot, but before he is there the rainbow has moved quickly away and is far beyond.

He never can overtake it; it moves more swiftly than any one can
see. Sometimes these songs are sung for runners before a great race
in order to bless them and give them the speed of the rainbow.

There are many mountain-songs, and of the songs here given
there are six, all to the same music. Each song is sung four times,
once for each mountain, and the singers must make no mistake
in their sequence nor miss a word. We always sing of the mountains in this order—East, South, West, and North, for it is thus
that the sun moves.

The mountain protects man like a god. When a man sings of
the mountain, then, through the singing, his spirit goes to the holy
place beyond the mountain, and he himself becomes like the mountain, pure and holy, living eternally, forever blessed.

DSICHL BIYIN

Be-ye-la-naseya,
Be-ye-la-naseyo,
Be-ye-la-naseya,
Ho-digin-ladji-ye-ye,
Be-ye-la-naseya,
Ka' Sisnajinni
Bine dji-ye-ye,
Be-ye-la-naseya,
Dsichl-nanitaï
Bine dji-ye-ye,
Be-ye-la-naseya,
Sa-a naraï
Bine dji-ye-ye,
Be-ye-la-naseya,
Bike hozhoni
Bine dji-ye-ye,
Be-ye-la-naseya,

The above is repeated three times, substituting for the mountain name, Sisnajinni, the names,
in order, Tsodsichl, Doko-oslid, and Depenitsa.

The five songs that follow are the same as the first, excepting that the refrain, Be-ye-la-naseya,
is replaced everywhere by a different refrain. These refrains are as follows:

Second song: Be-ye-la-nadesta
Third   song: Be-ye-nikiniya

Fourth song: Be-ye-la-naïshtatl
Fifth   song: Be-ye-la-nanistsa
Sixth   song: Be-ye-la-nanishta

Like the first song, each of these has four verses, one for each mountain. There are thus twenty-four stanzas. The first song only is written in the Navajo language under the music, since the refrains of the other five songs exactly correspond in the number of syllables. The names of the four mountains mentioned in four successive singings of each song are written in their proper place below the music, but in the English version the four mountain names must be used without the Indian prolongation by extra syllables. See music page 377.

MOUNTAIN-SONGS

Each song sung four times, with substitution, in the sixth line, of the name of another mountain

I

Swift and far I journey,
Swift upon the rainbow.
Swift and far I journey,
Lo, yonder, the Holy Place!
      Yea, swift and far I journey.
To Sisnajinni, and beyond it,
      Yea, swift and far I journey;
The Chief of Mountains, and beyond it,
      Yea, swift and far I journey;
To Life Unending, and beyond it,
      Yea, swift and far I journey;
To Joy Unchanging, and beyond it,
      Yea, swift and far I journey.

II

Homeward now shall I journey,
Homeward upon the rainbow; ·
Homeward now shall I journey,
Lo, yonder the Holy Place!
      Yea, homeward now shall I journey.
To Sisnajinni, and beyond it,
      Yea, homeward now shall I journey;
The Chief of Mountains, and beyond it,
      Yea, homeward now shall I journey;

NAVAJO

To Life Unending, and beyond it,
>> Yea, homeward now shall I journey;

To Joy Unchanging, and beyond it,
>> Yea, homeward now shall I journey.

III

Homeward behold me starting,
Homeward upon the rainbow;
Homeward behold me starting.
Lo, yonder, the Holy Place!
>> Yea, homeward behold me starting.

To Sisnajinni, and beyond it,
>> Yea, homeward behold me starting;

The Chief of Mountains, and beyond it,
>> Yea, homeward behold me starting;

To Life Unending, and beyond it,
>> Yea, homeward behold me starting;

To Joy Unchanging, and beyond it,
>> Yea, homeward behold me starting.

IV

Homeward behold me faring,
Homeward upon the rainbow;
Homeward behold me faring.
Lo, yonder, the Holy Place!
>> Yea, homeward behold me faring.

To Sisnajinni, and beyond it,
>> Yea, homeward behold me faring;

The Chief of Mountains, and beyond it,
>> Yea, homeward behold me faring;

To Life Unending, and beyond it,
>> Yea, homeward behold me faring;

To Joy Unchanging, and beyond it,
>> Yea, homeward behold me faring.

V

Now arrived home behold me,
Now arrived on the rainbow;
Now arrived home behold me,
Lo, here, the Holy Place!
>> Yea, now arrived home behold me.

At Sisnajinni, and beyond it,
   Yea, now arrived home behold me;
The Chief of Mountains, and beyond it,
   Yea, now arrived home behold me;
In Life Unending, and beyond it,
   Yea, now arrived home behold me;
In Joy Unchanging, and beyond it,
   Yea, now arrived home behold me.

VI

Seated at home behold me,
Seated amid the rainbow;
Seated at home behold me,
Lo, here, the Holy Place !
   Yea, seated at home behold me.
At Sisnajinni, and beyond it,
   Yea, seated at home behold me;
The Chief of Mountains, and beyond it,
   Yea, seated at home behold me;
In Life Unending, and beyond it,
   Yea, seated at home behold me;
In Joy Unchanging, and beyond it,
   Yea, seated at home behold me.

HOGAN BIYIN

Song of the Hogans (Hozhonji Song)

Sung and told by Navajos of Arizona

THIS is one of the oldest and most revered of the Hozhonji songs. It tells of two blessed hogans, the first that ever were made — in the east, the hogan of Hastyeyalti, god of sunrise; in the west, the hogan of Hastyehogan, god of sunset. Long ago, the gods had no dwellings but met in the open, they say. Then they decided that they must have houses wherein they might hold their sacred rites and sing their holy songs. So the blessed hogans were made, and this song was

sung to consecrate them. Even so with the same song the Navajo
now consecrates a new dwelling. He may also sing it at any time
as a blessing upon himself or his people:

HOGAN BIYIN

Tsanti hogani-la,
    Hozhon hogan-e.

Hayiash-iye beashdje
    Hogani-la,
    Hozhon hogan-e,

Ka' Hastyeyalti-ye bi
    Hogani-la,
    Hozhon hogan-e;

Hayolkatli-ye be bi
    Hogani-la,
    Hozhon hogan-e;

Tan-alchkaï-ye be bi
    Hogani-la,
    Hozhon hogan-e;

Yotti-iltrassaï-ye be bi
    Hogani-la,
    Hozhon hogan-e;

Tro-altlanastshini-ye be bi
    Hogani-la,
    Hozhon hogan-e;

Tradetin-iye be bi
    Hogani-la,
    Hozhon hogan-e;

Ka' sa-a naraï,
Ka' bike hozhoni bi
    Hogani-la,
    Hozhon hogan-e.

Tsanti hogani-la,
    Hozhon hogan-e.

SONG OF THE HOGANS
(Hozhonji Song)

Lo, yonder the hogan,
    The hogan blessed!

There beneath the sunrise
    Standeth the hogan,
    The hogan blessed.

Of Hastyeyalti-ye
    The hogan,
    The hogan blessed.

Built of dawn's first light
    Standeth his hogan,
    The hogan blessed.

Built of fair white corn
    Standeth his hogan,
    The hogan blessed.

Built of broidered robes and hides
    Standeth his hogan,
    The hogan blessed.

Built of mixed All-Waters pure
    Standeth his hogan,
    The hogan blessed.

Built of holy pollen
    Standeth his hogan,
    The hogan blessed.

Evermore enduring,
Happy evermore,
    His hogan,
    The hogan blessed.

Lo, yonder the hogan,
    The hogan blessed!

I-iash-iye beashdje
   Hogani-la,
   Hozhon hogan-e;

Ka' Hastyehogan-i bi
   Hogani-la,
   Hozhon hogan-e;

Nahotsoï-ye be bi
   Hogani-la,
   Hozhon hogan-e;

Tan-alchtsoï-ye be bi
   Hogani-la,
   Hozhon hogan-e;

Nekliz iltrassaï-ye be bi
   Hogani-la,
   Hozhon hogan-e;

Tro-piyash-iye be bi
   Hogani-la,
   Hozhon hogan-e;

Tradetin-iye be bi
   Hogani-la,
   Hozhon hogan-e;

Ka' sa-a narai,
Ka bike hozhoni bi
   Hogani-la,
   Hozhon hogan-e.

Tsanti hogani-la,
   Hozhon hogan-e.

There beneath the sunset
   Standeth the hogan,
   The hogan blessed.

Of Hastyehogan-i
   The hogan,
   The hogan blessed.

Built of afterglow
   Standeth his hogan,
   The hogan blessed.

Built of yellow corn
   Standeth his hogan,
   The hogan blessed.

Built of gems and shining shells
   Standeth his hogan,
   The hogan blessed. ·

Built of Little-Waters
   Standeth his hogan,
   The hogan blessed.

Built of holy pollen
   Standeth his hogan,
   The hogan blessed.

Evermore enduring,
Happy evermore,
   His hogan,
   The hogan blessed.

Lo, yonder the hogan,
   The hogan blessed!

STORY OF THE TWO BROTHERS

Told by Navajos of New Mexico and Arizona

O F all the Divine Ones none is more revered than Estsan-Natlehi (She-Who-Changeth).[1] Highly honored, too, is her younger sister Yolkai-Estsan (White-Shell-Woman). Of the turquoise of the land was made She-Who-Changeth; of the white shell of the ocean was made White-Shell-Woman. Each sister bore a son; the child of She-Who-Changeth was the god Nayenezrani; the child of White-Shell-Woman was the god Tobajischini.

At that time there were in the world many *Anaye*, they say, gods unfriendly to man, evil beings, giants, monsters, who destroyed the people.[2] When the two young gods were grown, they wanted to slay the Anaye that the people might be saved.

Now the brothers[3] often asked of the mothers, "Who is our father?" The mothers always answered, "You have none." At last, one day, they set out to find him for themselves; they took a holy trail and journeyed on the sunbeams. It was Niltshi, the Wind, who guided them, whispering his counsel in their ears.

Their father was Johano-ai, the Sun. His beautiful house was in the east; it was made of turquoise, and stood on the shore of great waters. There he dwelled with his wife, his daughters, and his sons, The Black Thunder and The Blue Thunder. Until the coming of the strange brothers, the wife of the Sun had not known that her husband had visited a goddess on the earth. Nor would Johano-ai believe that the two gods were his sons until he had proved it by making them undergo all kinds of trials. But the youths came through each test unharmed, and then the Sun rejoiced that these were indeed his children, and promised to give them what they asked. The brothers told their father that they wanted weapons with which to slay the Anaye. So Johano-ai gave

---

[1] According to Dr. Washington Matthews, the goddess is thus named because she passes through endless lives, continually changing from old to young again—" it is probable that she is an apotheosis of nature or of the changing year."

[2] Many of the Anaye are personifications of the dangers that lie in nature.

[3] The two gods are called " brothers " in all versions of the myth. Another version makes both gods twin-children of She-Who-Changeth.

them helmets, shirts, leggings, and moccasins, all of black flint; and when this armor was put on, the four lightnings flashed from the different joints.[1]   He gave them for weapons a mighty knife of stone, and arrows of rainbow, of sunbeam, and of lightning.   So the brothers slew the Anaye, and after each victory they returned to their mothers rejoicing.

Then Johano-ai came to She-Who-Changeth and begged her to make for him a home in the west, where he might rest at evening after his long day's journey across the skies.   Long he pleaded with her, until at last she yielded and said, "I will go and make a home for you, if you will give me what I ask.   You have a beautiful turquoise house in the east, they say.   I must have just such a beautiful house in the west, only it must be beyond the shore and floating amid the waters; and around the house must be planted all kinds of gems, that they may grow and become many."

Johano-ai granted every wish, and now, beyond the mountains, the sun-god rests at evening in the gem-surrounded floating house of Estsan-Natlehi in the west.

HLIN BIYIN

Song of the Horse

Sung and told by Navajos of Arizona

JOHANO-AI starts each day from his hogan, in the east, and rides across the skies to his hogan in the west, carrying the shining golden disk, the sun.   He has five horses—a horse of turquoise, a horse of white shell, a horse of pearl shell, a horse of red shell, and a horse of coal.[2]   When the skies are blue and the weather is fair, Johano-ai is riding his turquoise horse or his horse of white shell or of pearl; but when the heavens are dark with storm, he has mounted the red horse, or the horse of coal.

Beneath the hoofs of the horses are spread precious hides of

[1] See "The Morning Star and The Evening Star," page 103; also foot-note, page 315.
[2] See mountain narrative, page 351.

all kinds, and beautiful woven blankets, richly decorated, called "naskan." In olden times the Navajos used to wear such blankets, and men say they were first found in the home of the sun-god.[1]

Johano-ai pastures his herds on flower-blossoms and gives them to drink of the mingled waters. These are holy waters, waters of all kinds, spring-water, snow-water, hail-water and water from the four quarters of the world. The Navajos use such waters in their rites. When the horse of the sun-god goes, he raises, not dust, but "pitistchi," glittering grains of mineral such as are used in religious ceremonies; and when he rolls, and shakes himself, it is shining pitistshi that flies from him. When he runs, the sacred pollen offered to the sun-god is all about him, like dust, so that he looks like a mist; for the Navajos sometimes say that the mist on the horizon is the pollen that has been offered to the gods.

The Navajo sings of the horses of Johano-ai in order that he, too, may have beautiful horses like those of the sun-god. Standing among his herds he scatters holy pollen, and sings this song for the blessing and protection of his animals:

HLIN BIYIN

Nizho'ko ani—hiye !
Ka' Johano-ai dotlizhi be lin-iye
    Nizho'ko ani—hiye,
Yotti bahostieli tsi bakaï yiki
    Nizho'ko ani—hiye,
Tshilatra hozhoni be jinichltan laki
    Nizho'ko ani—hiye,
Tro-tlanastshini-ye be jinichltan laki
    Nizho'ko ani—hiye,
Ka' pitistshi-ye pilch tashokishko,
    Nizho'ko ani—hiye,
Ka' ba tradetin-iye yan-a toitinyeko,
    Nizho'ko ani—hiye,
K'ean natelzhishko k'at tonidineshko,
    Nizho'ko ani—hiye !

[1] This bit of imagery undoubtedly depicts the clouds. The sunlight on meadow and spring is suggested in the pasturing of the sun-god's horses.

SONG OF THE HORSE

How joyous his neigh !
Lo, the Turquoise Horse of Johano-ai,
How joyous his neigh,
There on precious hides outspread standeth he;
How joyous his neigh,
There on tips of fair fresh flowers feedeth he;
How joyous his neigh,
There of mingled waters holy drinketh he;
How joyous his neigh,
There he spurneth dust of glittering grains;
How joyous his neigh,
There in mist of sacred pollen hidden, all hidden he;
How joyous his neigh,
There his offspring many grow and thrive for evermore;
How joyous his neigh !

NAYE-E SIN

War-Song

Sung and told by Navajos of Arizona

THIS is an ancient Navajo war-chant. It was sung by
the god Nayenezrani, the Slayer of the Anaye.[1] Nayenezrani made the ancient war-songs and gave them to
the Navajos. In olden times, when the Navajos were
going to war, the warriors chanted this song and then went out into
a wide plain and put the war-feather in their hair. These feathers
were very holy and were ornamented with turquoise. No woman
or child might ever look upon them, lest the warrior, in battle,
become like a child or a woman.

The war-chant tells how Nayenezrani hurls his enemies into the
ground with the lightning, one after another. The four lightnings
strike from him in all directions and return, for lightning always
looks as if it flashed out and then went back.[2]

" Whe-e-yoni-sin" means the songs the enemy sings against him.
They are the sorcerous songs and evil prayers of the foe.

[1] *Anaye.* See "Story of the Two Brothers," page 359.
[2] See foot-note, page 103.

NAVAJO

When chanting this song in time of war, the Navajo would re-place the words, "the old peoples of the earth" with the name of the enemy, whoever he might be—Moqui, Zuñi, or Ute:

<table>
<tr><td>NAYE-E SIN</td><td>WAR-SONG</td></tr>
<tr><td valign="top">

Pesh ashike ni shli—yi-na,
Pesh ashike ni shli—ya-e

Nayenezrani shi ni shli—kola
Pesh ashike ni shli—
          E-na

Pesh tilyilch-iye shi ke—kola,
Pesh ashike ni shli—
          E-na

Pesh tilyilch-iye siskle—kola,
Pesh ashike ni shli—
          E-na

Pesh tilyilch-iye shi e—kola,
Pesh ashike ni shli—
          E-na

Pesh tilyilch-iye shi tsha—kola
Pesh ashike ni shli—
          E-na

Nolienni tshina shi-ye
Shi yiki holon-e—kola,
Pesh ashike ni shli—
          E-na

Ka' itsiniklizhi-ye
    Din-ikwo
Sitzan nahatilch—kola,
    Din-ikwo
Pesh ashike ni shli—
          E-na

Tsini nahatilch ki la
Nihoka hastoyo-la
Whe-e-yoni-sin-iye

</td><td valign="top">

Lo, the flint youth, he am I,
    The flint youth.

Nayenezrani, Lo, behold me, he am I,
  Lo, the flint youth, he am I,
    The flint youth.

Moccasins of black flint have I;
  Lo, the flint youth, he am I,
    The flint youth.

Leggings of black flint have I;
  Lo, the flint youth, he am I,
    The flint youth.

Tunic of black flint have I;
  Lo, the flint youth, he am I,
    The flint youth.

Bonnet of black flint have I;
  Lo, the flint youth, he am I,
    The flint youth.

Clearest, purest flint the heart
Living strong within me—heart of flint;
  Lo, the flint youth, he am I,
    The flint youth.

Now the zig-zag lightnings four
    From me flash,
Striking and returning,
    From me flash;
  Lo, the flint youth, he am I,
    The flint youth.

There where'er the lightnings strike,
Into the ground they hurl the foe—
Ancient folk with evil charms,

</td></tr>
</table>

Yoya aiyinilch—kola,
  Pesh ashike ni shli—
                    E-na

Ka' sa-a narai,
Ka' binihotsitti shi ni shli—kola,
  Pesh ashike ni shli—
                    E-na

Pesh ashike ni shli—kola
Pesh ashike ni shli—ya-e.

One upon another, dashed to earth;
  Lo, the flint youth, he am I,
                    The flint youth.

Living evermore,
Feared of all forevermore,
  Lo, the flint youth, he am I,
                    The flint youth.

Lo, the flint youth, he am I,
                    The flint youth.

PRAYER BY THE GREAT WATERS

A First Visit of Navajos to the Sea

IN the winter of 1903 a small band of Navajos left their native deserts to come, at the invitation of some Californians, to a New-Year's festival at Pasadena. Such verdant country was never before seen by the Navajos. "Here might our flocks graze forever," they cried, as they looked with wonder on the green slopes and orange-laden trees of Southern California. The Indians were taken to the coast, to see for the first time the "Great Waters"—waters incredibly great, where "a man upon the shore could not see the farther side."

In reverent silence they gazed, while the chief stepped solemnly to the water's edge and with quiet prayer sprinkled sacred corn-pollen on each receding wave. Two priests followed, and stood absorbed in chant, while the rising tide washed up about their ankles. Then all the little band approached the water, praying and scattering their pollen-sacrifice.

"So much of water is there here," they prayed, "here where there seems no need. With us the need is great. As we give of our offering, so may there be given to us of these Great Waters."

Prayer by the Great Waters

"Two priests stood absorbed in chant, while the rising tide washed up about their ankles"

TRO HATAL

Song of the Rain-Chant

Sung and told by a Navajo "Chanter" (Medicine-Man) of Arizona

THE Navajo ceremonies are called "Chants." This is a song from the "Water, or Rain, Chant." The Navajos tell of the Male - Rain and of the Female - Rain. The Male-Rain is the storm, with thunder and lightning; the Female - Rain is the gentle shower. The two Rains meet on the mountains, and from their union springs all vegetation upon the earth.[1]

The Rain-Mountain is a distant mountain west of Zuñi, and it is the home of the Rain-Youth, one of the Divine Beings. The Rain-Youth made the rain-songs and gave them to the Navajos. This song tells of him with the rain-feathers in his hair, coming with the rain, down from the Rain-Mountain, through the corn, amid the song of swallows chirping with joy of the rain, and through the pollen which covers him, so that the Rain-Youth himself is hidden, and only a mist is seen. The Navajos say that it is well to be covered with holy pollen, for such pollen is an emblem of peace.

TRO HATAL	SONG OF THE RAIN-CHANT
Niye tinishten	Far as man can see,
Shichl tsha huiyish tin'shta—a-ye-na,	Comes the rain,
	Comes the rain with me.
Niltsan Dsichl-iye	From the Rain-Mount,
Biya ra-ashte,	Rain-Mount far away,
Shichl tsha huiyish tin'shta—a-ye-na,	Comes the rain,
	Comes the rain with me.
Tshi-natan a-tso-hiye	O'er the corn,
Betra-ko,	O'er the corn, tall corn,
Shichl tshahuiyish tin' shta—a-ye-na,	Comes the rain,
	Comes the rain with me.

[1] See " The Ceremonial of Hasjelti Dailjis," by James Stevenson. Extract from the Eighth Annual Report of the Bureau of American Ethnology, Washington, D. C.

Betra-ko
Ka' itsiniklizh-iye,
Ka' itahazla-ko,
    Shich*l* tsha huiyish ti*n*' shta—a-ye-na,

'Mid the lightnings,
'Mid the lightning zigzag,
'Mid the lightning flashing,
    Comes the rain,
    Comes the rain with me.

Betra-ko
Ka' trashjesh dotlizh-iye
Ka' enadetla-ko,
    Shich*l* tsha huiyish ti*n*' shta—a-ye-na,

'Mid the swallows,
'Mid the swallows blue
Chirping glad together,
    Comes the rain,
    Comes the rain with me.

Betra-ko
Tradetin-iye
Banga-toyishtini-ko,
    Shich*l* tsha huiyish ti*n*' shta—a-ye-na,

Through the pollen,
Through the pollen blest,
All in pollen hidden
    Comes the rain,
    Comes the rain with me.

Niye tinishte*n*
    Shich*l* tsha huiyish ti*n*' shta—a-ye-na.

Far as man can see
    Comes the rain,
    Comes the rain with me.

DSI*CH*LYIDJE HATAL

Song from the Ceremony of the Mountain-Chant

Sung and told by a Navajo "Chanter" (Medicine-Man) of Arizona

THE Holy Youth, Tsil*ch*ke Digini, loved a mortal maid, and to make her divine like himself, so that he might take her to wife, he sang holy songs over her. Thenceforth she was called Estsan Digini, The Holy Woman. Together the two gave these songs to the Navajos, to be used by them as a cure for sickness. During the ceremony of the mountain-chant, four runners are dressed to represent four holy beings— The Holy Youth, The Holy Woman, Alilorani (The Lightning Youth), and Digini-ossini (The Holy Believer).[1] The last two are The Holy Youth and The Holy Woman in other forms. These

---

[1] The translation of the last two names is of somewhat doubtful accuracy. According to Dr. Washington Matthews, "*Alili* means show, dance, or other single exhibition of the rites. It also means a wand or other sacred implement used in the rites." The mythical colored hoops for raising a storm are also referred to as *alili*. *Orani* may possibly be *hogani*, the "g" in the latter word being pronounced like the guttural "r."

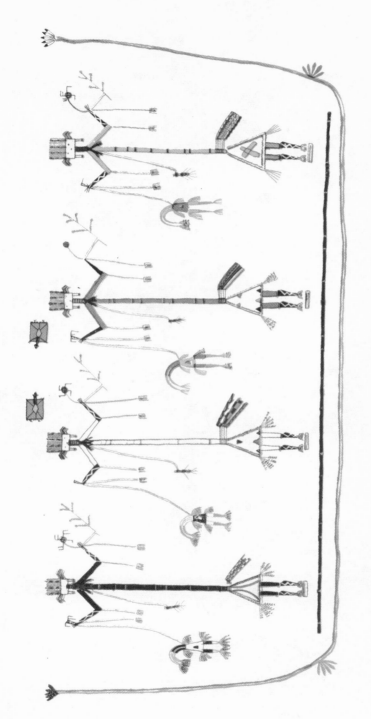

SACRED SAND-PICTURE

Sacred Sand-picture in the ceremony of the Mountain-Chant.

four runners carry sacred corn-meal in their pouches, to sprinkle upon medicine-men as a summons to attend the ceremony, each with his own songs and dances. At some part of the ceremony, one of the chanters (medicine-men) thus makes a sand-picture of the four Digini, or "Divine Ones," placing them from left to right: The Holy Youth, The Holy Woman, The Lightning Youth, and The Holy Believer. The sand-pictures[1] are made in this wise: Upon the floor of the hogan is spread fresh sand smoothed flat; then upon this background the medicine-man and his assistants make the symbolic figures, by sifting through thumb and finger colored powders ground from minerals and charcoal.

In the picture of the four Digini, the black streak at the bottom represents the hogan of The Holy Youth and The Holy Woman. Above the heads of the Divine Ones are the guardian bats of the hogan. A rainbow surrounds the picture, decked with sprays of prayer-feathers. Each figure stands upon a piece of rainbow, for it is upon the rainbow that the Divine Ones travel. Streaks of lightning are painted upon the legs, for lightning is the symbol of speed; around the neck hangs a whistle of eagle bone; while on the arms are bracelets[2] of eagle feathers, for the Divine Ones move swiftly, as with wings. The forms are naked except for the richly decorated sash and the "woman's belt." Their bodies are painted with clays of different colors. In the right hand each figure holds a pouch containing corn-meal, and in the left a small ceremonial basket and a sprig of spruce, which can be swallowed and drawn up again by those who have holy power. From the ears hang pendants of turquoise, and on the heads are five rain-feathers pointing upward towards the clouds. The medicine-men, while dressing the runners to represent the Divine Ones, chant the following song:

[1] Otherwise known as " dry-paintings."
[2] The bracelets are omitted, probably by error, from the accompanying sand-painting.

DSI*CH*LYIDJE HATAL	SONG FROM THE MOUNTAIN-CHANT
Baíyajíltríyish,	Thereof he telleth.
Tsílchke dígíni, Baíyajíltríyish,	Now of the Holy Youth, Thereof he telleth.
Ke-pa-nashjíni, Baíyajíltríyish,	Moccasins decked with black, Thereof he telleth.
Kla-pa-naskan-a, Baíyajíltríyishí,	And richly broidered dress, Thereof he telleth.
Ka' ka pa-stran-a, Baíyajíltríyish,	Arm-bands of eagle feathers, Thereof he telleth.
Níltsan atsoz-í, Baíyajíltríyish,	And now the rain-plumes, Thereof he telleth.
Níltsan-bekan-a, Baíyajíltríyish,	Now of the Male-Rain,[1] Thereof he telleth.
Ka' bí datro-e, Baíyajíltríyish,	Now of the rain-drops fallen, Thereof he telleth.
Sa-a naraï, Baíyajíltríyish,	Now of Unending Life, Thereof he telleth.
Bíke hozhoni, Baíyajíltríyish,	Now of Unchanging Joy, Thereof he telleth.
Baíyajíltríyish,[2]	Thereof he telleth.

[1] The Male-Rain is the heavy storm-rain, with lightning and thunder; the Female-Rain is the gentle shower. Both kinds of rain are prized in sickness for their cooling power.

[2] A second stanza follows, identical with the first, except that the word *estsan* (woman) takes the place of *tsílchke* (youth) and the word Níltsan-baad (female-rain) that of Níltsanbekan (male-rain). In the second stanza the refrain *baíyajíltríyish* is to be translated " thereof she telleth."

DINNI-E SIN

Hunting-Song

Sung and told by Navajos, near Fort Defiance, Arizona

ALL animals of the chase are the herds of Hastyeyalti, God of Sunrise. Hastyeyalti is god of game, and he made the hunting-songs and gave them to the Navajos. In the old days, before they were shepherds, the Navajos lived by hunting. The Navajo hunter sits quite still and chants a song, and the game comes straight to him.[1] When the animal is near enough, the hunter shoots him through the heart. The Navajos say that the deer like the song of the hunter, and come from all directions to hear it.

When a man starts to hunt he first prays to Hastyeyalti, then he sings a holy song to the god, and then he sings the hunting-songs. If he miss a word or make a mistake in the song he will have ill luck. But if his song be without error of any kind he will surely kill something.

In this song the hunter likens himself to the beautiful black-bird loved by the deer. The Navajos say that this bird alights on the animals and sometimes tries to make its nest between the horns. The refrain of the song tells of the coming of the deer—how he makes a trail from the top of Black Mountain down through the fair meadows, how he comes through the dew-drops and the pollen of the flowers, and then how, startled at sight of the hunter,

---

[1] This can readily be believed, for the Indian can be absolutely immovable. The measured chant attracts the animals, who, always curious, first come to find out what is the sound, and are then almost hypnotized, as it were, by the monotony and rhythm of the chanting. A young Navajo who had been educated away from the reservation told the recorder that he had been taught to look upon the ways of his people as foolish and superstitious. He did not believe in what the Navajos told him of their hunting. One day an old uncle took him to hunt. The two men sat motionless while the uncle chanted. Then the young man saw that the Navajos had spoken truly, for the deer walked straight to the hunters and fell their easy prey. " Since then," declared the young man, " I believe that the old people have wisdom that the white men do not always know about." Pueblo Indians say that before they start on the hunt they sing, bending every thought on prayerful wish for success. While they sing, the distant deer gather in council and choose to whom each will fall. To those who have been most devout in singing will the animals go. This idea is held by the Navajos also, as is shown in this song. Indians believe in man's power to draw to himself or to bring about that upon which he fixes his mind in song and prayer.

he stamps and turns to run. But the man kills him, and will kill yet many another, for he is lucky and blessed in hunting. The Navajos say that the male deer always starts with the left foreleg, the female with the right. This is an ancient song made by the god Hastyeyalti.

DINNI-E SIN	HUNTING-SONG
Ye shakaikatal, i-ne-yanga, Ye shakaikatal, ai-ye-lo, Ye shakaikatal, i-ne-yanga.	Comes the deer to my singing, Comes the deer to my song, Comes the deer to my singing.
Ka' aiyash-te tilyilch-ye Shini shlini ko-lo, Ye shakaikatal, i-ne yanga	He, the blackbird, he am I, Bird beloved of the wild deer. Comes the deer to my singing.
Dsichl-tilyilch-iye Bakashte Ka' ta-adetin 'shte lo, Ye shakaikatal, i-ne yanga	From the Mountain Black, From the summit, Down the trail, coming, coming now, Comes the deer to my singing.
Tshilatra hozhoni-ye Bitra 'shte lo, Ye shakaikatal, i-ne yanga	Through the blossoms, Through the flowers, coming, coming now, Comes the deer to my singing.
Bi datro-iye Bitra 'shte lo, Ye shakaikatal, i-ne yanga	Though the flower dew-drops, Coming, coming now, Comes the deer to my singing.
Ka' bi tradetin-iye Bitra 'shte lo, Ye shakaikatal, i-ne yanga	Through the pollen, flower pollen, Coming, coming now, Comes the deer to my singing.
Dinnitshe-bekan-iye Bitzil-le deshklashdji-lo Ye shakaikatal, i-ne yanga	Starting with his left fore-foot, Stamping, turns the frightened deer Comes the deer to my singing.
Bisedje Ka' shinosin-ku lo, Ye shakaikatal, i-ne yanga	Quarry mine, blessed am I In the luck of the chase. Comes the deer to my singing.
Ye shakaikatal, i-ne-yanga. Ye shakaikatal, ai-ye-lo Ye shakaikatal, i-ne-yanga.	Comes the deer to my singing, Comes the deer to my song, Comes the deer to my singing.

A second stanza follows, identical with the first, except that the word *baad* (female) takes the place of *bekan* (male), and the word *deshnash* (right) that of *deshklashdji* (left.)

Offering Sacred Corn-pollen on the Waters

NAESTSAN BIYIN

Song of the Earth

(Hozhonji-Song)

IN a ceremony for the healing of the sick, the Navajos sing of all things in the world, declaring them perfect as when first made—the heavens, winds, clouds, rain, lightning, rainbow, sun, moon, stars; the earth, the mountains, the corn, and all the growing things; in sequence of holy songs all forms of life are pronounced beautiful and good.

These songs are sung over the sick man, and the sufferer is thus placed in a perfect world, so that new and perfect life comes to him also. He is reborn into a state of wholeness. Thereafter he may wear a turquoise or bit of shell tied in his hair as a sign of his new birth.

This song is not a medicine-song but a Hozhonji-song. But like the medicine ceremony, it declares all things beautiful. It is highly revered and has great power to bless. It is a benediction on the created world. It tells how all things go in pairs, bending towards each other, joining and helping one another, as the heavens help the earth with rain.

Though the Navajos, like the Pueblos, have corn of many colors, white corn and yellow corn are the two kinds most often used emblematically in the songs. Of the white corn was made, in the beginning, First-Man, and of the yellow corn, First-Woman. The white corn is looked upon as male, and the yellow corn as female. Also, white is the symbolic color of the east, and yellow of the west.

"The Ripener" is he that makes the corn ripe. This is an insect that flies among the plants, possibly the wild bee. The Navajos say: "It has spotted wings, three on each side. It makes a very pretty noise and comes in the night-time. It eats corn-pollen and only comes when the corn is ripening."

The idea that, in nature, contrasting elements are complements and helpmates of one another is carried in the end of the song to the transcendent point of Everlasting Life, and the Happiness of All Things. Besides this, the earth or the sun is sometimes symbolically called *Sa-a narai* (Everlasting Life), and the sky or the moon, *Bike hozhoni* (Happiness of All Things, or Universal Blessedness).

Sometimes, after singing this Hozhonji-song, the Navajo sprinkles sacred pollen on the ground, calling the earth "Mother," and then scatters pollen upward to the sky, calling the heavens "Father."

NAESTSAN BIYIN	SONG OF THE EARTH (Hozhonji-Song)
Daltso hozhoni,	All is beautiful,
Daltso hozho'ka',	All is beautiful,
Daltso hozhoni.	All is beautiful, indeed.
Naestsan-iye,	Now the Mother Earth
Yatilyilch-iye,	And the Father Sky,
Pilch ka' altsin sella	Meeting, joining one another,
Ho-ushte-hiye.	Helpmates ever, they.
Daltso hozhoni,	All is beautiful,
Daltso hozho'ka',	All is beautiful,
Daltso hozhoni.	All is beautiful, indeed.
Sisnajinni-ye,	Sisnajinni,
Tsodsichl-iye,	Tsodsichl,
Pilch ka' altsin sella	Meeting, joining one another,
Ho-ushte-hiye.	Helpmates ever, they.
Daltso hozhoni.	All is beautiful,
Daltso hozho'ka',	All is beautiful,
Daltso hozhoni.	All is beautiful, indeed.
Ka' Doko-oslid-iye,	Now Doko-oslid
Ka' Depenitsa-ye,	And Depenitsa,
Pilch ka' altsin sella	Meeting, joining one another,
Ho-ushte-hiye.	Helpmates ever, they.
Daltso hozhoni,	All is beautiful,
Daltso hozho'ka',	All is beautiful,
Daltso hozhoni.	All is beautiful, indeed.
Ka' Tshalyilch,	And the night of darkness
Hayolkatli-ye,	And the dawn of light,
Pilch ka' altsin sella	Meeting, joining one another,
Ho-ushte-hiye.	Helpmates ever, they.

NAVAJO

Daĭtso hozhoni,
Daĭtso hozho'ka',
Daĭtso hozhoni.

All is beautiful,
All is beautiful,
All is beautiful, indeed.

Ka' Hastyeyalti-ye,
Ka' Hastyehogani-ye,
  Pĭlch ka' altsin sella
  Ho-ushte-hiye.
    Daĭtso hozhoni,
    Daĭtso hozho'ka',
    Daĭtso hozhoni.

Now Hastyeyalti
And Hastyehogan
  Meeting, joining one another,
  Helpmates ever, they.
    All is beautiful,
    All is beautiful,
    All is beautiful, indeed.

Ka' natan-alchkaï-ye,
Ka' natan-alchtsoï-ye,
  Pĭlch ka' altsin sella
  Ho-ushte-hiye.
    Daĭtso hozhoni,
    Daĭtso hozho'ka',
    Daĭtso hozhoni.

And the white corn
And the yellow corn,
  Meeting, joining one another,
  Helpmates ever, they.
    All is beautiful,
    All is beautiful,
    All is beautiful, indeed.

Tradetin-iye,
Anĭlchtani-ye,
  Pĭlch ka' altsin sella
  Ho-ushte-hiye.
    Daĭtso hozhoni,
    Daĭtso hozho'ka',
    Daĭtso hozhoni.

And the corn-pollen
And the Ripener,
  Meeting, joining one another,
  Helpmates ever, they.
    All is beautiful,
    All is beautiful,
    All is beautiful, indeed.

Ka' sa-a naraï,
Ka' bike hozhoni-ye,
  Pĭlch ka' altsin sella
  Ho-ushte-hiye.
    Daĭtso hozhoni,
    Daĭtso hozho'ka',
    Daĭtso hozhoni.

Life-that-never-passeth,
Happiness-of-all-things,
  Meeting, joining one another,
  Helpmates ever, they.
    All is beautiful,
    All is beautiful,
    All is beautiful, indeed.

    Daĭtso hozhoni,
    Daĭtso hozho'ka',
    Daĭtso hozhoni.

    Now all is beautiful,
    All is beautiful,
    All is beautiful, indeed.

Dsichl Biyin

Dsichl nant-e-tai,....
Chief of all mountains,

Pi-ki yo-......ye,
Thi-ther go....... o,

Sa-a na-rai,.
Living for-ev-er,

Pi-ki yo-......ye,
Thither go....... o,

Bi-ke ho-zho-ni,
Blessings be-stow-ing,

Pi-ki yo-....ye,
Thither go....... o,

Tso-ya shich ni........la!
Calling me "Son, my son."

[375]

Dsichl Biyin

Pi-Ki   i   ya
Thi-ther   go   I,

Pi-Ki   ya ya'
Thi-ther   go   I!

Ko la   ra   ne

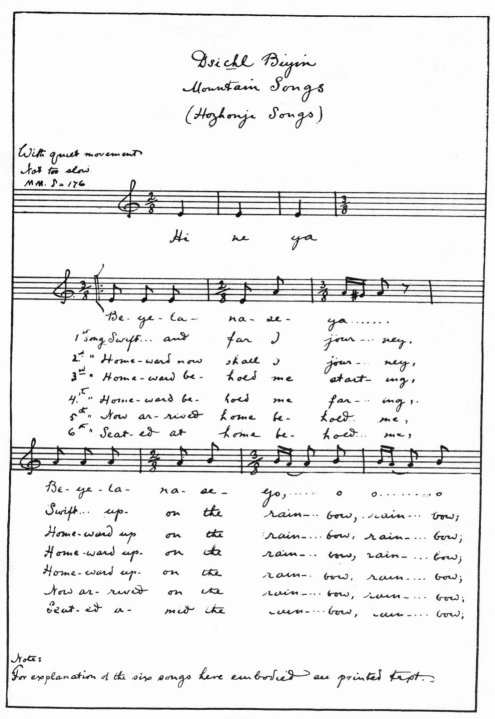

Dsichl Biyin
Mountain Songs
(Hozhonji Songs)

Note:
For explanation of the six songs here embodied see printed text.

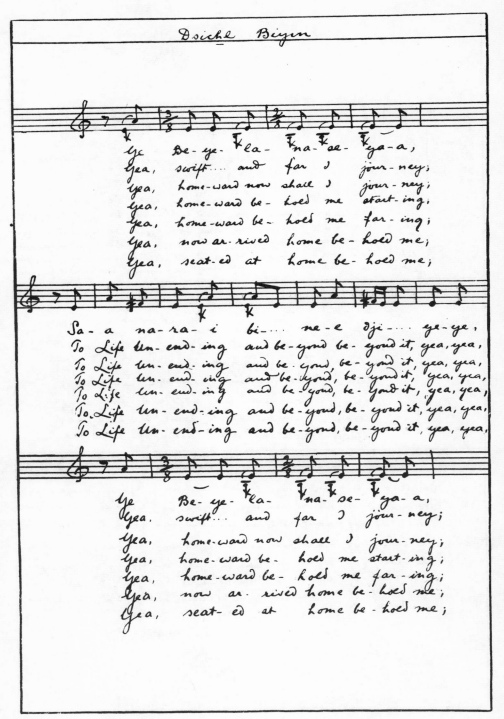

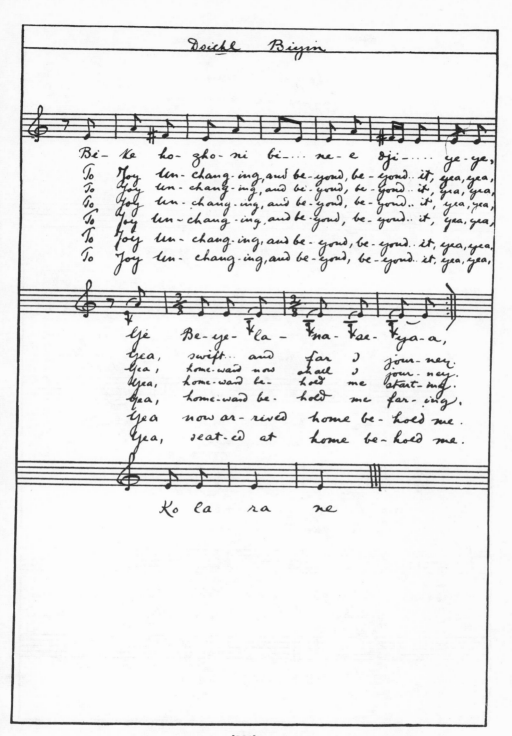

Dsichl Biyin

Bi—ke ho—zho—ni bi—...ne—e dji—...ye—ye,
To Joy un—chang-ing, and be-yond, be-yond it, yea, yea,
To Joy un—chang-ing, and be-yond, be-yond it, yea, yea,
So Joy un—chang-ing, and be-yond, be-yond.. it, yea, yea,
To Joy un—chang-ing, and be-yond, be-yond.. it, yea, yea,
To Joy un—chang-ing, and be-yond, be-yond.. it, yea, yea,
To Joy un—chang-ing, and be-yond, be-yond.. it, yea, yea,

Ye Be-ye-la—na-tse-tya-a,
Yea, swift... and far I jour-ney.
Yea, home-ward now shall I jour-ney.
Yea, home-ward be-hold me start-ing.
Yea, home-ward be-hold me far-ing.
Yea now ar-rived home be-hold me.
Yea, seat-ed at home be-hold me.

Ko la ra ne

[381]

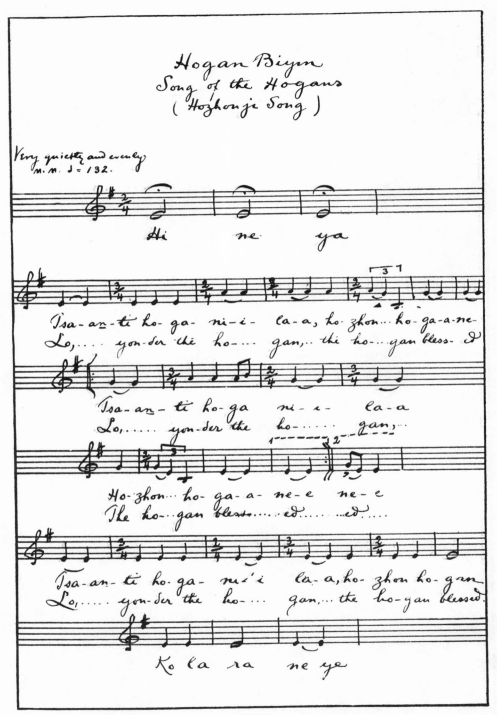

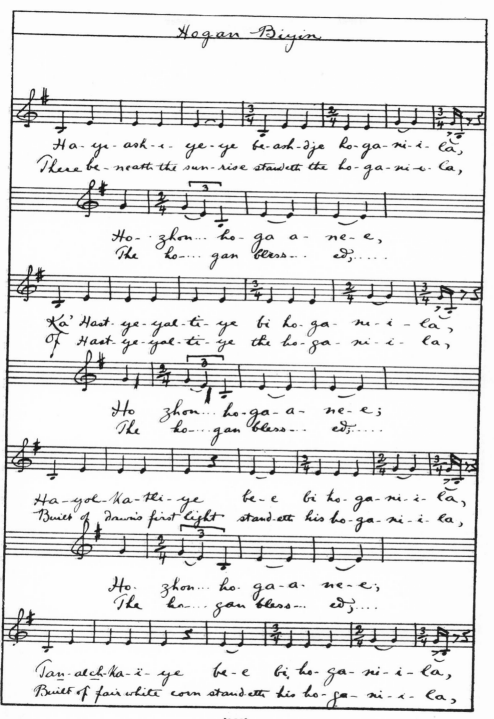

Hogan Biyin

Ha - ye - ash - i - ye - ye be-ash-dje ho-ga-ni-i-la,
There be-neath the sun-rise standeth the ho-ga-ni-i-la,

Ho - zhon... ho - ga - a - ne - e,
The ho-... gan bless... ed,.....

Ka' Hast-ye-yal-ti-ye bi ho-ga-ni-i-la,
Of Hast-ye-yal-ti-ye the ho-ga-ni-i-la,

Ho zhon... ho-ga-a- ne- e;
The ho-...gan bless... ed;.....

Ha-yol-ka-tli-ye be-e bi ho-ga-ni-i-la,
Built of dawn's first light stand-eth his ho-ga-ni-i-la,

Ho. zhon... ho. ga-a. ne-e;
The ho...gan bless... ed;....

Tan-alch-ka-i-ye be-e bi ho-ga-ni-i-la,
Built of fair white corn stand-eth his ho-ga-ni-i-la,

Hogan Biyin

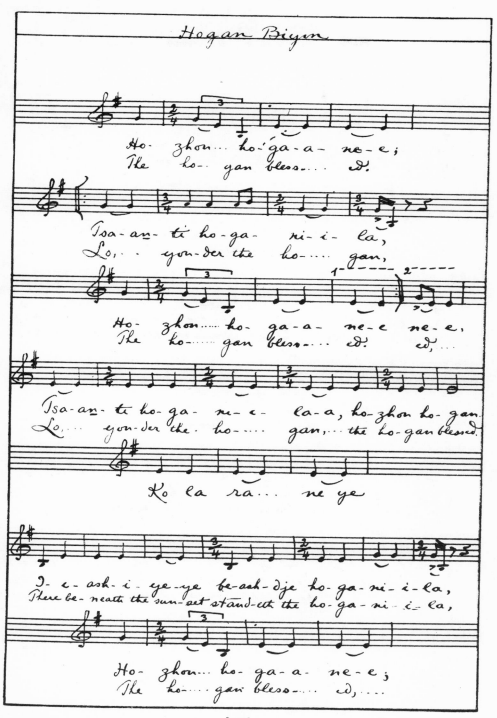

Hogan Biyin

Ho- zhon.... ho-'ga-a- ne - e;
The ho-- gan bless-.... ed.

Tsa-a<u>n</u>- ti ho-ga- ni - i - la,
Lo,.. yon-der the ho-..... gan,

Ho- zhon..... ho- ga-a- ne-e ne-e,
The ho-..... gan bless-.... ed. ed,...

Tsa-a<u>n</u>- ti ho-ga- ni-e- la-a, ho-zhon ho-gan.
Lo,... yon-der the. ho-..... gan,... the ho-gan blessed.

Ko la ra... ne ye

I- e- ash- i- ye- ye be-ash-dje ho-ga-ni-i-la,
There be-neath the sun-set stand-eth the ho-ga-ni-i-la,

Ho- zhon... ho- ga-a- ne-e;
The ho-.... gan bless-.... ed,....

Hogan Biyin

Ka' Hast-ye-ho-ga-ni bi ho-ga-   ni-e la,
Of Hast-ye-ho-ga-ni the ho-ga- ni-i- la,

Ho   zhon ho-ga-a-   ne-e;
The ho----gan bless----ed;....

Na-ho-tso-ï- ye   be-e bi ho-ga-ni-i-la;
Built of af- ter- glow stand-eth his ho-ga-ni-i-la,

Ho   zhon---ho-ga-a-   ne-e;
The   ho---gan bless--- ed;....

Tsan-alch-tso-ï-ye   be-e   bi ho-ga-ni-i-la,
Built of yel-low-corn stand-eth his ho-ga-ni-i-la,

Ho zhon---ho-ga-a-   ne-e;
The   ho---gan bless- ed;....

Ne-Kliz il-tsas-sa-ï-ye   be-e bi ho-ga-ni-i-la,
Built of gems and shin-ing shells stand-eth his ho-ga-ni-i-la,

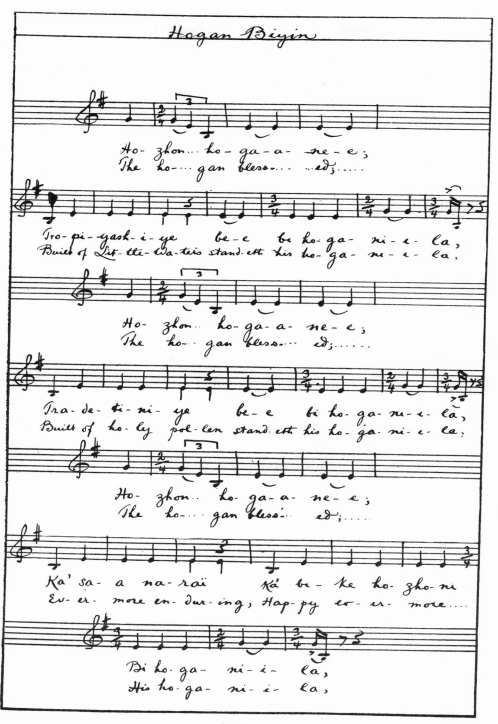

Hogan Biyin

Hogan Biyin

Ho zhon... ho- ga- a- ne- e,
The ho-----gan bless---- ed,.....

Tsa-an- ti ho- ga--- ni- i- la,
Lo,..... yon-der the ho------ gan,

Ho zhon... ho- ga-a- ne- e, ne- e,
The ho-----gan bless---- ed,.....- ed, ...

Tsa-an- ti ho- ga- ni- i- la-a ho-zhon ho-gan.
Lo,..... yon-der the ho------ gan,.... the ho-gan blessed

Ko la ra...... ne

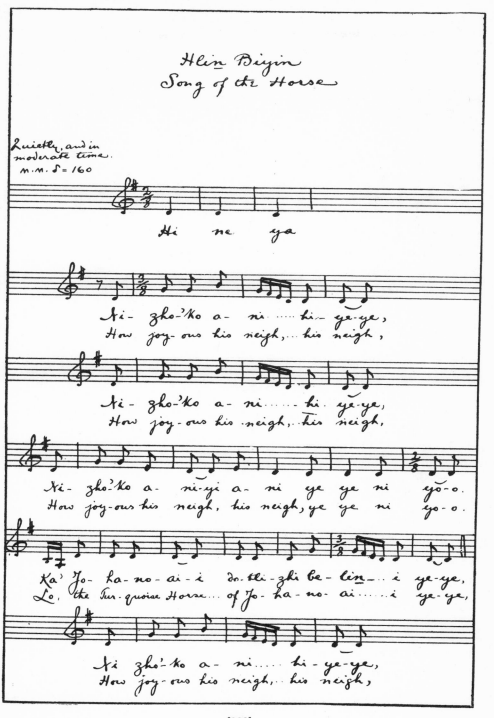

Hlin Biyin

Ni-zho'-ko a-ni-yi a-ni ye ye ni yo-o
How joy-ous his neigh, his neigh, ye ye ni yo-o.

Got-te ba-hoo-tiel-i tsi ba-Kai yi-ki yi,
There on pre-cious hides out-spread .... stand---eth he; ....

Ni-zho'-ko a-ni .... hi-ye-ye,
How joy-ous his neigh, .. his neigh, ..

Ni-zho'-ko a-ni-yi a-ni ye ye ni yo-o.
How joy-ous his neigh, .. his neigh, ye ye ni yo-o.

Tshi-la-tra ho-zho-ni be-e jin-ichl-tan la-Ki yi
There on tips of fair fresh flowrs feed-eth feed-eth he; ..

Ni-zho'-ko a-ni hi-ye-ye
How joy-ous his neigh, his neigh.

Ni-zho'-ko a-ni-yi a-ni ye ye ni yo-o.
How joy ous his neigh, his neigh, ye ye ni yo-o.

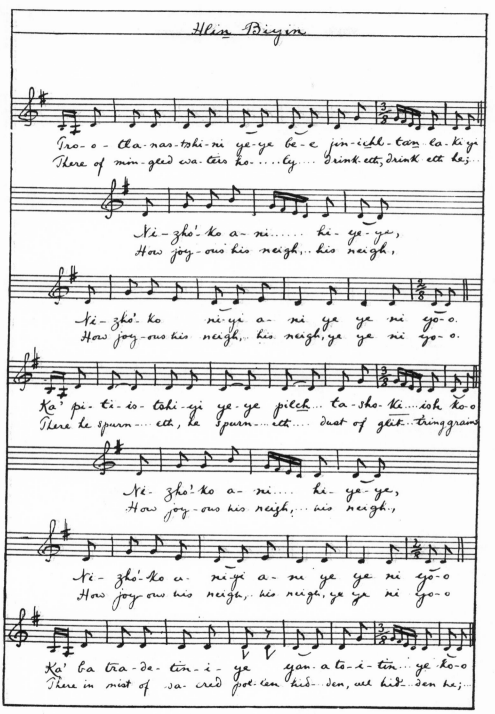

Hlin Biyin

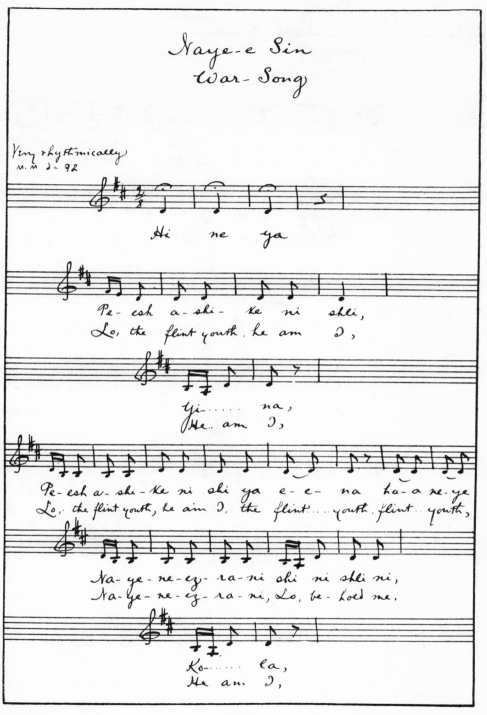

Naye-e Sin
War-Song

Naye-e Sin

[394]

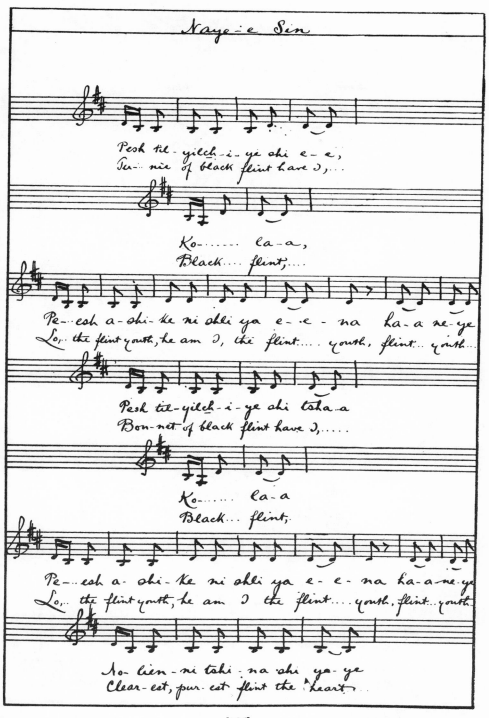

Naye-e Sin

Naye-e Sin

Shi-ye-ki ho-lon-e—
Liv-ing strong with-in me—

Ko——— la-a
Heart of flint;

Pe—esh a-shi-ke ni shli ya e-e-na ha-a ne-ye
Lo,.. the flint youth, he am I, the flint.. youth, flint.. youth..

Ka'i-tai-ni-Kli-zhi- ye
Now the zig-zag light-nings four

Sin i-kwo-o si-tan na-ha-tilch....
From me flash,... strik-ing and re-turn-ing;

Ko——— la-a,
From me flash;...

Pe—esh a-shi-ke ni shli ya e-e na ha-a ne-ye
Lo,.. the flint youth, he am I, the flint.. youth, flint.. youth..

Naye-e Sin

Naye-e Sin.

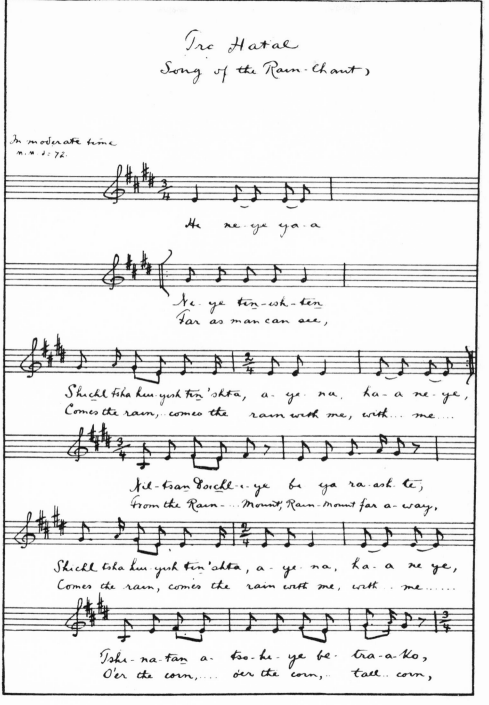

Tro Hatal

Skichl tsha hui yish tin'shta, a-ye-na, ha-a ne-ye,
Comes the rain, comes the rain with me, with... me...

Be-tra-ko..... Ka' i- tai-ni-Klizh-i-ye,
'Mid the light-nings, 'mid the light-nings zig-zag,

Ka' i-ta-haz-la-ye-Ko,
'Mid the light-nings flash-ing,

Skichl tsha hui yish tin'shta, a-ye-na, ha-a ne-ye,
Comes the rain,... comes the rain with me, with.... me.....

Be-tra-ko...... Ka' trash-jesh do-tlizh-i-ye.
'Mid the swal-lows, 'mid the swal-lows, swal-lows blue

Ka' e-na-det-la-a-ko
Chirp-ing glad to-ge----ther,

Skichl tsha hui yish tin'shta, a-ye-na, ha-a ne-ye,
Comes the rain,... comes the rain with me, with... me......

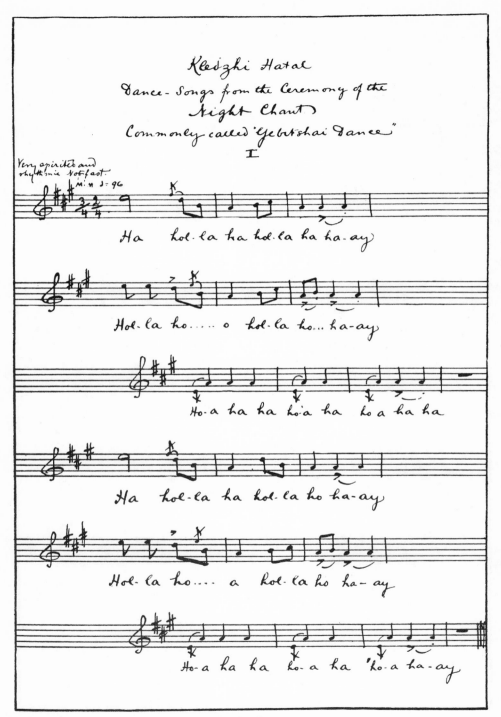

Kledzhi Hatal
II

Kledzhi Hatal

I...hi o i...hi ho

Ho ho ho ho ho ho ho hi yi

Ha..pi hi-yi hiya ho ho yong o

Ha pi hi-yi hiya ho o yong

Hi ya ho o..yong a ho li......i ho ho i hi he

I............hi-i-yi ho li ho li ho..li...i

Ho li....i ho ho i hi hi

[405]

Doìchlyìdje Hatal

Song from the Ceremony of the Mountain Chant

This song is sung in two stanzas, identical, except that the first stanza
pertains to the male divinity, the second, to the female. The differing words
are bracketed in the text.

M.M. ♩ = 58

Hi ne yan-ga

Ai ya ai... ya ai ye ye ye

Bai-ya-jil- tri-yish,
There-of {he (she)} tel-leth,
2nd stanza

ai ya ai.....ya ai ye ye ye

Bai-ya-jil- trish-dja,
There-of {he (she)} tel-leth,

Ai ya ai ye ye ne yo o

[408]

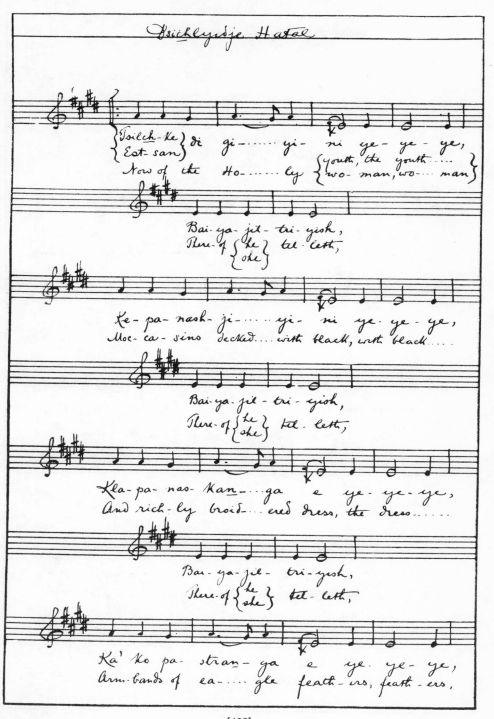

Dsichlyidye Hatál

Sa-a na-raï...... e ye-ye-ye,
Now of Un-end.....ing Life, of Life....

Bai-ya-jil-tri-yish,
There-of {he she} til-leth,

Bi-ke ho-zho.......... ni ye ye ye,
Now of Un-chang...ing Joy, of Joy....

Bai-ya-jil-tri-yish,
There-of {he she} til-leth,

Ai ya e ye ye ni yo o

Ai ya ai....ya ai ye ye ye,

Bai-ya-jil-tri-yish,
There-of {he she} til-leth,

[412]

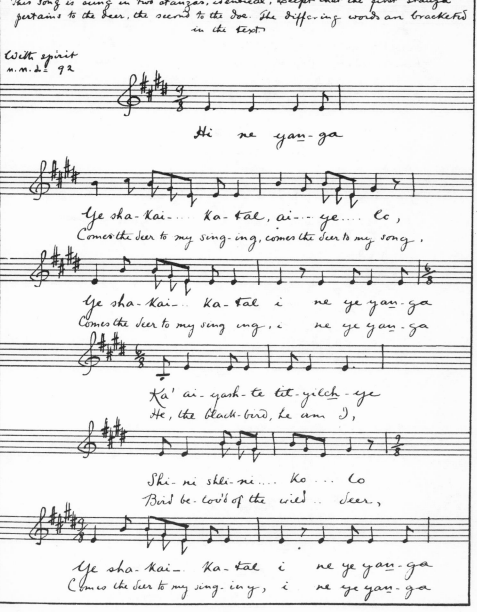

[413]

Dinni-e Sin

Dsichl-ta-yilch-i-ye   ba-kash-te-ye Ka'ta-a-de-
From the Mountain Black,   from the summits, down the trail....

ti-ni....'shte.... ĕo,
Com-ing.. com-ing now,

Ye sha-kai-.... ka-tal i   ne ye yan-ga
Comes the deer to my sing-ing, i   ne ye yan-ga

Tohi-la-tra ho- zho-ni-ye bi-
Thro' the blos-soms, thro' the flow-ers,

tra-a...'shte... ĕo,
Com-ing.. com-ing now,

Ye sha-kai-.... ka-tal i   ne ye yan-ga
Comes the deer to my sing-ing, i   ne ye yan-ga

Bi da-tro-i- ye bi-
Thro' the flow-er dew-drops,

[415]

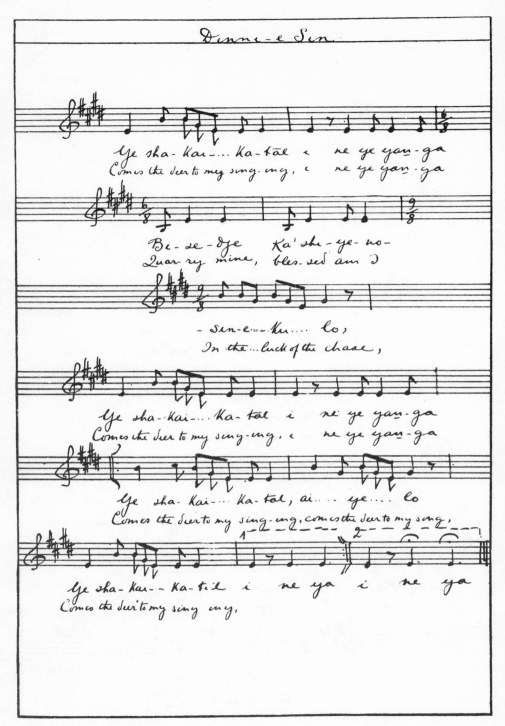

[416]

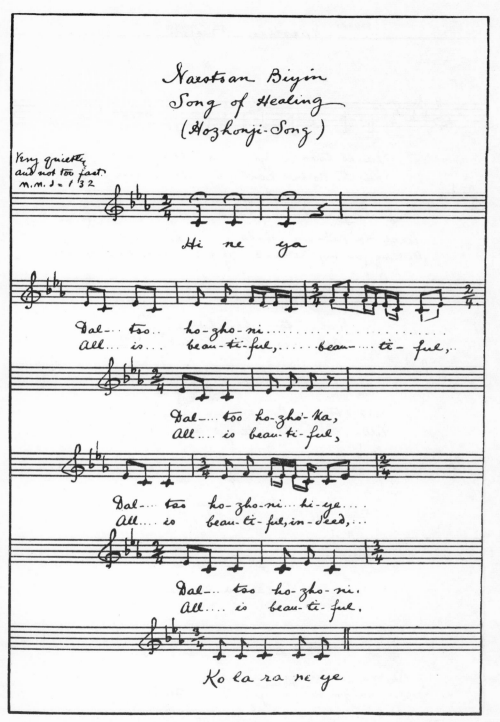

Naestian Biyin

Na - es - tsan - e - ye ... ya - til - yilch - i ye
Now the Mo - ther Earth, and the fa - ther Sky,

Pilch Ka' alt - sin sel - la.   Lo - ush - te hi ye ....
Meet - ing, join - ing one an - o - ther,   help - mates ev - er, they, ...

Dal - ... too ho - zho' Ka;'
All - ... is beau - ti - ful,

Dal - ... too   ho - zho - ni .... hi - ye, .
All ... is   beau - ti - ful, in - ... deed, ...

Dal - ... too ho - zho - ne .
All ... is beau - ti - ful.

Ko la za - ni ye

Ses - na - jin - ni - ye ye, Tso - dsich - i - ye,
Sis - na - jin - ni - ye - ye, Tso - ... dsich - i - ye,

[418]

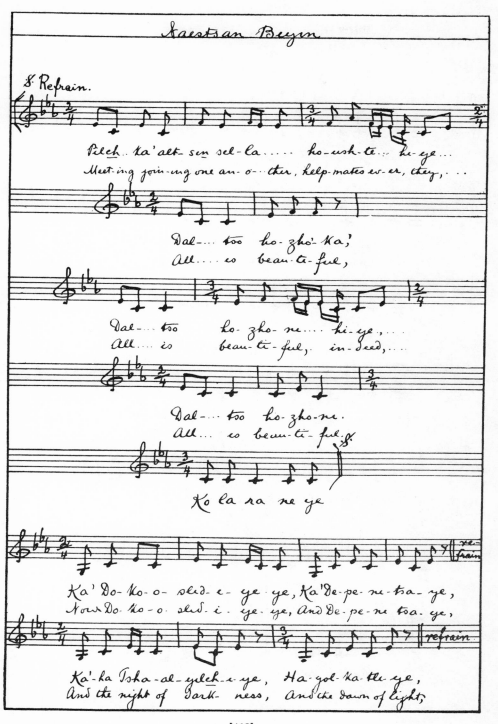

[419]

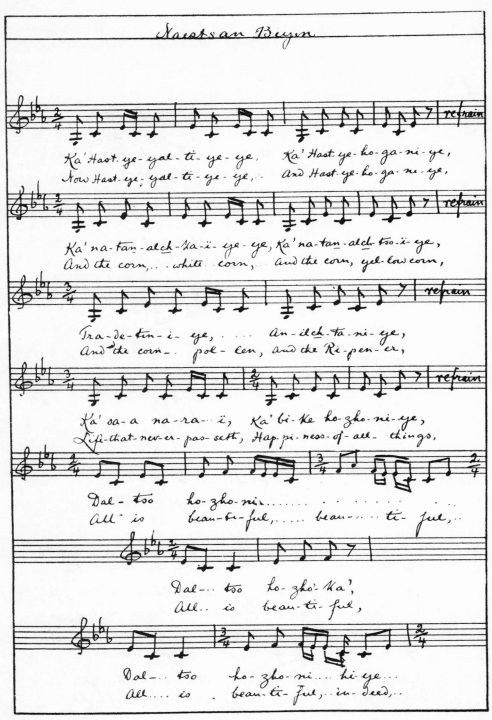

[420]

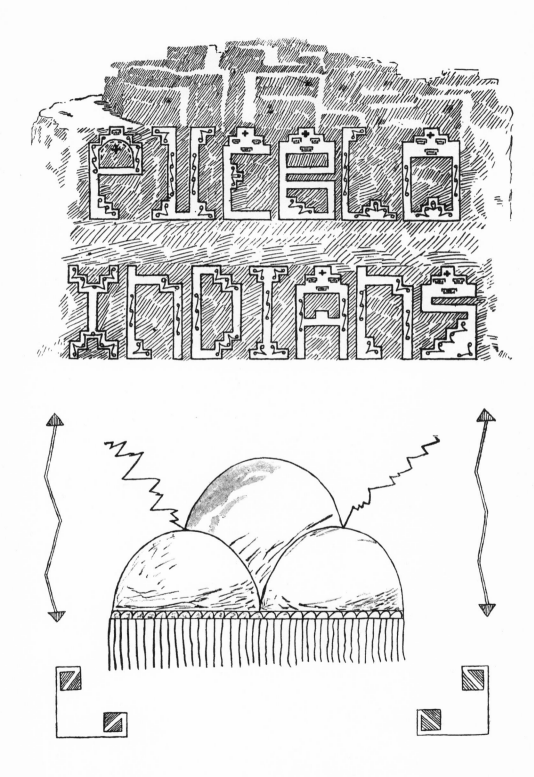

PUEBLO INDIANS TITLE-PAGE

The design at the bottom of the page is a symbolic figure which represents in conventionalized form clouds, lightning, and falling rain. The drawing, made free-hand, is by Gashhoienim, a Hopi Indian girl.

The lettering and decorations are by Hinook Mahiwi Kilinaka (Angel De Cora). Each letter is composed of the terraced cloud-form, typical of Southwestern Indian designs. Behind the words "Pueblo Indians" is seen a suggestion of a pueblo crowning a steep mesa. On each side of the cloud-design are lightning arrows. The page speaks of the village people, in whose agricultural life the great necessity is rain.

THE PUEBLO INDIANS

"P UEBLO" is a Spanish word meaning *town*, and is used to designate those Indians who live in villages or cities. Ancient Indian towns still inhabited, and ruins of yet older cities, lie strewn throughout New Mexico and Arizona, the home of the Pueblo people. Though the natives of the different Pueblos are of different linguistic stock, yet they closely resemble one another in their manner of life and in their thought.

The Pueblo Indians have ever been a peaceful agricultural folk, subsisting on the corn, vegetables, and fruits which by dint of ceaseless toil they force from the arid land. They have their own peculiar methods of desert-agriculture and their own system of irrigation.

Rumors of the wealth and splendor of the Indian towns attracted the Spanish explorers of the sixteenth century. Over the deserts marched the weary invaders, only to find a simple folk living as now in villages of stone and adobe. The Spaniards subdued the Pueblos and controlled them till, in the year 1680, the villages rose in concerted rebellion and drove out the hated conquerors.

The Pueblo Indians have attained to a very high grade of culture on the primitive plane. They excel in their own ancient industries, being skilled potters, weavers, basket-makers, and builders. Also they have in crude form veritable musical, poetic, and dramatic art. As with all Indians, religion is here closely interwoven with art and industry and with daily living. But with the Pueblo Indians, religious observance is perhaps more elaborately ceremonial than with most tribes. The Pueblos are rich in mythology and tradition, and their simple village life is framed in ancient customs both interesting and poetic. Symbol begins, for these Indians, with the hour of birth. In some villages it is the custom that the new-

[425]

born child shall not behold the outside world until, after a stated number of days, it is carried forth at dawn to see its father, the sun. As the first rays shine upon the child, prayers are uttered for the new life, while over the little one are solemnly repeated its newly given names. Thus at birth does the Pueblo Indian first look upon the world at birth of day. Existence, for him, begins, unfolds, and ends with symbol that is the very poetry of life itself.

The religion of this desert-dwelling, agricultural people expresses the supreme need — rain. Song and ceremony are one long invocation for the life-producing waters. Hard must the Pueblo Indian work, struggling against drought and sand-storm to procure the corn which is his sustenance.

Of these village-dwellers the Spanish conquerors narrated, "They have the finest persons of any people we saw." They are small and brown, delicate of feature, courteous of manner, gentle and refined. The native dress has beauty and charm, and is perfectly adapted to the climate and to the life of the people. But it is passing away before the effort to force all things Anglo-Saxon upon this unaggressive, beauty-loving folk.

The peaceful disposition of the Pueblo Indians and their native ancient systems of civic government have made of their villages well-ordered, thrifty, and industrious communities. The white visitor learns many a simple lesson from the life of these most ancient inhabited towns of the United States, the pueblos of the Southwest.

Zuni Indians

ZUÑI TITLE-PAGE

The designs are Zuñi pottery patterns. Painted by Ema-liya,
a Zuñi girl. The Zuñis, like most Pueblo Indians, are skilled
potters.
The lettering is by Hinook Mahiwi Kilinaka (Angel De Cora).

ZUÑI

ZUÑI is one of the most famed of all Pueblos. It is now generally agreed that the Seven Cities of Cibola, chronicled by the Spanish discoverers, were identical with the habitations of the Zuñi people. The pueblo lies on the level plain near an arm of the Little Colorado River. Around it rise the steep buttes and table-lands of New Mexico. To the east stands the great mesa[1] "To'yallanne,"[2] the sacred mountain of the Zuñis, ever hallowed by tradition and prayerful pilgrimage. Corn is the main sustenance of the Pueblo people. It is ground by the women in stone grinding-troughs, or "metates." These consist of a flat stone slab which is set into the floor of the house at a slight angle, and encompassed by stone gutters to receive the ground particles.

The corn is placed on the stone and is ground by rubbing over it another cubelike stone. The woman kneels to the work and sways back and forth with rhythmic swing. As she grinds she sings. There are usually two or three metates in each house, and two or three women often grind and sing together. Sometimes a woman will invite many others to her house to grind, spreading for her guests a mid-day feast. The visitors grind the corn of

NOTE FOR PRONUNCIATION OF ZUÑI TEXT

While in many Indian languages there are sounds not exactly the same as in the corresponding ones of European tongues, in the Zuñi occur sounds that have no counterpart at all in European languages. Such sounds, therefore, can be expressed by the Roman alphabet approximately only.

Unless otherwise specified, vowels have the Continental sound, and consonants the English.

[1] Table-land—plateau.
[2] According to Mrs. M. C. Stevenson, "Towa - Yallanne" (Corn - Mountain); according to Mr. Frank Cushing, "Toyalane" (Thunder-Mountain).

their hostess, taking their places in turn at the metates. Those who are resting swell the chorus of the workers, and the flutelike voices rise high and clear over the rhythmic scraping of the stones. In Zuñi, at such gatherings, the youths sometimes sing, or play the flute and drum, while the maidens ply the stones, and when the grinding is done the maidens dance.

The Zuñi grinding-songs here offered are old traditional songs. Two were sung by women whose white hair and quavering voices told of wellnigh fourscore years. All the songs were contributed by persons high in authority in the village, whose traditional conservatism forbids the mention of their names.

OCKAYA

Corn-Grinding Songs

I

OCKAYA	CORN-GRINDING SONG
Elu homa	O, my lovely mountain,
Yallanne !	To'yallanne !
Elu homa	O, my lovely mountain,
Yallanne !	To'yallanne !
Yallanne !	To'yallanne !
Awehlwia' kwai-i,	High up in the sky,
Imuna kwagia,	See Rain-Makers seated,
Lonan-eshto 'wiyane,	Hither come the rain-clouds now,
He-ya, ha-ya, he-ya !	He-ya, ha-ya, he-ya !
Liwamani	Behold, yonder
Iyuteapa	All will soon be abloom
Awiyane,	Where the flowers spring—
Hawilana litla.	Tall shall grow the youthful corn-plants.

Note.—Mrs. Stevenson, of the Bureau of American Ethnology in Washington, says that the Rain-Makers are the spirits of the dead Zuñis, who, dwelling in the nether world, come at the summons of the gods to make rain for the Zuñi people. The clouds are their masks, for their faces are too holy to be seen of men. So when impersonating the Rain-Makers in their dances, the Zuñis wear masks.

See "The Zuñi Indians, their Mythology, Esoteric Societies, and Ceremonies," by Matilda Coxe Stevenson, Twenty-third Annual Report, Bureau American Ethnology. "Outlines Zuñi Creation Myths," by Frank Hamilton Cushing, Thirteenth Annual Report, Bureau American Ethnology.

ZUÑI

II

Sung by the youths while the maidens grind the corn

OCKAYA

Elu honkwa lonan iyane !
Elu honkwa hliton iyane !
 Lekwa kela aiyan-towa
 Pene aiyaye
Maihoma antuna,
Holon-ellete
Lilthno kela
Kiawe-kwai-i nuwane !

CORN-GRINDING SONG

Lovely ! See the cloud, the cloud appear !
Lovely ! See the rain, the rain draw near !
 Who spoke ?
'Twas the little corn-ear
High on the tip of the stalk
Saying while it looked at me
 Talking aloft there—
" Ah, perchance the floods
 Hither moving—
Ah, may the floods come this way !"

III

In this song the rainbow is imagined as the Rainbow Youth,
and he is described as " brightly decked and painted." The swallow
is the summoner of rain. The Zuñis say he " sings for rain !"

OCKAYA

Amitola tsina-u-u-ne
Elu, elu toma wahane
Kiawulokia pena wulokia.
Kesi liwamani
 Hliton iyane !
Kesi liwamani
 Hlapi hanan iyane !

Letekwan atowa
Awuwakia litla.
Hi yai—elu !

CORN-GRINDING SONG

Yonder, yonder see the fair rainbow,
See the rainbow brightly decked and
 painted !
Now the swallow bringeth glad news ·to
 your corn,
Singing, " Hitherward, hitherward, hither-
 ward, rain,
 " Hither come !"
Singing, " Hitherward, hitherward, hither-
 ward, white cloud,
 " Hither come !"
Now hear the corn-plants murmur,
" We are growing everywhere !"
 Hi, yai! The world, how fair !

SHOKO OTIÏKWE

SHOKO OTIÏKWE

Chuap-tono,
Chuap-tono,
Kela ite tsina-u?
Amitola-Tsawaki.
Ma honkwa hito:
Lonawe,
Hlitowe,
Uletchi
Ite tsina-u!

CORN-DANCE SONG

Who, ah know ye who—
Who, ah know ye who—
Who was't that made a picture the first?
'Twas the bright Rainbow Youth,
    Rainbow Youth—
Ay, behold, 'twas even thus—
    Clouds came,
    And rain came
    Close following—
Rainbow then colored all!

THLAH HEWE

Song of the Blue-Corn Dance

(Old Chief's Song)

THLAH HEWE

Hi—ah-hai, elu!
  Shi—elu!
Lowi-yuteapa,
Mateona kesi,
Lowi-yuteapa
Awiyane
Litla

SONG OF THE BLUE-CORN DANCE

Beautiful, lo, the summer clouds,
Beautiful, lo, the summer clouds!
Blossoming clouds in the sky,
Like unto shimmering flowers,
Blossoming clouds in the sky,
Onward, lo, they come,
Hither, hither bound!

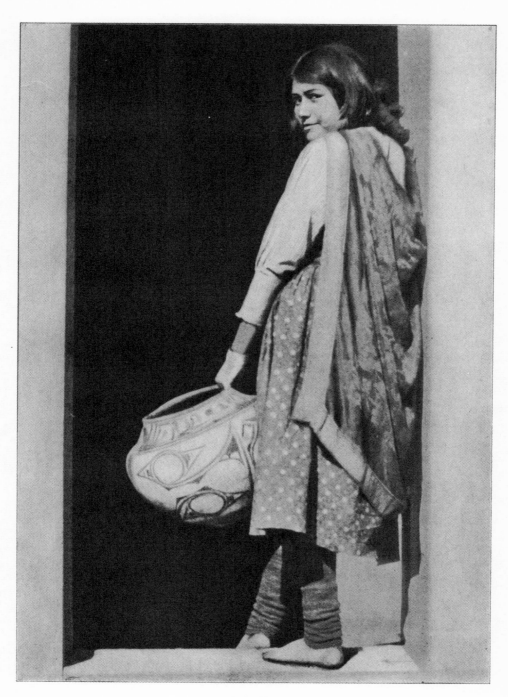

A Zuñi Maiden

Ockaya
Corn Grinding Song
I

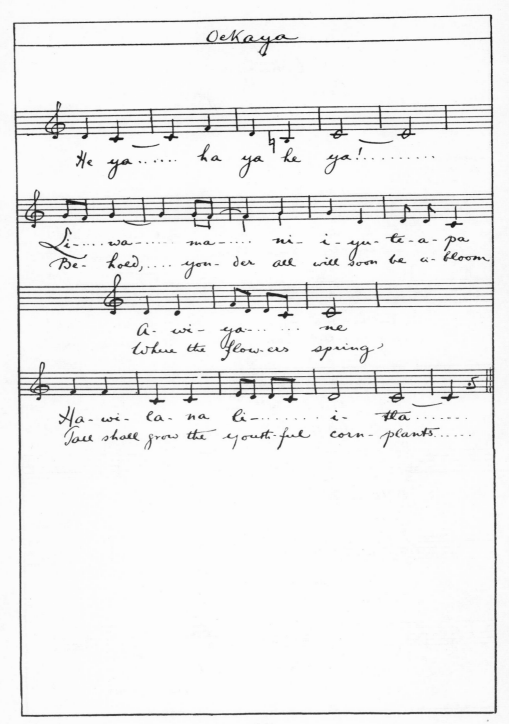

OeKaya

He ya..... ha ya he ya!.........

Li—....wa—...... ma—..... ni—i—yu—te—a—pa
Be—hold,.... yon—der all will soon be a—bloom

A—wi—ya—... ... ne
Where the flowers spring

Ha—wi—la—na li—.......i—tla.......
Tall shall grow the youth—ful corn—plants.....

Ockaya
Corn-Grinding Song
II

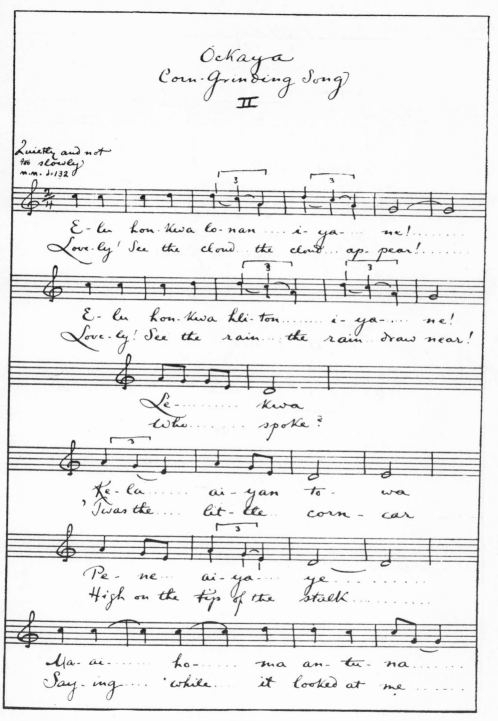

Quietly and not too slowly
m.m. ♩=132

E-lu hon-kwa lo-nan .... i-ya—— ne! ....
Love-ly! See the cloud the cloud... ap-pear! ....

E-lu hon-kwa hli-ton .... i-ya—— ne!
Love-ly! See the rain .... the rain draw near!

Le———— kwa
Who .... spoke?

Ke-la ..... ai-yan to wa
'Twas the .... lit-tle corn-ear

Pe-ne— ai-ya— ye ....
High on the tip of the stalk ....

Ma-ai ...... ho—— ma an-tu-na ......
Say-ing .... 'while it looked at me ......

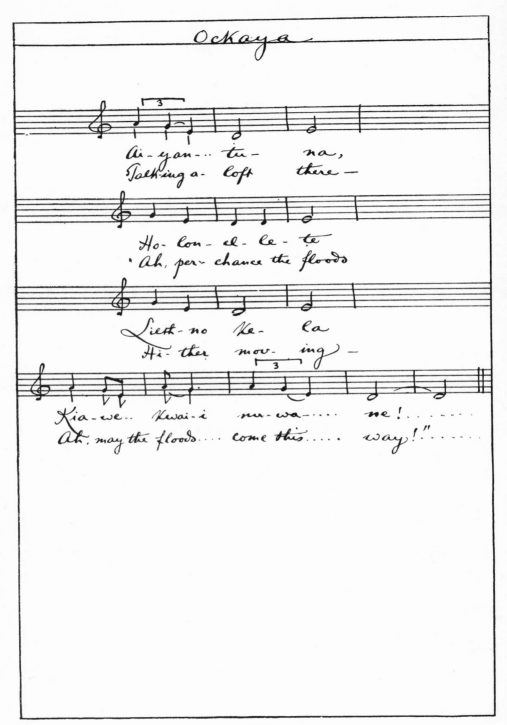

Ockaya

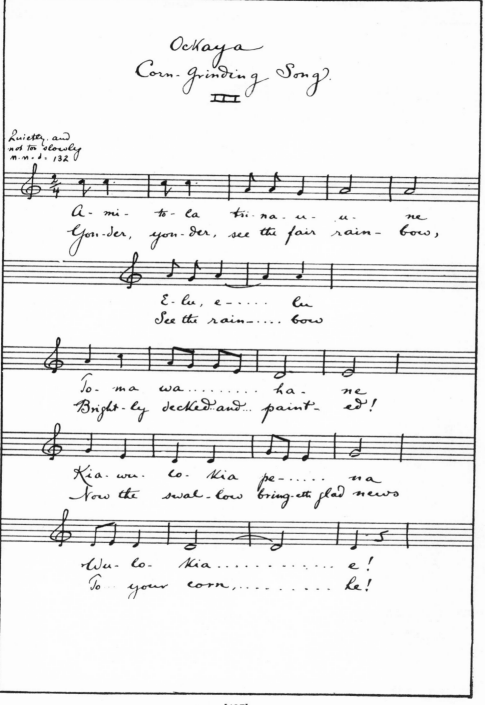

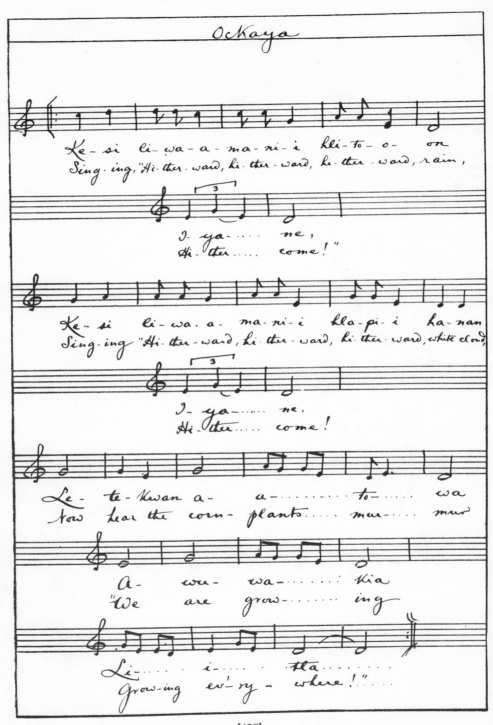

OcKaya

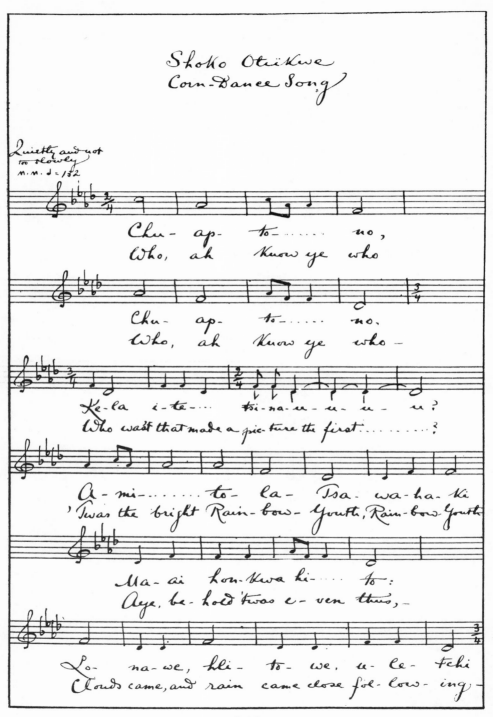

Shoko Otiikwe

I- te——— tsi-na-u———
Rain-bow then col-ored all!———

Ow hi i ya e he lu wi ya———

Hi i ya hi ai e lu ya ha

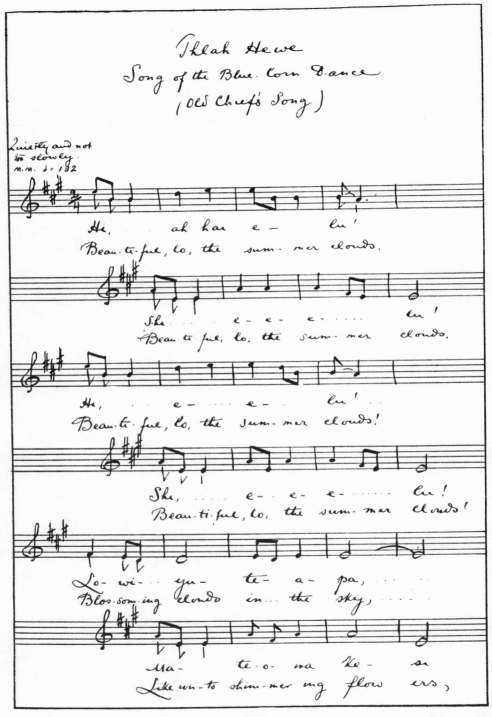

Thlah Hewe

Lo - wi - yu - te - a - pa
Blos-som-ing clouds in the sky,

A - wi - ya-ha - ne
On-ward, lo, they come,

Li - i-hi tta
Hi-ther, hi-ther bound!

a hi yi hai

E he lu wi ya

I yu hi yi a ha

Hi ya ha he

SAN

JUAN

ACOMA

SAN JUAN AND ACOMA TITLE-PAGE

The designs represent masks worn by the Pueblo Indians in
ceremonial costume. Upon the masks are painted symbols of
cloud, sun, lightning, rainbow, and rain. These drawings are
by a Laguna Indian, Idima (John Corn), of the Corn clan.
The lettering is by Hinook Mahiwi Kilinaka (Angel De Cora).

SAN JUAN

SAN JUAN is one of the largest of the upper Rio Grande pueblos, inhabited by people of Tañoan stock. The village was dedicated by the Spanish conquerors to St. John.[1]

ACOMA

Yaka-Hano Gatzina Yoni

(Corn-People Gatzina Songs)

THREE dance-songs from the pueblo of Acoma, New Mexico, have been contributed to The Indians' Book by an Acoma Indian. They are songs of the Yaka-Hano Gatzina, or Corn-People Gatzina. The Gatzinas are mythological beings who are impersonated in the ceremonials by dancers wearing masks decorated with emblems of clouds, lightning, rainbow, and with other symbols. The word *Gatzina* corresponds to the Hopi word *Katzina*,[2] only that with the Acomas the accent is placed on the first syllable, with the Hopis, on the second.

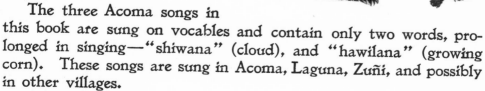

The three Acoma songs in this book are sung on vocables and contain only two words, prolonged in singing—"shiwana" (cloud), and "hawilana" (growing corn). These songs are sung in Acoma, Laguna, Zuñi, and possibly in other villages.

[1] For San Juan song, see page 449.   [2] See Hopi " Katzinas," page 482.

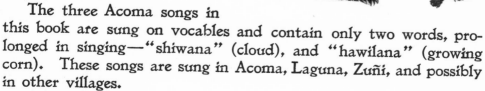

CORN HUSKING

Painted by Pan Yo Pin, a Tesuque Indian

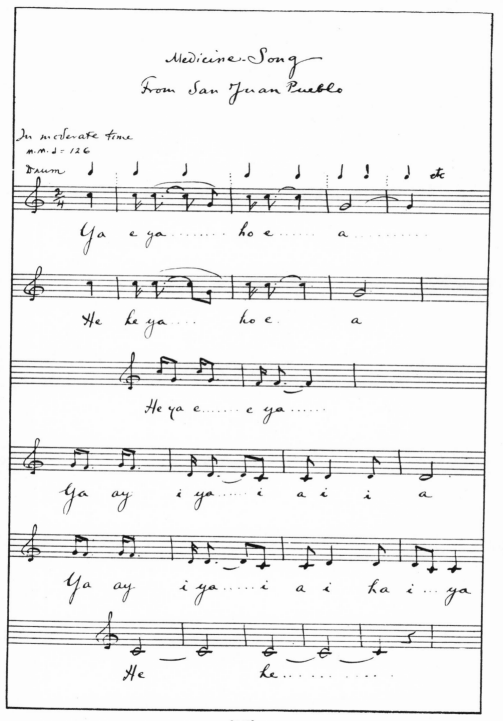

Gaka Hano Gatzina Yoni

Shi— i— i— i— wa— a— ha— na.....

Ha— a.... wi— i.... la— a— ha— na.....

Tempo primo

A— ni hio— o— o a— ni hio— o— o a— ni hio— o— o

meno M.M. ♩ = 104

A— ni ni ya ke   ah— ah ah ah ah i— yi hi yi hi yi

a ha   ha ah hi

[452]

Yaka Hano Gatzina Gone

Yaka Hano Gatzina Goni

III

M.M. ♩ = 108

Yo i.... a he ha yo.... i a

Yo i.... a yo i.... a a e a .... e he a

Ho e a ho e a ha a i hi yi

a ha i hi hi

Hi ne ya yo i.... te te na ni...... a

Yo i.... a yo i.... a a e ya.... e he a

[456]

LAGUNA TITLE-PAGE

The design represents a symbolic beast such as is painted on
the wall of the pueblo estufa (ceremonial council chamber).
The drawing is by a Laguna Indian, Idima (John Corn), of the
Corn clan.
The lettering is by Hinook Mahiwi Kilinaka (Angel De Cora).

LAGUNA

LAGUNA is one of the largest pueblos in New Mexico. The houses, like nearly all pueblo dwellings, are of two or more stories set back one above another in terrace form, so that the roof of the first story is at the same time the balcony of the second. On balcony and house-top the Pueblo Indian lives almost as much as within doors. Floating from the upper story of some whitewashed house may be often heard the song of the corn-grinder quavering in sweet, unusual melody to the rhythm of the stones.

The grinding-songs here offered are very old, and most of the words are archaic. The first song tells of "wonder-water," the welcome rain-water caught, after showers, by the hollows in the rocks so common in this country of strange erosion. The Laguna Indians thus explain these songs: "After rain, the water stands in hollows in the rocks. It is good, fresh water—medicine-water. It brings new life to him who drinks. In the song we say: 'Look to the southwest, look to the southeast! The clouds are coming towards the spring; the clouds will bring the water!' It is from the southwest and the southeast that we usually get our rains. The other song is about the butterflies, blue and red and yellow and white. We tell them to fly to the blossoms. At the end of the song we say, 'Go, butterfly, now go, for that is all!'"

The songs were sung by many Indians, among them an aged woman of authority well versed in the lore of her people.

NOTE FOR PRONUNCIATION OF LAGUNA TEXT

Unless otherwise indicated, vowels have the Continental sound, and consonants the English.

AIYA-GAÏTANI YONI

Corn-Grinding Song

I

AIYA-GAÏTANI YONI

I-o-ho, waitilanni,
I-o-ho, waitilanni,
Tzi washo iyani-i !
Yuweh puniakoekolika,
Yuweh haniakoekolika,
Tzi washo iyani-i !
I-o-ho, waitilanni,
I-o-ho, waitilanni,
Tzi washo iyani-i !

CORN-GRINDING SONG

I-o-ho, wonder-water,
I-o-ho, wonder-water,
Life anew to him who drinks !
Look where southwest clouds are bringing
    rain;
Look where southeast clouds are bringing
    rain !
Life anew to him who drinks !
I-o-ho, wonder-water,
I-o-ho, wonder-water,
Life anew to him who drinks !

II

AIYA-GAÏTANI YONI

Polaina, polaina,
Hai-ke-o-tzi-o-no-ho,
Kohochinishi,
Koeshkasi,
Hai-ke-o-tzi-o-no-ho,
Kukanishi,
Kasheshi,
Hai-ke-o-tzi-o-no-ho,
Ha-na-pu-ra-ni !
Polaina, polaina,
Hai-ke-o-tzi-o-no-ho,
Ha-na-pu-ra-ni !

CORN-GRINDING SONG

Butterflies, butterflies,
Now fly away to the blossoms,
    Fly, blue-wing,
    Fly, yellow-wing,
Now fly away to the blossoms,
    Fly, red-wing,
    Fly, white-wing,
Now fly away to the blossoms,
    Butterflies, away !
Butterflies, butterflies,
Now fly away to the blossoms,
    Butterflies, away !

CORN DANCERS

Painted by Pan Yo Pin, a Tesuque Indian

TUARI'S SONG

TUARI (Young Eagle) is at work far from his native village. When asked for a song, he said, "I will sing you my own song that I sing to my wife."

"But how can you sing to her when she is at home in Laguna and you are here?"

The Pueblo youth stared at the question, then answered, quietly, "I sing to her though I am far away, and she, too, sings to me. The meaning of my song is this: 'I am here, working for you. All the while I work I think of you. Take care of yourself, and take care of the horses, and the sheep and the fields.'"

"But your song has no words!"

"No, but that is what it means. So when I am far away we sing to each other, my wife and I."[1]

In the composer's mind the song is accompanied by the drum, and can be used as a dance-song for a dance of young men in the spring-time.

[1] See footnote, page 102.

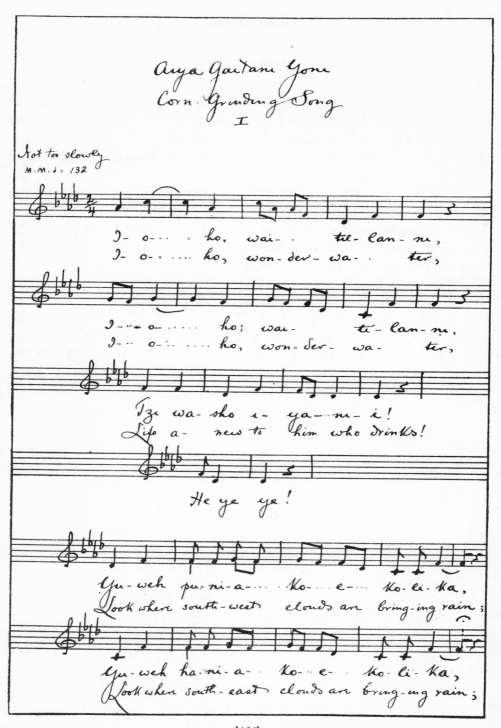

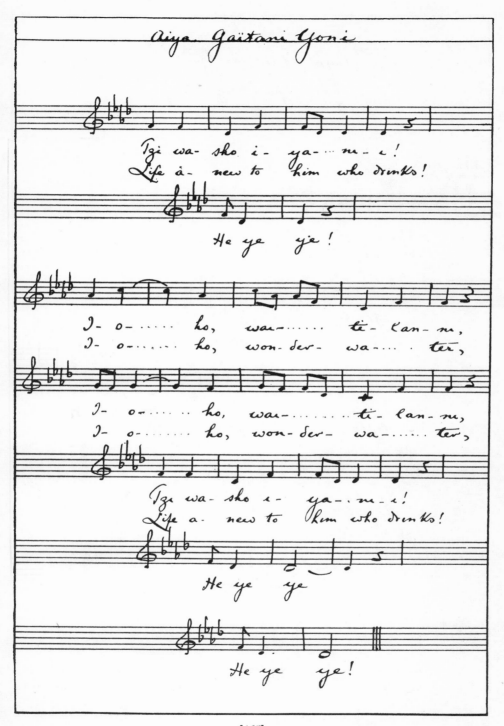

Aiya Gaïtani Yoni

Tzi wa-sho i- ya--ni-i!
Life a- new to him who drinks!

He ye ye!

I- o---- ho, war---- te- lan-ni,
I- o---- ho, won-der- wa-- ter,

I- o---- ho, war---- te- lan-ni,
I- o---- ho, won-der- wa-- ter,

Tzi wa-sho i- ya--ni-i!
Life a- new to him who drinks!

He ye ye

He ye ye!

Aiya Gaïtani Goni
Corn-Grinding Song
II

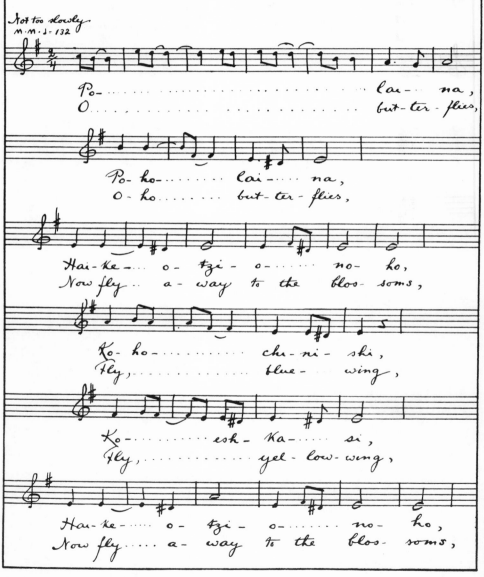

Not too slowly
M.M. ♩ = 132

Po-... lai- na,
O-... but- ter- flies,

Po- ho-......... lai- na,
O- ho......... but- ter- flies,

Hai- ke-..... o- tzi- o-..... no- ho,
Now fly... a- way to the blos- soms,

Ko- ho-..................... chu- ni- shi,
Fly,..................... blue- wing,

Ko-..................... esh- ka-..... si,
Fly,..................... yel- low- wing,

Hai- ke-..... o- tzi- o-..... no- ho,
Now fly..... a- way to the blos- soms,

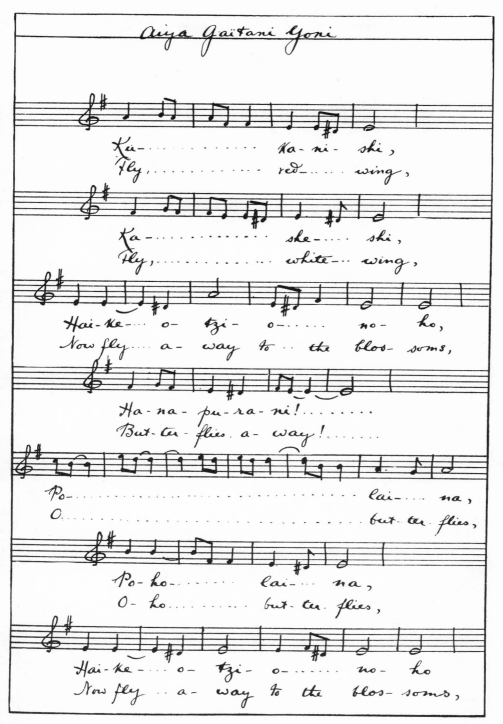

HOPI INDIANS

HOPI TITLE-PAGE

The round design in the centre of the page represents a pottery plaque, on which is painted a butterfly. This drawing is by Gashhoienim, a Hopi Indian girl.

The lettering and decorations are by Hinook Mahiwi Kilinaka (Angel De Cora). The decorations at the top and bottom of the page show the head and the antennæ of the butterfly; the letters are formed of the butterfly's body.

Nampéyo and Her Family

THE HOPIS [1]

I N northeastern Arizona, high on the summit of sheer cliffs, overlooking wide stretches of desert, and desert only, stand the seven villages of the Hopi Indians, the "People of Peace." Centuries ago, the gentle Hopis fled to the craggy heights to escape the ravages of wilder tribes. Here might the Hopi live at peace, creeping at dawn down the precipitous rock-hewn trail to labor in his field, and climbing up again at eventide. His village was his fortress, inaccessible and remote. Though some of the villages had been discovered by the Spaniards, yet since the Pueblo insurrection of 1680 the Hopis have had little contact with white men until quite recently. They are still a conservative folk, who, ever industrious and self-supporting, cling to their traditions and customs with dignity and reserve.

Song is the spontaneous expression of the people. It may be heard at all hours rising from the Hopi village or from the surrounding desert plains and cliffs. The shepherd driving his flock down the steep, rocky trail; the planter seeking his field at dawn; the woman at her task; the child at his play, all sing as naturally as the bird on the bough. Besides old traditional songs, the Hopis have

NOTE FOR PRONUNCIATION OF HOPI TEXT

While in many Indian languages there are sounds not exactly the same as the corresponding ones of European tongues, in the Hopi occur sounds that have no counterpart at all in European languages. Such sounds, therefore, can be expressed by the Roman alphabet approximately only.

Unless otherwise indicated, vowels have the Continental sound, and consonants the English.

q has a guttural sound.

ö is pronounced as in German.

ʊ has the sound of u in curd.

[1] Commonly called "Mokis" or "Moquis."

countless songs of the moment, which are composed and sung for a few years and then forgotten.

To seize on paper the spirit of Hopi music is a task as impossible as to put on canvas the shimmer and glare of the desert. Hopi music is born of its environment. The wind sweeping among the crags and whirling down the trail has carved its strange melody upon the Indian's plastic mind, even as it has carved upon the rocks, in curious erosion, the record of its presence. Its echo is heard in the song of the Hopi, yodelling through the desert solitudes. There, in that wide land, under the blaze of the Arizona sun, amid the shifting color of the tinted sands and the purple-blue of the sharp-shadowed rocks must the songs be heard to be heard truly.

Nearly sixty Hopi songs have been recorded, but because of their length and difficulty there is not here place for more than a few. These few have been chosen less for their quality than for the association with their composers, the song-poets of the cliff-perched Hopi pueblos.

THE SONG OF THE HOPI CHIEF

LOLOLOMAI, chief of the Hopi village of Oraibi, was well named *Lololomai* (Very - Good), for he had ever been the watchful father of his people. Eighty summers had shone upon him, yet he bore himself with the dignity of chieftaincy. Unlike many Hopis, he had travelled far and had been to see the great chief in Washington, in the land where "there were many clouds and the sun looked like the moon."

To The Indians' Book is here given the account of the white friend's talk with Lololomai, word for word, as written shortly after the visit:

I sought Lololomai to tell him of my purpose with the Hopi songs. My interpreter was a Hopi lad, who, though blind, led with sure foot the way up the steep, rocky trail to the village. The chief was seated on his house-top, spinning, for in Hopi-land it is the men who spin and weave. He rose and met us at the head of the ladder that led to where he sat.

An Evening Reverie on the House-tops

"I have come to talk with you, friend, on something that concerns your people," I said.

"Ancha-a ('Tis well)," he answered, solemnly, and motioned me to sit down with him.

"Lololomai," I said, "the Hopi children are going to school; they are learning new ways and are singing new songs—American songs instead of Hopi. Some of the children are very young—so young that there have been, perhaps, but three corn-plantings since they came into the world. These little ones will never sing the songs of their fathers. They will not sing of the corn, the bean-blossoms, and the butterflies. They will know only American songs. Hopi songs are beautiful; it is sad that they should be forgotten."

To all of this the old chief said, "Hao, hao (Even so, even so)," and nodded slowly.

"But," I continued, "there is one thing in the school good for all to have and to know, and that is *books*. Books can be of many kinds, Hopi as well as English. As yet your people have no books nor do they read or write. That is why your songs will be forgotten, why even your language may some day pass away.

"When you sing, your song is heard, then dies like the wind that sweeps the cornfields and is gone, none knows whither. But if you could write, you could put your song into a book, and your people, even to the children of their children, could know your song as if you yourself were singing. They could look upon the written page and say: 'Thus sang Lololomai, our chief, in the long ago. Thus sings Lololomai to-day.'"

The head drooped lower and the aged face was grave.

"But until the time shall come," I said, "when the Hopis shall themselves record their stories and their songs, some one must do this for them, else much will be lost—lost forever, like a wind-blown trail. So I have come from my far-distant home by the 'great waters' in the East to write the Hopi songs."

There was a pause. Then the old chief turned to me pathetically. There was a wistful yearning in the aged eyes, a cloud of trouble on the wrinkled brow.

"It is well," he said, "but will not the superintendent be angry if you do this thing? Are you sure that you will not bring trouble upon us? White people try to stop our songs and dances, so I am fearful of your talk."

"Be at rest, my friend," I said, "the great chief at Washington[1] is father of all the people in this country, as you are father of all in this village. He has given his permission for the writing of the Hopi songs. He is glad to have them written, for he, too, knows that Hopi songs are beautiful."

"Then it is well," replied Lololomai—"then it is well, indeed. But will you, friend, explain to me that which I cannot understand? Why do the white people want to stop our dances and our songs? Why do they trouble us? Why do they interfere with what can harm them not? What ill do we to any white man when we dance?"

"Lololomai, white men do not understand your dances or your songs. They do not even know one word of your language. When I have written your songs, I will write English words as well as Hopi, that white men may know of what you sing. When they understand, they will perhaps no longer want to stop your dances and your songs. To you, Lololomai, the Hopi chief, will I give the Hopi songs when they are written. You will keep them for your people with the other sacred things that are your trust. Then in the days to come the younger Hopis will read, and so the songs never will be forgotten."

Lololomai bowed his head. "Lololomai," he said, "pas lolomai (good, very good)."

"And now will you sing one of your own songs, that I may write it?" I asked. "Sing a song of your own making, for Lololomai's song should be the first."

The chief rested his chin on his hand and gazed before him over the desert in deep thought. "I am old," he said, "and I have made many songs and have forgotten many songs. It is as you say, the songs I made when I was young I remember now no longer. I will sing the last song that I made."

He rose and beckoned me to another sunny corner on the house-top, spreading a blanket for a seat.

---

[1] President Theodore Roosevelt, who, from the first, took great interest in the work.

HOPI

"This song," Lololomai explained, "was sung during our ceremony of thank-offering after the corn was garnered for the year.[1] The men go from one kiva[2] to another, all night long, dancing and singing. This is the song of the men from my kiva, the chief kiva. It tells how in my kiva the chief and his men are praying to make the corn to grow next year for all the people. That is the meaning of my song."

Then in rhythmic monotone the old man crooned beside me. Long and diligently I worked at the recording, with the glare of the hot sun on my paper. It was no light task to fix the chant in musical notation.

I saw this question in the chief's eyes: "I have sung the song; why does it take so long to make those black marks on the paper?" And I said, "Lololomai, you know that when the Hopi sets a trap for the blackbird, sometimes it is long before he can catch his fluttering prey. Your song is a wild blackbird to me, and it may be that the sun will move far along the sky before I have captured it."

When I had finished, I showed Lololomai the written page. The old man scanned the mysterious tracings, and, nodding slowly, repeated again and again, "Ancha-a, ikwatchi, ancha-a (It is well, my friend, it is well)." Then drawing his blanket around him, Lololomai stepped to the edge of the roof, and, facing the sun, sank upon his knees with head bowed in his hands. What his act meant I knew not, for I had heard that Hopis stood erect to pray. But the swift instinct of sympathy said—the aged father of the village thus consecrates the new task for the Hopis.

The shadows on the village street grew long. The sun was sinking. Here and there a lone Hopi was returning from below with laden burro. Soon the trail would be dotted with home-coming Indians. We sat long in silence, Lololomai, the blind boy, and I. I watched the glow enfold the desert with the mystery of dying

[1] This ceremony is called *Wuwuchim-yungya*.

[2] The kiva is an underground council-chamber. There are many kivas, probably one for each clan, originally. Here the men come to meet in council or to spin and weave. Here also the new songs are learned and dances practised. But the most important use of the kiva is as a sacred chamber where altars are placed and secret ceremonial rites performed.

day. The chief's song was that sung when the corn was garnered. And I—with book and pencil I was gleaning in the Hopi fields in this the sunset hour of the people's native life. The time is short before night shall fall forever on the spirit of spontaneous song within the Indian.

Silent still, the blind boy and I took our downward way upon the rocky trail. To my companion, in his night, the deepening shadow bore no import, but a twilight sadness lay upon my spirit. I thought of the garnered Hopi corn. Will there be many more plantings of poetry and harvestings of song? Darkness closed in. But off beyond in silver glory rose the moon.

To Lololomai had been promised the songs of his people. But before the pledge could be fulfilled the old chief followed the western sun. The silent desert never again will waken to his voice. But for Hopis yet unborn The Indians' Book holds the song of the long-loved chieftain of Oraibi.

Note.—Grateful acknowledgment is due to the Hopi authority, Rev. H. R. Voth, of the Field Columbian Museum, Chicago, for assistance in the English rendering of Lololomai's song, and for explanation of its contents. The whole collection of Hopi text has received Mr. Voth's expert criticism. The spelling, however, is not Mr. Voth's, but one conforming to the general system adopted in this book for the spelling of Indian words. Also, since Hopi songs are capable of many different interpretations, the recorder has felt obliged to hold to versions acquired through her own research among the Indians, even where such versions are more or less at variance with those kindly given by Mr. Voth. Mr. Voth, therefore, is not responsible for possible errors in the translations.

WUWUCHIM TAWI

Wuwuchim-Chant

Composed and sung by Lololomai

I N the kiva of the chieftain is performed a ceremonial, symbolic corn-planting. The idea in this song seems to be that a ceremonial planting of a perfect corn-ear— that is, one completely filled with kernels—will procure even such perfect corn-ears in the crop of the next season. Muyingwa is the god of germination and growth. He lives underground beneath the kivas. In this song he would seem to be beneath the kiva of the chief.

The Hopi word translated as "double corn-ear" means a corn-ear more or less cleft. By "rain that stands" the Hopis mean rain seen to fall from a distant cloud, giving an appearance of upright lines.

The Hopis have different words for the different kinds of cloud. The *heyapo* cloud, translated here as "cloud that rushes," is the fast-driven scud that underlies heavy masses of rain-cloud.

WUWUCHIM TAWI

Yan itam, yan itam
Tokilnawita
Hahlai unangway
Na'kalmumuya.

Natwanlawu inamu
Ayam Muyingwa
Mongwi kive
Mokwa kaö
Chochmingwun;
Natwantaqö pom nikiang
Bavas nawita sitalwunguni.

Peyo amumi namusha,
Yoyowunuto heyapo o-omawutu!

WUWUCHIM-CHANT

Thus we, thus we,
The night along,
With happy hearts
Wish well one another.

In the chief's kiva
They, the fathers,
They and Muyingwa
Plant the double ear—
Plant the perfect double corn-ear.
So the fields shall shine
With tassels white of perfect corn-ears.

Hither to them, hither come,
Rain that stands and cloud that rushes!

PUWUCH TAWI

Lullaby

THIS lullaby is one of the oldest Hopi songs. It is sung in many of the Hopi villages, and there is perhaps scarcely a Hopi who has not been lulled to sleep with its refrain —"puva, puva! (sleep, sleep!)"

The mother binds her baby on a board to sleep. Then she fastens board and baby on her back, and, swaying to and fro, becomes herself a living cradle, gently rocking to sleep the little one. As she rocks, she sings this ancient crooning lullaby.

The song tells of the beetles asleep on the trail. In Hopi-land, the beetles carry one another on their backs in the hot sun. The Hopis say, "The beetles are blind; the beetles are sleeping." So the child upon its mother's back must close its eyes, and, like the beetle, see no more.

PUWUCH TAWI	LULLABY
Puva, puva, puva.	Puva, puva, puva,[1]
Hohoyawu	In the trail the beetles
Shuhpö pave-e	On each other's backs are sleeping,
Na-ikwiokiango,	So on mine, my baby, thou
Puva, puva, puva !	Puva, puva, puva !

POLI TIWA TAWI

Butterfly-Dance Song

Composed and sung by Tawakwaptiwa

OF all the Hopi poets, none sings a gladder song than Tawakwaptiwa (Sun-Down-Shining).[2] He is one in whom the gift of song wells up like living waters, a Hopi untouched by foreign influence, the child of natural environment, spontaneous, alert, full of life and laughter.

[1] *Puva*, sleep.
[2] Like many Hopi names, this one is almost impossible of literal translation. Sun-Down-Shining is the general meaning of the name, as given by the Indians.

Tawakwaptiwa

Poli Tiwa—Butterfly Dance

"He makes good songs," say the Hopis. "Everybody likes Tawakwaptiwa."

The poet's answer to the question, "How do you make your songs?" was like the answer made by many a Hopi singer: "When I am herding my sheep, or away in the fields, and I see something that I like—then I sing about it."

"This song," Tawakwaptiwa explained, "is sung in the Butterfly-Dance. It tells how the youths and maidens are playing in the fields."

"Yes," upspoke a second Hopi, "when the corn and melons are ripe, the youths in the field hold high the fairest fruit and summon the maidens with a call. Then the butterfly-girls come running, and try to wrest the prize."

"The 'butterfly-girls'?"

"Yes," answered Tawakwaptiwa, "so we call the Hopi girls, because their hair makes them to look like butterflies."[1]

Then the poet threw his blanket over his shoulder, and, stretching his hand before him, with quick commanding gesture he sang the second stanza of his song, the summons to the thunder.

"So the thunder will come," he explained, "so the rain will come, that the corn-maidens may grow high."

"The 'corn-maidens'?"

"Yes, the little young corn-plants are corn-maidens."

"When the corn is no longer little, but grown," said the second Hopi, "then come the corn-ears, and these are the children of the corn. We call the corn 'mother.' It nourishes us, it gives us life, —is it not our mother? Tawakwaptiwa's song tells how we want the rain, that the little corn-plant maidens may help one another to grow tall."

"How do they help one another?"

"Oh, by gathering the moisture under the ground with their little roots."

The Poli Tiwa (Butterfly-Dance) is a dance of youths and maidens. The leaders plan the changing figures and drill the

---

[1] The Hopi maidens wear their hair in glistening wheels at each side of the head. The head-dress really represents the squash-blossom, emblem of virginity.

dancers in the preparation that for several days precedes the performance. The dance begins at noon and lasts until sundown, many figures being performed with intermissions for rest and change of costume. The dance is held in the open plaza of the village, and the on-lookers usually mount the house-tops for their view. The unaccustomed eye quivers and falls beneath the mid-day glare and the glinting color of the scene; for many of the spectators are brightly clad and the dancers are elaborately decked. The maidens wear wooden tablets on the head, symbolic of clouds. They carry little sprigs and decorously dance with downcast eyes and scarcely moving feet. The youths shake rattles and lift high the knee with springing step. Silently the dancers move, while a chorus sings the dance-music and sounds a drum whose steady rhythm is like the pulse-beat of the quivering hot air.

POLI TIWA TAWI	BUTTERFLY-DANCE SONG
Humicita cingölawu,	Now for corn-blooms we wrestle,
Mozhicita cingölawu.	Now for bean-blooms we wrestle.
Itam totim nikiang	We are youths, 'mid the corn,
Uyi shonaka ngöti-timani	Chasing each other in sport,
Tuvevol manatu amumi.	Playing with butterfly-maidens.
Peyo, peyo!	Hither, hither!
Umumutani	Thunder will hither move,
Ita ayatani,	We shall summon the thunder here,
Uyi manatu	That the maiden-plants
Omi nawungwinani.	Upward may help one another to grow.

KATZINAS

THE Hopi "Katzinas" are intermediary deities who bring to the gods the Hopis' prayers.

Long ago the Katzinas lived upon the earth and danced in the plazas of the villages and brought the rain. But now they come no more, and so to bring the rain the Hopis themselves impersonate the Katzinas. They dress like them, wear masks to represent the faces, and dance and sing for rain even as the

Katzinas did of old. There are many kinds of Katzinas, and the Katzina dance-songs are innumerable. The wooden masks are painted with symbols full of meaning, and the border of the woven sash worn by the Katzina dancer tells of the earth in blossom with the rain-clouds sending water upon it.

ANGA KATZINA TAWI

Anga Katzina Song

Composed and sung by Lahpu

LAHPU is brother of Tawakwaptiwa, and both men are nephews of the chief Lololomai. The blood of aristocracy is in their veins, for they belong to the oldest clan in Oraibi.

Said Lahpu of his song: "This is the first song that I ever made. I had been a long time away, and so my heart was happy as I came through the fields. I saw the Hopi girls playing among the corn-plants, chasing one another and laughing and singing, and—I liked it; it was pretty, and I was happy, so I made this song about it."

ANGA KATZINA TAWI

Uyi shonaka yoki;
Tuvevoli manatu
Nanguyimani yoyang.
Yala puma tahinpa natayawina
Yang *uyi* shonaka !
  A-ha, ha-ha,
  O-ah, e-lo !
Yani puma tuwati
Tataw-yuyuwina yanga
  O-o, o-ho,
  O-he, e-lo !

ANGA KATZINA SONG

Rain all over the cornfields,
Pretty butterfly-maidens
Chasing one another when the rain is done,
  Hither, thither, so.
How they frolic 'mid the corn,
  Laughing, laughing, thus:
    A-ha, ha-ha,
    O-ah, e-lo !
How they frolic 'mid the corn,
  Singing, singing, thus:
    O-o, o-ho,
    O-he, e-lo !

KOROSTA KATZINA TAWI

Korosta Katzina Song

Composed and sung by Koianimptiwa

NO one had as yet heard this song when its author, a young poet, Koianimptiwa, first offered to sing it for the recorder. He had just composed it for a coming dance in May — "Corn - Planting Time" — a "Korosta Katzina Dance," in which the katzinas wear masks whereon is painted the rainbow.

Said Koianimptiwa: "My song is about the butterflies flying over the cornfields and over the beans. One butterfly is running after the other like the hunt, and there are many."

Even as the Hopis paint their faces for a ceremonial dance, so have the butterflies, for their flight over the corn-blossoms, painted themselves with pollen.

"The butterflies must go through many flowers," say the Hopis, "to make themselves so pretty."

Koianimptiwa is a true poet, and he spoke well when he said, "Not all men can make songs."

KOROSTA KATZINA TAWI

Sikya volima
Humisi manata
Talasi yamma
Pitzangwa timakiang
   Tuve-nanguyimani.

Shakwa volima
Mozhisi manata
Talasi yamma
Pitzangwa timakiang
   Tuve-nanguyimani.

Humisi manata
Amunawita
Tatangayata
   Tökiyuyuwintani.

KOROSTA KATZINA SONG

Yellow butterflies,
Over the blossoming virgin corn,
   With pollen-painted faces
Chase one another in brilliant throng.

Blue butterflies,
Over the blossoming virgin beans,
   With pollen-painted faces
Chase one another in brilliant streams.

Over the blossoming corn,
Over the virgin corn
Wild bees hum:

HOPI

Mozhisi manatu
Amunawita
Tatangayatu
Tukiyuyuwintani.

Over the blossoming beans,
Over the virgin beans,
Wild bees hum.

Umuh uyi
Amunawit
Yoi-umumutimani
Tawanawita.

Over your field of growing corn
All day shall hang the thunder-cloud;
Over your field of growing corn
All day shall come the rushing rain.

Umuh uyi
Amunawit
Yoi-hoyoyotimani
Tawanawita.

HE-HEA KATZINA TAWI

He-hea Katzina Song

Sung by Masahongva

HE-HEA KATZINA TAWI

Humisi uyi manatu,
Mozhisi uyi siqölöva,
Bavatalawinani,
Shakwa omawutu—

Hapi me—
Hesiqölöva
Sikia voli nangöyimani.
Mozhisiqölöva
Shakwa voli nangöyimani.

HE-HEA KATZINA SONG

Corn-blossom maidens
Here in the fields,
Patches of beans in flower,
Fields all abloom,
Water shining after rain,
Blue clouds looming above.

Now behold !
Through bright clusters of flowers
Yellow butterflies
Are chasing at play,
And through the blossoming beans
Blue butterflies
Are chasing at play.

MÚNGWU KATZINA TAWI

Owl Katzina Song

See Appendix, page 572.

HEVEBE TAWI

Hevebe-Songs

BOTH of these Hevebe[1]-songs are very old. The Hopis have an ancient custom that is a playful sport and at the same time a symbolic invocation for rain.

At the coming of the "yellow line," for so the Hopis call the dawn, there may sometimes be heard the Hevebe-song of the men, as they go in line through the village, from house to house, calling to the inmates to rise and pour water on them from the house-tops.

"Often we are fast asleep," explained a little butterfly-maiden; "the song wakes us and we hear the men and boys coming nearer and nearer. We hear the voices and the splashing water and the laughing. And quickly we rise and take our water-jars and go to the top of the house, to be ready when they reach us. It is fun! We try to get the coldest water to pour on them! But the old people scold. They do not like to be waked. In the song, the boys call themselves the 'dawnlight-youths.' We often call the Hopi boys 'dawnlight-youths,' as Hopi girls are called 'butterfly-maidens' and 'shower-maidens.' They are pretty names. And the dawnlight-youth is always happy because the sunlight is in his heart."

The custom is a symbolic invocation for rain. For even as the Hopi woman pours water from the house-tops upon the men, so will those above pour water on the Hopi fields.

[1] *Hevebe*, archaic Hopi word, possibly the name of a certain kind of cloud or cloud-deity.

HOPI

I

Sung by Masahongva

HEVEBE TAWI	HEVEBE-SONG
Nana hopipaqŭ Qöyangwunuka kuyiva.	Now from the east The white dawn hath arisen.
Nana hopipaqŏ Sikiangwunuka kuyiva.	Now from the east The yellow dawn hath arisen.
Angwu huwam Hawiwokialyata.	Please ye, please ye, Now awake ! Arouse yourselves; Look ye here, Oh, look on us !

Itamumi kuyivawicha
Itamumi umuh kuyap kuyi wutaya—
  Iyo, iyo !
  Iyo, iyo !
	Lift your water-jars and o'er us
	  Pour ye, pour:
	  Pour ye, pour ye,
	    Cold, cold !
	    Cold, cold !

Hevebeta peyowi !
  Wuta, wuta,
  Wuta, wuta !
	Hevebeta, come, oh, come !
	  Pour down, pour down,
	  Pour down, pour down !

Qöyangwun-talao ti' Sikiangwun-talao ti'	Come we, white dawnlight-youths, Come we, yellow dawnlight-youths
Tuhiyongva to, Nahiyongva to,	Bringing joy to ye, E'en as joyful, we,

Yanikitiwa
Pavön mamantu.
  Iyo, iyo !
  Iyo, iyo !
	Here where dwell the maids—
	Dwell the shower-maidens,
	  Cold, cold !
	  Cold, cold !

II

Sung by Kuwanyisnim

This is a Hevebe-song of little girls. The naked children stand in line before the houses and clap their hands in time to the song, while sprinkled by the elders from the house-tops. The little singers frolic and laugh as they frisk about and rub the water over their shining bodies. The children may sing and play thus at any time. Sometimes, when the scarce and welcome rain is falling, they run out into the shower and perform their playful ceremony under the downpour of the long-invoked clouds.

HEVEBE TAWI

Hevebeta, peyowi,
Hevebeta, hevebeta peyowi,
Wu-wuta, wu-wuta—
    Wuta, wuta—ow !
    Wuta, wuta—ow !

Tovi chi chi,
Tovi chi chi,
Tovi chi chi,
Shi-i-wa-hana, (Shiwana)
Shi-wa-wai-ya,
Shi-wa-wai-ya,
Wa-wa-wa-wa.

Wu-wuta, wu-wuta,
Anoshkaï anoshkaï,
Nuishi o-ou-ya-a,
Nuipa o-ou-ya-a.

Hevebeta, peyowi,
Hevebeta, hevebeta peyowi,
    Wu-wuta, wu-wuta.
    Wuta, wuta—ow !
    Wuta, wuta—ow !

HEVEBE-SONG

Hevebeta, come, come,
    Pour, pour down,
    Pour, pour down,
Pour down, pour down—ow !
Pour down, pour down—ow !

Hither, flying cloud,
Hither, flying cloud,
Hither, flying cloud,
Sprinkle me,
Sprinkle me,
Cloud, come bathe me !
Hither hasten,
Hither hasten,
Come, come, come, come !

    Pour, pour down,
    Pour, pour down,
Oh, change me now,
Oh, change me now
Into a cluster of flowers,
Into a cluster of showers !

Hevebeta, come, come,
    Pour, pour down,
    Pour, pour down,
Pour down, pour down—ow !
Pour down, pour down—ow !

The Flute Ceremony at Oraibi

LENE TAWI

Flute-Song

Sung by Masaveimah and Kavanghongevah

THE Flute Ceremony, like most Hopi ceremonies, is a prayer for rain and for water in the springs. It is held in August when water is most needed, and is performed in alternate years with the Snake Ceremony. On the ninth day of the ceremony, the priests hold sacred rites around a spring, some singing, while others play the same melody on large flutes. There are two flute societies in every Hopi village, the "Blue" and the "Gray." This song belongs to the Gray Flute Society.

LENE TAWI	FLUTE-SONG
Hao, hao, hao inamu ! Mashilenangwu mongwitu !	Hail, fathers, hail ! Chieftains of the Gray Flute, hail ! At the four world-points
Nananivo omawutu wawai inamu ; Nananivaqö yoi nanakwushani.	Ye call, ye summon clouds. From the four world-points upstarting, Shall the rain hither come.
Peyo yoi-umumutimani yanga ! Peyo yoi-hoyoyotimani !	Hither thunder, rain-thunder here, Hither the rain-thunder will come;
Uyi shonaka Hakame yang	Hither rain, moving-rain— Onward now, over all the fields, Moving-rain.
Uyi shonaka Bava-tala-winani.	And the wet earth, 'mid the corn, Everywhere, far and near, It will shine—water-shine.

LOLOLOMAI'S PRAYER

A Leaf from the Recorder's Diary

I was sunset when for the last time I climbed the steep trail to the village of Oraibi. The level desert seemed a lilac sea, and the outlines of the craggy table-lands were sharp against the flaming sky. Many weeks had passed since I had left the railroad to take the long two-days' drive across the "Painted Desert" to the Hopi villages, and in those weeks I had learned to know and to love the "People of Peace." To-morrow I must leave the desert and its freedom for my distant Eastern home, and so I sought Lololomai, the aged chief, to say to him and to his household a parting word. Thus I passed on a farewell visit through the ancient town, with its terraces of roofs, its open dance-plazas, and its odd corners.

The chief's house was near the end of the village. I opened the low door and entered a dark chamber of stone. The pale light of dying day came faintly through the narrow windows; a smouldering fire on the hearth threw flicker of light and shadow on a group of Indians seated on the floor. A nephew of the chief stood before the hearth; the firelight showed the brown, handsome face, velvet clothes and buckskin leggings. He had passed me on the trail on his fleet white horse, flourishing his riding quirt, and singing as he rode.

"Where is your uncle, the chief, Lololomai?" I asked of the young man, when I had made my greetings.

"He has gone with some men to clear the springs," was the answer. "The sand has filled the springs and our animals have no water."

"Then I shall not see him," I said, sadly. "I had come to bid him good-bye."

But Ponianömsi, the chief's sister, said, "I will bear your message to Lololomai, if you will leave your words with me."

Ponianömsi was of high importance in the village, for, with the Hopi, descent is reckoned on the female side, and as the chief is the father of his people, so is his sister the mother. Ponianömsi had the gentle courtesy of the Hopi and the added dignity of her position.

Her shoulders were square and firm; they had not bent beneath the
weight of the water-jar carried daily by the Hopi women from the
springs up the steep trail to the village. Mules had hauled water for
the household of the chief; Ponianomsi's small form was erect.

The hostess spread a roll of sheepskin on the floor for me to sit
upon, and I joined the group by the fire. I had brought, as a farewell gift, a jar of gray sand from the shores of the Atlantic. The
Navajos, neighbors to the Hopis, had asked me the year before to
bring them such sand. They had said, "If, in our ceremonies, we
use sand that comes from where there is so much water, that sand
will surely bring water to us here; it must help us in our prayers for
rain."

I had brought enough sand for Hopis as well as Navajos. "See,"
I said to the group at the fireside, "I have brought you something
from the great waters, even some of the very ground that lies beneath
the waters. The sand is silver there, not golden, like yours upon
the desert."

I opened the jar and poured the gray particles into Ponianömsi's
out-stretched palm. She stooped by the fire the better to see, and
slowly let fall the shining stream from one hand into the other.

"Where I live," I continued, "there is much sand like this and
there are great waters, so great that a man standing on the edge can
see no land upon the other side."

Ponianömsi closed her fingers over the sand and looked at me
with earnest eyes. The other Indians, too, children of the desert,
all gazed upon me with fixed look. The sand was passed from hand
to hand. Each Indian fingered it with reverence.

"There is a great water to the west of California: that you know.
But my home is by the Eastern waters, towards the rising sun. And
in my home the fields are green with grass, and trees grow tall. The
mountains there are not barren rocks like yours; they are covered
with waving forests. The sun does not shine always, as with you;
there are many clouds, and much rain falls. Sometimes it rains for
many days; then skies are gray, not blue."

"And are you going back to those great waters and that Eastern
land?" said Ponianömsi.

"To-morrow I must go," I said. Then spoke Talaskwaptiwa,

brother of the chief, with true Indian hospitality. "But you will come to see us many times?"

"Ah no," I answered, "I cannot come back soon again, nor can I come back often, for my home is far away."

"How far?" said Talaskwaptiwa. "How many days must a Hopi run before he find your land?"

"A Hopi must run for many moons to reach the great waters of the East," I answered. "The railroad train runs four days and four nights without rest, and the train runs in one hour as far as a Hopi does in a day."

The Indians fingered the sand in silence. It had come a long way.

"You would be surprised at so much green, if you could see my country," I said. "But my people would be as much surprised if they could see your corn. With us, corn is all yellow and white, not many colored, as with you. We have never seen corn blue and red and black like yours. Will you, in friendship, give me of your corn an ear of every color to take to my people?"

Ponianömsi rose, and with her Talaskwaptiwa. At the embers they lit a tiny bit of candle and picking up a woven basket-tray went to the store-room where the corn was neatly stacked in sorted piles of different colors. They brought me the full tray. Ponianömsi held it in the light of the fire. "See," she said, picking up in turn an ear of each color, "the blue, the black, the spotted, the pink, the red, the yellow, the white, the lilac, I have brought one of each kind."

All light had faded from the windows. The room was lit by the fire alone; night had come. Outside, the white horse whinnied and stirred the dust impatiently. I rose to go; Ponianömsi took my hand. "You will not forget me," I said. Ponianömsi answered, "We will pray for you, our friend, and when you are in your far-off home by those great waters, will you pray for the Hopis, that they may have rain?"

"I will pray for the Hopis that they may have rain and that they may be 'good in their hearts,'" I answered, using the Hopis' own prayer-phrase.

Talaskwaptiwa stood by the hearth, his face grave in the fire-light. I knew that the time was drawing near when the Hopis would plant their *bahos*, — emblematic prayer-sticks, into whose feathered ends prayers are breathed.   If any Hopis are absent at the time of the offering of bahos, those at home make bahos for them. So I said, "When the Hopis make their bahos, will they make one for me?"

Talaskwaptiwa looked up quickly; this was a strange request from a *Bahana*—an American.   But he answered, "We are spinning now in the kivas;[1] soon we shall make the bahos.   I will make a baho for you, and we will pray for you."

"Pray that I, too, may be good in my heart," I said, as I bent and kissed the cheek of Ponianömsi.

So we parted.   The young nephew left with me, for he, too, lived at the foot of the mesa.   Together we passed through the shadowed village, meeting here and there a hurrying barefoot Hopi flitting homeward through the dark.

The young man led his white horse by the bridle as we clambered down the rocky trail beneath the stars.   "When Talaskwaptiwa has made the baho, what will he do with it?" I asked.

"He will give it to Ponianömsi," answered the Hopi, "when all the women go to plant their bahos she will take it with her."

"And where do the women plant the bahos?"

"Over there—east!"   He pointed with his whip to the cliff above. "On the edge of the mesa they will plant the bahos when the yellow line[2] comes over the mountains."

"Why do they plant them at the coming of the yellow line?"

"Because they pray, and if they pray when the sun rises, the sun will carry the prayers up, up!"   His whip moved, in illustration, from horizon to zenith.

"And to whom do the Hopis pray?"

There was a pause, then, slowly, "It is that which makes the rain —that makes all things.   It is the Power, and it lives behind the sun."[3]

---

[1] Woollen cord, used to bind the bahos, is ceremonially spun by the men in the *kivas*—underground council chambers.

[2] The Hopi expression for dawn.

[3] Mrs. Matilda Cox Stevenson, of the Bureau of American Ethnology, in her classification of the Zuñi higher powers, tells of "A'wonawil'ona, the supreme, life-giving, bisexual power, who is referred to as He-She, the symbol and initiator of life, and life itself, pervading all space," also of "The Sun Father, who is directly associated with the supreme power; . . . he is the giver of light and warmth, and through the supreme power the giver of life." (See "The Zuñi Indians; Their Mythology, Esoteric Fraternities, and Ceremonies." Twenty-Third Annual Report, Bureau of American Ethnology, Washington, D. C.)

"And the katzinas?"

"The katzinas only take the prayers. We do not pray to them."

"Does the Power that lives behind the sun look like a man, or like anything that the Hopis have ever seen?"

The Hopi looked at me in surprise. "No, it is not a man; we don't know how it looks. We only know that it *is*."

"When Lololomai, the chief, prays, how does he pray? Will you tell me?"

"He goes to the edge of the cliff and turns his face to the rising sun, and scatters the sacred corn-meal. Then he prays for all the people. He asks that we may have rain and corn and melons, and that our fields may bring us plenty. But these are not the only things he prays for. He prays that all the people may have health and long life and be happy and good in their hearts. And Hopis are not the only people he prays for. He prays for everybody in the whole world—everybody. And not people alone; Lololomai prays for all the animals. And not animals alone; Lololomai prays for all the plants. He prays for everything that has life. That is how Lololomai prays."

We trod the rest of our downward way in silence. I looked up at the sky, so vast and deep, lit by the brilliant desert stars. As we neared the foot of the trail, I glanced back at the village-crested mesa. It loomed a great black shadow on the sky. To-morrow, the Hopi world would no longer be mine. Then, as though to seal in spiritual beauty the memory of the simple people of Oraibi, the wide night seemed to echo, "He prays for the whole world—for everything that has life."

LOLOLOMAI'S PRAYER

Painted by V. Shiye, a Cochiti Indian

(The symbolism is clear except in the figure representing the
animal world. Hands, feet, and head suggest the Indian belief in
the entity of life, human and animal; and the prayer feathers
attached to the forehead suggest that even animals have a spiritual
relationship to "the Power that lives behind the Sun.")

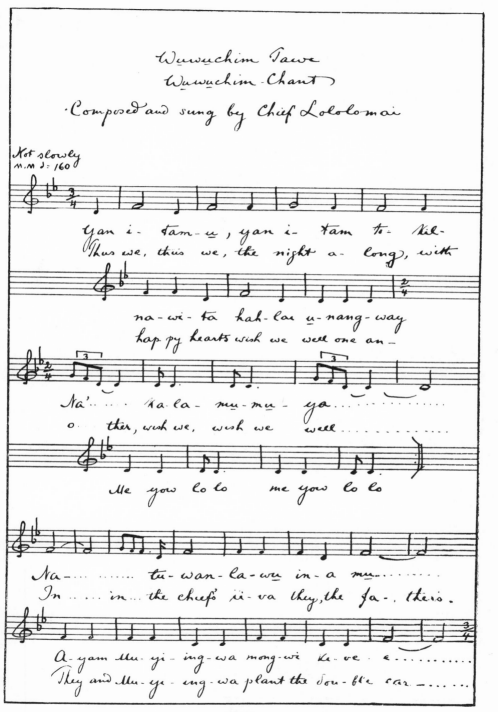

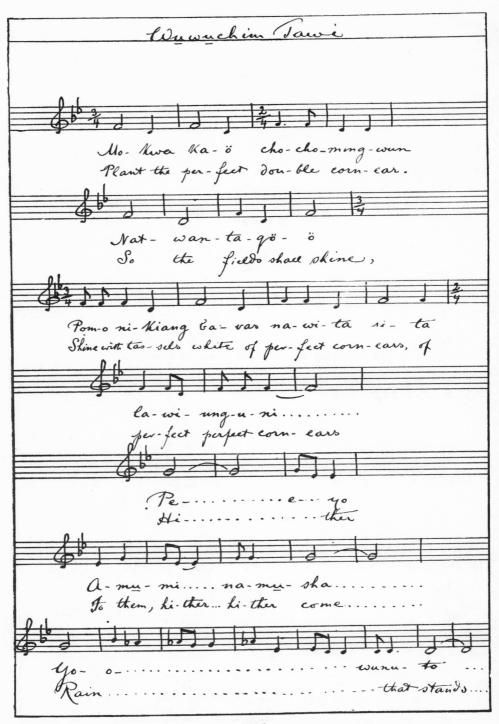

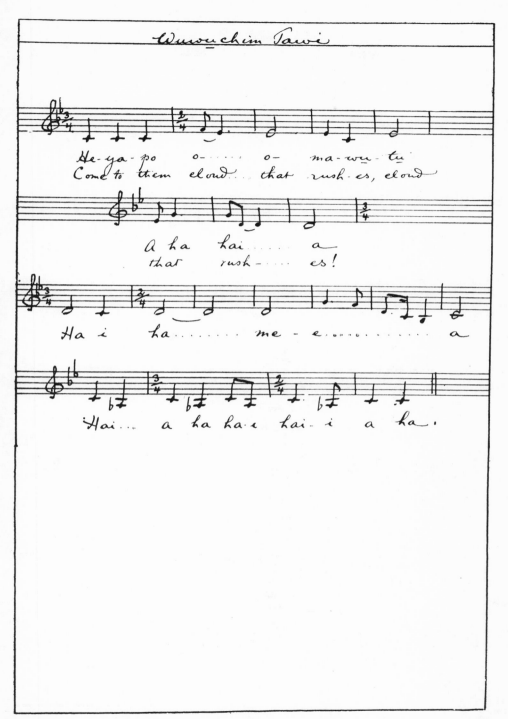

Wuwuchim Tawi

Pu- va,. . . . . pu- va,. . . . . pu-va!

The crosses over the notes indicate where the mother sways
forward in rocking the child; the circles, where she sways
back again to her normal position. The small crosses
signify a short half-sway forward, the long ones, a
long sway to a bent position which the mother
maintains until as indicated by the circle, she
sways back again.

Poli Tiwa Tawi

O- mi na-wung wi-na- ni............
lip-ward may help one an-o-ther to grow..........

Ha- a... ai ya- a- a- a- a

Ha- a.... ai ya- a- a- a a

Slower. m.m. ♩= 104   m.m. ♩= 168

Wi ya ha.. e........ ni ya ha

Slower. m.m. ♩= 104

E ni ya ha ha e ni ya

m.m. ♩= 168

Go- o- o- o

Slower m.m. ♩= 112   m.m. ♩= 168

·I- ya ha hi yi yi na hi yi yi na

* This triplet is a downward sweep of the voice.

[502]

Poli Tiwa Tawi

Poli Tiwa Tawi

Anga Katzina Tawi

Anga Katzina Tawi

Yang-a...... ah...... ai.............
Sing-...ing sing-ing... thus:............

O..... o-o   ho   o.......o...... he-e

E.... e..... lo   o..... o....... o- o   o

Ha.... u.... a-a- a ha........a-i ha.....a-a

Ha- a-i a- a- a

A...... a ha ha i....... i hi hi-i

Hi   hi yi hi yi hi!

* The refrain from here on represents the song of the maidens.

Korosta Katzina Tawi

Tu-ve- nang-u yi- ma- ni
In bril-liant, bril-liant throng

A ha-a-a i hi-i-i

Sha-kwa vo-li- mu-u- u-u
Blue but-ter-flies

Mo-zhi-si ma-na-tu yu-u-u-u u-i
O-ver the blossom-ing vir-gin beans,

Ta-la-si yam-mu-yu
With pol-len paint-ed fa-ces

Pi-tzang-wa a ti-ma- Kiang
Chase one an-other in bril-liant streams

Tu-ve- nang-u yi- ma- ni
In bril-liant, bril-liant streams

Korosta Katzina Song.

Korosta Katzina Song

[512]

Korosta Katzina Song

A-mu-na-wi ta-a-a
O-ver the vir-gin corn

Ta-a tang-a ya-tu
Wild bees wild bees hum

Tö-ki yu-yu-win-ta si
Wild bees hum, wild bees hum, hum

A ha-a-a i hi-i-i

Mo-zhi-si ma na-tu-u-u
O-ver the blos-som-ing beans

A-mu-na wi ta-a-a
O-ver the vir-gin beans

Ta-a tang-a ya-tu
Wild bees wild bees hum,

Korosta Katzina Tawi

[514]

Korosta Katzina Song

te-muh u- u- u- yi a- mu- na-wit yo-o- o- o- oi
O-ver your field of grow-ing corn all......... Day all day shall come

Yo- oi ho- yo- yo- ti- ma- ni......
Come the rush-ing rain, rush-ing rain,

Ta-wa-.... na.... wi-.... ta- a
Rush-ing rain, rush-.... ing.... rain....

Ai........ ai.... ha a.... ha ha- a

I........ hi i.... hi hi- i

Ho... o..... o..... o... ho ai- ai- ai- ai

E... e- e- e- e he lo- o- o- oi

[515]

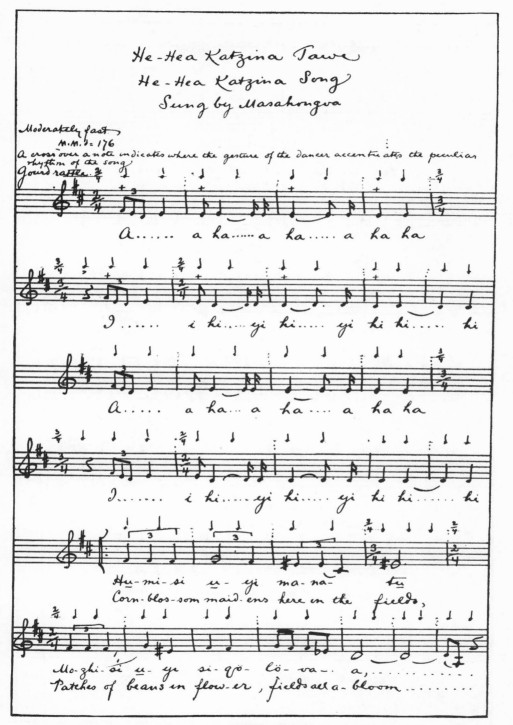

He-Hea Katzina Tawe
He-Hea Katzina Song
Sung by Masahongva

Moderately fast
M.M. ♩ = 176
A cross over a note indicates where the gesture of the dancer accentuates the peculiar rhythm of the song
Gourd rattle.

A...... a ha...... a ha..... a ha ha

I...... i hi.... yi hi.... yi hi hi..... hi

A..... a ha... a ha.... a ha ha

I....... i hi.... yi hi.... yi hi hi...... hi

Hu-mi-si u-yi ma-na- tu
Corn-blos-som maid-ens here in the fields,

Mo-zhi-si u-yi si-qö-lö-va- a,..........
Patches of beans in flow-er, fields all a-bloom..........

[517]

He-Hea Katzina Tawi

Ha-pi me
Now be-hold!

He-si gö-lö-va-a-a a-a-a a
Through bright clus-ters of flow'rs........

Si-kia vo-li nang-ö-yi-ma-ni-i-i-i-i
Yel-low but-ter-flies are chas-ing at play....

Mo-zhi-si-gö-lö-va-a-a a-a-a
And thro' the blos-som-ing beans..........

Sha-kwa vo-li nang-ö yi-ma...ni-i-i-i-i...
Blue.... but-ter-flies are chas-ing at play.....

O. ... ho.......... o......... o ho wa

E...... he........... e........ e he lo-oi

[520]

He-Hea Katzina Tawi

He-Hea Katzina Tawi

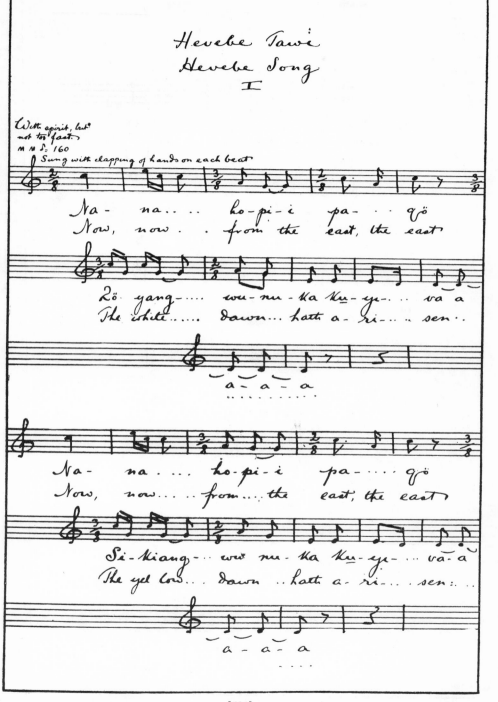

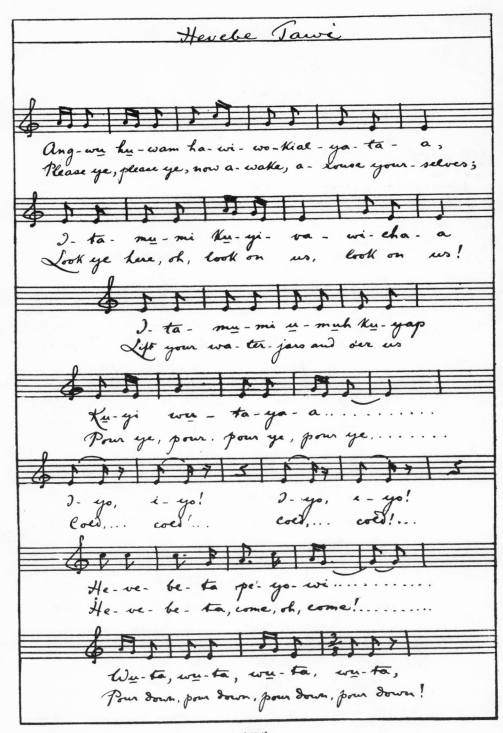

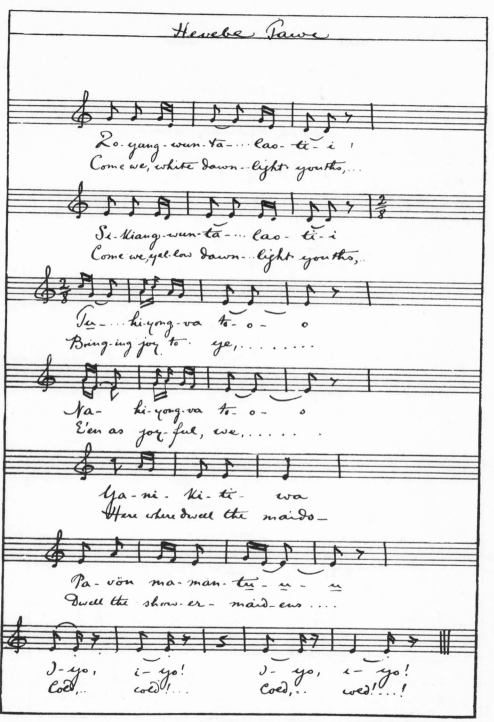

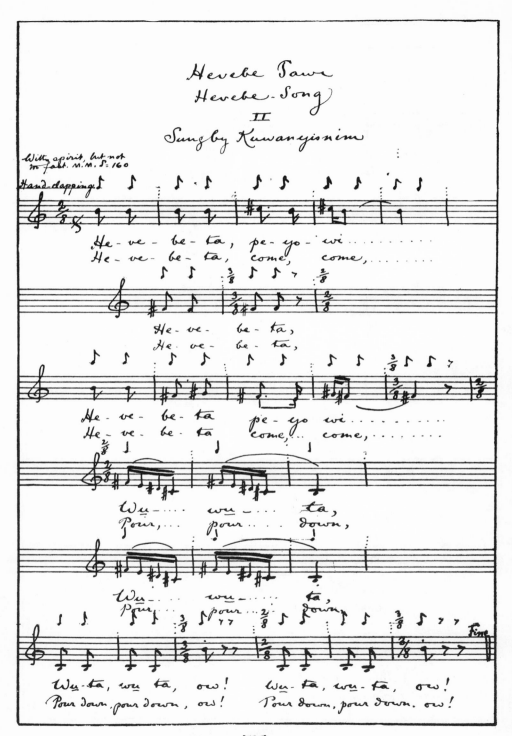

Hevebe Tawi

[530]

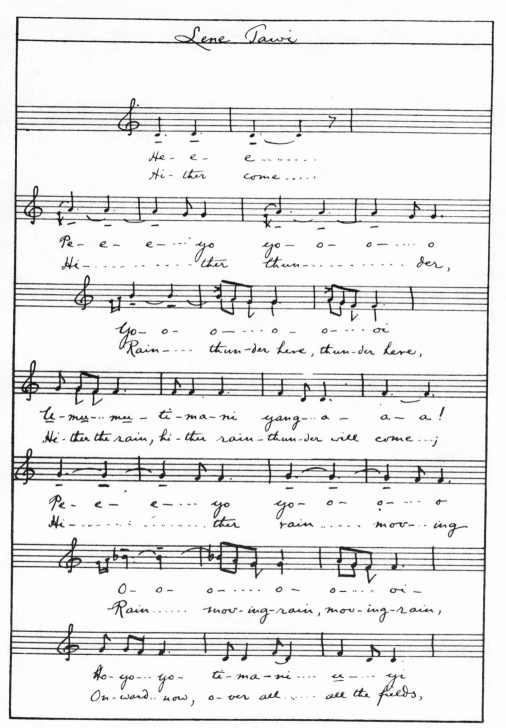

[531]

APPENDIX

T HE following paragraphs are from *The Discovery of America,* by John Fiske. The famous historian here sets the seal of authority on the value of the study and preservation of Indian thought:

"Aboriginal America is the richest field in the world for the study of barbarism. . . . Until we have become familiar with ancient American society, and so long as our view is confined to the phases of progress in the Old World, the demarcation between civilized and uncivilized life seems too abrupt and sudden; we do not get a correct measure of it. . . . But among the red men of America the social life of ages more remote than the lake villages of Switzerland is in many particulars preserved for us to-day, and when we study it we realize as never before the continuity of human development, its enormous duration, and the almost infinite accumulation of slow efforts by which progress has been achieved. . . .

"The folk-lore of the red men is found to be extremely interesting and instructive. . . . No time should be lost in gathering and recording every scrap of this folk-lore that can be found.

"The pueblos of New Mexico and Arizona are among the most interesting structures in the world. Several are still inhabited by the descendants of the people who were living in them at the time of the Spanish Discovery, and their primitive customs and habits of thought have been preserved to the present day with but little change.

"The house communities of the southern Slavs are full of interest for the student of the early phases of social evolution, but the Mandan round-house and the Zuñi pueblo carry us much deeper into the past. Aboriginal American institutions thus afford one of the richest fields in the world for the application of the comparative method, and the red Indian, viewed in this light, becomes one of the most interesting of men; for in studying him intelligently, one gets down into the stone age of human thought. No time should be lost in gathering whatever can be learned of his ideas and institutions before their character has been wholly lost under the influence of white men. . . . Some extremely ancient types of society, still preserved on this continent in something like purity, are among the most instructive monuments of the past that can now be found in the world. Such a type is that of the Moquis [Hopis] of northeastern Arizona. I have heard a rumor, which it is to be hoped is ill-founded, that there are persons who wish the United States government to interfere with this peaceful and self-respecting people, break up their pueblo life, scatter them in farmsteads, and otherwise compel them, against their own wishes, to change their habits and customs. If such a cruel and stupid thing were ever to be done, we might justly be said to have equalled or surpassed the folly of those Spaniards who used to make bonfires of Mexican hieroglyphics."

APPENDIX

NOTE

The interlinear translations here given have been made with care in the hope that the book may be of some aid in the comparative study of the linguistic stocks of the North American continent; yet they are offered as approximate only, for philological accuracy requires full and intimate knowledge of Indian languages—a knowledge which the recorder does not possess. Whenever an authority on the language of a given tribe has been found, his criticism has been solicited, as follows, and the recorder wishes here to express her grateful acknowledgment of the services so kindly rendered:

Penobscot and Passamaquoddy: Dr. J. Dynely Prince, Columbia University, New York.
Kiowa: Mr. James Mooney, Bureau of American Ethnology Washington, D. C.
Kwakiutl: Dr. Franz Boas, Columbia University, New York.
Zuñi: Mrs. M. C. Stevenson, Bureau of American Ethnology, Washington, D. C.
Hopi: Rev. H. R. Voth, Field Columbian Museum, Chicago, Illinois.

The words in Indian songs are often changed for euphony in singing, or they are prolonged for rhythmic and poetic effect by the addition of vocables. In the following pages the aim has been to present only actual words, omitting vocables and meaningless refrains.

WABANAKI

MALISEET DANCE-SONG

Now used at weddings

Kwe-hiu-wha-ni-ho
how are you: how d'ye do (used in songs—not the common expression—more a song-phrase than words with distinct meaning)

kshi-te-ka-mo-tik   **'lo**
dance hard   *if you please (abbreviation of l'lo the,*
                                                                        "l" twice sounded)

pilsh-kwe-sis-tok   **ski-no-sis-tok**
young girls: maidens   *young boys: youths*

PASSAMAQUODDY DANCE-SONG

Wagad-alo   **n'musums**
our   (no meaning—syllables affixed for song-euphony)   *grandfather*
sanow   **kchi**   **Blamswe-Zozep**   **ha-ba-mes-ba-na**
(meaningless syllables, as above)   great   François-Josephe (Francis-Joseph)   has been fishing

MALISEET LOVE-SONG

Boski-u   **klabin (sung, "ta-la-bin")**   **elmi niamwouik**
very often   *you look up*   *up the river*
elmi siguak   **tabegilok**   **chipduk**
next spring   *ice is breaking*   *you might (might· may be)*
knamihi   **skwelagweyan**   **ku we nu de nu**
you see me   *coming down the river*   *(meaningless vocables)*

Next spring, when the ice is breaking up, look often up the river.   You may see me coming down the river (" in my canoe," understood).

[535]

DAKOTA

WANAGI WACIPI OLOWAN
The soul when separated   *Dance*   *Songs*
from the body: Spirit

(*Ghost-Dance Songs*)

I

Ateyapi	**kin**	**maka**
Father	*the*	*earth*

owancaya   **lowan**   **nisipe lo**
everywhere   *to sing*   *commands you* (**ni**, *you;* **si**, *command;*
    pe, *plural form of* **pi**, *abbreviation of*
    pi-yela-yelo, *an emphatic ending*)

he	**eya**	**po**	**oyakapo**
this	*say*	(*imperative particle*)	*tell it abroad*

The Father commands all on earth to sing. Say this. Tell it abroad.

II

Ina	**hekuye**	**misunkala**
Mother	*come back: come home* (**he** *interjection;*	*my younger brother*
	ku *come home;* **ye** *a precatory form*	*little*
	of the imperative singular)	

ceya   **omani**   **Ate**   **heye**   **lo**
to cry   *walking about*   *Father*   *thus saith* (**heya** *to*   (*emphatic ending*)
to weep   *say this or that*)

III

He, he   **wanna**   **wawate**   **wasna**
(*exclamation*)   *now*   *I am eating, feasting*   *pemmican* (*dried buffalo-meat*
watinkte   *minced with wild cherries*
I shall eat   *and spices*)

WICASA ATAWAN OLOWAN
Man   *Looking at, or towards*   *Song*

(*Song of the Seer*)

Hocoka	**wan**	**cicuqon**
Centre of the camp—in this case,	*a*	*what I have given you*
the circle of warriors who are		*what I have prophesied*
gathered in the centre of the		*to you*
camp awaiting the prophecies		
of the Seer, or Holy Man, be-		
fore setting out to war		
yutonkal		**nunwe**
elsewhere		*let it be* (*let it be fulfilled*)

APPENDIX

TASUNKE-SKA OLOWAN
Horse   White   Song

(Song of the White-Horse Society)

Kola	taku	oteḣika	imakuwapi	lo
Friend	*whatever*	*hardship*	*charge me with*	*(emphatic ending)*
		difficulty	*put upon me*	
hena	**kowokipi**	**śni**	**waon**	**welo**
these	*fearing*	*not*	*I am*	*(emphatic ending)*

Friend, whatever hardships fall upon me, I fear them not!

(The song is also sung when one man tells another that whatever the hardship he will befriend him).

TOKALA OLOWAN
Fox   Song

(Song of the Fox Society)

Tokalaka	miye	ca	nakenula	waon	welo
Fox	*I*	*(connective)*	*a short time*	*I am*	*(emphatic ending)*

I am the Fox.   I am living but a short time.

TOKALA WACIPI OLOWAN
Fox   Dance   Song

Omani	kin	nayapapi	ca
Travellers	*the*	*you fled*	*and*
Agna-Iyanke	**hena**	**yunke-lo**	
Beside Runs	*there*	*lay (was killed)*	

yunkhe, *lying prone,* **lo** *(emphatic ending)*

You, the travellers, fled, and Runs-Beside lay killed.

WAKAN OLOWAN
Holy   Song

(The story of the Holy Song is here given in abbreviated form in the original Dakota)

Wakpa	can	śoka	el
creek	*wood*	*thick*	*at*
river or stream	*a tree*		
	trees		
ahi tipi	**na**		**memeya**
came into camp	*and*		*circle*
	also		
ahi	*moreover*	**ahiti**	
to bring to a place		*to come and pitch one's tent.* **Ti, tipi,**	
		a tent, house, dwelling	
etipi	**yun-kan**	**napsiyoḣli**	
camped at	*and then*	*finger-ring*	
na	**napoktan**	**ko**	**wicakila**
and	*bracelet*	*also*	*he asked of them*
ca	**kupi**	**na**	**wica kila**
and	*they gave*	*and*	*them he asked*

(**ku,** to give to any one;
pi (suffix) is usually
the sign of the plural)

inikaġa

sweat-lodge: new life (called "new life" because after the sweat-bath the man feels as though made over.   The sweat-bath is a sacred act of purification: **ini,** to take a vapor-bath, **inikaġa,** to make "ini.")

kaġapi
they made

.na
and

can
pole
(wood)

wan
a

paslatapi
set up

na
and

el
in

pte-hinca-ha
buffalo calf hide

wan
one
a

sayapi
red they painted

na
and

el
on

iyakaskapi
tied on to it

(iya-kaskapi
to it they bound

kaska
to bind

iyakaska
to bind to)

wicaśa
man

wan
a

eyanpaha
crier

icu
took

na
and

eyanpaha
*summon, cry out, or
herald*

si
bade him

na
and

tona
as many as

kużapi
*sick
(were, understood)*

hena
those

owasin
all

kuśela
close, near

u
to come

wicasi
told them
*(wica them tell;
si, command)*

na
and

can
*pole
(wood)*

kin
the

hute
*base
foot*

el
at

can
wooden

waksica
*cup
bowl
(used by medicine-men)*

egle
placed

na
and

lowan
sang

yun-kan
then

can
pole

etan
*from
(abbreviated form
of etanhan)*

mini
water

u
came

na
and

waksica
cup

el
at
(Poured or trickled into the bowl until it was full)

ożula
full

ca
and

kuża
sick

kin
the

wicaku
them gave

waksica
cup

etanhan
from it

mini
water

onqon
*where the water
was contained*

he
those

wicaśa
men

ota
many

yatkanpi
drank

tka
but

yahepapi
*they drank up
they drained*

sni
not

ohinni
always

ożula
full

asnipi
*cured
(they were cured)*

glapi
go home

na
and

owanżi
*be quiet
one or some (they);
"o" indicates the
locative form*

yankapo
*he commanded them to
stay in one place*
*(yanka to be in one place;
po, imperative particle)*

na
and

ake
again

lowan
sang

na
and

maka
*ground
earth*

el
on

owa
*wrote
drew*

na
and

iwankam
above

yuġata
his hand spread out

APPENDIX

yuṅkaṅ	**maka**	**el**	**owa**	**qon**	**he**
then	*ground*	*on*	*draw*	*that*	*it*
			(drawing)		
yawa	**yuṅkaṅ**	**ihaṅhaṅna**		**kiṅ**	**pte**
read	*then*	*next day*		*the*	*buffalo*
		morrow			
otapi	**kte lo**	**eya**	**yuṅkaṅ**		**ecetu**
plenty	*will be*	*he said*	*then*		*it was fulfilled*
	(lo (suffix) *is an emphatic*				
	particle)				
yuṅkaṅ	**ake**	**l'eya**	**ceži**	**kiṅ**	**hena**
then	*again*	*this he said*	*tongue*	*the*	*those*
		(le, *this;* **eya,** *he said)*			
oyoya	**kiṅ**	**na**	**cante**	**kiṅ**	**hena**
thighs	*the*	*and*	*heart*	*the*	*them*
(the best parts of the meat)					
ayustaṅpiktelo		**eya**	**na**	**waṅna**	**tiyata**
they leave shall		*he said*	*and*	*now*	*home to*
(lo, *emphatic particle)*					*at home*
glipi	**nahaṅ**	**pte-ha**	**etaṅhaṅ**	**ogle**	**wikcemna**
they came back	*and*	*buffalo-hide*	*of*	*shirts*	*ten*
			from		
topa	**(wikcemna-topa)**	**kaġa**	**na**	**peži**	
four	*forty*	*made*	*and*	*straw*	
na	**makahilila**				
and	*mud : clay (baked clay? " lilila " Teton form of " lilita," hot)*				
na	**ca-hli**	**icu**		**na**	
and	*charcoal*	*took*		*and*	
ca-hli	**wahiṅśa**	**na**	**mazasu**	**kaġa**	
gunpowder	*caps*	*and*	*wads*	*made*	
na	**wicaśa**	**kiṅ**	**wicaku**	**na**	**owasiṅ**	**iṅžiṅpi**
and	*men*	*the*	*to them gave*	*and*	*all*	*rose up*
na	**caṅ-noṅpa**	**waṅ**	**opagipi**	**na**	**wi**
and	*wooden pipe*	*a*	*filled*	*and*	*sun*
kiṅ	**on**	**iyat'aṅpi**	**l'eya**	**oyate**	**waṅ**
the	*with*	*lighted the pipe*	*this he said*	*people*	*a*
		(by the sun)	**(le,** *this;* **eya,** *he said)*	*tribe*	
waśte	**ca**	**piya**	**wakaġe**	**eya**	**na**	**waṅna**
good	*and*	*renew*	*I made*	*he said*	*and*	*now*
		regenerate			
		infuse new life			
wagnikte	**eya**				
I return will	*he said*				

WAKAṄ OLOWAṄ
Holy   *Song*

(Medicine-Song)

Oyate	**waṅ**	**waśte**	**ca**
people	*a*	*good*	*and*
nation			
tribe			
waṅna	**piyawakaġe**		**lo**
now	*I renew*		*(emphatic ending)*
	I heal		
	I make anew		

[539]

wankanta
On high—above

Tunkanṡila
Great Father
Grandfather (in this case the Supreme
Being)—literally, the Great Father

heya
thus said

ca
and

wanna
now

piyawakaġe
I make anew

OLOWAN
Song

Okicize
war
battle

iyotan
great
chief

micilaqon
I was thought

miye
myself
I, me

ṡni
(adverb of negation)
not, no

ṡe
used at end of sentence to
emphasize—i.e., it would
seem so, so it seems

iyotiyewakiye
condition
state

I was thought the greatest in battle. But it is no longer so. Now I am enduring hard-ships.

OMAHA WACIPI OLOWAN
Omaha   Dance   Songs

I

Natanhiwan
The charging enemy

winyan
woman

wakaġe
made

The enemy charged, but I made a woman of him!

II

Ho
(exclamation)

leciya
hither

nicopi
they called you

WIOṠTE OLOWAN
Love   Songs

I

Tokiya
where

amayaleso
are you taking me

higna-waya
to have for husband
(higna, husband)

cin
the

na
and

temahilaqon
that one dearly loves me

eṡa
so

wagnikte
I will go back

II

Inkpataya
up the creek

nawaẑin
I stand

na
and

ṡina
shawl
blanket

cicoze
to thee wave

ma-ya
(exclamation)

leciya
hither

ku wanna
come now

III

Koṡkalaka
young men

otapi
very many

tka
although.

niṡna
you alone

iyokipi mayaye
pleased me

iyotan
most highly, most
of all, chief

cilaqon
I esteemed you

wankiciyake
seeing one another

ṡni
(negative)
not

unqonkte
we must part

Although the youths are many, thou alone art pleasing to me. Above all others I hold thee.
We must part, not to see one another for a long time.

APPENDIX

IV

Eyas	hececa	ye	lakaś
Although	*thus*	*(an emphatic particle)*	*indeed, certainly, truly*

awanicigla waonqon		nape-mayuza	
I shall govern myself		*hands grasp me*	
I watched you			

First Version.—*Although it is thus, indeed (that I am in love), I will nevertheless guard my self-respect. Take me by the hand. I watched you. Take my hand and part.*

Second Version.—*That is the reason. I watched you. Take my hand and part.*

V

Ehake	wanmayakuwe		śice
last	*look upon me*		*term of endearment of a woman to a man*
	come to see me		*loved one*
			my love

tecililaqon	wanna	waya	wamanikte
I loved you	*now*	*school*	*I am going away*
ehake	wanmayakuwe	ehake	nape-mayuza
last	*look upon me*	*last*	*take my hand*
last time	*come to see me*	*last time*	

ŚUNKA OLOWAN
Dog   Song
Song of the Dog Feast

Sunka	wayatanin	(wayata	nin)
Dog	*may you eat!*	(*to eat*	*may it be*)

OKICIZE OLOWAN
War   Song

Kolapila	takuyakapi lo	maka	kin	mitawa
Friends my	*what you say*	*earth*	*the*	*mine*
yelo	epinahan	blehemiciye lo		(my kingdom)
(emphatic ending)	*I said*	*I exert me (emphatic ending)*		*(my domain)*

PAWNEE

TAWI' KURUKS
Song   Bear

("*Tawi'*" abbreviation of "*Tawio*")

Song of the Bear Society

Rerawha-a[1]	para	riku	ratutah	hi	tzapat
Those yonder coming	*almost*	*thus*	*I who did so*	*and*	*a woman*
rakuwaka	kuatutah		(ra, *the one who:*		iriritah
who would say	*oh, if I could do*		t, I: ut, *on be-*		*(as) those do*
	(kua, *oh, if:* t, I: ut,		*half:* ah, *to do*)		
	on behalf: ah, *to do*)				
rasakura[1]		rukuksa	rasakura		rura whia[1]
rays of sun		*which come down*	*rays of sun*		*which come moving*
					along the ground

[1] *The terminal "a" indicates "to come," i. e. direction towards the speaker.*

TAWI' KURUKS
Song   Bear

Song of the Bear Society

Nawa	Atira	ha	we	ra
Now	*the mother (Mother-Corn understood)*	*behold*	*she*	*cometh*
nawa	**Atius**	**ha**	**we**	**ra**
now	*the father (Father-Hawk understood)*	*behold*	*he*	*cometh*

IRUSKA

Songs of the " Iruska "—warriors who have won war honors

I

Narutitawe   **Atius**   **tiwaku**
a noun meaning a thing without an owner—   *Father*   *saith*
a lone thing, abandoned, forsaken, orphaned
asawaki   **ratawe**
spotted horse   *the one among them, i. e. the one among them, that does not belong there*

II

Hawa
again   **Atira**
tziksu weta tariruta   *Mother*
      (Mother-Moon understood)
spirit now I do for you: meaning, my spirit relies upon thee, I put my faith in thy power
(**tziksu**, *thinking power, mind, spirit*)

III

War-Dance Song of the Iruska

Atius   **si**   **tus kitawiu**
Father   *thou art he*   *thou ruling over*
karaku   **u-kitawiu**
there is not over thee any that is greater   *thou alone art ruler*

IV

Iruska Song of the Corn-Offering

Atius	ha	is-tewat	askururit	weta tsihakawatsista
Father	*behold*	*look thou*	*together*	*now we partake, eat*

SKIRIKI
Coyote

Coyote Warrior-Song

Ah   **tirus**   **takawaha**
(exclamation of adoration)   *yonder*   *expanse of heaven*
tiratpari
I walk or roam (I walk over the prairies)
tatàra kita-wira
I recognize thee as supreme ; meaning, I put my faith in the supreme power (**kita**, *above, over all,*
supreme)
hawa   **re-rawira**
again   *I am on the war-path (literally, "walking in*
      anger"; " war-path" is not a Pawnee expression)

[542]

APPENDIX

SAKIPIRIRU

Young Dog Dance-Song

Atius	esa	ruka	ratu	teriku
Father	*is*	*the one*	*me*	*I saw*

KISAKA

Song of Rejoicing and Thanksgiving

Nawa	Atius		iri
now	*Father*		*an expression meaning thanks, or with gladness or thankfulness*
ta-titska	**asuta**	**hawa**	**rurahe**
I wish	*should be*	*again*	*that which is good*
			(*long life, plenty in the fields, good gifts*)

O Father, while giving thanks I wish that that which is good may be again—or, that all good gifts may be renewed.

KITZICHTA

Lance Ceremony

Kitzichta: *A particular kind of lance from which comes the name given to the society and its ceremonies*

Nari-ru-rit riwaka
*it was said, or, some one said (***narit-ru** *somebody, they* · **riwaka,** *spoke, said*)

tzapat	tiwaku	Taku	kaki
woman	*this did say*	*dance (Lance-Dance)*	*no*
nariksha	**Kitzichta**	**ra**	**huriwi**
not real	*The Lance*	*yonder*	*walking around*
not true			
not true for you	(*The men who own the lance are walking around in the ceremony*).		

KEHARE   KATZARU
Dance   Spirit

Songs of the Spirit-Dance

I

Irittatu terit	na-	rittatu terit
I saw it	*verily*	*I saw it*
nawiru-tzawhio		**rhurhera**
*flag (***nawira,** *cloth ;* **tzawhio,** *that which floats in the air*)		*beautiful*

II

Ah	heru	tzu-ut	Atius	we	ta-ita
(*exclamation*)	*dear*	*sister*	*Father*	*now*	*knows you*
	beloved				

III

Ah	tziksu	rutatiku	we raku	retkaha	ra
(*exclamation*)	*mind*	*I am stirred*	*when it is*	*night*	*coming*
	spirit	*moved*			
	thinking-power	*touched*			
kaw-kaw		**rakuwak-tahu**		**operit**	**we ra**	**ti**
the caw of the crow		*cawing like a crow*		*star*	*when coming*	*I*
		imitating the sound of the crow		(*morning star*)		*that*
kuhruri	**operit**	**ti**	**ra-hu**		(*pronoun*)
wait	*star*	*that*	*coming*		

[543]

IV

Ruwerera *it is coming yonder*	**operit** *star (Evening Star understood in first verse, Morning Star in fourth)*	**rerawha-a** *they are coming yonder* (**re**, *yonder :* **ra**, *com- ing:* **wha-a**, *many*)
Atira *Mother (Mother-Moon)*	**Atius** *Father (Father-Sun)*	

CHEYENNE

WUCHTCHSE ETAN NO-OTZ
Red Fox   Man   Song

Ma-achis *old man*	**hevisa** *abbreviation of* **hevisochtzi,** *his teeth*	**naehio** *abbreviation of* **natomo-wonotziyi,** *I am afraid of him*

HOHIOTSITSI NO-OTZ
Morning   Song

Ehani *Our father*	**nah-hiwatama** *has had pity on me* *(is blessing me)*	**napave** *good* *(I am happy, blessed, at peace)*	**vihnivo** *on my way*

Our Father, the ruler of the sun, has been merciful to me.   Happily I go on my way in peace.

AOTZI NO-OTZ
Song of Victory

Honih-hio *wolves*	**tsi-wona-atz** *in the morning* (**wona,** *morning*)	**imio-missi-yo** *eating*

Wolves eat in the morning.

AOTZI NO-OTZ
Song of Victory

Tsivais *these*	**siyo** *many* *(people)*	**tsitonitoyus** *look*	**maitom** *red paint*	**tsihotonihos** *thickly piled on* *(those with red paint* *thickly piled on)*
tahta *in sight*		**nanias-sini** *we start off (plural form)*		

(the idea of daylight is also conveyed by this word)

AOTZI NO-OTZ
Song of Victory

Hetanu *box-wood bow* *(sacred bow)*	**dzinimat** *carrying* *(bow understood)*	**hitu** *this one*	**hominu** *elm*	**nimadzi** *carry*

Bearer of the Sacred Bow.   You should carry a bow of elm.

NAI NO-OTZ
Healing   Song

Taeva *at night*	**nama-eyoni** *holy man*	**tze-ihutzittu** *when I go my way*

APPENDIX

WAWAHI NO-OTZ
Swinging Song

Huchdjeho
wood-rats
etanio-o
men (the double o is plural form)

niochdziyo
come here
ini-stoni-wahno-tziyo
are drawing near

Mata-
Timber
ehenowe
thus they say

MESHIVOTZI NO-OTZ
Baby Song

Meshivotzis
baby

naotziyo
sleep
(a prolongation, for singing, of **naotz***)*

tsiso
little
(little one)

ARAPAHO

HASSE-HI NAAD
Raw-hide Song

(The name raw-hide alludes to the buffalo-hide, which is an important feature of the ceremony)

Hedawunaneina
he will have pity on us
that he may
may he (invocation)

hishish
sun

nisana
my father

HACHE-HI NAAD
Wolf Song
or
JACHU NAAD
Comanche Song

Nahani
behold
here
hani
probably for a long time
(it will be long ere you will see me)

chita-ini
look hither

hitha
there
hätinahawuni
you will see me

bäbian
far away

niyihana
I am going
(on the war-path understood)
haka
because
nihin
you say

KAINAWAD NAAD
Circle Dance Song

Seniesäna
I stepped into
I waded in, or through

niha-nawu
yellow water

nänäi
it was
that is
bäeno
turtle

nidjieh-hi
*lake (***hi,*** *added syllable for*
euphony in singing)

HO NAWAD NAAD
Crow Dance Song

Hesunanin
Our Father

ho-hu
crow
*(***ho,*** *crow;* **hu,** *syllable added in singing)*

bähinahnit-ti
*he is all (***ti,*** *added syllable*
for euphony in singing)

NAKAHU NAAD
Sleep Song
(Lullaby)

Cheda-e
term of endearment
(literally: little big-belly, meaning little boy, little tot)

nakahu-kahu
go to sleep

bebe
baby

[545]

GOCHOTI NAAD
Hand-Game Song

Natinachabena	**ni nananaechana**
seeking for horses	*now I am looking all around*
I seek my horses	

HICHAÄCHUTHI
Those with Clubs
(Hichaäch)
Clubs

Nanänina		**Nanakunithäna**	**nanänina**
I am		*White Horn*	*I am*
(second vowel " a " broadened	**Neyachat-Chawaat**	**chä**	**änitana**
for euphony in singing)	*Whirlwind Running*	*again*	*I am living*

KIOWA

GOMDA DAAGYA
Wind   Song
(Very old song, some words archaic)

A-doguonko	**do-peya**	**kuyo**	**kionte-go-k'ian**
the lazy youths	*at home*	*sitting about*	*loved ones*
(those who have remained		*(idly?)*	
in camp instead of going	**etbonholgon**	**ayi-ya**	**on-pali**
on the war-path)	*they can see them*	*somewhere*	*he is sick*
	whenever they wish		*home-sick*
on-dekia			*pining*
he is alone			*weary*

   The lazy youths idling at home in camp may see their loved ones whenever they choose.
But him whom I love is far away on the war-path, lonely and weary.

GOMDA DAAGYA
Wind   Song

Pako	**e'k'ianda**	**ayi apo**	**hayi**
but one	*lover*	*taken somewhere*	*somewhere*
(but one that I love)		*(he has gone on the war-path with other men)*	*afar*
ankom oyom giie			
an expression meaning, the time grows long, or he is lonely and weary			

GOMDA DAAGYA
Wind   Song

Agulkide	**dogul-ongu**	**ambonpoya**	**dogya**	**nokon**	**honde**
I envy	*young men*	*they are missing you*	*at home*	*me*	*nobody*
	(who are well off)				
imp'oya	**tont'-o-no**		**yai-dahe-ba kuyo**		
missing me	*has no thought of it*		*why are you sitting about silent and forlorn? why*		
	(nobody at home has		*do you not sing and lighten your hearts?* **(yai,**		
	any thought of mis-		*joy:* **dahe,** *singing:* **ba,** *plural ending for*		
	sing me)		*more than three ;* **kuyo,** *sitting about*		

   I envy you fortunate young men.   You are well off—you have loved ones at home who are
longing for you.   I have no one.   Nobody has a thought of missing me.   Why are you sitting
silent and forlorn?   You should be singing to lighten your hearts.

APPENDIX

KOALDA DAAGYA
Begging   Song

Inhote   **to**   **sai**   **tãlyi**   **k'anhoton**   **atzeyuda**
here   *tipi*   *(connective)*   *boy*   *spider*   *pet*
(in this)   *(sung, talyi)*

hondeta   **al**   **ahanda**   **goa-ain**
something   *(connective)*   *to eat*   *that is why we are coming*

ak'ainkotuna giat'akwot
give something for the sake of the child

(**ak'ainkot,** *any oily food:* **na,** *connective:* **giat'akwot,** *knock out, such as to knock something out of a box—to throw away*)

Within this tipi dwells a child with his little spider-pet. That is why we come to you. Give us something to eat for love of the child and his pet!

T'ÄPK'O DAAGYA
Antelope   Song

Ton   **k'an**   **giapowitzep**   **no**
wooden   *spoon*   *I lost it*   *and then*

tainkyowitte   **tain hol**
my grandmother   *whipped me*

komdombe   **tonok'o**
the interior edge of the tipi, near the wall   *lying on the ground and crying*
(to throw one's self on the ground in anger, crying)

tsainiya   **ode**
that was the time   *a prophet or holy man: one who has super-natural or divine power, who, through divine*
domgya   *aid, is always able to procure food in plenty.*
divine, miraculous power

I lost my grandmother's wooden spoon. She whipped me, and I threw myself on the ground, crying, beside the tipi wall. There it was that there came upon me in sleep the divine power to become a holy man, a worker of wonders, a winner of food.

OKUM DAAGYA
Stop-crying   Song

A-go-go   **t'oph'o**   **goan-kontono**
your mother   *(same as t'äpk'o)*   *she will bring it to you*
t'anba (*or* **tomba**)   *antelope*   **ok'un-balita**
tube near the heart of the antelope,   *a noun. meaning that which one*
the choice morsel   *eats when too hungry to wait*
    for the regular meal

Thy mother will bring thee the antelope, and the choice morsel shall be thine for a tidbit.

OKUM DAAGYA
Stop-crying   Song
(Lullaby)

Iapagya   **mainte**   **koain**   **zotom**
baby   *coming down the river*   *swimming*   *drift-wood*
    (with the current)

tonsädal   **tsainyi**   **polainyi**
legs   *rabbit (prairie dog?)*   *rabbit*

The baby is swimming down the river
Little drift-wood legs,
Little rabbit legs.
(Nonsense-rhyme)

GWU DAAGYA
War-path Song

Ameyaidonhonme ain honya mopoiko
that playful word you said to me I never can forget (**yai**, *playing* : **don**, *words* : **hon**, *negative*)
anti yayowut hoyano
I am waiting for the first lover

tsainko	**gompaomk'o**	**eyamkom**
horses	*sore back*	*that are being given for me*

The maiden, speaking in thought to her first lover, says:
That playful word you said to me, I never can forget. Thus I wait for my first lover.
The ponies that are now being given for me all have sore backs!

WINNEBAGO

WASH-CHING-GEKA NA-WA' NI-NA
Hare   Song   Own
Song of the Hare

Wa-le	**ki-zi-na-nap**	**chun-ka**
who	*reaches out with his tongue*	*great one*
wa-lai-na-nap	**sa-ah-zhe** **ai-le-la**	**hin-gi na-nap**
you gather them in	*used to* *they say*	*gather me in*

WI-LA NA-WA' NI-NA
The Sun   Song   Own

Wash-ching-ge	**hin-khu lush-ka-le**	**hi-tek-nik**	**wa-la-ka**	**hi-u-ni-nik**
hare	*to loosen me*	*little fathers (uncles)*	*your*	*little mothers (aunts)*
wa-la-ka	**cha-ku**	**ki-shkan**		**hi-la-ni-he kche-zhe**
your	*what*	*they do*		*will ever*

WAI-KUN
Fable

Mo-zhun-na-le	**pe-zhe**	**ya-ki-ske shun-non-nink na-gi-kche**
earth full this	*who*	*is there like little me*
ne-sha-na	**ma-chi-nik-gla**	**ya-ki-o-o**
I alone	*sky little the*	*can touch*

Throughout the earth, who is there like to little[1] me! I alone can touch the little[1] sky!

MA-O-NA
Song to the Earth-Maker

Ma-o-na	**wai-kan-chunk hi kche**	**hing-ge**
Earth-Maker	*holy am I to be*	*tells me*

MUN-KUN NA-WAN
Medicine   Song

The words of this song are ritualistic, and most of them are archaic. They are greatly changed in singing, being drawn out by the interpolation of vocables. The hidden meaning is understood only by the initiated. The few words that can be translated literally are the following:

Han-te (*sung*, ha-ha-ti-hi)		**hi-na-wi-na**
I went away and learned		*the spirit says, " Dream again, tell of me "*
ma-na-gle	**nach-kwang-l** (*sung*, ha-ha-wha-nan-g'le)	**shi-ke-ha-e-hi**
the world	*hear me*	*in the beginning*

---

[1] *Diminutive, like the German suffix, " chen."*

APPENDIX

HI-WA-SHI-DA
Dance

Ma-na-gle	**wu-hi-ni-gi-gi-na**	**ha-chi-je-na**
the world	*I have won*	*I am come now*
chi-na-gla	**wu-hi-ni-gi-gi-na**	**ha-chi-je-na**
the village	*I have won*	*I am come now*

MUN-KUN NA-WAN
Medicine   Song

(The words of this song are ritualistic, and do not occur in the spoken language of to-day)

Ma-ni-na		**le-ha-no**		**wunk-i-wi-zha**
medicine-arrow (**mana,** *arrow*)		*make it go, let it fly*		*upon the man* (**wunk,** *man*)
le-ha-no	**ma-ni-na**	**le-ha-no**	**hi-nuk-i-zha**	**le-ha-no**
let it fly	*medicine-arrow*	*let it fly*	*upon the woman* (**hinuk,** *woman*)	*let it fly*

HE-LUSH-KA NA-WAN
Warrior   Song
I

Shun-ke	**wo-djin**	**wi-ne**	**ko-la-wi-la**	**Pa-ni**	**ka-lai-la-dju-ka**
horses	*whip*	*your*	*comrades*	*Pawnees*	*they have gone*
shun-ke	**wa-na-ma-ne**	**Pa-ni**	**guch-la**	**Pa-ni**	**ka-lai-la-dju-ka**
horses	*urge them on*	*Pawnee*	*shooter*	*Pawnees*	*they have gone*

HE-LUSH-KA NA-WAN
Warrior   Song
II

Wa-we-la	**ha-dja-le**	**hi-cha-ko-lo**	**Pa-ni-na**
my trail	*you see*	*friend*	*Pawnees those*
wa-cha-la		**wa-we-la**	**ga-ske-na**
I saw		*my trail*	*it is thus*

See what a trail is mine! Friend, I saw the Pawnees. See what a trail is mine!

HE-LUSH-KA NA-WAN
Warrior   Song
III

Ho-chunk-gi-le	**hi-she-na**	**Pa-ni-na**	**hi-she-na**
Winnebagos these	*you say*	*Pawnees these*	*you say*
hi-ta-lo	**hi-she-na**	**Ho-chunk-gi-le**	**hi-she-na**
friends	*you say*	*Winnebagos these*	*you say*

HE-LUSH-KA NA-WAN
Warrior   Song
IV

Ho-wi	**lo-ki-wa-wi-le**	**lo-han**	**tt'eh-hi-ga**	**ma-shon**	**o-ni je-na**
around	*ride with him*	*many*	*kills*	*feathers*	*is looking for*

HE-LUSH-KA. NA-WAN
Warrior   Song
V

Ya-tt'-eh-la	**hamb-la**	**pin-na**	**hi-he-la**	**na-nach-kon-je**
when I speak	*day the*	*fine*	*so I say*	*you hear me*
Na-ju-zi-la	**Ho-chunk-la**	**zhe-skai-le**	**hi-he-la**	**na-nach-kon-je**
Yellow-Hair	*Winnebagos the*	*are all like this*	*I say*	*you hear me*

WA-GI-TT'EH NA-WAN
Mourner's Song

Pe-zhe-ga	ko-ni-ka	ya-ge-kche-ne-zhe
whom	*grandmother*	*to call I wonder*

WAK-JE NA-WAN
Scalp Song
Victory Song

Pa-jo-ka	nik-la	hi-zhuk	ha-ni-na	nan-na-ke-we-no
Winnebago name for Comanche,	*little*	*gun*	*my*	*you are afraid of*
a neighboring tribe				

WUNK-HI NA-WAN
Men about Songs
Songs about Men
(Love-Songs of the Women)

Na-ni	dega-go	e-dja	wa-de-kjela
mother	*my uncle*	*to him*	*I wish to go*

WUNK-HI NA-WAN
Men about Songs
Songs about Men
(Love-Songs of the Women)

Hi-zhan	ho-do-chuch-ka	zhe-ske	shu-nu-na	hi-zhan
whoever	*I look at*	*becomes*	*thus (love-crazed, understood)*	*whoever*
wa-ki-tt'-eh-ka	zhe-ske	shu-nu-na	hi-zhan	wai-zhi-zhi-ka
I speak to	*becomes*	*thus*	*whoever*	*I whisper to*
zhe-ske	shu-nu-na	hi-cha-ko-lo	hi-nuk	lo-in-na-gle
becomes	*thus*	*friend*	*women*	*ones who want*
wi-do-kan-na-na	hi-zhan	do-mai-ku-ka	zhe-ske	shu-nu-na
one under my power	*whoever*	*I touch*	*becomes*	*thus*

KWAKIUTL

KLAWULACHA
Song of the Totem-Pole

Pulnakwila-	kiash-	ila-	koi
flood growing	*real*	*causing*	*distant*

Wakiash-
(the literal meaning of the name "Wakiash" is Wa, river, kiash, real)

kiash-	o-	choi
real	*good*	*there*

(Wakiash, the man, is called "The River" because he is rich and generous, full of gifts as the river is full of fish)

hitlpalkwala-	kyilish-	kiash-	ila-	koi
flood noise	*the world*	*real*	*causing*	*distant*

Kalakuyuwish
name of a particular totem-pole, supposed to mean the "pole that holds up the sky." Also a name of the man, Wakiash, who takes the name of the totem-pole.

lach-nahkwulla-	choi
in the world	*there*

    Meaning:—*Wakiash causes the distant flood to rise, signifying that his greatness and generosity are overflowing. The totem-pole is making a noise (like the creaking of trees) because it holds up the sky and the sky is so heavy. Good in the world is Kalakuyuwish who raised up this pole.*

APPENDIX

PIMA

CHUHWUHT
World

Chuhwuht-tuh	makai (*sung*, maka-i)	chuhwuht-tuh	nato	himalo himicho
world	*creator*	*world*	*finished*	*now it is started*
	maker			

also holy man, or medicine-man

CHUHTEK-OHOHIK NIEH
Blue-Bird   Song
(The words of this song are very much changed for singing)

Hai-ya hai-ya hai-ya
(exclamation of sadness, meaning, "alas, woe's me!")

chuhtek-ohohik   nieh-nieh
blue-bird   song
(*sung*, cheh wahl ohi nieh-nieh)

nieh-nieh-i   a-to   ho-huk
my song   is all   gone
(*sung*, nieh ha nieh va yo-hu-ka)
va ha va ho-huk
will all be gone
(*sung*, va ha maw-haw va yu-ka)

HUHWUHLI NIEH
Wind   Song
(Medicine-Song)

Hanam
cactus
(a variety that has fruit which
the Indians eat)
kachuwuch (*sung*, ka-cho-wuch-chi)
they grow, stand

yo-osik   a-ai huh-wurt (*sung*, ya-hai huh-wurt)
blossom   swaying back and forth
kano (*sung*, kani-hu-va muh-muhk)   muk
way over   far
kano   ya-ha   kimoich (*sung*, ki-moi)
way over   ridges in the desert   o'er

APACHE

MEDICINE-SONG

Awbizhaye
little cloud
niniya
this is the way I go
     Upon a little cloud I ascend; thus I journey upward.
pass through the air.

shichl
me, I
tsago degi
this place holy

hadahiyago
going up
naleya
changing while going through the air
To a holy place I go, changing as I

YUMA

AROWP
Song

Amai
sky
tza mi na hi
it is he who sings(?)
     (I go on the straight road, meaning I am good and happy).

ariwa
thinly covered with clouds
hunya kwa pai va
I go up the grade ·

shakwakwa (*sung*, shakwa)
mocking-bird
hunya kwa hui pa
I go up on the level, or (straight) road

NAVAJO

DSICHL BIYIN
Mountain-Song, or Hymn

Piki yo ye	dsichl	nantai	sa-a narai	bike	hozhoni
meaning, I walk up to the	*mountain*	*chief*	*living forever*	*happiness*	*everywhere*
mountain, or, I walk thither			*life unending*		

[551]

The expressions **sa-a naraï** *and* **bike hozhoni** *occur in many songs, usually at the end.* (*According to Dr. Washington Matthews, their literal translation is, "In old age walking the beautiful trail." This scholar further states that the expressions are equivalent to saying, "Long life and happiness," and as a part of a prayer the phrases are a supplication for a long and happy life.*) *The present compiler has found the usual translation given by the Indians in the songs recorded by her to be, "living forever," or "life unending," and "universal happiness," or "the happiness of all things." The significance may of course vary slightly in different songs. In this instance the meaning is that the mountain gives long life and peace to man, calling him "grandchild," or "son."*

tsoya	shich ni la
grandchild	*with me*
son	*(called me)*

The mountain calls me "son." (*This, say the Navajos, is a blessing.*)

DSICHL BIYIN
Mountain-Songs, or Hymns

Be		**naseya**	**ho-digin**	**ladji**	**ka', or kat**
with		*I go everywhere*	*place holy*	*yonder*	*now*
(or, with it—the rain-		*(with the rainbow)*	*divine*	*there*	*(a word often used to begin*
bow is understood)					*a phrase; when used as the*
					ending of a word, it denotes
					emphasis, as "indeed")

Sisnajinni

The sacred mountain of the East. (*According to Dr. Matthews, the name probably means Dark Horizontal Belt, and the mountain is presumably Pelado Peak, Bernalillo County, New Mexico*)

bine dji	dsichl-nantaï	sa-a naraï	bike hozhoni
behind there	*mountain chief*	*life unending*	*happiness of all things*

Tsodsichl

The sacred mountain of the South. (*According to Dr. Matthews, the name is from* **tso,** *great and* **dsichl,** *mountain. Called San Mateo by the Mexicans, Mount Taylor by the Americans*)

Doko-oslid

The sacred mountain of the West. (*According to Dr. Matthews, the name seems to contain, modified, the words* **tro,** *water, and* **kos,** *cloud. Called by the Americans, San Francisco Mountain*)

Depenitsa

The sacred mountain of the North. (*According to Dr. Matthews, the name is from* **depe,** *sheep— Rocky Mountain sheep—and* **intsa,** *scattered all over. Depenitsa seems identical with the the San Juan Mountains of Colorado*)

The present compiler received from the Navajos slightly varying translations of the mountain names, but the thorough study made by Dr. Matthews of the subject, and the authority of his Navajo informants, make his version to be preferred.

Second song:	Be	nadesta
	With (*it*)	*I am going homeward.* (*I shall go home-*
		ward with, or upon, the rainbow)
Third song:	Be	nikiniya
	With (*it*)	*I start homeward*
Fourth song:	Be	naïshtatl
	With (*it*)	*I am on my homeward way*
Fifth song:	Be	nanistṣa
	With (*it*)	*I am come home*
Sixth song:	Be	nanishta
	With (*it*)	*I sit down*

APPENDIX

HOGAN BIYIN
Hogan Song, or Hymn

Tsanti	**hogani**	**hozhon**	**hogan**	**hayiash**	**beashdje**
behold	house	beautiful	house	sunrise	under
yonder	dwelling	blessed			

ka', or kat	**Hastyeyalti**	**bi**	**hogani**	**hayolkatli**
now	name of God of Sunrise	his	house	dawn-light, first light, coming light (**katli,** coming)

be	**bi**	**hogan**	**tan alchkaï**	**yotti-iltrassaï**
from	his	house	white corn	hides precious
made of			(from **natan,** corn, and **alchkaï,** white)	

(*According to Dr. Matthews,* **yotti,** *or* **yodi** *are "furs, skins, textile fabrics, and such things as Indians bartered among themselves, except food and jewels"*)

tro-altlanastshini, or tro-tlanastshi
all waters, waters from many springs

(*According to Dr. Matthews,* **tro-tlanastshi** *"is a mixture of all kinds of water—i. e., spring-water, snow-water, hail-water, and water from the four quarters' of the world. Water used to-day in some of the Navajo rites approximates the mixture as nearly as possible"*)

tradetin
sacred corn-pollen

(*According to Dr. Matthews, sacred pollen is obtained from various plants, but Indian-corn is the chief source of supply. The offering of sacred pollen almost always follows or accompanies prayer, and is a part of religious rites*)

sa-a naraï	**bike hozhoni**	**i-iash**
living forever	happiness everywhere	sunset
everlasting life		

Hastyehogan	**nahotsoï**	**tan-alchtsoï**
name of God of Sunset	yellow after glow or	yellow corn
	evening twilight	(from **natan,** corn, and **alchtsoï,** yellow

nekliz, or inkliz
gems

(**Nekliz,** *or* **inkliz,** *are shells of all colors, turquoise, cannel-coal, and many other stones prized by the Navajos, and from which they make their jewels. The expression as here used signifies the gems used in prayer*).

iltrassaï	**tro-piyash**
precious	little waters
	dew-drops (literally, **tro,** water; **piyash,** children)

HLIN BIYIN
Horse Song, or Hymn

Nizho'ko	**ani**	**Johano-ai**	**dotlizh**	**be**	**lin, or hlin**
from **nizhoni,** beautiful, happy,	voice	name of the Sun-God,	turquoise	his	horse
and **ko,** having		the Bearer of the Sun			

yotti
precious hides of buckskin, buffalo, beaver, and mountain-lion; and "naskan,"an elaborately decorated ancient woven blanket formerly worn by the Navajos. The Navajos say that the "naskan" was first found in the house of the Sun-God

bahostiel	**bakaï**	**yiki**
spread out	on top	on it (the horse stands upon rich hides that are spread out beneath him)

tshilatra	**hozhoni**	**be**
blossoms, tips of flowers	beautiful	with, from

jinichltan
he (Johano-ai) feeds him, pastures him (he feeds his horse on the tips of flowers)

tro-tlanastshini, *or* **tro-tlanastshi**
mixed waters—waters of all kinds: spring-water, snow-water, hail-water, and water from the four quarters of the world; such waters, as nearly as possible, are used in the Navajo religious ceremonies

ka', *or* kat   **pitistshi**   **pilch**
now   *fine particles, shining grains of mineral used*   *with*
in religious ceremonies, possibly mica

tashokishko
mist, dust (meaning: when the horse of the Sun-God goes, he raises a dust of these glittering particles)

ba, *or* **bi**   **tradetin**   **yan**
his, his own   *sacred pollen (here, flower-pollen)*   *on*

toitinko
covered, hidden (when the horse runs, the sacred corn-pollen belonging to the sun is all about· him, like dust, so that he looks like a mist. The Navajos sometimes say that the mist on the horizon is the corn-pollen offered to the gods)

k'ean   **natelzhishko**   **kat**   **tonidineshko**
they   *increase*   *now*   *eternally (the herds of Johano-ai
increase eternally, growing
ever more and more)*

NAYE-E SIN
Enemy   Song
(War Song)

Naye, *from* **anaye,** *translated by Dr. Matthews, " alien gods "*

pesh   **ashike**   **ni**   **shli**   **Nayenezrani**
flint   *youth*   *suffix, meaning person*   *I am*   *name of the war-god, the slayer
of the alien gods*

shi   **ni**   **shli**   **pesh**   **tilyilch**   **shi**
I, me, my   *person*   *I am (***shi ni shli,** *I am)*   *flint*   *black*   *my*

ke   **pesh**   **tilyilch**   **siskle**   **pesh**   **tilyilch**   **shi**   **e**
moccasins   *flint*   *black*   *leggings*   *flint*   *black*   *my*   *tunic*

pesh   **tilyilch**   **shi**   **tsha**   **nolienni**
flint   *black*   *my*   *helm, hat, head-dress*   *finest kind of transparent flint,
highly valued by the Navajos*

tshina   **shi**   **yiki**   **holon**   **ka',** *or* **kat**   **itsiniklizh**   **din**   **ikwo**
alive   *me*   *in it (?)*   *within*   *now*   *zig-zag lightning*   *four*   *(no meaning)*
(within me)

sitzan nahatilch
*from me: coming back to me (the four lightnings strike, or flash from me and return. " for,"
say the Navajos, " lightning always looks as though it flashed out and then went back ")*

tsini   **nahatilch**
there where the lightning strikes (word for common use, **tsitte)**   *and comes back to me*

nihoka   **hastoi**
on the earth   *old men: old people (probably an ancient evil*

whe-e-yoni-sin   *people, before the coming of the Navajos)*
*" the songs the enemy sings against me " (instead of fighting, the old people would sometimes sing
sorcerous songs and pray evil prayers against their foe)*

yoya   **aiyinilch**
under: down: in the bottom   *in the ground (there where the lightning strikes,
the old enemies, with their evil songs and
charms, are cast into the ground. The
Navajos say " he hurls them into the ground*

ka'   **sa-a narai**   *with the lightning, one after another ")*
now: verily: indeed   *living forever*

ka'   **binihotsitti**   **shi ni shli**
verily   *the brave one, he whom all fear (***tsitti,** *fear)*   *I am*

APPENDIX

TRO HATAL
Water Chant
(Song from a ceremony called the "Water-Chant")

Niye tinishten	**shichl**	**tsha huiyish**	**tinl shta**
as far as may be seen	*with me*	*coming*	*water*
		(the rain comes with me)	*rain*

Niltsan Dsichl
rain mountain
(a mountain west of Zuñi—the
  home of the Rain-Youth)

biya ra-ashte
from behind
(biya, *bottom, base)*

tshi-natan
corn
(natan, *corn;* **tshi-natan,**
  word used in poetry)

tso	**betra**	**ka', or kat**	**itsiniklizh**	**ka'**
great	*among*	*now*	*zig-zag lightning*	*now*
tall	*through*	*indeed*		
big		*verily*		

(the rain comes with me through the tall corn)

itahazla	**betra**	**ka'**	**trashjesh**	**dotlizh**	**ka'**
streaks of lightning	*among*	*now*	*swallows*	*blue*	*now*
	through				

enadetla	**betra**	**tradetin**	**bantoyishtin**
chirping together	*among*	*pollen*	*hidden*
	through		*covered all over*

(through the pollen, hidden in pollen)

DSICHLYIDJE HATAL
On the Mountain Chant
(Mountain-Chant)

Baiyajiltrish	**tsilchke**	**digin**	**{ estan digin }**	
thereof he telleth	*youth*	*holy*	*{ woman holy }*	*second stanza*

ke	**pa**	**nashjin**	**kla**	**pa**
moccasins	*upon*	*black*	*dress (?)*	*upon*

naskan
the word, as here used, is translated by the Navajos thus: " The pretty work on the dress : the
  embroidery (of quills)." General meaning, the beautiful adorned woven dress

ka'
now (probably inserted to fill out the rhythm)

ka pa-stran
arm-bands, or bracelets, of eagle feathers

niltsan	**atsoz**	**niltsan-bekan**	**{ niltsan-baad }**	
rain	*feathers*	*rain male*	*{ rain female }*	*second stanza*

ka'	**bi**	**datro**	**sa-a narai**	**bike hozhoni**
now	*his : her*	*drops (drops after rain :*	*life unending*	*happiness of all things*
		fallen drops)		

DINNI-E SIN
Game Song
Deer

Ye shakaikatal
he starts, coming towards me with it
he walks towards me with it—" it " referring to the song

ka'
now

aiyash-tilyilch
a beautiful blackbird
(tilyilch, *black)*

shi ni shli	**Dsichl-tilyilch**	**bakashte**	**ka'**	**ta-adetin**
I am	*mountain black*	*on top*	*now*	*trail*
	(Black Mountain)	*(where the trail starts)*		

'shte	**tshilatra**	**hozhoni**	**bitra**	**'shte**
abbreviation of **yushte**	*flowers of all kinds,*	*beautiful*	*among*	*coming*
or **ho-ushte,** *coming*	*blossoms, tips of flowers*	*pretty*		

bi	**datro**	**bitra**	**'shte**	**ka'**	**bi**	**tradetin**
their	*dew-drops*	*among*	*coming*	*now*	*their*	*pollen*

bitra	'shte	dinnitshe	bekan	⎰ baad ⎱ second stanza
among	coming	game	male	⎱ female ⎰
		deer		

(ceremonial word used in poetry or rites)

bitzil	deshklashdji	⎰ deshnash ⎱ second stanza	bizedje
foreleg	left	⎱ right ⎰	the kill
			quarry
			(game killed by the hunter)

shinosin
they want me (meaning, the game choose to come to me.   The hunter is blessed and lucky in hunting)·

NAESTSAN   BIYIN
Earth   Song, or Hymn

Naestsan
(according to Dr. Matthews, the Earth-Mother, or the Woman Horizontal—estsan, woman)

daltso   **hozhoni**
all, everything   *beautiful, blessed, happy, perfect*

hozho'ka'
from hozhoni, beautiful ; ka', or kat, suffix, denoting emphasis, meaning " indeed," or " forever"

naestsan   **yatilyilch**
the Earth-Mother   *the Sky-Father (according to Dr. Matthews, literally, the Upper Darkness)*

pilch   **ka' altsin sella ho-ushte**
with: facing one another   *joined together : bending towards one another : complements, or helpmates of one another :*
                                          (ho-ushte, or yushte, coming)

Sisnajinni, Tsodsichl, Doko-oslid, Depenitsa,
names of sacred mountains bounding the Navajo land

tshalyilch	hayolkatli	Hastyeyalti
darkness : night	*dawn*	*name of God of Sunrise*
Hastyehogan	**natan-alchkaï**	**natan-alchtsoï**
name of God of Sunset	*corn white*	*corn yellow*
tradetin **anilchtani**	**sa-a naraï**	**bike hozhoni**
sacred pollen " The Ripener"	*life unending*	*happiness of all things*

ZUÑI

OCKAYA
Corn-Grinding Song
I

Elu	homa	yallanne	awehlwiawe, or awehluyawe	kwai-i
beautiful	*my*	*mountain*	*clouds*	*coming out*
lovely			*(cumulus clouds)*	*rising*
fair				
imuna		**kwagia**	**lonan-eshto**	**'wiyane**
sitting		*up in the sky*	*rain-clouds coming*	*coming*
(expression used in song)		*(refers to the Rain-Makers)*		*(one after another)*
liwamani	**iyuteapa**	**awiyane**	**hawilana**	**litla**
yonder	*poetic word for flowers*	*coming*	*young corn growing up*	*here*
			(Laguna word)	

OCKAYA
Corn-Grinding Song
II
Sung by the youths while the maidens grind the corn

Elu	honkwa	lonan	iyane	lekwa	kela
beautiful	*indeed, perchance, or implying*	*cloud*	*coming*	*said*	*first*
lovely	*a wish "O would that—"*				
fair					

[556]

APPENDIX

aiyan-towa		pene	aiyaye	maihoma	antuna
little corn-ear on the tip of the corn-stalk		*talking*	*up there*	*at me*	*looking*
holon-ellete	lilthno	kela	kiawe-kwai-i		nuwane
perchance (?)	*here*	*first*	*water coming out*		*moving, coming*
with wish or hope implied	*this way*		*floods*		*going*

OCKAYA
Corn-Grinding Song
III

Amitola	tsina-un	elu	toma wahane	kiawulokia	pena
rainbow	*painting*	*beautiful*	*your corn (?)*	*swallow*	*talking*
	painted	*lovely*			
		fair			

wulokia	kesi	liwamani	hliton	iyane	kesi	liwamani
swallow	*now*	*yonder*	*rain*	*coming*	*now*	*yonder*
		hither				*hither*

hlapi hanan	iyane	letekwan	atowa	awuwakia	litla
white clouds	*coming*	*it said*	*corn*	*all growing*	*here*

SHOKO OTIÏKWE [1]
Corn-Dance Song

Chuap	tono	kela	ite tsina-u	amitola	tsawaki	ma honkwa hito
who	*you*	*first*	*make a shadow*	*rainbow*	*youth*	*thus it is, or thus it was*
			draw a picture			*—or it was in this wise*

lonawe	hlitowe	uletchi		ite tsina-u
clouds	*rains*	*under or behind, coming one after another ;*		*make a shadow*
		modern use of word means saddle-		*draw a picture*
		blankets, or folds, one over another		

1st Version.—Who was the first to paint a picture? It was the Rainbow-Youth. It was
even thus: first clouds, then rain, one after the other—then the Rainbow-Youth painted on them.

2d Version.—Who was the first to cast a shadow? It was the Rainbow-Youth. Ay, thus
it was: first clouds, then rain—then from behind the Rainbow-Youth cast his shadow (*probably
meaning that the rainbow is the shimmering reflection of the Rainbow-Youth*).

THLAH HEWE [2]
Song of the Blue-Corn Dance
(Old Chief's Song)

Elu	shi	lowi-yuteapa	uteapa
beautiful	*see !*	*cloud flowers*	*(archaic word for flowers,*
lovely	*or listen*		*y added for euphony)*
fair	*(exclamation to call attention)*		

cloud flowers are blooming in the sky, or the clouds are blooming like flowers

mateona	kesi	lowi-yuteapa	awiyane	litla
at this time	*now*	*cloud flowers*	*coming*	*here*

(**awiya,** *coming; final* ne *added for euphony*)

[1] (*According to Mrs. M. C. Stevenson, of the Bureau of American Ethnology, Washington,
the word "Shoko," is from "Shokona," the flute of Payatamu, god of music, flowers and
butterflies.*)

[2] (*According to Mrs. M. C. Stevenson, of the Bureau of American Ethnology, Washington,
"Thlah hewe" is a ceremonial for rain and the growth of corn. The singular of the word is
"Thlaha," rabbit-skin blanket. The name signifies fecundity. This song is one used in the
"Thlah hewe" ceremonial, one of the most sacred of the Zuñi festivals. The words are spelled
'Hlahewe and 'Hla'ha, according to the Bureau of American Ethnology*).

LAGUNA

AIYA-GAÏTANI YONI
Corn-Grinding   Song

I

I-o-ho		waitilanni		tzi washo iyani-i
(meaningless vocables)		*wonder-water*		*what life now*
yuweh	puniakoekolika		yuweh	haniakoekolika
yonder	*southwest*		*yonder*	*southeast*

AIYA-GAÏTANI YONI
Corn-Grinding   Song

II

Polaina		hai-ke-o-tzi-o-no-ho		kochinishi (*sung* kohochinishi)
butterfly (archaic word)		*now fly away to the blossoms*		*blue*
koeshkasi	kukanishi		kasheshi	ha-na-pu-ra-ni
yellow	*red*		*white*	*now go! away!*

HOPI

WUWUCHIM TAWI
Wuwuchim   Song

Yan	itam	tokilnawita	hahlai	unangway	na'kalmumuya
thus	*we*	*(all) night along*	*happy*	*heart with*	*wish well one another*
natwanlawu	inamu	ayam		Muyingwa	
they plant	*my fathers*	*yonder*		*Muyingwa, god of germination and growth*	
mongwi	kive		mokwa		kaŏ
chiefs	*kiva, in the*		*double*		*corn-ear*
chochmingwun		natwantaqŏ			pom
perfect (one)		*if (they) plant (that)*			*that*
nikiang	bavas		nawita		sitalwunguni
but: yet	*field*		*along*		*blossom, tassel, will shine*
peyo	amumi		namusha		yoyowunuto
hither	*to them*		*here*		*rain-standing*
heyapo					o-omawutu
scud underlying heavy masses of rain-cloud					*clouds*

PUWUCH TAWI
Sleep   Song

Puva	hohoyawu-u	shuhpŏ pave-e	na-ikwiokiango	puva
sleep	*beetles*	*on the road (trail)*	*they carry one another*	*sleep*
			on their backs	

POLI TIWA TAWI
Butterfly-Dance Song

Humicita	cingŏlawu		mozhicita		cingŏlawu
corn-blossoms	*wrestle*		*bean-blossoms*		*wrestle*
itam	totim	nikiang	uyi		shonoka
we	*are youths*	*but*	*corn-plants*		*among*
ngŏti-timani		tuvevol			manatu
we shall chase each other		*butterfly*			*maidens*
amumi	peyo	umumutani		ita	ayatani
with	*hither*	*it shall thunder*		*we*	*shall send*
uyi	manatu	omi			nawungwinani
corn-plant	*maidens*	*upward*			*shall grow together*

APPENDIX

ANGA KATZINA TAWI
Anga   Katzina   Song

Uyi	shonaka	yoki	tɐvevoli	manatɐ	nanguyimani
corn-plants	among	rain	butterfly	maidens	chasing one another

(rain all over the cornfields)

yoyang	yala	pɐma	tahinpa	natayawina
raining (after the rain is over)	behold	they	how	flitting about

(enjoying themselves)

yang	ɐyi	shonaka	yani	pɐma
all over	corn-plants	among	thus	they
tɐwati		tataw-yɐyɐwina		yanga
also		singing enjoy themselves		all over : there

KOROSTA KATZINA TAWI
Korosta   Katzina   Song

Sikya	volimɐ	hɐmisi
yellow	butterflies	corn-blossom : blossoming corn
manatɐ	talasi	yammɐ	pitzangwa	timakiang
maidens	pollen	?	faces	painted
tɐve-nanguyimani		shakwa		volimɐ
bright, chasing one another brilliant		blue		butterflies
mozhisi				
bean-blossoms : blossoming beans				

(etc., as before)

hɐmisi	manatɐ	amɐnawita
corn-blossom : blossoming corn	maidens	over
tatangayatɐ	tŏkiyɐyɐwintani	(etc., as before)
wild bees	humming	
ɐmɐh	ɐyi	amɐnawit	yoi-ɐmɐmɐtimani
your	plants : field	over	rain-thunder
tawanawita	ɐmɐh	ɐyi
all day (tawa, sun ; 'nawita, over)	your	field
amɐnawit	yoi-hoyoyotimani	tawanawita
over	rain on-moving	all day

HE-HEA KATZINA TAWI
He-hea   Katzina   Song

Hɐmisi	ɐyi	manatɐ	mozhisi	ɐyi
corn-blossom	plant	maidens	bean-blossom	plant
siqŏlŏva	bavatalawinani	shakwa	omawɐtɐ
patch, cluster	water will shine, the wet earth will shine with water after rain	blue	clouds
hapi me	hesiqŏlŏva	sikia voli	nangŏyimani
behold	patch, or cluster, of yellow flowers	yellow butterflies	chase one another
	(hesi, a certain yellow flower)		
mozhisiqŏlŏva	shakwa voli	nangŏyimani
patch, or cluster, of bean-blossoms	blue butterflies	chase one another

HEVEBE TAWI
" Hevebe "- Song

I

Nana-hopipaqŏ	qŏyangwɐnɐka	kɐyiva
now from the east (hopaqŏ, east)	the white dawn	has arisen
nana hopipaqŏ	sikiangwɐnɐka	kɐyiva
now from the east	the yellow dawn	has arisen

angwu huwam hawiwokialyata
so now *an expression of politeness, analogous to the* *arouse, bestir yourself*
English " and it please ye "

itamumi kuyivawicha itamumi umuh kuyap
to us ; at us *come look* *to us* *your* *cup ; vessel*

kuyi wutaya iyo hevebeta peyowi
of water *pour* *cold* *a kind of cloud (?)* *come*

wuta qŏyangwun-talao tiyo sikiangwun-talao tiyo
pour *the white dawn-light* *youth* *the yellow dawn-light* *youth*

tuhiyongva to nahiongva to
we please every one, or, we surprise others *we please ourselves, or, we surprise ourselves*

yanikitiwa pavŏn-mamantu
thus it has been said, or, thus dwell *corn-stalk maidens. or, shower-maidens*

HEVEBE TAWI
" Hevebe"- Song
II

Hevebeta eyowi wuta tovi chi
a kind of cloud (?) *come* *pour* *(archaic or foreign : translated, " the clouds are moving*
here," or " the cloud deities are seated in the sky ")

Shiwana Shi-wa-wai-ya wuta
(Laguna word used for the masked dancers, who probably *(corruption of Shiwana)* *pour*
impersonate clouds, or cloud deities ; also means cloud)

anoshkaï nuishi o-ou-ya-a nuipa o-ou-ya-a
(archaic Hopi or foreign word *make of me a cluster of flowers* *make of me a cluster of*
translated by the Hopis, *(shi, or si, means flower, or* *showers (pa is water)*
" Come, bathe me ") *blossom)*

LENE TAWI
Flute - Song

Hao inamu mashilenangwu mongwitu nananivo
hail *my fathers* *gray flute* *chiefs* *at the four world-points*

omawutu wawai inamu nananivaqŏ yoi
clouds *call : want* *my fathers* *from the four world-points* *rain*

nanakwushani peyo yoi-umumutimani yanga peyo
will start to come *hither* *rain-thunder it shall* *yonder moving along, or,* *hither*
all over, here, there

yoi-hoyoyotimani uyi shonaka hakame
rain-moving will move *the plants* *among* *everywhere*

yang uyi shonaka bava-tala-winani
far and near *the plants* *among* *the earth will water-shine*

CONTRIBUTORS

WABANAKI

Bedagi, Big Thunder.
Joseph Nicolar.
Blamswe-Zozep Tene, Francis Joseph Dana.
Asawhis, John Salis.

DAKOTA

Maza Blaska, Flat Iron.
Tatanka-Ptecila, Short Bull.
Matoisto-Nakipin, Bear-Arm-Necklace.
Wicapi, Star.
Wambli-Waste, Good-Eagle.
Tasunke-Hinto, Blue Horse.
Tasunke-Ciqala, Little Horse.
Capa-Tanka, Big Beaver, Frank Goings.
Tatanka-Hinapawi, Buffalo-Appearing
Wicapi-Wakan, Holy Star, Julia Yellow-Hair.
Tasunke-Hinsa, Sorrel Horse.
Malipiya-Tatanka, Sky Bull.
Mato-Wankantuya, High Bear.
Huhuseca-ska, White Bone.
Zintkala Maza, Iron Bird.
Mato-Nazin, Standing-Bear.

PAWNEE

Sakuruta, Coming Sun, James R. Murie.
Letakots-Lesa, Eagle Chief.
Lesa-Kipiliru, Young Chief.
Lukitawika - wari, Rider - Around - the - Great-
  Heaven-Domed-Lodge.

CHEYENNE

Wihu-Hwaihu-O-Usz, or Hiamovi, High Chief,
  or High Wolf.
Honihi-Wotoma, Wolf-Robe.
Nahios-si, Three Fingers.
Mochta-Wontz-tz, Starving Elk.
Wihunahe, Chief Woman.
Mowihaiz, Magpie, Leonard Tyler.
Wupcha-e, White Cap.
Wowesta, White Buffalo Woman.
Hotuwasu, Little Buffalo Bull.

ARAPAHO

Nakos, Sage.
Wageoh, Maud Shawnee.
Nawadek, Susie Sage.
Nabilase, Jessie Sage.
Gelbini, Cappie Webster.
Waatina Bichut, Black Shirt.

KIOWA

Owik'uyain, The Home-Comer.
Apiatan, Wooden Lance.
T'e-ne-t'e, Eagle Chief.
Sah-mount, Samon.
Guwekondgieh, Black Wolf.
Potine, White Beaver.

WINNEBAGO

Hinook Mahiwi Kilinaka, Angel De Cora.
Chash-chunk-a, Wave, Peter Sampson.
Nek-hu-wi-ka, South Wind, Jacob Russell.
Wa-che-li-man-iga, Surly Walker, James Mal-
  lory.

KWAKIUTL

Klalish, Charles James Nowell.

PIMA

Visak-Vo-o-yim, Hovering Hawk.
Katarina Valenzuela.
Hal Antonio.
Ataloya.

APACHE

Geronimo.
Fleming Lavender.
Rivers Lavender (Gumanchiä.)

MOJAVE-APACHE

Hukutgodga.
Somurturgigu-a.

YUMA

Chiparopai.

ZUÑI

Ema-liya.

LAGUNA

Tuari, Young Eagle.
Idima, John Corn.

HOPI

Lololomai, Very Good.
Tawakwaptiwa, Sun-Down-Shining.
Lahpu, Cedar-Bark.
Koianimptiwa.
Masahongva.
Kuwanyisnim.
Masaveimah.
Kavanghongevah.
Gashoienim.

Also various Indians from the Navajo tribe, and from the villages of Acoma and San Juan.

YUMA CREATION MYTH

The creation legend of the Cochans is ancient, but the interpolation of the white man is, of course, a later addition to the tale. According to the Cochans the white man is "in the west," for the first white men seen by the Yumas were the Spaniards who came from California, which at that time was still a part of Mexico. It will be seen throughout the legend that the Cochans believe that they themselves migrated to their present home from the north.

People! Behold, thus it was in the beginning:—All was water: there was no sky, no land, no living thing. Then, as the waters moved, the waves dashed spray aloft, and foam; and the foam and the spray thickened into mist and rested above the waters and became the sky. But there was neither sun, nor moon, nor star. All was darkness. Kokomaht (God) dwelt beneath the waters—a nameless being made out of the Nothing—and he was two. And the twain made thunder beneath the waters, and the waters heaved, and up through the floods rose the first of the twain. As he passed through the waters he closed his eyes; then when he had risen he bathed his eyes and opened them and saw. So thus he stood upon the waters, seeing, and named himself Kokomaht, maker and father of all.

And the second of the twain called to Kokomaht from beneath the waters, and asked, "How went you up:—with closed eyes, or open eyes?"

And Kokomaht made answer falsely, thus: "As I came through the floods I opened my eyes."

Now the second believed, and as he rose he opened his eyes, and the waters rushed in upon his eyes, and behold! when he had come up through the waters he was blind. Kokomaht then named him Bakotahl, the Blind. And Kokomaht was good, and Bakotahl was evil.

So the twain stood upon the waters in the midst of darkness, for as yet there was no land. Kokomaht asked of Bakotahl, "Where is the north?"

Bakotahl knew not, and pointed to the south. "No," said Kokomaht, "that is not the north."

But Bakotahl found not the north, for he was blind. Then said Kokomaht, "Behold, I will show you how to make four directions. This is north." And he pointed to the north. Then he walked upon the waters four steps northward and stood for a moment, and then came back to his starting-place. Then he said, "Lo, this shall be west!" And he walked upon the waters four steps westward, and stood for a moment and then came back to his starting-place. Even so he made the south, stepping four times southward; and the east, stepping four times eastward; and then at last he stood still at the central starting-place.

Then Kokomaht took the hand of Bakotahl (because the Blind One knew not the directions) and he pointed with it north, west, south, east. But the Blind, who saw not, would not believe. But he said nothing.

Then Kokomaht said, "Lo, now I will disperse the waters and make Earth!"

And the Blind, believing not, said, "How will you do this thing? Think you that you can make Earth in truth?"

"Yes, that can I," said Kokomaht.

And the Blind said, "Let me be the first to try this thing."

But Kokomaht answered, "Nay, I will not."

And Kokomaht turned and faced the north and stooped over the waters and with his hand stirred the waters to a whirlpool. And the waters rose and then went down, and as they ebbed land appeared. And Kokomaht seated himself upon the earth.

Now Bakotahl was bad of heart because he might not make the land. He would have liked to go elsewhere. But he, too, seated himself upon the earth. Then he thought, "I will take of this earth and make a being, with head, arms, legs, feet and hands." So he made of clay an image like a man; but it was not right. The hands were not divided into fingers or the feet into toes. When the image was finished Bakotahl laid it behind him where Kokomaht might not see it.

Now Kokomaht said in his heart, "I will make man." And he took clay and made an image with head, arms, legs, hands and feet: it was perfect. "This is man," he said. Then he made another image, and this one, too, was perfect. "This is woman," he said. And he took the first image and lifted it and swung it back and forth four times, northward, and stood it upon its feet upon the earth. And behold, it was a living man! And he took the second image and swung it back and forth four times northward, and stood it on its feet upon the earth. And behold, it was a living woman!

Now Bakotahl had in this time made seven images, but he himself knew not what they were. And Kokomaht saw them and said, "What have you made there?"

And Bakothal answered, "Lo, these are men that I am making."

Then Kokomaht said, "Lift your hand and touch and feel these that I have made."

And Bakotahl felt of the man and the woman that Kokomaht had made. They were perfect, with face, eyes, hands and fingers: they were perfect.

And Kokomaht said to the Blind, "What then seek you to make of these that you have made?"

And Bakotahl answered, "Of all these I shall make men."

Now on the hands of his images the Blind had made no fingers, nor upon the feet had he made toes. Kokomaht said, "What will they do if they are hurt in battle? Behold, they have no fingers!"

Bakotahl said, "If they are hurt, they will heal themselves."

Kokomaht said, "Behold, I have made fingers, yea, even finger-nails. If one finger is hurt, it can be cut off, and there yet will be four fingers left. And my people can hold things, for they can put their fingers together, as one, even like the hands of your creatures, or they can spread their fingers apart. All things can they do with their hands."

And Kokomaht looked upon the images of Bakotahl and beheld how they were sore imperfect, and he lifted his foot and spurned them into the waters.

Now Bakotahl was angered and hot with rage, and he leaped into the water, to make Sickness that should destroy the people of Kokomaht. And as he went down beneath the waves there was a noise as of thunder. Out from the waters he blew a whirlwind[1]; but Kokomaht lifted his foot and stepped upon the whirlwind and quenched it. But the whirlwind was very strong and when Kokomaht lifted his foot a little breath of the whirlwind slipped out, and this it is that has brought all sickness to the people of the earth.

Now Kokomaht was alone, save for the one man and the one woman, and these twain were the Cochans (Yumas). Then Kokomaht made two people more, man and woman, and these were the Cocopahs. Then he made the Diegueños, man and woman, and the Mojaves, man and woman. Then he stopped and pondered. He had made people of four kinds. And now he worked again and made the Apaches, then the Maricopas, then the Pimas, then the Coahuillas,

---

[1] Several Southwestern tribes believe that the whirlwind brings sickness, and among some tribes medicine-men destroy the sickness by piercing the whirlwind with an arrow.

again people of four kinds. Then he labored again, until he had made, in all, people of twenty-four kinds, and the last twain that he made were the white people.

Now behold all these living beings on the earth who knew not how they should live. And the first man, the Cochan, said to Kokomaht, "Behold, we know not how to live!"

And Kokomaht answered, "Think in your heart. You cannot be always a lone and separate being. Join with another, and bring forth children."

And Kokomaht begat a son, to teach the people, and the child was conceived of the Nothing and born without a mother, yet was he in form even as a man; and Kokomaht called him Komashtam'ho. And when the people understood, they lived no more apart as man and woman, but joined each with the other, and reared children unto themselves. Now when thus there were many people upon the earth, Kokomaht said, " Behold what I will do! It is dark; I will make light." So he made the Moon, and then the Morning Star.

Now the son, Komashtam'ho, as he waxed older began to ponder and think in his heart that he too would one day make something. The different kinds of people were now grouped in different places on the earth. But Kokomaht knew that his own work was finished.

Now behold, among the people was a woman, Hanyi, the Frog, and her heart was bad toward Kokomaht, and she fain would destroy him. So she crept down under the earth. Now Kokomaht knew her heart, for he knew all things, even the hearts of all the people he had made. But it was thus: Kokomaht himself willed to die, that he might teach men how to die, even as he had taught men how to live. For he knew that all men must die, else would the world be too full of people.

Now Hanyi crept down into the ground beneath the place where Kokomaht was standing, and she pulled out his breath till his throat was dry, and he wandered this way and that, knowing not whither he went. For Hanyi was a sorceress, and she had the power of the frog; for the frog has great power: if you throw it into the fire, it cannot be burned, it will jump here and there and then jump out. Kokomaht sickened, and lay down, and thought soon to die. Now there was no day or night, but only moonlight all the while; for as yet was there no light save that of the moon and of the one star.

So Kokomaht lay dying, and he called all his people about him, and they gathered, all save the white man, who lingered by himself in the west. The white man was crying because his hair was curled and his skin was white. Komashtam'ho looked up and beheld the white man sitting by himself in the west, weeping thus, and Komashtam'ho rose and went to him, and took a stick of wood, and set another stick of wood across it and said, " Here, you may ride this! " And behold, it was a horse! So he comforted the white man with gifts to ease his crying. For the white man was the youngest of all peoples; he was made the last, and he was even as a child, petulant and wilful, crying for all that he saw, and never appeased until all had been given to him. So unto the white man did Komashtam'ho give all the good things of the earth, for the Indians were older and could better bear deprivation and hardship.

So Kokomaht died, to show men the road of death, even as he had shown men the road of life. And now Komashtam'ho pondered in his heart how he might change the world so that there would be night and day. And he spat on his hand, and with his finger he rolled the spittle to a disc, and he took the disc and threw it to the east. Then he said to all the people, "This is the Sun, and it will move from the eastern sky to the western."

Then he thrust the sun down under the earth, and the darkness returned. And now he spat on his finger and sprinkled the sky, and lo, there were many stars. Then he told the people, " Behold, these are stars. But you will see them only at night. In the day, you never will see them."

But the people believed not, for Kokomaht, who had made all things, was dead.

APPENDIX

Now Komashtam'ho would burn the body of Kokomaht; but as yet there was no wood for poles and logs—there were no cottonwood or willow trees, as now. So Komashtam'ho summoned the wood from the north, and when it was come he made a great funeral pyre.

Now Kokomaht, whilst he had lain nigh unto death, had called unto him the Coyote, and had said, " Take my heart. Be good. Do what is right."

And the Coyote thought that Kokomaht meant that he should take the heart from Kokomaht's body, and eat it.

Now all was ready for the burning, but Komashtam'ho knew that the Coyote had it in his heart to eat the heart of Kokomaht. So when the sun was rising, Komashtam'ho said to the Coyote:

"Go, fetch the light wherewith to kindle the fire." And the Coyote leaped four times to the east and lifted his hand and reached toward the sunrise. And now, while the Coyote was thus gone seeking light, Komashtam'ho quickly took a stick and fitted it into a hole in a piece of wood, and twirled the stick between his palms till fire sprang from the end of it. Thus did Komashtam'ho show the people how to make fire, and so was the first fire kindled for the burning of Kokomaht. And Komashtam'ho lit the funeral pyre, for he would that Kokomaht's body should be burned before the Coyote might return. Behold, all the people were gathered save the white man, and he desired not to see the burning and stayed afar. But the people wept not, or mourned, for as yet they understood not what death was. Now the fire had been burning but a little time when the Coyote returned. The people closed in together about the pyre because they knew that the Coyote would try to leap upon the pyre to take the heart of Kokomaht. Among the people was the Badger, and he was so low of stature that the Coyote, at a bound, leapt over him, even upon the pyre, and seized the heart of Kokomaht. Then he leapt off at the other side, and ran swiftly away. All the animals who were fleet of foot chased him, but none could catch him.

Then Komashtam'ho called aloud after the Coyote: "You will nevermore do good. You will be a wild man with no dwelling house, and naught to call your own. You will steal, for you will of yourself own nothing, and for your thefts you will be killed."

Thus Komashtam'ho proclaimed it before all the people, and they knew henceforth what the Coyote was.

The people stood all around the burning pyre and then they began to weep and cry. They understood not sickness and death, but Kokomaht had shown them that men must sicken and die. Yet the people could not believe that Kokomaht would not longer live among them, and they looked for him to come again. Then Komashtam'ho said:

" You will nevermore see Kokomaht. He has died. If he were to live, all men would live, and the world would not hold all the people who would be alive. This is why Kokomaht has died—to teach you."

And the people wept. They thought that the Frog was afar, for she had run away from the people in the same direction as the Coyote. The people would fain have killed the Frog because she was a sorceress; the Frog knew this, so she hid herself under the ground. But now when the people wept, she came out and listened, and when she heard the people grieve she went down into the ground again and resolved, out of fear of the people, to move elsewhere. So the frog lives ever out of sight.

Now by the burning of Kokomaht all the country round about was set in flames and there was a mighty heat from the fire, so that forever afterward the land is hot.

When the great fire was over and all had been burned, the people sat together in the same place. But the Cocopah Indians wanted not to be close to the Cochans, and they stayed apart from them, and the Maricopas wanted to be near to the Cocopahs. But the Mojaves, Apaches and Dieguienos drew nigh to the Cochans, and so to-day these tribes live near together. Now, as the people sat, they saw a little whirlwind forming near the place where Kokomaht had been burned. And the people rose up and said, " What is there? "

And Komashtam'ho answered, " That is Kokomaht. His spirit is now soul only, and that is he. He will be elsewhere than here—maybe north, or west, or east, or south. He will never tire nor hunger, and he will always be happy. People, grieve not."

Thus he taught the people. When he had told them this, they understood and watched, and saw a whirlwind all around the place where the fire had been. Komashtam'ho said:

" He will always be happy, but I—I am not happy. Would that he were alive! "

Now the Cochans believe that when they die, they go not to this place or that, as the white people teach, nor are they punished or rewarded. In death all men are equal. When they die, they are again with those whom they love and who belong to them, no matter how bad or how good they may be. But the life after death is fair, and corn grows plentifully, and all are young and strong—happy with those who love them and whom they love—and that is all.

Komashtam'ho now chose a man, Marhokuvek, to help him to think and to plan all things that now must be made and all that now must be done. Marhokuvek thought; then he looked upon the people and said to them:

" Because you all have lost your father, you should cut your hair as a sign of mourning."

So all the people cut their hair. And Marhokuvek called the birds and the animals and cut their hair—for in the beginning the animals were persons, even as men. Now when this was done, Komashtam'ho thought, and he said:

" These animals and birds look not well thus: I will make of them persons no longer, but animals." And now when they were just wild animals, Komashtam'ho said:

" I would fain kill them all." But Marhokuvek said:

" Nay, do not that! "

So they called the Rain, for Komashtam'ho would cause a flood that should destroy the animals. Now many of the beasts perished in the flood, but not all, for if there should come so great a flood that all the animals would drown, the Indian peoples would die of the cold, for their country is hot because of the burning of Kokomaht and so the Indians cannot bear cold. Marhokuvek told Komashtam'ho to spare the animals for the sake of the people, and Komashtam'ho stopped the rain. So the world is full of animals as well as men, but the animals are wild, and since that time men and animals live no more together, but are fearful of each other.

Now Kokomaht had had a dwelling house in the north. And Komashtam'ho would not that the house should stay when Kokomaht was dead. For when a man dies and his spirit goes forth, the spirit of all that he possessed should follow him into the other life; therefore the people destroy the earthly belongings of the dead man, that the souls of these things may be still the property of him who is gone. Also, when a man has passed to where no man may behold him, it is not good to look upon anything that had belonged to him who is gone. The sight of such a thing calls to mind the dead one: we see his house, but him no more, and this keeps the heart ever sad and makes such constant sorrow that he who is still alive sickens with pining and with grievous thoughts. What we cannot help we should not ponder upon, lest we grow weak of heart. Therefore the Yuma Indians burn all that belonged to the dead man, the house and all his things, and move elsewhere to a dwelling that holds no memory of the absent one. Never again may the name of the dead man be spoken, and life for the remaining ones begins anew upon another road.

So Komashtam'ho would destroy the house of Kokomaht. He took a pole and thrust it into the ground before the house and shook it from side to side, this way and that, four times till it pierced so deep that behold! water was all around the end of it. Then he thrust the pole along making a rut, southward, and struck the house with the pole, and it broke and fell. And the waters flowed all along the rut made by the pole, and behold! this flowing water was the Colorado River.

Now the people without fingers or toes that Bakotahl had made were beneath the waters, and as the river passed by the Indian peoples these people of Bakotahl's making arose and floated down upon the river. And behold! they were ducks, and water-creatures, with webbed hands and feet. Komashtam'ho stood beside the river, and knew who these creatures were, and he tried to catch them. But they would not come near, and kept only in the water. Then Komashtam'ho called to the young—the little fledglings, but they answered not, nor came; so he said:

"You have wings, but you may not fly as other birds. You shall remain forever near the water, as water-fowl." And to this day water-fowl are frightened of men, and come not near when they are called, but speed quickly away.

Now Kahk, the Crow, was a good farmer. After the river was made. he brought corn and seeds of all kinds. He flew southward to the Gulf of California, stopping four times by the way and crying, "kahk, kahk!" And at each of these four stopping-places a mountain arose. So he brought seeds from the south, that the people might plant after the overflow of the river.

Some say that the mountains of the earth other than these four were made in the beginning by Kokomaht. When the land was not yet dry Kohomaht pushed the wet clay to this side and that with his hands, heaping it into mountains. Others say that the waves broke on the newly risen land, and, as they dashed up over the country, they destroyed not the land, but stayed as they were, hardened into mountains.

Now the peoples had been divided; some had gone here, some there; but Komashtam'ho would keep the Cochans ever under his protection. So he said:

"Behold, I am now only one, so I cannot thus be with you always, for I must sometimes be elsewhere. So I will become four. I will change my name: I will no more be Komashtam'ho, but Eshpah-kohmal, White Eagle." And Komashtam'ho changed and became as four eagles. The Black Eagle, Eshpah-kwinyil, went to the west, where the sky always is dark with clouds and rain. The Brown Eagle, Eshpah-etsikwitsa, went to the south. This eagle has little power; he only dips in the water and catches fish to eat. The fourth eagle was called Eshpah-kwamait, which means Eagle-Unseen, for no man sees that eagle. The White Eagle was ever in the north, even from the time when Komashtam'ho changed himself.

When Komashtam'ho thus had become four, he dwelt no more among the Yuma people as a man, because all the peoples were divided: some had gone to the north, some to the west, some to the south and some to the east; so he might no more be in just one place. Yet he would ever guard and protect the Cochans, and in dreams give them power from Kokomaht. So Kokomaht teaches the people through Komashtam'ho in dreams, saying to them: "Think on me; follow my word, and bid the sick remember me!"

Bakotahl, the Blind, is under the earth, and all men know that he is evil. He is lying down beneath the ground, nevermore to come out, but sometimes he moves, and then the earth trembles and shakes; when he turns over, there is a noise as of thunder, and the earth opens and mountains crack and fall. And people say, "Lo, the Blind One stirs below!"

Kokomaht helps the good, but Bakotahl helps the wicked, and this is why in the beginning Kokomaht lied to Bakotahl and blinded him. For Kokomaht knew that Bakotahl was evil, and Kokomaht willed only good to men. All good is under the protection of Kokomaht.

Lo, this is the story of the making of all things, and of the beginning of the Cochans. People, behold, this is all!

THE WORDS OF *CHI*PAROPAI: SHOWING THE INDIAN'S OUTLOOK UPON THE TRANSITION PERIOD

The following paragraphs are a true record of a talk with Chiparopai. It should be stated, however, that the recorder has made no study of the religious beliefs of the Yumas, nor of the Yuman mythology, and therefore cannot say how nearly Chiparopai's individual thought conforms to that of her people. Chiparopai's words are offered as giving the point of view of the Indian himself upon the changes that confront him in the life of to-day.

Chiparopai was sitting in the shade of a thatched shed. It was spring, and the lemon tree beside her was just breaking into blossom. In contrast with this budding freshness drooped the aged form. Chiparopai was bent, but her strong frame still showed the vigor of the Indian. Over each shoulder hung a heavy plait of gray hair. The brown face was firm and round, the dark eyes gentle and thoughtful.

Chiparopai glanced up inquiringly as I drew near. " They told me you were looking for me," she said.

I held out my hand. " I have looked for you for many weeks," I answered. " The other Indians have told you this, I know. I love your people and I want to know them."

" You love Indians? " was the slow response, followed by a long look. Then the brown eyes softened and Chiparopai said simply, " Sit down: I will tell you what I can. What is it that you want to know? "

" Will you tell me of yourself? " I asked.

" My life has been long and full of change," was the answer. "Once when I was a child our people were fighting with the Cocopas, and I was alone with my mother in our melon patch. I was stolen by the Cocopas and traded to a Mexican for a pony. The Mexican sold me to a white man, who took me north to California. All my youth I worked among strangers till at last a great longing came over me to see my own people again, and I came home and married. My husband died and I put my little boy in the government school[1] and went away again to work, for we were poor. So I grew old. Then my son came to find me; he had grown to be a young man. He said, ' Mother, come back to live with us. If you are ill, then I am near. Never mind if we are poor. What good is life if we are not happy? And the best happiness is to be together.' So he brought me back to live with my people. White people think that money is everything; we Indians think that happiness is more. Yes," she added, slowly, "you teach my people to believe that *money* is the greatest thing. We used to care to be happy in our homes."

Chiparopai broke off and her eyes took on a dreamy look. The Yuma of to-day seemed to fade from her mental vision, and the olden time rose before her—the time when the glittering desert stretched out vast and silent with never a white man's house upon it; when the Colorado River wound its rushing course between green cottonwood trees, unspanned by bridge, unnavigated by steam, as yet, all unexplored.

" Long ago," she began softly, as though unmindful of my presence, "long ago there were many of us. Before the Americans took our land we lived along the river, up and down, and on both sides. Now we only have the reservation. But when I was young my home was in the valley; it is all white people's farms now."

Schools for the Indians are maintained on the reservations by the government or by missionaries. There are also several non-reservation boarding schools.

APPENDIX

She gazed before her with wistful sadness. Then a sudden spasm of coughing racked her bent frame.

"*Chiparopai*," I cried, " why is it that so many of your people cough?"

She shook her head, then answered simply, " I cannot tell; it seems as though you white folk bring poison to us Indians. Sickness comes with you, and hundreds of us die." She paused again pathetically. " Where is our strength? Look at me; my father and mother never knew what sickness was, but I, I cough always. In the old times we were strong. We used to hunt and fish. We raised our little crop of corn and melons and ate the mesquite beans. Now all is changed. We eat the white man's food, and it makes us soft; we wear the white man's heavy clothing and it makes us weak. Each day in the old times in summer and in winter we came down to the river banks to bathe. This strengthened and toughened our firm skin. But white settlers were shocked to see the naked Indians, so now we keep away. In old days we wore the breech-cloth, and aprons made of bark and reeds. We worked all winter in the wind— bare arms, bare legs, and never felt the cold. But now, when the wind blows down from the mountains it makes us cough." The voice was low and solemn. " Yes—we know that when you come, *we die*."

" It will not always be thus, my friend," I said. " Try to believe that a better day will come."

"Ah, well—white people do not mean to harm us—maybe. But you do not understand my people, and" she added slowly, "*you never even try*. You want now to divide for us the little land that we may still call our own. You never ask us what *we* would like, or would not like. We are ruled by your laws and you never try to make plain to us what these laws mean. White people came upon our land and built a chapel for us there. Did they ask us if we wanted it? Did they pay us for the land? Perhaps *we* would rather have had the land for our farms. They want us to have their religion. Would it not be fairer if they built their chapel on their own land and asked us then to come to it? You want our children to go to the schools that you have for us. Do you come to us old people first and tell us about the schools, and explain to us what the schools are for, so that we may understand? We Indians only know that schools will make our children like white people, and some of us ——" she paused, then said quietly, " some of us do not like white people and their ways.

" Of course I know that schools are good and that white people mean them to help my people. Schools are good; it is right for everyone to learn all he can from everyone. But white people should be more gentle with the older Indians if we cannot quickly understand. Our lives are sad—and we love our children. If I came to take your children to some strange place to learn things of which you knew nothing, would you like it? If I, an Indian woman, took your children to the desert to make them grow like Indians, would you like it? We Indians have the same love for our brown children that you have for your white ones. Explain to us all the new things that you mean for our good; take the trouble to know us a little if you really want to help and teach us. You do not understand our customs. You do not understand the way we think and feel. A white man laughed when he asked me why we cared when the white people sheared us like sheep.[1] Are we not men, too? Should not each man think and dress as suits his life? We *like* long hair. Is it not beautiful? Why have we not a right to what is ours? We never interfered with you until you interfered with us. How does our long hair harm you? Your men wear stiff

---

[1] Some years ago Washington issued an order that the hair of all Indians should be cut short. The hair cutting had to be done by force. This order with its enactment created such indignation and disturbance among the Indians that it was revoked. In a message to employees, the present Indian Commissioner advocated tolerance of hereditary customs of the Indians, and said that so long as the Indians were properly clad, they should be allowed to dress as best suited their taste and comfort and the climate in which they lived. However, there lingers among many government officials and missionaries a prejudice against any form of native dress. (Written in 1909.—*Ed.*)

clothes and hard collars. Your dress seems foolish and uncomfortable to us, as ours may to you. Yet you would not like it if we took your collars off."

"Not all white people are thus. Some of us would gladly know of your religion. You, too, believe in the Great Spirit."

*Chi*paropai gazed quietly at me for a moment, then said:

"Is there a people who does not? How would we know how to live if we did not believe in something greater than ourselves? What would teach us?"

She pointed to the lemon tree beside her. "Who tells the tree when it is time to put out its little leaves? Who tells those blackbirds that warm weather has come, and that they may fly north again? Birds and trees obey something that is wiser than they. They would never know of themselves. Often I sit alone in the desert and look at the lilies and all the pretty little pink flowers,[1] and I say, 'Who told you that spring was here and it was time for you to come? and I think, and I think, and always the truth comes back to me the same. It is the Something Greater that tells all things how to live. We are like the flowers. We live and die, and of ourselves we know nothing. But the Something Greater teaches us—teaches us how to live."

"And when we die?" I asked.

"Then it is all happiness. When we *die* we are all alike. There is no difference then."

"And when you burn your dead in those great funeral pyres, and burn the house and everything belonging to the dead man, what is your reason; will you tell me?"

"The body is nothing now. We burn it to set the spirit free. If there is old age or disease, all this is burned away from the spirit with the body. And we burn all the dead man's things so that he may have them in the other life.[2] If his people love him very much, they burn all their things too, so that he may have those also. And if we are rich enough we buy or make new things so that he may have as much as possible in the other life."

"And what does 'the Speaker' say when he talks so solemnly at the funeral pyre?"

"The Speaker tells of the man that is dead. He tells what a great man he was—how strong, how brave. And he tells of the trees, how they grow tall and straight and send out wide branches—then how they grow old and slowly decay, until at last they fall. This, he says, is the life of man—this is the life of man."

The voice dropped, and we sat long in silence till the cool patch of shade that had sheltered us shifted away. I glanced up; the sun had moved, and I knew that I had far to go. I took *Chi*paropai's hand.

"I looked for you long and now we are friends," I said.

"We are friends," *Chi*paropai repeated. "I live far from here—many miles out on the reservation, where I can feel the air wide around me, and look off far. I must always be where I can feel the air. But I must see people too, so I live by the wells where many come and go; I have little to offer, but if you will come you are welcome to all that I have.

"You say you want to know my people? There is but one way. Live among them. See them in their fields, planting and harvesting; see them with their children; hear them sing! In old days we were a happy people and we had many songs. You can never know the Indians by looking at them only. If you would really know us, come. You are welcome to all that I have."

[1] In spring the deserts of Arizona and California are covered with wild flowers.

[2] Many Indian tribes believe that material objects have spiritual life as well as material form, even as man has both spirit and body.

APPENDIX

YUMA LULLABY

Ash'var' Homar' Tashmatsk'   "Song for putting Child to sleep"

*Meaningless syllables.

HOPI OWL SONG

"Mungwu Katzina Tawi"   "Owl Katzina Song"
Free English Translation

A "Stop-crying song" for naughty children is supposed to be sung by the Owl-Katzina, a mythological being represented in Hopi ceremonials by a masked dancer. In the Refrain, at the end of the song, the "me" of bleating goats and the foreboding hoot of the Owl suggest to the child the terror of the flocks at the approach of the Owl-Katzina.

Mung-wu,.. Mung-wu,.. ku-to-zhit a-mum, Na mi po-ci,
Owls,...... Owls,...... big owls and lit-tle, Star-ing, glar-ing,

no-no-va-o-ya; Si-kiang-put-a tai kiang...... o!
eye-ing each oth-er; Children, from your boards, oh,....... see!

U-mu-yu.... wi-kia-la-wu, wi-kia-la-wu;
Now the owls are look-ing at you, look-ing at you;

Ha-ki, wi-norzh tu-ya.... ta, Tu-va-tso-ta.... sho-wa-ni.....
Ha-ki, wi-norzh ti-ya.... ta, Nu-ying-ya-ta.... sho-wa-ni.....
Say-ing, An-y cry-ing child, Yel-low eyes will eat him up.....
Say-ing, An-y naught-y child, Yel-low eyes will eat him up.....

Ka-ung-u pa-kiang-o.... pu.... va qö ö, Ka-ung-u sho-wa-ni....
Nu-ung-u pa-kiang-o.... pu.... va qö ö, Nu-ung-u sho-wa-ni....
Sleep, do not cry, sleep, do not cry, O children, look, Then we will pass you by...
But if you cry, but if you cry, O children, look, We'll eat you bye and bye.

Mé.... é.......... h'm h'm h'm h'm h'm* a.... ha i.... hi hi,
Mé.... é.......... hoo hoo hoo hoo hoo

a.... ha i.... hi hi yi;   h'm h'm h'm h'm h'm* Ho ho ho ho ho!

* Sung with closed lips.

[572]

INDEX

ABBREVIATIONS

INDEX

Dance, Dances, Dancing (Wi.), 255; see Hi-wa-shi-da.

Dance-Song (Ap.), 328; (M.), 334, 335.

———— of the Fox Society (D.), see Tokala Wacipi Olowan.

Dance-Songs (Wa.), 9.

———— from the Ceremony of the Night Chant (N.), see Kledzhi Hatal.

Darkness Maiden, mythic personage (N.), 351.

Dawnlight-Youths (H.), 486, 487.

Dawn Maiden, mythic personage (N.), 351.

——— Youth, mythic personage (N.), 351.

Death (D.), 50, 61; (Pa.), 113, 114; (C.), 152, 153, 154.

Deathless One, mythic personage (M.), 331, 332, 333.

———— and the Wind, story (M.), 331.

De Cora, Angel (Wi.), see Hinook Mahiwi Kilinaka.

Deer (Wi.), 244, 248; (N.), 369, 370.

Depenitsa, sacred mountain (N.), 351, 353, 372, 552.

Digini, "Divine Ones," mythic personages (N.), 367.

Digini-ossini, the Holy Believer, mythic personage (N.), 366.

Diné, "The people" N. name for themselves, 347.

Dinni-e Sin, Hunting-Song (N.), 369, 370, 413, 555.

Divine Beings (Pa.), 99; (N.), 365.

Divine Ones (N.), 352, 367.

Dog (D.), 58, 59; (C.), 150.

—— Feast (D.), 59.

—— Society (Pa.), 112.

—— Soldiers (Pi.), 31; (D.), 50.

Doko-oslid, sacred mountain (N.), 351, 353, 372, 552.

Dorsey, Dr. George A. (Ar.), 198.

Drawings by Indians, xxii., xxviii.

———— by High Chief, 149.

Dream, Dreams, Dreamer, Dreaming (Pi.), 31; (D.), 43, 60, 61; (Pa.), 109, 112, 114; (C.), 158, 159, 161; (Ar.), 200, 202; (Ki.), 226; (Wi.), 261, 263; (Pi.), 314; compare also Spirit, Trance, Vision.

Dry-paintings, sand-pictures, so-called (N.), 367.

Dsichl Biyin, Mountain-Song (N.), 352, 353, 354, 355, 356, 377, 552.

—— ———, Mountain-Song (Hozhonji Song), (N.), 350, 352, 374, 551.

Dsichlyidje Hatal, Song from the Ceremony of the Mountain-Chant (N.), 366, 368, 408, 555.

Dwellings (Wa.), 3; (Pi.), 39 (f.); (Pa.), 94; (Ar.), 197; (Ki.), 222; (Kw.), 298; (N.), 348; (Pu.), 425, 461.

E

Eagle, xv.; (Pa.), 97, 98; (C.), 165.

—— Chief (Pa.), see Letakots-Lesa.

—— —— (Ki.), see Te'-ne-t'e.

Eagle's song, xv.

Eagle symbol, xv.

Earth, as the common mother (Wa.), 11; (D.), 41; (N.), 372; compare also Story of the First Mother (Wa.), and Stories of Wash-ching-geka, the Little Hare (Wi.).

Earth-Maker (Wi.), see Ma-o-na.

——, Song to the (Wi.), see Ma-o-na.

Eaton, George, a Wi. Indian, 258.

Echo, in myth (Kw.), 302.

Echo Mask (Kw.), 301.

Education of Indians, national policy for, xxxiii.; see also Indian children at government boarding-school (D.).

Elephant (Wi.), 248, 249.

Elk (D.), 40; (Wi.), 244, 248, 251.

—— Chief (Wi.), 253.

Ema-liya, Z. contributor, Zuñi Indians' Title-page, facing p. 426; 561.

Emergence, Navajo Story of the, 350 (f.); compare also Story of Gomoidema Pokoma-Kiaka (M.).

Estsan Digini, Holy Woman (N.), 366.

Estsan-Natlehi, deity (N.), 359, 360.

Evening Star (Pa.), 94, 99, 100, 101, 102, 103, 104, 107.

F

Fable (Wi.), see Wai-kun.

Father, Prophet of the Ghost-Dance Religion (D.), 43, 44, 45, 46, 47, 48; (Pa.), 112; see also Prophet.

Father-Crow (Ar.), 201.

Father-Hawk (Pa.), 97; (f.), 107, 108.

Father-Sky (N.), 372.

Father-Sun (Pa.), 116; (Ar.), 198.

Female-Rain (N.), 365, 368.

First-Man, mythic personage (N.), 351, 371.

First Mother (Wa.), 4.

First-Woman, mythic personage (N.), 351, 371.

First Woman who made the Son of God (M.), see Story of Gomoidema Pokoma-Kiaka.

Fiske, John, quotation from, 533.

Flat Iron, D. chief, see Maza Blaska.

Fletcher, Alice C., xxii. (f.); (Pa.), 102, 107 (f.).

Flint (Pa.), 103; (Wi.), 248, 249; (N.), 360, 363, 364.

—— Youth (N.), 363, 364.

Flute (Wi.), 261; (Z.), 430.

—— Ceremony (H.), 489.

—— Song (H.), see Lene Tawi.

Fly, Flies (Wi.), 246; (M.), 333.

Foolish One (Wi.), see Wak-chung-kaka.

Fort Laramie, treaty signed at (C.), 148.

Fox (D.), 51.

—— Men (Pi.), 31.

—— Society (D.), 61.

Frog (Kw.), 299, 300, 302.

Frog-folk (M.), 330.

G

"Gaigwu," Ki. name for the tribe, 221.

Game of Barter (Wa.), 7.

Games (Wa.), 7; (C.), 158, 161, 162; (Ar.), 201, 202; (M.), 332.

INDEX

INDEX

Mooney, James, 41 (f.), 535.
Moose (Wa.), 11, 12.
Moqui, 363.
Moquis, see Hopis.
Morning Song (C.), see Hohiotsitsi No-otz.
—— Star (Pa.), 93, 94, 99, 100, 101, 102, 103, 104, 107.
—— —— Clan (Pa.), 99, 100.
Mother-Corn (Pa.), 97 (f.), 103, 107, 108.
—— Earth (N.), 372.
—— Moon (Pa.), 110, 116.
Mountain Lion, mythic Star Beast (Pa.), 101.
—— Song (N.), see Dsichl Biyin.
—— Songs (N.), see Dsichl Biyin.
Mountains, sacred (N.), see Sacred Mountains.
Mouse, Mice (Wi.), 253; (Kw.), 300, 301.
Mowihaiz, Magpie, C. contributor, 164, 188, 192, 561.
Mun-kun Na-wan, Holy Song (Medicine-Song) (Wi.), 254, 255, 256, 270, 274, 548, 549.
Murie, James R. (Pa.), see Sakuruta.
Music, Indian, see Indian Music.
Muyingwa, H. deity, 479.
Mystery-power (D.), 39, 40.

N

Nabilase, Jessie Sage, Ar. contributor, 201, 211, 561.
Naestsan Biyin, Song of the Earth (Hozhonji Song) (N.), 371, 372, 417, 556.
Nagi, D. word for soul, 61.
Nahios-si, Three Fingers, C. chief, contributor, 156, 157, 159, 160, 178, 179, 180, 561.
Nai No-otz, Song of Healing (Medicine-Song) (C.), 159, 160, 179, 544.
Nakahu Naad, Lullaby (Ar.), 201, 211, 545.
Nakos, Sage, Ar. chief, contributor, 199, 200, 204, 206, 561.
Naskan, beautiful woven blankets (N.), 361.
Navajos, 347; singing of, xxviii.
Nawadek, Susie Sage, Ar. contributor, 201, 211, 561.
Naye-e Sin, War-Song (N.), 362, 363, 393, 554.
Nayenezrani, N. deity, 103 (f.), 349, 359, 362.
Nek-hu-wi-ka, South Wind, Jacob Russell, Wi. contributor, 244, 254, 265, 270, 561.
Nicolar, Joseph, Wa. contributor, 4, 561.
Niltshi, The Wind, N. personification, 359.
Nolmihigon, Wa. word for clown, 7, 8.
Nowell, Charles James (Kw.), see Klalish.
N'Skawewintuagunul, Songs of Greeting (Wa.), 7; (for music, see Penobscot Song of Greeting, Passamaquoddy Song of Greeting).
Nu-u-sinim No-otz, Hand-Game Songs (C.), 161, 182, 183, 184, 185, 186, 187.

O

Ockaya, Corn-Grinding Songs (Z.), 430, 431, 433, 435, 437, 556, 557.
Offering, ceremony (C.), 151.
Ogallalla, members of the band, contributors of D. songs, 38.
Okicize Olowan, War-Song (D.), 59, 60, 89, 541.

Okum Daagya, Lullabies (Ki.), 228, 229, 238, 239, 547.
Old Chief's Song (Z.), see Thlah Hewe.
—— Tale (C.), 158.
Olowan, Song (D.), 55, 79, 540.
Omaha Dance (D.), 55, 56.
—— Dance-Songs (D.), see Omaha Wacipi Olowan.
—— Wacipi Olowan, Omaha Dance-Songs (D.), 55, 56, 80, 81, 540.
One-Above (Pa.), see Tirawa.
One-On-High (Ar.), see Ichebeniatha.
One-Who-Never-Died (M.), see Sekala Ka-amja.
Oraibi, H. village, 474, 483, 490, 494.
Orani, possible derivation of (N.), 366 (f.).
Organizations of the Plains Indians, 31.
Otter (Pa.), 97, 98, 101; (Wi.), 256.
Owik'uyain, The Home-Comer, Ki. contributor, 223, 228, 236, 238, 239, 561.
Ohwiwi No-otz, Song of the Offering Ceremony (Sun-Dance Song) (C.), 151, 166.

P

Painted Desert (H.), 490.
Paiute (D.), 42, 44, 45.
Pajoka, Wi. name for Comanche, 260.
Pani, synonyme for Pawnee, 93.
Parfleche, satchel of dressed hide, xv.
Passamaquoddy, a tribe of the Wabanakis, 3.
—— Dance-Song (Wa.), 10, 24, 25, 26, 535.
—— Song of Greeting (Wa.), 16.
Pathway of Departed Spirits, Pa. designation of the Milky Way, 99.
"Pawnee Shooter," a Wi. Indian, 258.
Pawnees, 93.
Pellote, mescal button (C.), 162.
Pemmican, Indian dish (D.), 48.
Penobscot, a tribe of the Wabanakis, 3.
—— Barter Dance-Song (Wa.), 8, 17.
—— Dance-Song (Wa.), 9, 19.
—— Medicine-Song (Wa.), 9, 21.
—— Song of Greeting (Wa.), 14, 15.
—— War-Dance Song (Wa.), 8, 18.
People of Peace, H. designation of themselves, 473, 490.
Peyote (C.), see Pellote.
Pimas, 313.
"Pitistchi" (N.), 361.
Plains Indians, 31, 41, 42, 93, 94; singing of, xxviii.
Plum-tree, as symbol (Ki.), 226.
Pony (D.), see Horse.
Potine, White Beaver, Ki. contributor, 225, 561.
Prayer, Prayers, Praying, xxiii., xxiv.; (Pl.), 33; (D.), 39; (Pa.), 113; (C.), 149, 151, 152, 154, 161, 162; (N.), 362, 364, 369; (H.), 490, 491, 493, 494.
Prayer by the Great Waters (N.), 364.
Prayer-Sticks (H.), xxiii., 492.
Prince, Dr. J. Dynely, 535.
Prophet, Paiute, of the Spirit-Dance Religion (D.), 42, 44, 45; (Pa.), 112 (f.); see also Father.

INDEX

Song of the Antelope Ceremony (Ki.), see T'a'pko Daagya.
— — — Bear Society (Pa.), see Tawi' Kuruks.
— — — Blue-Corn Dance (Z.), see Thlah Hewe.
— — — Bow-and-Arrow Society (C.), see Honimiyotzu.
— — — Buffalo-Dance (C.), see Mahoeva No-otz.
— — — Buffalo-Hide Ceremony (Ar.), see Hasse-hi Naad.
— — — Club Society (Ar.), see Hichaä-chuthi.
— — — Dog-Feast (D.), see Sunka Olowan.
— — — Dog Society (D.), see Sunka Olowan.
— — — Earth (Hozhonji Song) (N.), see Naestsan Biyin.
— — — Hare (Wi.), see Wash-ching-geka Na-wa' Ni-na.
— — — Hogans (Hozhonji Song) (N.), see Hogan Biyin.
— — — Hopi Chief (H.), 474.
— — — Horse (N.), see Hlin Biyin.
— — — Lance Ceremony (Pa.), see Kit-zichta.
— — — Mescal Rite (Ar.), see Hachayachu Naad.
— — — — — — (Ki.), 133.
— — — Mocking-bird (Y.), see Arowp.
— — — Offering Ceremony (C.), see Ohwiwi No-otz.
— — — Rain-Chant (N.), see Tro Hatal.
— — — Red Fox Society (C.), see Wuch-tchse Etan No-otz.
— — — Seer (D.), see Wicasa-Atawan Olo-wan.
— — — Spirit-Dance (Ghost-Dance Song) (Ar.), see Kainawad Naad.
— — — Sun (Wi.), see Wi-la Na-wa' Ni-na.
— — — Totem-Pole (Kw.), see Klawulacha.
— — — White-Horse Society (D.), see Tasunke-ska Olowan.
— — — Wolf (D.), 54.
— — — World (Pi.), see Chuhwuht.
— — Victory (C.), see Aotzi No-otz.
— — sung by Geronimo (Ap.), 327.
— — to the Earth-Maker (Wi.), see Ma-o-na.
Songs, contributing of, xxi., xxii., xxiii.; recording of, xxii.; sacred to occasions, xxii.; Pa. stanzas in, 100 (f.).
— — of Greeting (Wa.), see N'Skawewintua-gunul.
— — Loneliness (Wa.), 12.
— — the Dakotas, 60.
— — — Fox Society (D.), see Tokala Olo-wan.
— — — Iruska (Pa.), see Iruska.
— — — Spirit-Dance (Ghost-Dance Songs) (D.), see Wanaĝi Wacipi Olowan.
— — — Spirit-Dance (Ghost-Dance Songs) (Pa.), see Kehare Katzaru.
— — Victory (C.), 154.
"Sons of the River" (Y.), 339.
Sorrel Horse (D.), see Tasunke-Hinsa.

South Wind (Wi.), see Nek-hu-wi-ka.
Southern Star (Pa.), 99 (f.).
Spanish explorers (Pu.), 425.
Spiders (Wi.), 247.
Spirit, Spirits (Pl.), 31; (D.), 39, 46, 53, 61, 62; (C.), 161, 165; (Ar.), 200, 202; (Wi.), 244, 246, 253, 254, 262, 263; (Ap.), 324; (N.), 353; compare also Dream, Trance, Vision.
— animal (Pl.), 31.
— camp, Spirit-encampment (D.), 45, 46.
— companions (D.), 46.
— Dance (D.), 44, 48; (Ar.), 198, 200; (Ki.), 223; see also (D.) History of the Spirit-Dance, Wanaĝi Wacipi Olowan.
— Land (D.), 45.
— man (D.), 45.
— world (D.), 42, 43, 48; (Ar.), 200.
Standing Bear (D.), see Mato-Nazin.
Standing Rain, Pa. name for maiden, 104.
Star, a D. Indian, see Wicapi.
— of Morning (Pa.), 116.
— — Evening (Pa.), 116.
Starving Elk (C.), see Mochta-Wontz-tz.
"Step," Pa. designation of stanza, 100 (f.).
Stevenson, James (N.), 347 (f.), 365.
— , Matilda Cox (Z.), 429, 430; (H.), 493; 535.
Stories of Wak-chung-kaka (Wi.), 245.
— — — and Wash-ching-geka (Wi.), 244.
— — Wash-ching-geka (Wi.), 247.
Story of Gomoidema Pokoma-Kiaka (M.), 330.
— — the First Mother (Wa.), 4.
— — — Moose (Wa.), 12.
— — — Two Brothers (N.), 359.
— — Wakiash and the First Totem-Pole (Kw.), 299; for stories, compare also (D.), Holy Story; (D.), Short Bull's Narrative; (Pa.), Morning Star and the Evening Star; (C.), Old Tale; (Wi.), True Story; also stories connected with the various songs, passim.
Sun (Pa.), 94, 96, 103; (C.), 151, 165; (Ar.), 198; (Wi.), 250; (Pi.), 316; (M.), 331; (Pu.), 426; (H.), 493.
Sun-Dance (C.), 151; (Ar.), 198.
— — Song (C.), 151; (Ar.), 198.
Sun-Down-Shining (H.), see Tawakwaptiwa.
— Father, Z. deity, 493 (f.).
Sungmanitu Olowan, Wolf Song (D.), 54, 78.
Sunka Olowan, Song of the Dog-Feast (D.), 58, 59, 88, 541.
— — — , Song of the Dog Society (D.), 50, 69.
Supreme Being (Pl.), 32; (C.), 154.
Surly Walker (Wi.), see Wa-che-li-man-iga.
Swallow (N.), 365, 366; (Z.), 431.
Sweat-Lodge (D.), 52.
Swinging-Song (C.), see Wawahi No-otz.
Symbolism of color (N.), see subject-matter on pages 351, 371.

T

Talaskwaptiwa (H.), 491, 492, 493.
Tañoan stock, people of (S.), 447.

INDEX

ET us recognize in all things the value of our opposites. Old age seems justly to be the summing-time of life, the only philosophic decade; yet should we never forget the child nor the child-race who live so near to God that truth flows to them from a still untainted channel. For of such is the Kingdom of Heaven. Do we tend to become a people continually busy with the world's affairs, let us remember that the sources of spiritual truth have arisen oftenest among the contemplative peoples of the Orient, and let us then turn to the contemplative dark-skinned natives of our own land. If not in the hope and expectancy that are born of friendship, at least with tolerance and without scepticism let us stop long enough to hear the broken fragments of a message which they might have brought in its entirety to all their brethren in the world."—From *Genius and Primitive Man.*